MOVING AWAY FROM SILENCE

Thomas Turino

MOVING AWAY FROM SILENCE

Music of the Peruvian Altiplano
and the Experience of Urban Migration

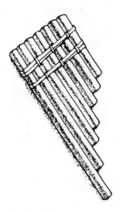

THE UNIVERSITY OF CHICAGO PRESS

Chicago & London

Thomas Turino is associate professor of music at the
University of Illinois, Urbana.

The University of Chicago Press, Chicago 60637
The University of Chicago Press, Ltd., London
© 1993 by The University of Chicago
All rights reserved. Published 1993
Printed in the United States of America
02 01 00 99 98 97 96 95 94 93   1 2 3 4 5 6
ISBN (cloth): 0-226-81699-0   ISBN (paper): 0-226-81700-8

Library of Congress Cataloging-in-Publication Data

Turino, Thomas.
    Moving away from silence : music of the Peruvian Altiplano and the experiment
of urban migration / Thomas Turino.
        p.   cm. — (Chicago studies in ethnomusicology)
    Discography: p.
    Includes bibliographical references and index.
    1. Folk music—Peru—Conima (District)—History and criticism.
    2. Folk music—Peru—Lima—History and criticism.   3. Rural-urban
migration—Peru.   I. Title.   II. Series.
    ML3575.P4T87   1993
    761.62′688508536   dc20   92-26935
                                                                                         CIP
                                                                                         MN

♾ The paper used in this publication meets the minimum
requirements of the American National Standard for Information
Sciences—Permanence of Paper for Printed Library Materials,
ANSI Z39.48-1984.

For Elisabeth

CONTENTS

Contents

ILLUSTRATIONS

PLATES *(following page 168)*

ACKNOWLEDGMENTS

Like musical performance in Conima, the research for, and the writing of, this book has been a collective endeavor at various times. I would like to express my gratitude to all the Conimeño musicians who shared the pleasure of performing with them in Conima, Lima, and Huancané: the members of Qhantati Ururi, Tarkas de Putina, Pitus de Checasaya, Centro Social Conima, and Unión Hilata. Filiberto Calderón took me into his home. He also taught me a great deal about music and life in Conima, as did my *compadre* Jorge Apaza, his father Samuel, his brother Leo, and the rest of their family in Conima. Aldemir Calderón, Manuel Pomare, and Juan Quispe had important roles in guiding my work in Conima. In Lima, my compadres in Centro Social Conima, Toribio Mamani and Benito Pomare, welcomed my wife Elisabeth and our son Matthew into their families; many other Centro Social members welcomed us into their homes and into their lives: Fabian Mamani, Fidel Cataricora, Filomeno Mamani, Oscar and Hilda Mamani, and Hermanjildo Chambi. Bernabé Quispe, a member of both Unión Hilata and Asociación Juvenil Puno in Lima, took particular interest in my study and helped me in countless ways. Although my oldest friend and teacher in Peru was not directly involved with the current study, I would like to thank Julio Benavente Díaz for providing so many insights into the beauty of Peruvian music and the complexities of Peruvian life.

I am indebted to my teachers at the University of Texas at Austin for their help and support at an earlier stage of this work. Gerard Béhague served as the director of my doctoral dissertation (1987) and throughout my years at Texas provided major encouragement and guidance for my Peruvian research. Richard Schaedel also served as a mentor and as a valuable member of my graduate committee, as did Greg Urban, Richard Adams, Henry Dietz, Steve Slawek, Steve Feld, and John Grubbs; their comments and suggestions still resonate throughout this book.

Special thanks go to Stephen Blum, Patricia Sandler, Charles Capwell,

Timothy Rice, and Larry Ward, who read earlier drafts of this book and spent many hours providing thoughtful, detailed criticism and concrete suggestions for improvement. Jaime Montaño, an early member of Asociación Juvenil Puno and a key player in many of the situations that I describe, also read an earlier draft and provided valuable criticism and clarifications. Especially in chapters 5 and 6, parts of Montaño's lengthy commentary on the draft are incorporated into the text. Alma Gottlieb, Samuel Araujo, Fred Lau, Robert Templeman, and Lise Waxer read parts of earlier versions and provided helpful commentary; Inni Choi drew the maps included in the text. Conversations about writing ethnography with Bruno Nettl, Veit Erlmann, and Paul Berliner influenced this book's final form. To these friends, students, and colleagues, I owe a special debt of gratitude.

My fieldwork for this study was supported by a Fulbright Fellowship, which I gratefully acknowledge; Dr. Koth de Paredes and the other members of the Fulbright staff in Peru facilitated my work in many ways. Earlier field research in southern Peru, which influenced the present study, was supported by an Inter-American Foundation Fellowship. I would also like to thank the University of Illinois Research Board for financial assistance in the final stages of this project.

My wife Elisabeth and son Matthew, who at the time was six months old, accompanied me to Peru. Matthew is now seven, and he finds it inconceivable that I have been working on the same project for as long as he has been alive and for much longer than our daughter, Cristina, has been with us. I would like to offer a heartfelt word of thanks to my family for their patience, to Matt for coming home every day and asking, "Is your book finished yet?" and for their enthusiasm when it finally was.

INTRODUCTION:

FROM CONIMA TO LIMA

IN THE ANDEAN villages along the northeastern shore of Lake Titicaca in Puno, Peru, daily life is very quiet. Depending on the time of year and the agricultural tasks to be performed, routines are established and one day passes much like another. The family I lived with in the District of Conima usually rose before dawn, ate a small breakfast, and then did chores around the house until seven. Being on a different schedule, I frequently awoke to the sound of Filiberto sweeping, or to the sounds of his grandson, the only child in the house, playing with toys of his own invention. Before the family went out to the fields to work, another more substantial meal was served—some variety of potato soup, which was much like the one eaten the day before and the one that would be eaten upon returning. After sundown, the families in Conima closed themselves in. Light, warmth, and smoke were provided by a fire in the chimneyless kitchen where we gathered for the evening meal and then entertainment: listening to the transistor radio. The volume was kept low, barely audible, to save batteries.

Occurring on the average of once a month in Conima, festivals are the reverse side of life's cloth. They break other routines and are the focus of conversation long before and long after they are held. Fiestas begin with the preparations of the sponsors, the sewing of costumes, the cutting of panpipes, the composition of new musical pieces, hours of cooking, and the washing of shawls. They end with hangovers, sore feet, new engagements, fatigue, and the desire to get back to everyday tasks. In Conima, music and dance are at the center of festivals, which are at the center of communal social life.

One afternoon in May of 1985 I was talking with Filiberto about the fiesta of Corpus Christi that had once been important in Conima. In his matter-of-fact way, he told me that the fiesta was no longer celebrated:

> The community authorities used to make sure that somebody
> took the *cargo* [role of fiesta sponsor] and that the music and

1

dances were performed. Now they do not seem to care and the dances are being forgotten. They have left us in silence.[1]

I had already been conscious of how silent Conima could be in periods between fiestas. Having lived much of my life in or near cities in the United States, I often enjoyed the quietness, but sometimes it also augmented a kind of loneliness. After this conversation, silence took on new meaning for me, just as its antidote—music—came to stand for a whole way of life and for the bond that held communities together.

The music and dances of Corpus Christi are not the only ones being forgotten in Conima. Over the past three decades, more and more young people are moving away from their villages. There are now fewer people in the district to take the fiesta sponsorship roles, to play panpipes and flutes, and to perform the dances. The departure of many younger people and their frequent visits home, have been important catalysts for altering the timbre of life in the rural communities. Many young people move to highland cities and to the lower lands on the eastern slopes of the Andes; but the national capital of Lima, located on the Pacific coast, has historically been the primary magnet for highland migration.

○

In Lima, a constant din of noise—cars, trucks, horns, construction—hangs in the air like a white sheet, almost like silence. The color too is like this. In the winter months, rainless clouds cover the sky as cement covers the ground, and as sand hills cover the horizon around the squatters' communities that surround the city. Even the trash—newspapers turning around in the early wind of damp mornings—is gray.

Regardless of the time of year, routines are established among the Conimeños and other highland migrants who have settled in Lima. For six days a week, one day passes very much like another: up before dawn, a small breakfast to the sound of radio or the glare of TV, a one- or two-hour bus ride to Callao, or central Lima, or one of a thousand other places. Sometimes there are seats on the bus, but usually there are not. Each day the migrants wake up to people pushing in around them. All day they work. The maids clean up after their employers, the municipal workers clean up after the city, the construction workers carry cement, the furniture makers spray lacquer on tables, and the shoe shiners polish shoes. On the ride home, their clothes compare badly with those of people in cars stopped at a light. For Limeños, each face is the same as all facing out the same bus window, looking down on those they have come to serve.

2

But on Sunday it is different. The migrants ride the bus with others of their highland home. Carrying bags filled with glittering costumes and panpipes under their arms, they enter what on other days is a school, a vacant lot, or a parking lot. A brass band is warming up, a panpipe ensemble is playing in the corner. A young woman, who on other days works as a maid, dons a gaudy sequined vest and velvet skirt—'costume of light.' Her face brightens, and there is lightness and grace in her walk. For one afternoon a week she becomes a star; she is transformed and she is beautiful. Her dance group moves into the center of the lot to perform for people from her highland home. Other horns fade behind the blast of trumpets as they dance.

Fiestas, music, and dance are as essential to many Andean migrants in Lima as they are to the people in the villages from which they came. In both places the performance of music and dance brings people together and celebrates the specialness of the occasion and of their community. There is even a certain similarity between the dry, hard, barren altiplano and the huge gray expanse of cement in Lima, between the silence of the rural communities and the white noise of the capital. Against either backdrop, the bright costumes, the sounds of panpipes, and the choreographed movement circumscribe an alternative space for social life and for living.

In regard to more specific processes, institutions, and meanings surrounding Andean musical performance in Lima, however, something new is being created. In the city, the migrants draw on ideas and styles of behavior learned from a multitude of heterogeneous sources—from their parents and neighbors in the highlands while growing up, from Limeños, from North American and Argentinian soap operas, from migrants of other regions, from radio announcers, ad infinitum. They adapt, alter, combine, and create cultural resources in unique ways, and for very specific reasons, the search for security, feelings of self-worth, and some kind of livable space not least among them.

The widespread performance of indigenous highland music in Lima is relatively recent. When I asked residents (the term highlanders in Lima use to refer to themselves) from the department of Puno why they had not performed the indigenous panpipe and flute music in the capital prior to the 1970s, a frequent reply was "vergüenza" (shame, embarrassment). In Peru, the social order inverts the physical order. Andeans who live at 12,500 feet above sea level, or who come from there, find themselves at the bottom of a social, political, and economic hierarchy that is anchored on the coast and traditionally embodied, both in actual and symbolic terms, in the Spanish-criollo ("white," Hispanic-American) capital, Lima. Many migrants were, and still are, reluctant to be openly involved with cultural practices that would identify them as having come from the rural highlands. The long history of the domination of, and prejudice against, people identified as "Indians" in Peru is well documented, as is their resistance (e.g., Tschopik 1968:37–41; Hickman 1975:24–25; Allen 1988:24–32; Stern 1987; Turino 1991a).

In their efforts to create positive self-images and a livable space for themselves and their children in Lima, highland residents are profoundly constrained by dominant social attitudes. A process of negotiation emerges in these struggles over social and self representation, and the stakes are high. As in other harshly hierarchical societies, social identity in Peru determines whom people can marry, possibilities for economic improvement and security, the ability to care adequately for one's children, and, more subtly, feelings of self-worth and pride. The language a person speaks and the way it is spoken; styles of clothing, movement, and social interaction; and the music one listens to and performs are all fundamental cultural resources for defining and negotiating social position (Herzfeld 1987). In Peru, music has been particularly important in such processes of self and group definition.

By 1985 the huge demographic shift from the highlands, and a continuing crisis within the Peruvian state, had led to a new orthodoxy about the positive value of Andean identity among highland residents in Lima. But given the background of prejudice and the subtle and not so subtle forms of oppression, it is still striking that by 1985, many Puneño regional migrant clubs had already formed panpipe ensembles in the capital. On almost any Sunday afternoon, 'folkloric festivals' were organized by various clubs in different parts of the city. The festivals, centered on a formal performance contest, were based on the *ayni* (traditional highland) system of reciprocal aid maintained among the clubs. In the city, walls of cement kept out people who did not want to pay the entrance fee to that week's host club. But the walls also provided privacy, a kind of safety, separating the memory, or perhaps the imagining, of Puno from the rest of Lima and the rest of life.

After a migrant-club fiesta in Lima in 1986, a group of Conimeño residents (people from Conima who live in Lima) were particularly exuberant because they had won the contest for panpipe performance that evening. Once outside the protective wall of the school patio where the festival had been held, some of the younger members of the Conimeño club wanted to walk to their bus stop playing panpipe music. A heated argument ensued between these musicians and other club members who did not want to perform panpipes in the streets of Lima. Those who refused walked off alone to the taunts of those who stayed behind to play: "Are you ashamed of your own music? Are you ashamed to play in the street?"

For the musicians who wanted to play, the others' refusal was tantamount to a denial of who they were and where they were from. Several of these Conimeño residents viewed the playing of panpipes openly in the street as a politically potent form of self-assertion; others, still in the festival spirit, wanted to do it for fun. Conversely, some of the reluctant club members had been deeply affected by long-standing traditions of racism against people defined as 'Indians' in Peru.

The positions of the various factions within the Conimeño regional club, often deeply felt, are understandable. This book is an attempt to understand them. It is also an attempt to understand the value and meaning of the panpipe (*siku*) and other flute (*pinkillu, tarka,* and *pitu*) traditions performed by the people of rural Conima and the Conimeño residents in Lima. Throughout this study I am interested in the specific qualities of Conimeño music that make it a particularly powerful medium for bringing people together, for articulating who they are, for furthering their political goals, and for making their lives meaningful. Most important, the book explores how musical activities have figured into people's struggles to maintain or alter their ways of life during a period of dramatic social upheaval in Peru—an upheaval that was brought on by economic and social crisis and by tremendous urban migration.

A COMPARATIVE MUSICAL ETHNOGRAPHY

Using Conimeño musical traditions as the unifying thread, the stories in this book unfold around a comparison of various groups of people: older Aymara-speaking musicians in rural Conima (part I); their children who have migrated to nearby highland cities (part II); young, urban, middle- and working-class highlanders from Puno who have migrated to Lima and served as the vanguard of the urban panpipe movement (part II); and rural Conimeños in Lima who have organized themselves in regional clubs (part III). All these groups are involved with the "same" panpipe and flute traditions, although their musical practices and conceptions about what the music means differ in important ways. The fieldwork among these various groups was conducted in Conima, Lima, the city of Puno, and the town of Huancané between November 1984 and July 1986.

The idea of doing a comparative musical ethnography of an indigenous rural highland region, and of migrants from that region in Lima and other cities, was inspired by nineteen months of previous fieldwork in Cusco and

5

Puno, Peru, during 1977 and 1981–82. Given the mobility of twentieth-century Peruvian life, bounded rural ethnographies are no longer practical; much of what influences rural indigenous musicians and musical style is ultimately traceable—through medium-sized highland cities—to Lima itself as the hub of the national society. Throughout this study I trace the paths of interaction.

By the 1970s, scholars had begun focusing attention on Andean migrants in Lima and the regional clubs as a primary center of highland musical activity; many writers used music as an index of the transformations taking place in the capital—the so-called "Andeanization of Lima" (see Schaedel 1979; Matos 1984; Doughty 1970, 1972; Degregori 1981, 1984; Nuñez and Llórens 1981; Llórens 1983; Altamirano 1988; de Soto 1989:3–4). Because of the pronounced regional variations in highland traditions, however, cultural studies of Andean migrants in the capital cannot be carried out in sufficient depth without a detailed knowledge of their place of origin (Altamirano 1984). I have tried to balance the view of the Conimeño migrants' musical practices with an equally detailed discussion of musical life in Conima.

COMPARATIVE ETHNOMUSICOLOGY

From the beginning, ethnomusicological work has been implicitly and sometimes explicitly comparative (Hornbostel 1975 [1905]; Merriam 1977; Nettl 1983:52–64). In the very act of doing ethnomusicological research, or reading about the members and music of another society, we inevitably call up myriad comparisons with our own musical experience and social understanding; we approach new experiences or ideas against the backdrop of what we already know.

Such implicit, almost automatic, comparison is potentially positive insofar as it broadens the boundaries of *what we are able to think* by giving us alternative ideologies, discourses, and experiences to think with.[2] From my perspective, this is a major objective of ethnomusicological work in general and of this book in particular. During my stay in Conima I was introduced to new ways of thinking about what music, musical participation, and social life can be; these alternatives seem worth sharing.

The danger of "writing cultures" to the specifications of our own personal and social needs, and according to our own cultural dispositions and knowledge, is by now well known (e.g., Clifford and Marcus 1986; Bourdieu 1977; Said 1989; Rosaldo 1989). As with comparison itself, we inevitably conduct ethnographic research and write from our particular subject positions. These endeavors, however, are usefully informed by a kind of ongoing self-analysis, paralleling the psychoanalysis that psychoanalysts typically undergo before beginning professional practice. Throughout this writing I have tried to make my own positions clear (both to myself and to the reader), and to point out where they differ from those of the people I am writing about.

More explicit use of comparative methods has been in place since the inception of ethnomusicology. Early on, comparative musicology was often fueled by Eurocentric evolutionary theories. In 1964, Alan Merriam dismissed the older comparative approach supporting such theories, but still assumed "that one of the aims of ethnomusicology is to produce data which can be compared and that therefore the broader aim is generalization about music which can be applied ultimately on a worldwide basis" (1964:53). Merriam suggested that comparative method "must be cautious, that like things must be compared, and that the comparisons must have bearing upon a particular problem and be an integrated part of the research design" (1964:53).

Alan Lomax's cantometrics project (1968) is one of the best known examples of conscious, systematic comparison in its attempt to correlate singing styles with modes of economic and social organization on a worldwide basis. Beginning around the same time, more ethnographically grounded comparative approaches were being used by ethnomusicologists to address similar issues. For example, David Ames (1973) compared musical life among the Igbo and Hausa in two specific West African locations in relation to issues of economic and social stratification and specialization. Similarly, in 1984 Steven Feld suggested that ethnomusicological comparison be derived from intensive local ethnographic research and framed in terms of a series of general questions and areas of inquiry.

The present study is explicitly comparative, grounded ethnographically at the local level, and I have compared similar phenomena among various groups of people. Compositional processes, musical ensemble organization, rehearsals, styles of decision making, public speech and interactional styles, musical repertory, tuning systems and other parameters of musical style, musical occasions, religious practices, and conceptions about music are compared among older Conimeños in the highlands, their children, the Conimeño residents in Lima, and the young urban Puneños in Lima and Puno. Detailed comparative research among these groups has proven useful for understanding how musical practices articulate with different social, economic, and political formations; it places the specificity of each group, as well as the relations among them, in stronger relief.

THE CONCEPT OF CULTURE

In the main, ethnomusicological comparison has been "cross-cultural," with regions, entire nations and societies, or more specific ethnic groups commonly providing the units of analysis. This, in turn, has been based on the assumption of cultural homogeneity within such entities, allowing for their comparison *as units*. In contrast, I have chosen to analyze similarities and differences between groups of people, as well as between individuals who typically would be thought of as belonging to the same "culture," the same ethnic group, or at least the same society. The Conimeño club members' conflict over playing panpipes in the streets of Lima, described earlier, is an example. Although these people come from a single region and even the same villages, they represent a multiplicity of subjective cultural positions. This raises critical questions about how we think and write about the concept of culture itself.

From the perspective taken here, "culture" can be located only in relation to the lives of concrete individuals as articulated through action at specific moments. It involves the *resources* (ideas, dispositions, practices, material objects, and modes of expression and behavior) that individuals select, create, or absorb through socialization to fashion their lives. Subjective cultural positions are simultaneously individual and social and are located at the multiple points where the individual and social intersect. As with Bourdieu's notion of the *habitus*, subjective cultural positions dialectically structure (shape tendencies) and are structured by the conditions within and through which people live their lives (Bourdieu 1977). Following from this, and from the work of Anthony Giddens (1979), the notion of structure, itself, implies a *process* involving concrete actors—operating within a context and with goals and constraints—rather than a superindividual *thing* (see Karp 1986:135).[3]

Cultural positions and processes involve not only homogeneity and coherence but also the ways differences and contradictions are articulated, negotiated, explained, and utilized (Hall 1986a, 1991a, 1991b). In 1983, Bruno Nettl accurately characterized a common ethnomusicological concern with studying and describing the "typical" aspects of a whole society, in part to aid cross-cultural comparison (p. 9). In a sense, this remains a concern in the present work, and yet the level of analysis has fundamentally shifted, and hence the boundaries for defining "the typical" have also changed. In this book, "cross-cultural" comparison is extended to the study of similarities *and differences* among neighbors, among club members, among parents and children, and among people in Conima, Lima, and a variety of other locales.

MUSIC, CULTURE, AND SOCIETY

Against the backdrop of musicological "Great Man" approaches to history and Kantian views of the autonomous nature of art, ethnomusicologists have long been interested in the possibility of establishing meaningful links between music and the society that produces it (see C. Seeger 1977 [1951]; A. Seeger 1980). Publications like Leppert and McClary's *Music and Society* (1987) indicate that this remains an issue currently, yet scholars from the "anthropological side" of ethnomusicology supplied the pertinent point of departure for such analyses decades ago—the assumption that music making *is* social behavior and action, and that it articulates broader social values and ideologies (e.g., McAllester 1954:3; Merriam 1963; Blacking 1967:5). More recent work has suggested that social practices and the signs people use for self-representation and for interpreting the world not only reflect or articulate internalized dispositions and worldviews but also operate dialectically in the ongoing construction of internalized dispositions (Bourdieu 1977, 1984; Turino 1988; Sugarman 1989). This idea is central to my analysis of the importance of musical practices in social life.

By the late 1970s, a number of detailed ethnographic studies gave accounts of the integral relationships between music and other social domains in regard to style, practices, underlying dispositions, and worldview (Kaeppler 1978; A. Seeger 1979, 1980, 1987; Keil 1979; Becker and Becker 1981; Feld 1982, 1984, 1988; Turino 1989). The best of this work, often influenced by structuralism, presents elegant depictions of the tight coherence of cultural practices, aesthetics, and ethics across various realms of social life in small-scale settings. Typically, however, these studies do not stress individual subject positions within the depiction of specific groups, nor do they emphasize the more discrete levels of disagreement, contradiction, and conflict. They also tend to isolate the specific social setting from its broader regional, national, international, and historical contexts.

The present study grows out of this tradition of ethnomusicological work. It continues to investigate the rich coherence between different types of practices, dispositions, and knowledge among specific groups of people, but I have also tried to extend the theoretical approach by giving more attention to individual variation and agency, and to the historical links among local, regional, national, and international forces. As in my previous work (1984, 1987, 1988, 1990a, 1991), I remain fundamentally concerned with how musical and other social practices articulate with specific relations of social power, with situations of "internalized domination," and with statist projects to construct hegemony in the Gramscian senses of the term.

9

Social Power and Musical Practice

Antonio Gramsci uses the concept of hegemony in various ways. Importantly, the concept refers to a dominant group's (or alliance's) ability to establish a position of leadership by winning the consent of allied and subordinate groups through articulating common interests and goals—by establishing linkages across *different* identities and social positions. Gramsci contrasts hegemony with the need to use coercion in situations of domination, and identifies it within the realm of civil society (1971:12). He also discusses hegemony as "the 'spontaneous' consent given by the great masses of the population to the general direction imposed on social life by the dominant fundamental group; this consent is 'historically' caused by the prestige (and consequent confidence) which the dominant group enjoys because of its position and function in the world of production" (1971:12).

The concept, thus, comes to be associated with cultural, moral, and ideological leadership, and at one point Gramsci characterizes the state as a kind of educator. He writes, "Every state is ethical in as much as one of its most important functions is to raise the great mass of the population to a particular cultural and moral level, a level (or type) which corresponds to the needs of the productive forces of development, and hence to the interests of the ruling classes" (1988:234).

Yet hegemony should not simply be glossed as "ideological domination" (Hall 1986a), since in some instances consent is "won;" that is, subaltern people may actively link themselves to ruling groups or the state in response to concessions made. Moreover, hegemony operates in conjunction with economic power and is backed by the potential use of force, and hence is never purely "ideological" (cf. Gramsci 1971:12, 1988:197, 210–11; see Forgacs in Gramsci 1988:422–24). The notion of "ideological domination" is related to, although not the same as, Gramsci's concept of hegemony as "spontaneous consent" that results, in part, from the "educative function" of the state.

The concepts of "ideological domination" and "spontaneous consent" raise analytical problems inherent in the notion of false consciousness (being "educated" to act against self-interest). They also often result in descriptions of subaltern peoples as overly passive and open to manipulation. Yet for my work it has been important to retain the concept of hegemony as consent that is "won," as well as ideas about the more subtle (and often related) processes involved in "ideological domination," "internalized domination," or what Bourdieu has called "symbolic violence" (1977:190–97).

In situations where there is extreme social prejudice, for example, subaltern individuals are often schooled from infancy with images of their own inferiority or marginality, supporting the privileged position of elite groups. These messages—involving the relative status of the indices of group identity such as music, language, and clothing styles—are sometimes subtly absorbed by subordinate people vis-à-vis the state or elite groups as "educator." When internalized, these ideas form part of people's "commonsense" notions about the world and about themselves. According to Gramsci, *common sense* is "strangely composite," comprising a heterogeneity of old, current, and futuristic ideas, which may be partly imposed or absorbed passively from the outside or the past (1971:324). As Forgacs has noted, "Many elements in popular common sense contribute to people's subordination by making situations of inequality and oppression appear to them as natural and unchangeable" (in Gramsci 1988:421; cf. Bourdieu 1977). For this reason, political struggles frequently involve a contest to define or influence common sense (views of "the natural," or worldview), and this is done through the use of redundant imagery in the full range of semiotic domains (language, music, gesture, visual codes, etc.).

The value of this line of thinking for music scholars, and in the present study, is that it relocates cultural practices and semiotic domains such as music making at the center of social and political life (as politicians, rulers, and revolutionaries have long recognized; see the section on Velasco in chapter 6). It is important to emphasize that Gramsci describes hegemony as a temporary condition that must be actively maintained when, and indeed if, it has been established—it cannot be taken as a given in situations of domination. This is also true for the notion of internalized domination. The temporary, nonguaranteed, contestable nature of hegemonic relations and internalized domination returns our attention to the importance of musical and cultural forms and practices *as strategic resources* that can affect and be affected by the interplay of social forces within specific historical conjunctures.

From Problems of Musical Change to Conjunctural Analysis

"Culture" is not a thing or a system to which people belong; rather, I use the concept to refer to the complex, fluid, and often amorphous resources and processes of lived human relations, identity, and understanding. Many ethnomusicological studies concerned with urban migration, "westernization," and other situations of "culture contact" have focused on issues of musical and cultural change. If one abandons the notion of "culture" as a thing or a system, however, ideas about the "dynamism of culture" and typologies of "musical change" become increasingly difficult to use (cf. Blacking 1978; Kartomi 1981; Nettl 1985). Put simply, "cultures" and "musics" do not come into contact or change, *people do.*[4] Among Conimeño residents in Lima, for example, we cannot talk about cultural continuity and change, because, after twenty years in the city, there is no unitary cultural baseline—neither Conimeño nor Limeño, Andean nor Western—from which continuity or change can be understood. Rather, we have new groups of individuals, variously self-defined, who must be understood on their own terms in relation to their composite experiences, resources, and specific circumstances.

This book, then, is explicitly *not* about cultural or musical change in regard to the Conimeños who move down from the mountains to Lima; it is about similarities and differences relative to other social groups, and about creativity in relation to particular social needs, constraints, and conditions. This distinction is not merely semantic; it draws attention to an analytical emphasis on people, practices, and specific historical moments rather than on products and superorganic notions of "culture" and "music."

Analytically, however, it is equally important to relate the particular historical moments and positions of specific groups to the more permanent (stable) aspects of the social, economic, and political terrain. As suggested by Antonio Gramsci,

> a common error in historico-politico [and cultural] analysis consists in an inability to find the correct relation between what is organic [relatively permanent] and what is conjunctural [appearing as occasional, immediate, almost accidental]. This leads to presenting causes as immediately operative which in fact only operate indirectly, or to asserting that the immediate causes are the only effective ones. In the first case there is an excess of "economism," or doctrinaire pedantry; in the second, an excess of "ideologism." In the first case there is an overestimation of mechanical causes, in the second an exaggeration of the voluntarist and individual element (1988:201–2).

From this perspective, my analysis moves back and forth from the "relatively permanent" features of the social formation to the occurrences of specific conjunctures to illustrate how individual/small group agency interacts dialectically with broader structural patterns and constraints in the shaping of social and musical life (see Grossberg 1992:52–60).

Introduction

ESSENTIALISM AND THE ESSENTIAL

The construction of new identities and cultural practices—and similarly, the defense of existing ways of life—involves creative, ongoing processes that call into question the fixed, essentialist conceptions of culture and identity that studies emphasizing culture contact, assimilation, and continuity and change require.[5] As Christopher Waterman suggests, "All human identities, no matter how deeply felt, are from an historical point-of-view mixed, relational, and conjunctural" (1990b:367). This statement also applies to the cultural practices that people invent to articulate identity and to the ideologies that they inherit, absorb, and create to interpret their world (Keil 1985; Romero 1990; Blum 1990; Erlmann 1990; Meintjes 1990; Uzzell 1979).

At the same time, the sadness that many older people in Conima express about the passing of their way of life—as in Filiberto's reference to the silencing of Corpus Christi—returns our attention, not to the essentialist, but to the deeply felt *essentialness* of localized community and tradition.[6] It is important for us to understand what is lost as well as gained by moving away from Conima into a situation ever more closely defined by worldwide capitalism, racist attitudes, and hierarchical, nonreciprocal human relationships. These forces have profoundly affected the quality of the Conimeños' traditions and lives. Their efforts to struggle against, or work within, the play of these forces make the specific stories told here relevant to people's experiences and struggles throughout much of the contemporary world.

THE ETHNOGRAPHIC CONTEXTS

The highland District of Conima, the urban sprawl of Lima, and the roads and provincial towns in between constituted the ethnographic setting for my fieldwork (November 1984 to July 1986) and for this study. Residence in any one of these places would have provided some understanding of the ways in which musical resources are used to represent, reproduce, and transform social relations, as well as of the role of individuals as the embodiment and makers of social and musical history (see Rice 1987:476). But in Peru, at least, and I would guess more generally, bounded, synchronic musical ethnography in an isolated rural setting is no longer a tenable methodology because of the circular links among these different types of spaces (Erlmann 1990, 1991; Waterman 1990a). The emphasis on synchronic analysis also seems unrealistic since social action and ways of seeing the world are historically constituted, just as they constitute history (Sahlins 1981; Blum 1991).

Lima, "the city of kings," and the indigenous villages of the southern sierra, sometimes referred to in Peru as the *mancha india* (Indian region; literally, Indian stain), may be thought of in the abstract as two distinct and contrasting spaces. But they are also bound as one, and bound to a multitude of places known as Peru by history, the state, the political economy, the military draft, a system of public schools, radios, and roads—just as Peru is bound to other nations through capitalist and political relations (the struggles with the International Monetary Fund and the "war on drugs" being recent examples).

Previously, I conceptualized the contexts of ethnographic work metaphorically as ever-expanding concentric rings with pathways that cross and connect them (Turino 1990a). This idea and other spatial and place-oriented metaphors for context, culture, and social structures should probably be reconceptualized because even these imply a fixity that is not realistic (see Blum 1990). Important to the notion of *context* in semiotics—those features of the situation that inform the meaning of signs (E. Hall 1977)—are the aspects that individuals carry around inside: memories, past experience, the knowledge of specific codes. This internalized portion of the ethnographic context is movable and constantly on the move.

My own field experience mirrored the increasingly transitory lives of some Conimeños. My time was split between Conima and Lima, with stopovers of different lengths in the cities of Puno and Juliaca and the provincial capital of Huancané, Puno, where many Conimeños live. I came to know the bus and truck drivers who move people, goods, and information between Juliaca and Conima. I became known by them and other people along the route as the *gringo* who played music with Putina and Qhantati Ururi of Conima, and who had a house built for him on Filiberto's land.

My family remained in Lima most of the time, and I traveled back and forth constantly, alternately spending a month or six weeks in each locale. Upon my return from my first stay in the highlands, my seven-month-old son did not recognize or remember me. But rather than being disruptive to my relationships with the Conimeños in both places, as I feared it might, my constant movement between Conima and Lima was seen as normal for a person my age. Moreover, I became another valuable link for the Conimeño residents in Lima and people in the hometown: carrying messages, goods, and recordings of new highland compositions between them. Just as I performed with a community ensemble in Conima, I became a formal honorary member of the regional association, Centro Social Conima, in Lima. Because of the differences between the lives of proletarian workers in Lima and peasants in the highlands, and because of ecological and spatial differences, distinct styles of research and personal relationships emerged (see chapter 10), just as different forms of musical life are generated by these same conditions.

Conima was chosen as the site of research because the panpipe style from this district had become particularly prominent in Lima, even among Limeño university groups and migrant clubs from other parts of Puno. It was an obvious style to study given my interest in the dynamics among different types of social groups.

The choice was also made for me. The first time I heard Conimeños play, at a festival in Lima in November 1984, I thought it the most beautiful and powerful music that I had ever heard in Peru.

THE DISTRICT OF CONIMA

Located in the Province of Huancané, Puno, the District of Conima is situated on the Peruvian *altiplano* (high plain) on the northern shore of Lake Titicaca, between the District of Moho and the Bolivian border.[7] A glance at a map helps to explain Conimeños' contention that their home is a forgotten corner of Peru (see maps 1 and 2). A dirt road running along the shores of Titicaca, linking the cities of Juliaca, Puno, and La Paz, Bolivia, crosses the district, but it is much less traveled than the paved Peruvian-Bolivian route to the south of the lake. No mail service or other regular forms of communication, except transistor radios, linked the district with the rest of the country during my stay. In cases of emergency, messages could be broadcast to Conima from radio stations in Juliaca or Puno, but travelers provided the only way of sending messages out. For a number of months in 1986 the rain-swelled lake flooded the road, and all overland access was cut off, so that boat travel across Titicaca became the only option.

There are some two million Aymara speakers on the Peruvian/Bolivian altiplano, and further south in Bolivia and in Chile (Briggs and Llanque 1982:13). The provinces of Huancané and Chucuito and certain communities in the Province of Puno are the Aymara-speaking areas in Puno, and the primary Aymara areas in Peru. Aymara speakers are clearly a minority in comparison with speakers of Quechua, the dominant indigenous language in the Peruvian highlands.

Although the terms "Quechua" and "Aymara" are frequently used by scholars, for convenience, to refer to the two major Andean ethnic groups, these social categories do not serve as the basis for social solidarity among rural villagers. Rather, when left to themselves, rural people in southern Peru usually define their identities according to localized communities and

15

Map 1. The departments of Peru.

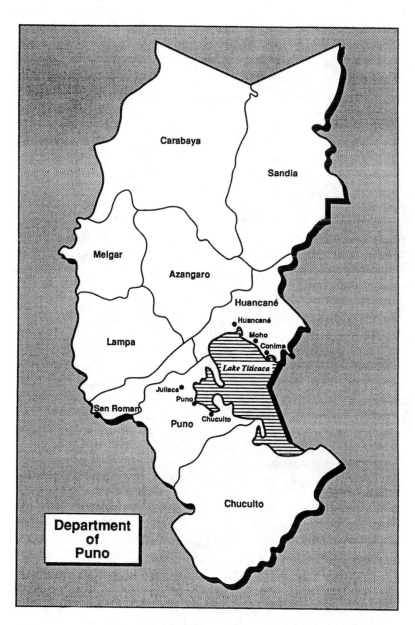

Map 2. Puno.

regions. Likewise, among indigenous Andeans, cultural practices vary according to specific locations. Hence, while the people of Huancané are linked culturally in some ways with Aymara-speaking communities to the south of the lake in Puno and in Bolivia and Chile, there are also marked regional differences (see Carter 1967; Solc 1969; Allen and Albó 1972; Tschopik 1946; Hickman 1975; Grebe 1980; Buechler and Buechler 1971, Buechler 1980). There are also many similarities and differences in worldview and cultural practices between Aymara- and Quechua-speaking communities in different areas that do not neatly correspond with the language spoken. In southern Peru, then, both social identity and cultural practices must be understood in local terms.

Political and Economic Organization

The District of Conima is divided into six indigenous *ayllus* (political-geographical-religious social units; see Bastien 1978; Allen 1988).[8] The town of Conima, serving as the district capital, and Tilali, another town on the opposite side of the district, are considered to be socially and geographically external to the ayllus. According to a census taken by the members of the Guardia Republicana in 1985, the population for the district was 9,501.[9]

Conimeños conceptualize the district as a whole in two halves with three ayllus each. This binary division is formalized in that the three ayllus on the "Conima side" (versus the "Tilali side") are linked in a *suyos* (quarters) system of land distribution and crop rotation cross-cutting the individual ayllu territories. The social separation of the two sides is, at present, clearly articulated by their independent celebration of most fiestas, whereas in the past, according to Conimeños, the entire district celebrated major fiestas together. An active separatist movement among ayllu dwellers of the Tilali side is working to establish a distinct political district with the help of migrants from these ayllus in Lima, who act as brokers with the central government.

The ayllus themselves are subdivided into sub-ayllu and smaller community units through a similar process of factionalism. For example, the community with which I worked most closely, Putina, is part of Ayllu Sulcata on the Conima side of the district. Sulcata is divided into Upper Sulcata, Central Sulcata, and Lower Sulcata, with the communities of Putina and Huata making up the latter. Within Lower Sulcata, the communities of Huata and Putina exhibit feelings of competition and mistrust yet may function as a cooperative unit in some contexts, and this is true for the sociopolitical units at other levels.

Being part of a single, formalized ayllu subdivision, Huata and Putina have the same rotating political and religious leaders, share a school, and do cooperative communal work projects (*faenas*) together for the school. But in fiestas, the major public forum for articulating community relations and group identity, each community has its own musical ensemble that competes most directly with the other's. Fiesta and ritual occasions that involve only these two communities take place in a special centrally located (neutral) place on the border between them, so that neither will benefit more than the other from the rituals enacted. This is also the case for fiestas involving Central and Lower Sulcata (chapter 4).

The older people who live in the ayllus are mainly involved in small-scale subsistence agriculture and animal husbandry, and remain largely outside the national cash economy. They maintain a labor-intensive style of agriculture, with pre-Columbian technology such as the use of digging sticks (Guaman Poma 1980). The year is divided conceptually into a wet season, roughly from November to April, and a dry season from April through October. Planting takes place from August through October, and the main agricultural rituals occur during the rainy season in February and March.

Conimeños conceptualize their landholdings at three levels of altitude: high, medium, and lake levels. Families usually have agricultural plots in all three, providing a type of insurance against total crop failure. In wet years when the lake rises, the crops on the pampa next to the lake may be lost or damaged, but those higher up will survive. In drought years, the higher *chakras* (agricultural plots) will not produce, but those on the pampa are a safeguard. The chakras at median altitude tend to produce most consistently. People's landholdings are usually just enough to feed the family, and the all-too-common event of crop failure in either the pampa or at the higher altitudes brings frequent hardship and suffering.

The difficult climatic conditions on the altiplano, in conjunction with population expansion and an increasing awareness of other economic options, have spurred a dramatic trend of emigration to cities and to lowland areas of Puno where cash crops such as coffee and coca are produced. Migration has led to a major depopulation of the district during much of the year. Among older people who stay in Conima, there is at once understanding, bewilderment, pride, and sadness regarding young people's emigration.

One day while we were sitting on his patio, an older man in Putina remarked, "My land once belonged to my grandfathers, but now my children have all gone away." Perhaps it was the quiet of the afternoon or the presence of a foreigner instead of his children that had brought the thought to mind. He went on to say, "Some of them should stay home and take care of the house, but they all want to leave, so what can I do? When I die my [adobe] house will fall down and go back to the earth."

Women, children, and older people are the main inhabitants of the district during the dry season (when there is work on the lower Andean slopes), except during fiesta times, when some people return. Children of school age stay with their grandparents or mothers, while the younger men and women go elsewhere to seek employment. People working in the lower regions of Puno and in nearby highland cities return relatively frequently to Conima and often still consider it home base, whereas migration to the distant coastal cities of Lima and Arequipa is more permanent. The people who work nearby remain part of family and community life and are a source of cash for the family members who remain at home. Young men who come back from the local cities, however, can also be a source of tension (chapter 6).

Local Tradition among the Older People in Conima

In terms of social practices and ways of seeing the world, there is a dramatic split between the younger generation and older people in Conima—a split apparently more pronounced than in earlier eras. For people growing up since the 1960s, continual contact with the outside world has been a more profound part of their experience: the constant movement of people and ideas in and out of Conima; the advent of the transistor radio. They grew up during a time when educational and agrarian reforms and the official state discourse of President Juan Velasco (1968–75) promised reduced marginalization and upward social mobility for Andean peasants (chapter 6).

The former isolation of the district as well as the generally recognized chauvinistic tenacity with which Aymara-speaking communities value their heritage (Albó 1974:68) help explain the older generation's conservatism relative to people of more mestizo regions of Peru (see Romero 1990). That people in Huancané still speak Aymara is an example of this tenacity, since many groups adopted Quechua—the state language—during and after the Inca period.

Older Conimeños' maintenance of a distinct local identity and worldview, however, must also be understood in regard to the politics of domination since the colonial era in Peru. The "Indian" identification was partially constructed and maintained by the colonial and republican states, and by members of local elites, in order to retain the indigenous segment of the population as serfs, as a labor pool for the mines, and for tribute payment (Hobsbawn 1990:67; Kubler 1946:371; Tschopik 1946:510).

20

People and cultural practices identified as "Indian" have been systematically separated out, marginalized, and oppressed by the state and local elites for much of Peru's history. Often denied access to opportunities and upward social mobility within the larger society, indigenous Andeans in southern Peru bolstered their own social unity at the local level as a means of defense, and distanced themselves culturally and, when possible, geographically (Schaedel, Escobar, and Rogríguez 1959:13). In some highland regions, such as Conima, this bilateral process of social separation—dialectically generated by both elites and indigenous people themselves—partially accounts for the maintenance of strikingly distinctive local practices. This is particularly true for people whose ideas and styles of living were formed before things began to open up in the 1960s.

The T'inka and Local Divinities

In almost all realms of social practice in Conima, with the exception of the use of mestizo clothing style, distinctive local traditions are evident among older ayllu dwellers.[10] Spiritual beliefs and practices are a prime example. The Christian God, Jesus, Mary, and certain saints have been incorporated into the local religion in extremely complex ways (chapter 4). They are considered additional sources of power, but are usually invoked only at times of major crisis or during certain fiestas along with the local sources of power. In practice, most Conimeños place much more emphasis on maintaining relationships with the local divinities, and "religious" aspects permeate daily life to such a degree that a secular/sacred dichotomy is largely irrelevant. Many of the local forces that I would translate as "supernatural" (for example, places of power on the land, on mountains, or in rivers) are conceived as part of this world; things we consider mundane (the earth itself) are thought of as alive and powerful.

In order to maintain active, reciprocal relations with the most important forces operating in the region, Conimeños include rituals known as *ch'alla* and *t'inka* in almost all social and musical occasions. Ch'alla, almost always performed before social drinking, involves words and an offering of drops of alcohol to the female Earth, to local places of power, and to the ancestors. People in Conima explained that they must give back to those that provide them with life and sustenance.

During the t'inka, a ring of cigarettes is arranged around a pile of coca on a woven cloth, with two cups of alcohol placed on opposite sides of the weaving. Those present (elders first) place selected leaves of coca into the cups while addressing the particular divinity to which the cup is to be offered.

The ritual is repeated three times with the pair of cups. The first time, the contents of one cup is thrown to Condor Mamani (a single divinity of the home and family); that of the other is thrown in the direction of the *cabildo* (a place of power on a family's or community's land). The contents of the second pair are offered to an *achachila* (the divinity of a specific mountain, also translated as "place" and sometimes thought of as a special type of ancestor), and to the *aviadores* (like achachilas but not tied to a specific place). The third time, the contents are offered to Pachamama (Earthmother) and to the ancestors (sometimes called *almas*).[11] Afterward, the coca and cigarettes are shared.

Some people said that the spiritual forces addressed in the t'inka can have both positive and negative influences on people's daily lives, depending on the relationships maintained with them through the ritual performances. Reciprocity between these forces and the communities stands out as a central idea. The emphasis on balance and reciprocity is articulated in social relations, and in relations between people and their ecological environment. The reciprocal offering of coca, which takes place among the participants in a t'inka after the cups are offered, is a type of social communion that realizes this idea.

While almost all older people in Conima participate in these rituals regularly, their meaning may vary for specific individuals. The father of my *compadre*, Jorge Apaza (my wife and I are the godparents of his daughter), is a healer and a specialist in spiritual matters. Relationships with the local as well as Catholic divinities had a special importance in his life. He articulated a strong belief in the power of the achachilas, Pachamama, the ancestors, and other local forces, and characterized them in an orthodox manner that had been echoed by other people within the district. One day when I was speaking with another acquaintance about the nature of the local divinities, however, he responded, "Maybe they are as people say, and maybe they are not. We are only people; how can we know about such things?"

I do not interpret this comment as pure skepticism. Rather, this man simply seemed to be expressing the idea that some things are difficult to know—for particular local people who, for whatever reason, probe such matters in distinct ways, and certainly for ethnographers who attempt to describe complex realms of belief and feeling.

Social Style in the Ayllus of Conima

For their subsistence, older Conimeños depend on the earth and the weather, and they take care to maintain reciprocal relations with these forces. Likewise, tied to their land, surrounded by the land of their neighbors, they depend on other community members in reciprocal labor (such as *ayni*) and social relations. To be excluded is to be left in silence; to be included is to uphold one's responsibilities and to act like a normal human being, which is to say, an *hak'e* (the Aymara word for 'person,' which is how the people of the ayllus refer to themselves).

In commonplace interactions as well as in heightened situations of performance, Conimeños place fundamental value on the solidarity and unity of their social groups (which are situationally defined). They also tend to emphasize the unique identity of their community. This is done primarily through musical repertory and style during performances in the larger district-wide fiestas, the main context for interaction and competition among different communities. As Rodrigo Montoya has accurately observed, Quechua and Aymara speakers in the rural Peruvian highlands perceive their identity concretely in terms of their localized ayllu or community (1986: 254). Abstract concepts of a Quechua or Aymara society are foreign to their daily discourse, as are notions involving ethnicity, except in interactions with mestizos.[12]

Rural Conimeños often stress the collective over the individual. Most older people simply do not like to stand out as individuals in public social settings, and this includes musical performance. In the ensembles there is no place for highlighted soloists; when in public, individual composers will usually attribute their pieces to the ensemble as a whole (chapter 3). The circle formation used by musical ensembles and for most group activities in Conima is significant for maintaining and reproducing egalitarian relations. A Conimeño would not be comfortable on an elevated platform facing and conducting an orchestra, a classroom, or a meeting. In the ayllus, speaking style is soft and indirect. People generally avoid eye contact during conversation, and when talking in groups, a speaker will look at the ground so as to address no one in particular and everyone at the same time.

In addition to downplaying individuality, the emphasis on group solidarity has led to a social style within communities that has conflict avoidance as a guiding principle. People do not typically confront or criticize others publicly, or call attention to them within group interactions. Obviously tensions exist, and people are certainly criticized in private, among family or trusted friends. This difference between public and private behavior, however, underlines the fact that community solidarity is an ideal, part of an ideology that, precisely because of its constant public articulation, becomes deeply internalized.

As Albó notes, and as I have observed in Conima, an outcome of the emphasis on pacific, egalitarian community relations is that public political and religious offices rotate equally among adult male community members, and equality of opportunity is given precedence over individual competence for specific tasks, roles, and rights (Albó 1974:69).[13] This disposition affects attitudes toward musical participation and production in basic ways: any man has the right to join with his community ensemble, regardless of his musical ability and knowledge.

The egalitarian, participatory social style in Conima is also clearly evident in decision-making meetings. Albó's description of the process of reaching consensus in Bolivian Aymara-speaking communities closely mirrors what I have observed in Conima:

> These assemblies are a forum of collective expression and pro-
> cess for decisions that surprise the observer for the degree of
> participation and the feeling of democracy. They are contexts
> usually calm and quiet in nature in which the same theme (or
> idea) is repeated over and over by the different participants until
> they arrive at a certain community consensus explicitly assimi-
> lated, or if consensus is not arrived at, until the point when
> people begin to leave for their houses. (Albó 1974:69)

In Conima, group decisions are reached in a quiet and nonconfrontational manner; there are usually no debates, no hashing out of disagreements, and no direct rejections of ideas or the people who presented them. The issue on the floor is treated as neutral material to be shaped by each interested party in turn until an implicit consensus is reached. Consistent with the desire to avoid conflict, if consensus cannot be obtained, people begin to ignore the issue, turning to other matters, or they simply begin leaving for home. Consensus decision making provides exact parallels to the process of communal-musical composition in Conima (chapter 3), and Albó's mention of the repetitive nature of decision-making meetings is particularly important.

By stressing egalitarian social relations, I do not mean to imply that differences of wealth, status, or prestige do not exist. Older people who have served community offices in the ayllus, and older people in general, are granted special respect and privileges. A difference in status between men and women also seems apparent in public leadership roles, the playing of musical instruments, and other areas. Finally, individual knowledge and ability are also granted special respect. These examples do not contradict the notion of general egalitarian relations, however, in that heightened prestige does not create a situation of asymmetrical social power.

Richard Adams defines social power as "that aspect of social relations that marks the relative equality of the actors or operating units; it is derived from the relative control by each actor or unit over elements of the environment of concern to the participants" (1975:9–10). Social power allows individuals to use the things that they control in order to have their way in spite of the resistance of others. This is precisely what does not usually occur within community relations in the ayllus. Prestige is granted to certain individuals and groups by the community, and the prestige depends on this allocation. If an individual or group attempted to use prestige to their own advantage while ignoring the welfare of others, the allocation would be rapidly withdrawn. This is particularly well illustrated by styles of leadership in musical ensembles (chapter 2). The relations among the different communities in Conima are also egalitarian in nature.

In Conima, the other side of the solidarity coin is factionalism within, and explicit competition between, social groups (Albó 1974). If there is a serious problem within a group that cannot simply be ignored (the typical Conimeño way of dealing with conflicts), the dissenting parties split off. Factionalism within and competition between social units in Conima are pronounced at all institutional levels, as I pointed out earlier in describing the division of the district as a whole and the continual splitting of ayllu and sub-ayllu groups. Like community identity, competition is most clearly manifested in public through musical performance by the ensembles, who serve as champions for their villages during larger festivals.

Hak'e-Mestizo Relations in Conima: Issues of Ethnicity and Class

Conima, like most rural highland districts in Peru, is socially, culturally, and economically divided between the *pueblo* (town) and the communities belonging to the ayllus. The town of Conima serves as the political-administrative center of the district as well as the link with Peruvian national society. The edifices and functionaries of political and ideological domination are located in its central plaza: the Catholic church (now closed all but a few days a year because of a lack of personnel), police headquarters, and the town hall. The buildings surrounding the central plaza, the site of major fiestas, house a number of small stores that sell processed foods, coca, alcohol, and manufactured goods that have been imported from the coast via Juliaca. While each ayllu or subdivision has its own grammar school, the two high schools of the district are located in the towns of Conima and Tilali.

The town of Conima is largely inhabited by mestizos and the families of the former landholding class (Velasco's 1969 agrarian reform broke up the three haciendas of the region). These people refer to themselves as *vecinos* (literally, neighbors), *vecinos notables* (notable neighbors), or *gente decente* (the decent people). They are referred to as *mistis* (mestizos) or *q'ara* (a negative term to denote outsiders) by the people of the ayllus. Because of the steady migration of vecinos to highland and coastal cities,[14] rural people are moving into town from the ayllus to fill the vacancies. These people, often called *cholos* in the anthropological literature (Schaedel, Escobar, and Rodríguez 1959), are distinguished from the mestizo vecinos in Conima on the basis of class and quasi-ethnic criteria. At the same time, people in the ayllus scoff at the air of superiority assumed by these new town dwellers and comment how this or that one has changed his Aymara surname but fools no one.

The mestizos who live in the town are bilingual Spanish/Aymara speakers but speak Spanish among themselves. They wear Western-style clothing, and the majority are Catholic, although some have converted to Protestantism in recent years. The mestizos' worldview, sifted through a rural-provincial outlook, is largely tied to the national, Western-oriented culture. They take care to distinguish themselves from the people of the ayllus and verbally disdain indigenous practices such as coca chewing and indigenous rituals.

Before Velasco's agrarian reform (1969), the asymmetrical power relations between mestizos and indigenous Andeans were based on the mestizos' commercial links with the outside and their greater ability to control and usurp land with the aid of state force: the armed police and military. The legal system also supported land snatching by mestizos and the forced, un-paid labor of indigenous people. Social prejudice and negative attitudes toward indigenous arts and cultural practices were a central part of the ideological apparatus that rationalized and helped underwrite the domination of Andean peoples. Although most of Conima was free of haciendas, the social relations and attitudes engendered by the larger system of domination were carried over to define "ethnic" relations within the district.[15] Velasco's land, educational, and social reforms have helped reduce mestizo privilege, making their attempts to distinguish themselves all the more vigorous—moves played out, by this time, mainly in terms of social style and cultural capital (chapters 5 and 6).

On the other side, the people of the ayllus frequently harbor a great mis-trust of and dislike for mestizos and, with the exception of certain ritualized relations such as *compadrazgo* (coparent relations), avoid social interaction with them whenever possible. One night after a fiesta performance I was drinking with Filiberto and Manuel in a small store on the plaza. We were sitting on a bench, passing the bottle and a single glass among us, when a policeman and two mestizos entered. I was holding the bottle and glass when the mestizos began to engage me in conversation. After a few minutes, I turned to hand the glass to Manuel but was surprised and somewhat annoyed to find that both he and Filiberto had silently vanished—as if through the wall—leaving me alone to extricate myself from what could have become a difficult situation. Stories abound of indigenous people being thrown out of stores, beaten by mestizos, and harassed by police in the not so distant past. Acts of violence between drunken policemen and people from Conima occurred during my stay.

Social Mobility

Referring to social mobility in the Department of Puno prior to 1959, Richard Schaedel writes:

> Historically speaking, movement of the Indian towards the middle and upper classes by passing through the different stages of urbanization or "cholofication" has been the usual means of vertical movement. At no time does it appear to have been considerable. The main development seems to have been the maintenance of the two ethnic lines of origin: on the one hand, the middle and upper classes with Spanish and Mestizo backgrounds, and on the other the Cholo and Indian groups. (Schaedel, Escobar, and Rodríguez 1959:13)

Over the past two decades, the situation in Conima has changed substantially, and movement from indigenous to mestizo status may take place within a generation. For example, while vecinos in Conima defined the older musicians with whom I worked as "Indios," a few of the musicians' sons, through education, by becoming completely bilingual, by moving to urban centers, and, most significantly, by becoming "professionals" (schoolteachers, white-collar clerks, etc.), were redefined by these same vecinos as "mestizos." This was dramatically demonstrated on several occasions when one of these young professionals returned home for a fiesta. The young man was welcomed as a guest at a private indoor party attended only by mestizos; meanwhile, his father remained outside on the patio with the contracted musicians and was basically treated like a servant by the host (see chapter 5). This same young man, who married a mestiza from another region, rarely came home because, as his father explained with a mixture of hurt, anger, and sarcasm, his son was ashamed of his "ignorant" parents in front of his wife.

27

If occupational and economic status is improved, one moves up in the hierarchy and ultimately becomes redefined as mestizo. This is somewhat circular, however, because to improve one's socioeconomic position, one nearly always must take on the features of mestizo culture: language, literacy, occupation, and social style. Ethnicity as it intersects with class, then, is clearly a construct that can be manipulated with effort. Urban migration is the prime way to "move up" within the rural hometown (chapter 10), but simultaneously, within the cities where they go to live, most people from rural peasant backgrounds find themselves back down on the lowest rung of the ladder. According to the criteria defining social position in Peru, and particularly in Lima, being from the rural highlands—that is, being an "indio" or "cholo"—was and is a tremendous liability for movement within criollo society.

LIMA: THE CITY OF KINGS

Lima, founded in 1535 as the capital of the Spanish Viceroyalty of Peru, is a huge city that, with its port of Callao, had a population of about six million in 1984 (Matos 1984:67). Like most large modern cities, particularly in Latin America, it is characterized by dramatic contrasts. Practically all of Peru's wealthy elite reside in enclaves within the metropolis, as do some of the nation's poorest people. On any day in the central part of the city, women dressed in the latest European fashions can be seen driving Mercedes past ragged, hungry highland families who live in the street. The National Symphony performs regularly, as do rock groups, salsa bands, and highland-migrant ensembles that play music from every rural corner of the nation.

The city is built on a sandy desert oasis on the Pacific coast. It almost never rains, although from April to October the capital is constantly shrouded in cold, damp fog and clouds. The metropolitan area of Lima-Callao has forty-five separate districts (see Henríquez et al. 1985:30–31). The symbolic and administrative heart of the criollo capital is the Plaza de Armas with its governmental palace and the Plaza San Martín in the center of old Lima. Many of the central districts of old Lima are in a state of decay; beautiful wooden colonial balconies rot on unpainted walls. On the sidewalks below, passage is blocked by street vendors who sell cigarettes, pencils, batteries, hairbrushes, plumbing supplies, car parts, clothing, books, and pirate cassettes (de Soto 1989).

Driving southwest to the coast from the District of Lima, one passes through the older fashionable districts of San Isidro and Miraflores, where private police can be seen guarding the residences of those made fearful by the increasing political and criminal violence. Desperation has continued to rise on all sides throughout the 1980s, as have the activities of guerrilla movements such as Sendero Luminoso.

Demographics and Social Change

In less than fifty years Lima has gone through a series of dramatic transformations because of migration, the population explosion, and Peru's economic decline. As recently as 1940, Lima-Callao had 645,172 inhabitants (Henríquez et al. 1985:12) as compared with six million by 1985. People of both the lower and upper classes reminisce about what a different place Lima was in the 1940s. For example, one elderly Puneño of the working class moved to the District of La Victoria when it was still on the outskirts of the city and "practically all *chakra*" (agricultural fields). The central market and violent slums grew up rapidly around his neatly kept house, and now he is afraid to leave the sanctuary of his home. Lower-income families in many parts of the city live in similar daily fear, but are unable to move because of their financial circumstances.

A dramatic contrast between the 1940s and the 1980s is also felt by criollos of the upper classes. In the 1940s and 1950s their position, birthright, and authority were not openly questioned; the sidewalks were clean and were not cluttered by *ambulantes* (street vendors), and there was not a beggar's hand extended at every turn. During 1984–86, though, kidnapping and organized political violence aimed at members and emblems of the elite were escalating. The growing concentration of the underclass in Lima had come to affect the elite directly, perhaps for the first time.

In Peru as a whole, a major transformation has taken place. By 1984, close to 65 percent of the population was urban, whereas in 1940 this same percentage of the population was defined as rural (cf. Matos 1984:43; de Soto 1989:7). Traditionally, Lima has been the major destination for internal migration (Henríquez, Blanes, and Valleras 1979:51), with the majority of migrants coming from the Andean highlands (Dietz 1976:10; Matos 1968:22, 46). It has been estimated that between 1976 and 1981, Lima's stable population grew by 40,000 inhabitants each year because of migration (Henríquez et al. 1985:14).

Conimeños suggest that, initially, the most common reasons for urban migration were rural population growth, land shortage, and the economic insecurity of a peasant's existence (chapter 7). Other factors such as access to better education and health services are also commonly cited by highland migrants. By now, because of the depopulation of many rural areas, it would seem that ideological factors generating migration can no longer be denied. Fundamentally, these include the idea that an urban-Western way of life is superior to the Andean. Public education in the rural areas and the media have promulgated such ideas. For all but the most romantic observer, the choice of urban life would seem logical, and yet the insecurity, hardship, and frequent failures encountered in Lima by many migrants raise difficult questions (chapter 7).

The heaviest migratory movements from the sierra prior to 1961 were from departments closer to the capital: Ancash (88,136 migrants living in Lima in 1961), Ayacucho (73,203) and Junín (62,630). The number of Puneño migrants living in Lima in 1961 was relatively small, 14,881 (Henríquez 1980: anexo cuadro 2). The major migratory flow from Puno, which began in the 1960s, was later than that from the departments mentioned above. Henríquez estimates that between 1961 and 1972, 28,578 Puneños migrated to Lima (1980: anexo cuadro 2), almost double the number that had come to Lima before 1961 and were living there in that year.

Pueblos Jóvenes

To accommodate this demographic explosion, the city expanded outwardly in tremendous proportions. The upper class formed new enclaves further out of town (Schaedel 1979:405). The middle class situated itself somewhat outside the city core, in districts such as Lince and Pueblo Libre. Some members of the lower and working classes remained in the inner-city slums and low-rent districts (Millones 1978:12–13; Schaedel 1979:405), but in addition, these groups have banded together to form *barriadas* or *pueblos jóvenes* to the north and south of the city.

The pueblos jóvenes (a euphemism from the Velasco era for *barriadas*, or squatter settlements) are communities that are usually established through land invasions. Groups organize and then, in a single night, move en masse to the selected area of unused land at the edges of the city. Houses of straw mats are erected on the sand immediately, and someone must always remain at the site to maintain the claim. The land invasions are illegal to a greater or lesser extent, depending on the stance of the government in power (de Soto 1989). In 1985 under the American People's Revolutionary Alliance (APRA) government of Alan García, an attempted land invasion near the airport was foiled by government troops, who burned the straw huts and removed people forcibly. During the military government of Juan Velasco (1968–75), a more lenient approach was taken, sometimes involving relocation. In and after this period, many new pueblos jóvenes were established in the "northern cone" and "southern cone" of the city (see Matos 1968; Collier 1978). In 1972, an estimated 783,093 people lived in pueblos jóvenes in Lima (23.7 percent of the population) as compared with 1,171,839 (25.5 percent) in 1981 (Henríquez et al. 1985:19)—although exact figures may be difficult to obtain because of the informal nature of these settlements.

If a land invasion succeeds in the initial phase (i.e., the people are not evicted), community organizations begin to petition the government for legal land rights. Once this is accomplished, they begin to petition for services such as water, electricity, and transportation, all of which may take several years to establish. Within a single pueblo joven, homes at all stages of construction may be seen, ranging from huts made of straw mats to nicely finished two-story houses. This is the case in Mariano Melgar, the pueblo joven where many Conimeños live. In spite of the unsavory reputation of the pueblos jóvenes as crime-ridden, dangerous locations, many are well-organized, orderly neighborhoods. The formation of pueblos jóvenes represents the major strategy for people of the lower and working classes to own their own homes, and they are decidedly a step up from the inner-city slums (Dietz 1976; Collier 1973:25; Millones 1978; de Soto 1989).

Economic and Political Relations in Lima

Besides the physical changes in Lima, there have been major political, economic, social, and cultural changes that have resulted from mass highland migration and Peru's economic paralysis. Traditionally throughout Peru, but particularly in Lima, official political, economic, and sociocultural institutions were oriented toward upholding and protecting the privileged position of the Peruvian criollo elite (see Schaedel 1979; *Caretas* 1983:29). The Peruvian upper classes used both official and unofficial channels to maintain their dominant position. Bureaucratic webs were cast around those who were not well connected to people in power, and those who did not look, talk, and behave like members of the urban-criollo group. Infinite inaction was used to deny rights, privileges, licenses to conduct business, titles to buy land, and so on to people identified as Indio or *provinciano* (from the provinces; see de Soto 1989). The cultural markers that distinguish social groups were thus extremely important components of the power structure, and assimilation in cultural terms was a central strategy for upward social mobility.

31

In regard to criollo-highlander relations in Lima in the 1940s (and before), Schaedel writes that

> the patterns of acculturation that the dominant urban *criollo* society imposed upon the migrants were fairly well observed. These amounted to a series of informal constraints, reinforced by discriminatory attitudes that the *criollos* practiced upon the migrants. Attributes of indigenous origin were simply not tolerated in Lima (e.g. Indian dress, barefootedness, coca chewing, Quechua speech); the opportunity structure was open at the level of domestic servant and apprentice or helper to the skilled *maestro* category of manual worker. Forms of speech governed the relationship of subordination in transactions (e.g., tu versus Ud.). It was clear that migrants who came to Lima in this decade, and certainly more obviously so in previous decades, were obliged to adopt *criollo* ways and suppress their ethnicity, and part of the *criollo* way was to accept their role as manual workers and subordinate people. (Schaedel 1979:402)

By the 1960s, however, highlanders in Lima were becoming increasingly aware of their power in numbers. They began organizing many different types of grass-roots movements to solve their own problems, in the face of official unwillingness or inability to do so (see Uzzell 1974a, 1974b, 1980). The organized land invasions for the creation of pueblos jóvenes offer a clear case in point, as do the formation of street vendors' unions and community-based food-relief programs and cooperatives. Certain highland regional associations—a focus of this study—have come to serve similar functions, but they must be understood within this larger context of grass-roots movements and the harsh conditions that forced them into existence.

Problem solving outside the usual official channels has become generally known as "informality" (e.g., see Salcedo 1984; Matos 1984; de Soto 1989). This name comes from the term "informal sector," referring to unlicensed and untaxed businesses. While Lima is Peru's principal industrial center and has the major portion of the salaried population in the country (Henríquez et al. 1985:32), the growth of industry and of formal-sector jobs had not been able to keep pace with the booming migrant population. Heightened crisis in the Peruvian economy—the external debt, a declining formal GNP and investments—during the 1980s made matters worse. Numerous "informal" businesses have sprung up as a result, including everything from shoe shining and selling candy on the street to the manufacturing of furniture and car parts. Many new businesses, even some of a fairly substantial nature, remain in the informal sector due to the bureaucratic difficulties of obtaining licenses (*Caretas* 1983; de Soto 1989). While the figures are difficult to substantiate, it was estimated that in the 1980s between 30 and 40 percent of Lima's population was working as a part of the informal economic sector (Henríquez et al. 1985:32; Wendorff 1985:138, 143; de Soto estimates 48 percent nationwide, 1989:12).

The swelling migrant population has led to a boom of highlander-owned and operated businesses (some in the formal sector, but more often in the informal), and it also provided a market to support them. By the 1980s, highlanders had created substantial networks through which newcomers gained employment. This contrasts with earlier decades when criollos controlled the job market and migrants were forced into the position of supplicants for employment. One Conimeño who owns his own construction company in Lima told me that he hires only highlanders, "because criollos are lazy and do not know how to work." This is not an isolated case, and the change in control over the hiring and firing, as well as the reverse prejudices voiced, indicate an important alteration in highlander/criollo power relations.

Rather than seeing "informality" as proof of the value of laissez-faire capitalism as de Soto seems to, I believe in most cases it should be interpreted as people hustling for survival in a bad situation that provides no other options. I also do not wish to underplay the fact that many highland resident families remain economically marginalized and, by 1990, are in particularly desperate straits because of Peru's economic collapse and President Alberto Fujimori's countermeasures. But it is important to emphasize that, by the time of my fieldwork, the criollo-controlled economic sector was no longer the only game in town. This situation, perhaps more than any other, led highland residents to reconsider the value of Andean identity and social unity.

Because of their massive numbers, *provincianos* (highland residents) in Lima also had gained economic clout in the form of consumer power in the formal sector during the mid-1980s. Provinciano and criollo commercial concerns alike turned increasing attention to the provinciano market. This was indicated first by radio and then by television advertising. More radio and television time has been devoted to entertaining and selling to provinciano audiences, and hence there is more highland music on airwaves that, before the 1950s, were dominated by foreign and criollo musical styles (Cotler 1983:198; Doughty 1972:44).

In political terms, the huge provinciano population in Lima became a force that could no longer be ignored, and this is certainly the case during the 1980s, after democratic process had returned. The surprising victory of Alberto Fujimori over Mario Vargas Llosa in the 1990 presidential election is the most dramatic illustration to date. One observer has written: "In different circumstances, or in a different country, [Fujimori's] campaign might have evaporated swiftly. But Peru is a country marked by racism and class hatred, in which to the great majority of the population the fact that he was an Oriental meant, above all, that he was not white, and was therefore one of them" (Guillermoprieto 1990:122).

During my stay, candidates for municipal and national offices campaigned at regional migrant-club functions, and, as is described in chapter 9, the government had to take highlanders increasingly into account when courting public opinion and acceptance.

Velasco

The change in this century from a local land-based economic structure to greater reliance on a commercial-industrial base led the nation to economic crisis and to deep dependence on foreign capital. In response, the government of President Juan Velasco (1968–75) undertook sweeping economic and social reforms. These included the land reform that undid the highland hacienda system in favor of peasants; the legalization of Quechua as an official language; media reforms that favored the diffusion of Peruvian music and views, including those of highlanders; and an educational reform that penetrated the rural highlands to a greater degree than ever before. In a conscious effort to establish hegemony, this government's pro-Andean position softened the marginality of highland culture by the mid-1970s (Schaedel 1979:408).

Puneños, both in the sierra and in Lima, frequently identified the Velasco era as the time when prejudice against their highland heritage began to diminish. Simultaneously, efforts such as educational reform had particular success in diffusing urban-national values to young people in rural areas. Perhaps more important, Velasco's policies generated the idea that opportunities for young rural people within the national society were now more available, making the choice to join the nation more appealing.

Greater economic autonomy and political power among migrants, and the legitimation of Andean culture within state discourse since Velasco, has reduced the impetus to deny highland heritage in Lima. But the migrants' discovery that the formal opportunity structures in the capital were still largely closed to them—and, in any event, were crumbling—inspired alternative problem-solving strategies. The bolstering of regional-highland unity and identity for the creation of self-help networks became one viable course of action for an increasing number of migrants. Given the regionally specific nature of Andean music, and the paramount importance of music and dance as artistic and community activities in the highlands, Andean music took on new value in the city as a fulcrum for migrant identity and social action.

Among Puneños, playing panpipes in Lima—behind walls or in the streets—represents a political choice, as they themselves recognize (see chapter 9). Many of the middle-aged Conimeño residents that I knew had not touched a panpipe or Andean flute during their first ten or fifteen years in Lima. They did not simply "bring their culture with them," as descriptions of migrants in Peru and in other societies often suggest. Rather, because of changes in the political, social, and economic conditions in Lima—primarily changes in power relations—and their own needs, Puneño migrants rediscovered the potency and importance of the highland musical traditions as emblems and as a means for uniting, and actually creating, their communities in the city.

As in Conima, the Conimeño residents in Lima use musical traditions from the home district to create and represent their community and identity. In Lima the residents emphasize that they are Conimeños, and they name their regional associations accordingly (Centro Social Conima, Unión Progresista Conima). Their main goal in musical performance is "to sound like Conima." But what it *means* to be a Conimeño in the highland district and in Lima differs radically, and some understanding of the contrasts can be gained though studying the differences in musical practice, value, occasions, and style.

PART ONE
Music in Conima

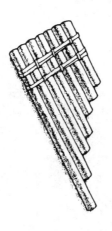

O N E

Instruments, Aesthetics, and Performance Practice

ONE MORNING SEVERAL weeks before the Easter fiesta, Filiberto emerged from his storeroom with an old flour sack filled with delicate cane, neatly grouped by size and tied with string. It was the relatively late hour of eight, and his wife had already gone to work in the fields. Filiberto seemed particularly content not to be doing agricultural work that day; he told me that he never liked it very much. Moving leisurely like a man on holiday, he rolled a large stump into the sunshine on his patio, placed the bag of cane on one side and his measuring sticks and a bag of coca on the other, and sat down, spreading a thick cloth and tools on his lap.

Filiberto likes to make all sorts of things, from houses to dustpans, and he is good at it. One time, when I returned to Conima after a stay in Lima, I was surprised to find that he had built me a one-room adobe house next to his. Embarrassed by my gratitude, he told me that it had not been much trouble, and anyway, he said, "I like to build houses." Filiberto sometimes takes on building projects for townspeople for wages. Because of his skill, he is also a particularly valued participant in communal work projects and in *ayni* (reciprocal labor) relationships. Above all, however, he is known both in and outside the district for his ability to "cut cane"—to make musical instruments, a specialized skill in Conima.

It may take Filiberto two days or more to cut a tuned consort of panpipes for twenty-four people. Working slowly and deliberately so as not to waste precious material, he places a notched measuring stick into each tube, marks and cuts the cane at the proper notch, and then smooths the edge with a stone. Once all the tubes are cut, he begins to assemble the different instruments, constantly checking the tuning of newly constructed panpipes against others already finished. He raises the pitch of tubes that blow too flat by trimming the blowing end, those that play excessively sharp must be replaced.

Instrument makers in Conima cut only the *tropas* (tuned consorts) of panpipes (*sikus*) and side-blown flutes (*pitus*). The other two main instrument types used in the district, *pinkillus* and *tarkas* (duct flutes), are purchased from makers outside the district—usually at markets on the Bolivian border or in the town of Huancané. I cannot say why Conimeños do not make the duct flutes, except to speculate that they require more tools and different knowledge.

Usually only one man within each of the different communities in Conima inherits the measuring sticks and knowledge for making the pitus and sikus. The proper tuning and voicing of an ensemble are considered crucial to a good performance, and a community's measuring sticks are carefully guarded for fear that other groups in the district will "steal" their tunings (determining the relative range and tuning variances among the voices), a key to the sound by which they distinguish themselves publicly. As an instrument maker approaches old age, he considers the younger men within the community very carefully before deciding to whom he will pass his knowledge and tools. One older panpipe maker told me that he was at a loss regarding a successor. He threatened to go to the grave without teaching anyone if a younger man did not materialize whom he could trust to be "responsible and serious." While I do not take this threat literally, it does speak to the specialized, esoteric conception of wind-instrument making, and the importance of a community's "unique" tunings as an expression of group originality and identity.

In contrast, many men know how to build drums used for panpipe performance (*bombos*), and they are often made collectively by ensemble members (of plywood and goatskin). Drums are fairly uniform in sound and construction among the different communities, and thus they do not have the same significance for distinguishing community identity.

When economically feasible, a community's fiesta sponsor purchases the necessary cane for making panpipes and side-blown flutes, or buys a tropa of pinkillus or tarkas at a local market, depending on the instrument associated with the upcoming festival that he is hosting. At the beginning of a fiesta, the instruments are given to the musicians as gifts for their participation, and many men in the ayllus have a collection of instruments from past years. After a fiesta has passed, however, instruments may be treated in a rather cavalier fashion. While visiting friends in Conima, I frequently saw instruments lying about in random corners of rooms or on their patios—sometimes broken or taken by children as playthings. Although Filiberto preserved his old instruments and had a particularly large collection, many

Conimeños did not seem to cherish instruments as objects in and of themselves. They granted them importance only before and during a festival for their use-value: bringing the specific celebration to life and the community together. At these times instruments were handled with care, almost tenderness.

MUSIC IN CONIMA

There is an average of one fiesta a month in the District of Conima (appendix 1 includes a calendar of fiestas and associated musical traditions). The people of the ayllus often plan variable life-cycle celebrations such as weddings around these times, thereby extending some festival periods to a week or more. The communities in the district have varied customs regarding the dances they perform and the fiestas they celebrate, although all the communities participate in Carnival and Todos los Santos (November 1–2). Each community has its own performing ensemble. Music is largely a nonspecialist activity, but only men perform instruments.[1] In Conima during the 1980s, five Andean wind instruments were the mainstay for ayllu festival music: sikus (double-row panpipes); five-hole pinkillus; six-hole pinkillus (vertical cane duct flutes); tarkas (carved wooden duct flutes); and pitus or falawatus (transverse cane flutes). Examples of these instrumental traditions from Conima and elsewhere in Peru may be heard on *Mountain Music of Peru, Vol. 2* (SF 40406; see discography).

These instruments are all played in large ensembles in which only the same type of melodic instrument is used (tarkas with tarkas, sikus with sikus, and so on). The ensembles can range from twelve to, on exceptional occasions, fifty players.[2] Between four and eight panpipe musicians accompany the ensemble with drums, usually bombos (also called *wankara*—large, deep-sounding, double-headed wooden drums). Pitu and tarka groups are accompanied by Western snare and bass drums, and the pinkillu ensembles have a separate *caja* (large, deep-sounding, indigenous, wooden snare drum) section, with drummers almost equal in number to the flute players.

In Conima, each instrument has between two and seven musical genres that are specific to it and that, like the instruments themselves, are linked to different fiestas, costumed dance dramas, and times of year (see appendix 1). Except for life-cycle fiestas (which have variable dates), panpipes are performed in the dry season (April–October) and duct flutes (pinkillus and tarkas) are associated with the rainy season. These same seasonal associations frequently apply to panpipe and duct-flute performance in indigenous

41

communities throughout Puno and in Bolivia (Baumann 1981, 1982a, 1982b; Buechler 1980:40–41, 358–59), although, as always in the Andes, there are local variations.[3]

CONTEMPORARY INSTRUMENTAL TRADITIONS IN CONIMA
Major Panpipes Styles in Puno

Various single- and double-row panpipe traditions are found throughout the contemporary Andean highlands—from Ecuador to northern Chile and Argentina—and in the Amazonian region. (See appendix 2 for historical background on the different instruments covered in this chapter.) Although panpipes are found in Peru as far north as Cajamarca (e.g., the single-row *antara*, or *andara*, played solo in pipe and tabor fashion), Puno is the sierra region where the performance of double-row panpipes is most pronounced (Instituto Nacional de Cultura 1978:192–219). The large ensemble panpipe and other wind styles of Puno are actually more closely linked to Bolivian traditions than to musical styles to the north in Peru.

In Puno, the names of double-row panpipes often correspond to the names of the dances and genres performed. The major indigenous traditions in the department include *ayarachis*, *chiriguanos*, and *sikuris*.[4] The ayarachi style is performed by Quechua speakers near Lampa, in three parallel octaves with drums resembling the *cajas* of Conima (Cuentas 1982a; Bellenger 1983). The chiriguano style (distinct from the tradition of the same name in Bolivia) is performed on huge panpipes around the provincial capital of Huancané for the Fiesta de la Cruz (May 3) by people from the local ayllus. The consort is likewise made up of three parallel octaves, but the ensembles do not use any percussion (see Valencia 1981; Bellenger 1983).

Although the double-row panpipe is known generically in Peru by the Aymara term *siku* (and by the Spanish word *zampoña*), the word *sikuri* refers to a specific type of panpipe ensemble in Puno, a specific musical genre, and the musicians that play this tradition. Sikuri ensembles, with local stylistic variations, are found throughout Huancané and also in the Province of Puno (Valencia 1980). In recent decades it has been diffused more widely because of an urban panpipe movement (chapter 6). It is presently the only panpipe style performed in Conima and is discussed at length below.

Unlike these three indigenous panpipe traditions, the *sikumoreno* double-row panpipe style is usually more closely associated with mestizo culture and contexts. According to Américo Valencia (1983:65), the style is also referred to as *mistisikus*, (misti = mestizo), indicating this ethnic association. The term *moreno* is related to other ornate mestizo costumed dances, known generically as *trajes de luces* (costumes of light), which have come to Puno from Bolivia (e.g., Rey Moreno). Sikumorenos are performed in various parts of the Department of Puno and in the Department of Tacna. Despite the association with mestizos, it is also the main panpipe style among Aymara speakers in the provinces of Puno and Chucuito. This may be related to the fact that the main transportation route connecting the city of Puno with La Paz, Bolivia, runs through these provinces, making them less isolated than Huancané, to the north of the lake.

Sikumoreno ensembles use two or three parallel octaves, Western snare and bass drum, and cymbals. In the cities of Puno and Juliaca, and in larger towns, the musicians typically wear ornate costumes in the traje de luz style. Sikumoreno music is usually considered livelier and more upbeat than the indigenous styles because of the use of snare drum and cymbals, its faster tempos, and the more staccato—punchy—blowing style. The choreography, consisting of small, quick forward steps and intricate figures, differs from the sikuri dance in Huancané—a slow, natural walk in circle formation. As discussed in chapter 6, the sikumoreno style was the first large-ensemble panpipe tradition to catch on in a major way among Puneño migrants in Lima.

The Sikuri Tradition in Conima

The siku used in Conima is the typical stairstep variety, with each tube cut successively shorter and stopped at the lower end by a natural node in the cane. The delicate cane comes from the tropical forest region. The two rows of the siku are known as *ira* (the one that leads, the shorter of the pair with six or seven tubes) and *arca* (the one that follows, with seven or eight tubes). In some Andean regions, the ira and arca panpipe rows are said to be considered male and female, respectively (Grebe 1980; Jiménez 1951; Baumann 1982b), but the Conimeño musicians I questioned did not seem to think of the ira and arca rows in this way.

A single instrument pair is tuned so that the pitch series alternates between the two rows, requiring two musicians to interlock their respective ira and arca parts to create a melody. The tuning of octaves on a single instrument, or of unisons and octaves among the instruments of a tuned consort, can vary considerably. For example, the following middle-sized (*ankuta* or *malta*) panpipes were cut as a single consort by Filiberto, who is generally considered the best maker in Conima. Moving low to high, from E^{b4} to $C\#^6$, the figures given are in (+ or −) cents, and the pitches placed in columns would be blown simultaneously.[5]

43

IRA:		F#−44	A+20	C#−47	E−41	G#−35	B−34	
ARCA:	E−46	G#−45	B−30	D−45	F#−44	A−37		C#−76
IRA:		F#−37	A−13	C#−35	E−45	G#−36	B−39	
ARCA:	E−41	G#−48	B−25	D−37	F#−85	A−44		C#−52
IRA:		F#−19	A+24	C#−26	E+11	G#−33	B−46	
ARCA:	E−29	G#−27	B+8	D−27	F#−52	A−7		C#−82
IRA:		F#−6	A+17	C#−20	E−14	G#−86	B−48	
ARCA:	E−24	G#+3	B−30	D−33	F#−48	A+19		C#−17

Fig. 1. Ankuta panpipe tunings.

The type of tuning variance for any given unison or octave illustrated in figure 1 is fundamental to the distinctive color of indigenous Andean wind ensembles throughout southern Peru. It should be understood as an allowable range for any given pitch that results in an extremely dense sound quality—rich with overtones and combination tones. When cane is available, each panpipe row will be constructed with a second resonating row placed behind it (its *requinto*); these corresponding tubes are tuned roughly an octave higher, with about the same range of variance as shown in figure 1. Air spilled over into the resonating tubes fills out the sound of the instrument and points to the same basic aesthetic preference for a dense, sonorously rich and varied sound (see Keil 1987).

Sikuri ensembles usually play in a large circle formation. The paired musicians who interlock their ira and arca parts typically stand next to each other and listen most closely to their partners. Sometimes long-lived partnerships form between certain players in a group. Each member of the pair usually holds his note, slightly overlapping with his partner's, so that there are no gaps of silence in the melody. A relatively gentle attack, a crescendo for the center of the pitch, and then a gradual decay also aid in blending the ira and arca parts. When a musician has sequential melodic tones on his panpipe, slurs are used and distinct articulations are avoided, as is vibrato. Ideally, each tube is blown so that it is filled with air, creating a relatively smooth, even sound. Honking on the panpipes—forceful blowing, creating harsh overtones and filling only the mouth of the tube with air—is considered bad playing in Conima, although it occurs sometimes on the larger panpipes, which are harder to blow.[6]

The contemporary Conimeño sikuri style is most clearly distinguished from other panpipe traditions by the particular harmonic voicing used. The voicing of panpipe ensembles is produced by cutting the instruments to different lengths, so that the corresponding tubes of each voice will sound in specific harmonic intervals when played in parallel fashion—corresponding tubes played at the same time. Each voice has its own name, starting with the smallest: (1) *suli* (ultimate); (2) *ankuta* (youth, young female, young female animal) or *malta* (middle); and (3) *sanja* or *tayka* (mother, old woman, old female animal).[7] Terminology for the names of instrumental voices varies regionally; I will consistently use Conimeño nomenclature.

At present there are three basic schemes for parallel voicing used by sikuri groups in the Province of Huancané. These include ensembles with three parallel octaves (suli, malta, sanja). The other major double-row panpipe traditions of Puno—sikumorenos, ayarachis, and chiriguanos—also use three parallel octaves, as did the single-row *loke pallapalla* and *kallamachu* panpipe ensembles in Conima. A second type of voicing that distinguishes the sikuri style ideally has three voice groups with two voices each, as shown in figure 2 (pitches refer to the lowest tone of each panpipe voice).

This type of voicing also characterizes the kantus style of Bolivia (Baumann 1985). The third type of voicing, that of the Conimeño sikuri tropa style, differs as shown in figure 3 (data are given for the largest tube of each voice, the actual pitches may vary).

This harmonic framework, ideally involving nine voices and the number of pairs indicated above, is in reality contingent on a series of factors such as who shows up for a performance and whether or not a fiesta sponsor can afford the cane for a new tropa (chapter 3). The group that I played with, Qhantati Ururi, often dropped the suli voice. Moreover, during my research, the bajosanja and contrasanja voices were used infrequently due to a shortage of cane of sufficient length. A tropa cut for me, however, did include a

Panpipe Voice	*Pitch* (+ / −)
Suli	E5
Contrasuli	B4
Malta (or ankuta)	E4
Contramalta	B3
Sanja (or tayka)	E3
Contrasanja	B2

Fig. 2. Sikuri tropa in parallel 4ths and 5ths.

Panpipe Voice	Length (cm)	Pitch (+ / −)	No. of Pairs
Suli	13.50	E5	1
Bajosuli	15.85	C#5	1
Contrasuli	19.35	A4	1
Malta (ankuta)	27.00	E4	4–6
Bajomalta	31.70	C#4	1
Contramalta	38.70	A3	1–2
Sanja (tayka)	54.00	E3	1–2
Bajosanja	63.40	C#3	1
Contrasanja	77.40	A2	1

Fig. 3. Conimeño sikuri tropa.

suli, a bajosanja, and a contrasanja, since Filiberto felt that it should be complete.

This sikuri tropa style is said to have originated in Conima as the innovation of a local town mestizo (chapter 5). While it is likely that the addition of thirds was derived from Western/mestizo musical practice, the harmonic configuration is not conceived in terms of stacked root-position triads. Rather, all the voices are heard in relation to the central malta voice and voice group (each voice group is thought of as a unit). Conimeño musicians consistently state that the malta is the principal melody-carrying voice, with the other voices heard as 'accompaniment,' and the malta is strongly foregrounded in volume, with as many as four to six pairs performing it. The concept of tonic is not applicable since sikuri music is not tonal, but the final of the malta voices serves a similar function, as the melodic goal for the entire consort. Conimeño musicians also suggest that the higher and lower voice groups should be symmetrically balanced in volume around the prominent center group. Therefore, the larger, softer contramalta and sanja panpipes are doubled to balance the louder, shriller sulis if enough personnel is available and new cane has been purchased, allowing the panpipe maker to have a hand in determining the voicing.

Sikuri ensembles traditionally perform for Pascuas (Easter), Santa Cruz (May 3), San Isidro (May 15), La Virgen de la Asunción (August 15), San Miguel (mestizo patronal fiesta, August 29), and weddings and other life-cycle events such as the *primer corte de pelo* (child's first haircutting, a pre-Columbian tradition). The life-cycle festivals may occur at any time of year and are usually held around the time of a major community festival, when people are already gathered and ready to celebrate. In 1985, I was aware of three weddings in different communities during February between Candelaria and Carnival.

Three sikuri genres, *lentos* or *sikuris* (slow pieces), *ligeros* (fast pieces), and marches, are used for social dancing and processions during many of these fiesta occasions. Some events, however, call for specific genres. In the Easter celebration, a particular genre called *choclo* (corn on the cob, referring to the quick steps taken close together in the dance) is played. This is the only time the multiple bombos are replaced by a Western snare and bass drum in Conimeño sikuri ensembles. In fact, the change in drum accompaniment is the only musical marker that distinguishes choclos from ligeros; the same pieces will be performed in both styles. On May 3, the genre *imillani* (a dance for the "coming out" of young girls) is performed, accompanied by cajas (played by the panpipe musicians). The *satiri* genre, to accompany a dance drama representing the agricultural cycle, is played on May 15 with bombos.

Pitus: Side-Blown Flutes

Side-blown flutes are played in many areas of the Peruvian highlands as well as in the Amazonian region (Instituto Nacional de Cultura 1978:219–25; see appendix 2). In contrast to the unison transverse flute styles most typically heard in Peru, Conimeño ensembles play in parallel polyphony. Two types of tropas are used, depending on the particular Conimeño community, as shown in figure 4.

Conimeños make their flutes of cane (1–2 mm thick), with six non-equidistantly placed holes on the upper side. They tune them roughly to a diatonic series (using sequential fingerings), but with the same type of tuning variance described for the sikus. The tayka measures about 58.5 cm with a diameter of about 2 cm; the ankuta (type 2) is about 43 cm in length; and the suli measures 30.5 cm with a diameter of 1.4 cm.

	Type 1	*Type 2*
Suli	C4	C4
Ankuta	G3	F3
Tayka	C3	C3

Fig. 4. Pitu tropas (lowest non-overblown pitches).

47

As in the case of sikuris, pitu musicians state that the central ankuta is the main melody-carrying voice. Ideally it is foregrounded in volume, with fewer of the louder sulis being used to balance the lower, softer taykas. The pitu is primarily overblown in the high register (only the second octave and beginning of the third octave are used). It is played with a soft embouchure, creating a breathy sound which contributes to a well-blended ensemble; both the tuning variance and the overblowing technique augment the density of sound, a prominent characteristic of all the wind traditions in Conima. With the exception of occasional trills, downward-cascading slides (usually at cadence points or at the end of long-held pitches) are the main type of ornamentation used. As in all Conimeño wind performance, vibrato and sharp articulations (tonguing) are avoided.

Pitu ensembles presently accompany two different costumed fiesta dances: *achachk'umu* (or *auki auki*, hunchbacked old man) on May 3 for the Fiesta de la Cruz, and *pastorcitos* (shepherds) at Christmas. For performance in annual fiestas, then, the pitus are not associated with a particular (rainy or dry) season, unlike the other instruments in Conima. Formerly, pitu ensembles accompanied various other dance-drama traditions during the Fiesta de la Virgen de la Asunción (see appendix 1), as well as wedding processions, but these dances are no longer performed, and sikuri music has replaced pitus during weddings.

Duct Flutes: Pinkillus and Tarkas

Cane and wooden duct (block, fipple) flutes are found in a large variety of forms and sizes and are known by a number of regional names throughout the Andean highlands (Instituto Nacional de Cultura 1978:225–45). Conimeños perform three types: the tarka, the five-hole pinkillu, and the six-hole pinkillu. The two pinkillus are similar, but Conimeños consider them separate traditions. They have distinct repertories and contexts of use, and are not played together in ensemble.

The five-hole pinkillu played in Conima, and throughout Huancané, is made of cane about 2 cm in diameter and approximately 43 cm long. The six-hole cane instrument is slightly larger: 3 cm in diameter and 53 cm in length. Each is half stopped on the bottom, with all finger holes located on the upper side of the flute. The larger six-hole variety is pitched slightly lower. While Conimeños generally considered it more 'sentimental' or serious than the brighter, happier five-hole pinkillu, I am not sure that the instruments' ranges alone are responsible for this association.

The pinkillus are performed in what may be described as "wide unison."

When a new tropa of pinkillus is purchased, the fiesta sponsor, or an experienced musician who accompanies him, carefully selects instruments that are well tuned. Testing the instruments of several tropas myself, I found that the instruments were tuned with much less variation in pitch than the instruments (sikus and pitus) made in Conima. It is therefore striking that in performance, pinkillu players produce the same type of pitch variance on unisons that is characteristic of pitu and siku ensembles. To get a similar effect, the pinkillu players would have to blow with a variety of different intensities producing pitches up to 20 or 25 cents sharp and flat of the median pitch series—resulting in a spread of about a quarter tone. "Wide unison" is the result not only of variance among the flutes' fundamental pitches but also of the variety of overtones and combination tones that augment the density of the ensemble sound. Since the basic tuning of the instruments would allow playing in close unison, pinkillu performance suggests that this range of variation in tuning is simply a part of Conimeños' musical sensibility—it is the sound they want to hear.

The pitch series on both pinkillu types is obtained by the use of nonsequential fingerings and consistent overblowing, producing the second and part of the third octave. On the five-hole pinkillu, the stop farthest from the mouthpiece always remains open, and the one closest always remains closed. The use of the overblowing technique corresponds with a general Andean aesthetic preference for high vocal and instrumental tessitura. Like the pitu, both varieties of pinkillus have a lower octave available, but Conimeños consistently choose to play these flutes only in the overblown octaves.

As in Conima, wind instruments are pitched relatively high and/or are usually overblown in most contemporary Andean communities (Vásquez and Vergara 1988:137). In Quechua-speaking communities, where vocal performance is much more important than it is in Conima, women are the preferred singers, particularly young women, and falsetto is common. In an earlier study of the *charango* in southern Peru, I found that indigenous performers tended to use smaller instruments and higher-pitched tunings than their mestizo counterparts because of the desire for high tessitura. My mestizo charango was frequently criticized by peasant musicians for being pitched too low and for being too 'hoarse.' They said it did not "cry out like a cat" as charangos should.

In Conima, the forceful overblowing technique also results in a breathy sound, rich with overtones, which augments the dense sound quality; this contrasts with the cleaner timbre preferred in mestizo or Western flute performance. Ornamentation such as trills and glissandi is kept to a minimum in pinkillu performance, although community groups use ornaments subtly to distinguish ensemble style.

During my visits to Conima, the pinkillu ensembles usually included from eight to fifteen flute players and a separate section of drummers, slightly fewer in number, who performed cajas with two padded mallets. The caja is a low-pitched, indigenous-style, double-headed snare drum played with the heads perpendicular to the ground. It measures about a meter in diameter and 30 cm high. The timbre of these low-pitched snare drums provides a striking contrast to the stridency of the flutes and also augments the density of the ensemble sound. Consistent with all wind performance in Conima, the pinkillu ensembles play in a closed circle formation—either walking in a circle or stationary and facing inward.

Conimeños use five-hole pinkillus to play the *wifala* genre for a large-circle courting dance during Candelaria (February 2), the *carnavales* (or *pinkillada*) genre during Carnival (dates vary in February and March), *todos los santos* for the fiesta of the same name (November 2), as well as the *achuqallu* game-dance genre for variable roof-raising fiestas throughout the year. The six-hole pinkillu is played on New Year's (January 1) in a fiesta celebrating the change of ayllu political officials. It is also played during Candelaria, the same musicians switching between the five- and six-hole flutes depending on the nature of the particular events within the fiesta (chapter 4). Although the six-hole pinkillus are usually played in wide unison, at one point during Candelaria in the village of Japisi some of the musicians performed the melody a parallel fifth below the main melodic line.

The other type of duct flute played in Conima, but only during Carnival, is the tarka. The tarka is constructed out of a single piece of carved wood with a cylindrical bore; the six stops are located on the upper side. This instrument, which is played in Peru's southern departments of Puno and Tacna, came from Bolivia to the Province of Huancané as recently as the 1930s, according to various local accounts. Until that time, Carnival music had been performed only on the five-hole pinkillu. By 1985, most ayllu ensembles on the Conima (versus the Tilali) side of the district had changed to the newer instrument.

During the 1985 and 1986 Carnivals, the tarka ensembles comprised approximately twelve to twenty flute players accompanied by Western snare and bass drums. As in pitu performance, the snare drum plays straight rolls, while the more syncopated bass drum pattern largely follows the melodic rhythm. A tarka tropa traditionally consists of three different sizes played in parallel polyphony (for the lowest non-overblown pitches); see figure 5.

Suli	E4
Ankuta	B3
Tayka	E3

Fig. 5. Tarka tropa.

Ideally, a greater number of the larger, softer taykas are balanced against only one or two of the shrill sulis. In recent years, however, the sulis have been dropped from certain community ensembles; the reason is obscure, since musicians themselves say that the ensemble sounds better when it is complete. Two sizes of tropas are used in Conima: a smaller variety, *cura-huara* (tayka = approximately 47 cm), which is most common in Puno generally, and the *salinas* type (tayka = approximately 57.5 cm.) which is most popular in Conima.

Each flute is tuned in a diatonic scale, and sequential fingerings are used. The instrument is blown very forcefully, and due to its construction, this splits the octave and produces a particularly dense, reedy sound. A Peruvian friend jokingly referred to the tarka as the Andean saxophone. The second octave is produced by overblowing. Two genres are performed during the week-long Carnival celebration: *tarkiadas* or *carnavales,* and faster dance music known simply as *wayno,* a term indigenous Peruvians often use almost synonomously with "music" or "song."[8]

Other Musical Traditions in Conima

Although much less important than the wind instruments just discussed, there are several brass bands in the ayllus of Conima; the brass instruments were learned during the musicians' mandatory military service. These groups occasionally play at ayllu weddings and for mestizo-organized fiestas. Unlike the music performed by the other ayllu ensembles, the brass band repertories consist largely of mestizo dance and religious pieces that are not specific to the district. Brass bands have become important to musical life in rural communities throughout Peru and Bolivia; they range from large professional ensembles that travel widely to more informal, less active local groups like those in the District of Conima.

String music is not currently performed in Conima—surprisingly, not even among the mestizos in town. Localized *charango, bandurria,* diatonic harp, and violin traditions are important in Quechua-speaking peasant communities in the central and southern Peruvian highlands.[9] Mestizos throughout the nation specialize on these and other stringed instruments such as the guitar and mandolin. In Puno's Aymara-speaking areas, and throughout the rest of the department, town mestizos perform in large string ensembles known as *estudiantinas*,[10] but to my knowledge the charango is the only stringed instrument commonly played by rural Aymara speakers in Peru (primarily on the south side of the lake). The total absence of strings in the ayllus of Conima is typical of other indigenous communities in Huancané.

Various writers have noted the relative lack of vocal music in Aymara communities as compared with Quechua areas, where singing is one of the most prominent musical activities (e.g., Buechler 1980:97; Tschopik 1946:555). This observation holds for Conima, where I heard local songs in an ayllu festival only once, during Candelaria (chapter 2). Popular waynos were sung, accompanied by drums, for a costumed dance known as tundiqui (or *los negritos*—see Buechler 1980:42) during the Easter fiesta in the town plaza. Very occasionally, young vecinos (town mestizos) would sing popular texts with panpipe performances in the town plaza, but older players from the ayllus did not appreciate or participate in this practice. These were the only instances of vocal music that I heard, either in public or private settings, during my stays in Conima.[11] Also in striking contrast with many Quechua-speaking regions in Peru, music was not used to accompany agricultural or other types of work activities in Conima (e.g., see Romero 1990).

Only several decades ago, two distinctive types of panpipes, *kallamachu* and *loke pallapalla*, used to be played in Conima. Unlike all the other types of panpipes documented in Puno, they are single-row instruments. Whereas the pitch series of the more famous double-row Andean panpipe alternates between the two rows and requires an interlocking technique, single-row instruments contain a complete scale, with each musician performing the entire melody. The lokepallapalla and kallamachu panpipes have the traditional stairstep shape, with each tube cut to a different length. The consort of each comprises three sizes (tayka, ankuta, suli) played in parallel octaves. The kallamachu musicians used to accompany themselves on cajas in pipe and tabor fashion, while the lokepallapalla ensemble used no percussion.

According to musicians in Conima, the lokepallapalla used to be played for the Easter festival by young boys. This single-row instrument (with seven tubes) was considered easier to play since it did not involve the interlocking technique, and it was the instrument that boys in Ayllu Sulcata learned before graduating to sikuri music in their late teens. I was told that the kallamachu panpipe used to be played by a single community (Cambria) in a dance representing people of the *puna* (places of higher altitude) during the festival on May 3 (chapter 4).

Like these single-row panpipes, the more widely diffused *chokela* (vertical cane end-notched flute and dance of the same name—see Cuentas 1982a; Hickman 1975:96–101) was played until recently in various ayllus of Conima for the Fiesta de la Cruz (May 3). Older musicians in Conima explain the loss of these instrumental, and other dance, traditions as the result of emigration and the increasing lack of interest in local traditions among the young men who stay behind.[12] Strikingly, the Conimeño music-dance traditions that have disappeared were those performed for dry-season festivals— the period when many men are away working on the lower eastern slopes of the Andes (see appendix 1). As these celebrations grew smaller, and hence less important, Conimeños living in nearby cities—who typically return for major fiestas—also stopped coming.

The one instrument associated with the dry season that has remained vital is the siku. During the 1980's, sikuri music became the most popular local musical style among young Conimeños because of its prominence in the cities. Pascuas (Easter), the most important festival for sikuri performance, still draws people back to Conima from all over, precisely because of the popularity of this music. But the young men who return, and those who stayed behind, do not want to play lokepallapalla. They want to play sikus with Qhantati Ururi, Q'keni Sankayo, and Juventud Conima—local groups that have gained prominent reputations in urban panpipe circles. Thus, both the abandonment and the vitality of specific local traditions must be understood in the context of migration and the musical activities of migrants in the cities—topics taken up in parts II and III.

AESTHETICS AND PERFORMANCE PRACTICES
Talking about Music

About a mile east of the district capital near the community of Putina, the road to Bolivia winds higher above the lakeshore and is flanked on the opposite side by the steep slope of Cambrapi Mountain. During the day, people use the road to walk to another chakra where work is needed, or to take their sheep to pasture. For most people who remain in the ayllus, time is not money. Meeting on the road, men may stop if the day is fine and, after greeting each other, pull out their *chuspas* (woven bags) or plastic bags used to carry coca. The green leaves are offered in companionship, and words of respect are whispered to the achachilas, the earth, and the ancestors. The men may stand, chewing silently, for some time before beginning leisurely conversation about destinations, work, and weather. During times when men gather, such as at rehearsals, during meals at festivals, or even when meeting on the road, the talk frequently turns to fiestas, the high points of Conimeño social life.

Usually these discussions simply recount the details of a recent fiesta: the quantity and quality of alcohol, coca, and food provided by the fiesta sponsor, the number and energy of the musical ensembles that performed, a particularly enjoyable fistfight that occurred, or an amorous tryst that seems to be moving toward marriage. But sometimes conversations may take a critical turn, comparing the different musical groups that participated and their strengths and weaknesses.

Making critical commentary about ensembles other than one's own is an accepted pastime in Conima, because of the competition among different ayllu groups. If Conimeños openly discuss their own group's performance, it is typically done in positive terms and in such a way that no particular musician is mentioned. Even praise of a community member may cause internal competition or jealousy, making people reluctant to stand out from the group in any way. If a problem is already brewing within the community, however, negative comments about a musician can be used effectively. A conflict over land rights made one man in Sulcata a target for public criticism, and his deficient musical abilities were added to the list of shortcomings.

In 1985–86, during discussions about musical ensembles from other communities, certain types of observations were made repeatedly. The highest praise an ensemble could receive was that "they sounded like an organ" (*sonaban como un órgano*) or "they play like a single instrument" (*tocan como un instrumento*). Conversely, people criticized sikuri groups because the small, strident suli panpipe voice 'escaped' (stood out) too often during a performance, disturbing the unified fabric of the ensemble's sound. The small size of the suli requires special breath control and restraint. Not only is it the easiest panpipe to overblow, but it also has a propensity to stand out because of its shrill, loud quality. (Other voices, however, sometimes 'escape' as well.)

Other comments such as "Nothing but contras and sanjas" and "I could not hear the ankutas" were made derisively if the different voice parts were not properly balanced, so that the 'sweetness' of the ensemble's sound was diminished. Some of the ayllu ensembles typically fell short of the twenty-four to twenty-six players Conimeños say are needed to complete the voicing of an ensemble; even the best groups did not have enough musicians for some of the less important fiestas. Smaller groups, such as Cambria, would emphasize the ankuta, sanja, suli, and contra voices, and the players of the larger ensembles tended simply to dismiss them as being of lesser quality because they were 'incomplete.' Groups also received negative evaluations because their instruments were 'false' (out of tune).

Groups might be criticized because they played a given genre too slowly or too fast, or because the accompanying drums did not help the music 'run,' (*correr*, swing, groove) and thus it was less 'danceable' (*bailable*). But ensembles were also praised for playing with great strength, and especially for the quality and originality of their compositions and performance style. When people said, "They certainly have their own *toque* [manner of playing]!" these were words of high praise. Finally, musical ensembles received a positive evaluation when they remained in the plaza performing for the people for extended periods, thus contributing to the overall success of the fiesta. It was a matter of pride to be the last ensemble to leave the plaza on fiesta days. Groups that left early had little chance of being considered that year's best ensemble in the many discussions that took place once the fiesta was over. This type of commentary highlights some of the most important aesthetic and ethical dispositions guiding musical performance in Conima.

Ethics, Aesthetics, and Performance Practice

When Conimeños say that a good ensemble is one that "plays like one instrument" and that no individual's instrument should "escape" from the dense, integrated fabric of the ensemble's performance, they are talking about sound, but they are also articulating a certain vision of the relationship between the individual and the community. In Conimeño musical ensembles there is no place for highlighted soloists; in general, people are no more anxious to draw attention to themselves during music making than they are in any other public setting. The reasons for not wanting to stand out are *pragmatic* (fear of arousing disapproval or jealousy), *ethical* (consistent with the ethos of egalitarian relations and how a Conimeño should behave), and *aesthetic*[13] (ideals about how an ensemble should sound), illustrating the unity of ethics and aesthetics. The understanding of aesthetics—articulated both verbally and musically—as a part of an individual's or group's ethics is important to the conceptualization of musical practice as social practice in the chapters that follow.[14]

Related to the stated value of "playing as one" in Conima is the preference for a dense sound quality. This is expressed verbally by Conimeños when they say that there should be 'no holes' (gaps, periods of silence) in an ensemble's music. By "dense sound quality" I mean a consistent overlapping and blending of discrete sounds to produce a thick unified texture (Schafer 1977:159), as well as to a fuzzy aura around musical pitches in contrast to a clear or sharp sound. Both of these features contribute to an ensemble's ability to "sound like one instrument." Conimeños' desire for a dense sound quality relates to the way instruments are made (panpipe resonating rows, tarka construction), performance techniques (loose embouchure on the pitu, overblowing, filling siku tubes with air), and the wide variance in tuning unisons, octaves, and other harmonic intervals (sometimes approaching a quarter tone). In sikuri performance, musicians consistently overlap their (ira or arca) pitches with those of their partners' so that there will be no holes in the melody.

Although melodies are basically performed in "wide unison" or a style approaching parallel polyphony, and there is no place for the soloist per se, certain ornamental and improvisatory techniques provide ample leeway for individual expression within ensemble performance. In the primary improvisatory technique for siku performance, for example, expert malta players who perform the ira row improvise harmonic accompaniment to the arca part, and vice versa. Sometimes the use of this technique approaches the production of a counter melody. Simultaneously, the contramalta or sanja players may hold certain pitches longer than the other voices while the contrasuli players may perform variants on the basic melodic line; a number of people may overlap various versions of the standard cadence and bridge formulas. In pitu performance, descending ornamental slides played at cadences, and while other musicians sustain long pitches, are available for individual expression and function to create overlap. Flute players will also perform relatively subtle variants on the basic melody as is done by the sikuris. These improvisatory techniques add additional, lively, textural layers to the dense overlapping of sound. Conimeños indicate that, ideally, skillful improvisation is woven into the ensemble fabric to 'add flavor' but that it should not stand out.

While Conimeños may talk about music in these normative ways and may articulate these ideals through musical performance in certain instances, they also play music to let loose, to celebrate, and to compete with other community ensembles. As people's enthusiasm and energy rise, or as a competition becomes particularly fierce, panpipes sometimes do escape, articulations become sharp, people become carried away with ornaments and slides, but the richness of possibilities, the density, and the power of the music also grow. In particularly electric moments during fiestas, *other* ethical-aesthetic priorities come into play and are expressed directly through musical sound and behavior. There is no advantage to granting more or less weight to verbalized aesthetic ideals—spoken at certain times and places, and for specific reasons—over those articulated directly through musical practices. In the following chapter I turn to a discussion of how ethics and aesthetics, musical practice and broader patterns of social practice are articulated together within musical ensemble organization.

T W O

The Collective and Competitive Nature of Musical Performance

ONE MORNING MATEO, a respected musician from Sulcata in his early fifties, asked the whereabouts of an American friend who was visiting me in Conima at the time. I told him that Ralph was back in his room playing fiddle. Mateo asked with whom he was playing, and when I said that Ralph was practicing by himself, he looked up in surprise and asked, "What would he want to do that for?" I explained that North Americans often practice music by themselves and play for their own enjoyment. He looked puzzled, so I asked if he thought this odd. He replied, "Well, we do not do it."

Although musical performance is generally a collective, public activity in the rural villages of southern Peru, Conima represents the extreme case. During my time in the district, only once did I hear a flute being played at full volume outside of formal fiesta or rehearsal occasions, whereas in other Peruvian regions I encountered rural people performing music alone for their own enjoyment any number of times.[1] In Conima, even practicing or learning music alone in private is rare; older Conimeños humorously accepted my doing so, but never really understood it.

When interviewing friends in their homes, I found them reluctant to demonstrate techniques or sounds on their instruments by themselves. They protested that the music "does not sound right" or "is not the same" when performed solo. On the occasions when individuals did perform for me privately, they usually played at a volume just above a whisper. Sometimes men compose new pieces on their instruments at home by themselves; but when I observed Filiberto doing this, he also played at a whisper.

By social definition, musical performance is a collective activity in Conima that takes place only in public festivals; within their traditions, the making of acceptable musical sounds is not something that can be done alone. Music is also integrally associated with movement and dance during fiestas. When musicians talk about playing for an upcoming fiesta they almost always say, "We are going to dance [*bailar; thuqt'aña*]," rather than "We are going to

58

play [*tocar; phusaña*]." The musicians' emphasis on dancing is important because it highlights the activity in which the entire community, including women, can participate together.

THE MUSICIANS

In the larger fiestas celebrated in the town plaza as well as festivals that occur in particular ayllus, men of a given community come together voluntarily as a musical ensemble. Most older men in the ayllus have some degree of skill in playing all the different wind instruments (a situation that has changed with the current younger generations), and anyone so inclined is welcome to join the ensemble on an ad hoc basis. In this respect, the wind instruments played in Conima are not specialist traditions. Nonetheless, within each community some individuals are known for their particular dedication to, and performance abilities on, one or more of the instruments. Regardless of who else shows up to play, these men form the core of their community ensemble, and the *guías* (Aymara *irpa*, 'guide') for the different instruments also play particularly important roles.

Conimeños recognize different levels of ability in musical performance and composition. In private conversations with me, people were happy to discuss the special abilities and knowledge of particular individuals in their communities, although they generally did not speak about such things in group settings. Conimeños explained that performance skills were accessible to anyone. If some men were better players than others, it was because they had a greater interest in, and dedication to, musical matters, and because they participated regularly; advanced age and long experience were also advantages. Performance skill, then, was described largely as a matter of personal choice and inclination; the idea of talent did not seem to enter in.

In the realm of composition, however, special abilities are recognized that seemed to parallel Western notions of innate talent. Certain people are known for being able to produce original musical ideas ("he takes them from his head"), whereas others, even seasoned players, told me that they are simply unable to do this. Like instrument makers, individuals with the ability to create original musical ideas are highly regarded in their communities. They have a prominent role in shaping their ensemble's sound and repertory, and thus are able to strengthen their community's hand in musical competition.

The Guía: Ensemble Guide

Musical ensembles in the ayllus are anchored around the figure of their guía. This is not a formal position; rather, the guía is a person who is implicitly recognized as the 'musical guide' by the other musicians according to a number of criteria. The guía should be a skilled performer, have detailed knowledge of the tuning, voicing, and repertory of the tradition in question, and be able to set the correct tempos and initiate the tunes. Since he is usually among the most skilled composers, he also has major responsibility for shaping the ensemble's repertory. Within the same community, the role of guía often shifts from one person to another for the different instruments, because of individual expertise and interest. For sikuri ensembles there are two guías, one for the ira and the other for the arca panpipe row. In sikuri ensembles, the guías play bombos and frequently the ankuta voice, since it carries the main melody.[2]

Perhaps the most important criteria for the role of guía involves certain personal qualities of leadership. A guía can function well only if it appears that he is not leading and that he has no desire to do so. A guía commands authority and respect with ability, but he himself usually does not emphasize his abilities; he must let others continually choose him to guide the group. Guías typically behave in a noncritical, nonconfrontational manner and cannot explicitly exercise authority—for in so doing they will lose it. The word "guide" itself (rather than "conductor" or "leader") seems particularly appropriate to the nature of the role. An incident that took place during Carnival 1986 will illustrate the point.

On Tuesday afternoon during the festival, the guía of Tarkas de Putina began issuing increasingly insistent commands to the other musicians, acting more like a boss than a 'guide.' From other things that occurred during the fiesta, I would guess that this behavior resulted from a combination of too much alcohol and a desire to impress me with his musical expertise. The other musicians' initial response to his behavior was surprise, but this soon turned into annoyance expressed through laughter. For a time the guía became even more aggressive, insisting on certain tunes and becoming impatient when the group did not come together quickly enough to begin them. This continued for about thirty or forty minutes, during which time the other players simply began to ignore him. Finally, without any discussion, several other men jointly took over calling the tunes and leading the performance; the deposed guía, drunk and angry, walked off to join some other men.

By the following day the guía had come to his senses. That afternoon he was again guiding the performance, the events of the day before apparently forgiven. It is easy to see, though, that if his unusual behavior had continued, he would not have remained guía for long.

Filiberto is one of the most respected sikuri guías and musicians in Conima. He is particularly effective because his energy, ability, and love for the music shine through during rehearsals and composition sessions, and when he is playing. Filiberto is a modest, good-humored, soft-spoken man who is liked by all who know him. The musicians in his ensemble seem to follow his lead simply as a matter of course and grant his opinions special attention—precisely because he is slow, even reluctant, to offer them.

During fiesta performances, Filiberto's actions as guía are often rather subtle. When the ensemble has rested after its last tune, he casually picks up his bombo and moves into the space where the group had been performing. He may softly tap the drum several times, as if testing the skin tension, or blow his panpipe to himself as if recalling a tune. Gradually, other musicians take notice and begin forming the performance circle. Filiberto is able to recall a large number of panpipe tunes, and other members of the group naturally look to him when deciding what they should play next. Many pieces are not known by titles; Filiberto generally initiates a tune by whistling the first phrase softly. Then as he makes eye contact with the other drummers, they raise their sticks together and begin the piece with the first stroke of the drums.

During fiestas, the players are often content to continue drinking and talking between numbers; someone has to take the initiative to get them playing again. Filiberto simply assumes this responsibility more often than other people, although he seems just as happy when others begin rounding up the group or suggest tunes. When his ensemble is engaged in an intense musical competition with another group, the atmosphere and pace becomes less relaxed, and the musicians' attention becomes riveted on Filiberto and Aldemir, the arca-siku guía. At such times the position of the guías becomes more pronounced.

The Maestros

The people recognized as the core group (my term) of a community ensemble have many of the same qualities as the guía. They perform well on the instruments, know the repertory, and, perhaps, have some compositional ability. Most important, they must be dedicated to the ensemble and to the music, and this requires that they show up regularly for rehearsals and fiesta performances. It is the core musicians that attend the opening rehearsal at the sponsor's house, where the new instruments will be handed out and the new pieces for that year's fiesta will be composed (chapter 3). It is this group that constitutes the foundation of the ensemble, which, ultimately, must depend on voluntary "collaboration."

Although a fiesta sponsor specifically invites the guía and the core musicians to the rehearsal at his home one or two nights prior to a fiesta, all men in the community are welcome at this occasion. In some respects rehearsals are regarded as a chore, due to the lengthy process of composition that takes place during these sessions; typically only those most dedicated to the music and the ensemble attend. Regular attendance at rehearsals largely defines who the core players are.

Because of the ethics of collective participation, however, any man in the community may perform with his ensemble during fiestas, whether he has attended the rehearsal or not. In addition to joining the ensemble for the pleasure of playing, some men who are not necessarily skilled or dedicated performers may take part to enjoy the alcohol, food, and coca served to the musicians throughout the festival. The number of "ad hoc" (noncore) musicians varies greatly from one community and one fiesta to another; the generosity of the sponsor, the season, and the importance of the festival influence participation. Carnival usually draws a lot of participation, and in Tarkas de Putina, ad hoc players who had not attended the formal rehearsal equaled the number of core musicians in 1985 and 1986.

Although any man from Putina may participate in the tarka ensemble, not everyone is equally welcomed by all the other performers. A friend in the group, who was particularly enthusiastic about playing tarkas during Carnival, complained to me privately about one man who joined us in 1985. My friend objected that the man could not really play very well, that he did not care about the music but only joined the ensemble for the alcohol that would be offered, and that "he spoils [*malogra*] the music." The man did join the group, however, and my friend's opinions were not voiced publicly.

Given the fusion of communal ethics and musical aesthetics in Conima, it is difficult to untangle what bothered my friend most—the perception that the man spoiled the music or that he did not care about it. It is probable that both aspects were involved. For Conimeños, performance ability is directly tied to a person's level of dedication, but because musical sound is not usually assessed separately from the total gestalt of the occasion, the spirit one brings to a musical performance may be as important to being considered a good player as the sound produced.

Although individual musical abilities and contributions to a performance are discussed privately, there is no overt differentiation of status between the core musicians and other men who join the ensemble during a fiesta. The Spanish term *maestros* (master, as in "master craftsman") sometimes seems to be used to refer to the men I am calling the "core group" of musicians.

For instance, after I had composed a tarka piece that was accepted by Tarkas de Putina during my second year with them, someone commented, "You have become a maestro." But during fiesta performances, the same term was used to refer to all the men playing in the ensemble—regardless of ability or whether they had attended the rehearsal or were composers.

The presence of ad hoc players usually adds volume and spirit to the ensembles, and this is greatly appreciated. At the same time, these players can hinder a group from reaching other aesthetic goals. Since few, if any, ad hoc players attend the rehearsals, they are not immediately familiar with the new pieces composed during these sessions. This puts constraints on composition itself, and consequently on the extent to which innovation and originality can be expressed (chapter 3). Most ad hoc players do not receive new instruments from the fiesta sponsor. Instead, they come with instruments that they already have, which may not be in tune or may not be the voice needed for balancing the group's sound. Finally, since participation is not limited to skilled performers, ensembles may have difficulty achieving the well-integrated sound that Conimeños appreciate.

As in all facets of life, musical performance in Conima involves compromises among the performers' various aesthetic-ethical dispositions as well as an articulation of their priorities. When faced with tradeoffs, Conimeños typically place greater importance on maintaining open, nonhierarchical ensembles than on ensuring the favored tuning and voicing that would guarantee a well-blended sound. Not everyone joins the ensemble out of love for the music, or out of community spirit. Such people may be criticized privately, but to confront them publicly or discourage their participation would do more violence to the aesthetics of collective musical life than the sounds of panpipes 'escaping' or flutes that are out of tune. I believe that, for Conimeños, ideas about musical sound are so integrally meshed with notions about community that the two cannot be easily separated.

Fiesta Sponsorship

In addition to the musicians, the person taking the role of fiesta sponsor (*alférez*, sometimes also called *guía*) is particularly important for organizing fiesta performances. All the men are expected to sponsor each of the fiestas celebrated in their village once in their lives. An individual typically sponsors only one event in any given year, and usually the different sponsorship roles are stretched out over time because of the financial burden involved. At the end of each festival, peer pressure is used to strong-arm someone into publicly taking the role for the following year.[3] Because of temporary and permanent emigration, the pool of possible sponsors has diminished. If no one will undertake the extremely heavy financial and organizational responsibility for the coming year, the community's performance in that fiesta may be discontinued indefinitely. Since sponsors are located during the fiesta itself, when the continuity has been broken it becomes even more difficult to find someone who will again take up the task.

This is a primary way that performance traditions and entire fiestas pass out of existence in Conima, and people in the ayllus, particularly older people who have done their service, see it as a great tragedy. The reluctance to assume sponsorship roles is augmented by a change of values that seems to accompany the process of temporary migration itself. People who spend some, or much, of their time outside the community may develop more individualistic attitudes and begin to place higher priority on their own economic well-being than on their duties to the community. Greater economic and social independence from the community reduces the influence of peer pressure.

Normally, the sponsor's duties include supplying food, alcohol, and coca for a variety of occasions during the fiesta. He must ensure musical participation by formally inviting the guía and a group of core musicians to perform. If a costumed dance is involved, the sponsor usually organizes the dancers. It is also customary for the sponsor to purchase a new consort of instruments for the musicians.

Differences in sponsors' wealth affect the quality of fiestas and of musical performance. Wealthier community members are better able to purchase a new, well-tuned consort of instruments, thereby affecting the musical performance. If a sponsor is known for being both well-off and generous, he is more likely to attract greater musical participation because of the quality and quantity of food, drinks, and coca that can be expected. The wealth of individual sponsors varies both within and across communities over a series of fiestas, however, and negates any stabilized mark of economic differences between the villages. Great expenditure leads to enhanced individual prestige, but it also has an economic leveling effect (see Harris 1973). Elders who have met all their responsibilities to the community gain heightened respect and prestige in decision-making meetings and in other contexts; however, checks by people in the same position, as well as from the community at large, keep fiesta sponsorship from becoming a base of individual social power.

During fiestas, the sponsor has the role of host, and the musicians have the status of honored performers and guests. Throughout the fiesta, the musicians are granted prestige by the entire community, since it is they who make the fiesta come alive through musical performance. While ultimately it is the sponsor's responsibility, community members and dancers also reciprocally offer coca, drinks, and food to the musicians to keep them content and playing. I have attended fiestas where, when insufficient alcohol and coca were provided, some musicians began to drift away early, leading to the fiesta's, and the sponsor's, failure.

MUSICAL COMPETITION AND ENSEMBLE STYLE

Upon entering the plaza of Conima during the night before Easter, during the Carnival celebration, or on other major occasions during 1984–86, a visitor would encounter between four and eight community ensembles performing in their customary locations around the square.[4] It was at such times that musical competition—a primary impetus for creativity and originality of ensemble style—became explicit.

On the opening day of Carnival in 1985, for example, seven ensembles (two five-hole pinkillu groups and five tarka ensembles) timed their arrivals close to midday and, after taking an initial turn around the plaza, established themselves in their performance locales. The initial entrance into the plaza was considered particularly important for impressing spectators.[5] The best of the newly created compositions was selected by the guía and the core musicians for that moment (thus, it usually became the group's emblem piece for that year's fiesta), and the musicians paid special attention to the quality of their performance during the entrance.

Early in the afternoon on the opening day, the musicians and dancers of each community socialized separately among themselves and with the other people who came from their village. The ensembles alternated periods of music and dancing with extended times for drinking and resting, so that they staggered their performances with other ensembles in close proximity. As the afternoon wore on, crowds of spectators (people not represented by specific ensembles) began to form around the groups that had the best dancers and music.

When an ensemble started to draw a crowd, the guía took care to select their best pieces, and they began to play louder and longer, often simultaneously with neighboring ensembles, so as to hold their audience. The spectators' animation increased with drink and the music, and they, in turn, gradually contributed to the rising excitement by joining the dance with the ensemble of their choice. Some ensembles, now purposefully playing at the same time as their neighbors, attempted to outlast and outplay them in sheer volume and intensity. The times between concluding one piece and beginning the next became rushed; all musicians kept their eyes focused on the guía and the ensemble core so as to begin together. By around half past three it had become clear where the main centers of action were, and more people were drawn to the ensembles that had already attracted a crowd. A particularly intense competition between the closely situated tarka ensembles of Huata and Putina drew the largest number of spectators. The music in this corner of the plaza was almost nonstop, and the dancers formed wild, fast-moving chains around the musicians.

The animation of the fiesta continued to escalate until around six P.M., when fatigue began to take its toll and people started leaving for home. Groups that had failed to draw a crowd also began leaving early but were hardly missed as the hardy continued to move around the more popular ensembles. The intensity—a product of interaction among the musicians, dancers, and spectators—receded as spontaneously as it had begun. After seven o'clock, even some of the ad hoc musicians of the best ensembles began to slip away, until only the core members of one or two groups remained with some diehard revelers. Finally, sometime around eight o'clock the guía of the last remaining group, Tarkas de Putina, indicated that it was time to leave. After we took a final turn around the plaza, the sound of our emblem piece could be heard through the darkness as we moved off toward home: tired, happy, and, like other groups, certain that we had been the best.

Musical Competition

Usually only one ensemble performs in the fiestas celebrated within a single community; hence musical competition is not an issue during these occasions.[6] After large, district-wide festivals such as Carnival, however, Conimeños devote a great deal of discussion to determining which ensemble was the best. The informal nature of the competition, which does not involve official judging or trophies, allows a number of communities to believe, or at least publicly assert, that their ensembles had been most popular. Meanwhile, a general consensus about the relative success of the different groups will be found among town and ayllu dwellers who were not represented by ensembles. Everyone becomes aware of these decisions, regardless of whether they are publicly accepted by communities that were involved.

The competitive nature of musical performance in Conima is typical for fiesta performance throughout the Peruvian highlands, in both indigenous and mestizo communities. Usually, the competition is in the informal-consensus mode, although formalized performance contests, as discussed in parts 2 and 3, are spreading increasingly from urban centers to rural towns throughout the highlands. As will become clear later, the adoption of formal contests by migrants in Lima signals new relations to, and attitudes about, musical performance.

People in Conima use various criteria for assessing the ensembles. A major issue is the length of time and amount of energy expended in performing, and thus providing entertainment for the people in the square. It is a matter of honor, as well as a show of stamina, to be the last group to leave the plaza. Ensembles are also obviously evaluated by the quality of their sound— tuning, fullness, balance, and blend—as well as the energy and spirit with which they perform. Loud volume is important to attract and hold a crowd when various groups are performing simultaneously, and it is also an indication of stamina and spirit; at times the competitions become like musical shouting matches. The value placed on loud volume favors larger groups, and it also affects instrumental performance practice.[7] Although sikus, for example, should be blown with a relatively gentle attack and, to create a well-blended sound, staccato overblowing is avoided, these values are balanced with the ideal of forceful playing, which, in the heat of a competition, may lead to overblowing.

The originality and distinctiveness of performance style and, even more crucial, of repertory are particularly important criteria for evaluating the ensembles. Groups that enter the plaza without a newly composed emblem piece for each major fiesta, or groups that are perceived as copying the style or repertory of another ensemble, are criticized and even ridiculed as unoriginal and unskillful—especially by the musicians who feel that their music is being imitated. In Conima, the competitive nature of musical performance is closely linked to the strong value of community solidarity, which has, as its corollary, emphasis on distinguishing one's community from others. Musical originality and competence are perceived as important demonstrations of social competence and unique identity. For this reason, ensemble style markers and original repertory are jealously guarded, and imitation of other groups is disparaged. Musical innovation is, in itself, highly valued as a means of capturing the attention of the spectators and thereby providing a competitive advantage.

Ensemble Style

Within relatively narrow limits for variation, musicians consciously cultivate style markers to distinguish their groups, and these features tend to be recognized by Conimeños generally. When playing panpipes, all the community ensembles basically work within the same framework of nine voices, although the number and balance of voices can vary within and across communities from one fiesta to the next. They all perform the same musical genres called for by the given occasion in largely the same way. Aside from distinct repertories, Conimeños differentiate the sikuri style of Huata from that of Qhantati Ururi (associated with Sulcata; see chapter 5), for instance, in terms of two basic factors: Huata consistently plays at faster tempos, and Huata uses tropas that are tuned at a different pitch level from those of Qhantati Ururi.

Comparison of three similar performance contexts for these two groups over the span of a year confirmed these general observations. While tempos within a given genre vary slightly, depending on how the guía feels a particular piece should be played within a specific situation (during heightened competition, for example, tempos tend to increase), Huata did consistently perform faster. For instance, in the Easter fiesta of 1985, Huata played the choclo genre with an average quarter-note metronome marking of 96, while Qhantati varied between 84 and 90, with 88 being most common. For the genres used for social dancing, Huata tended to perform lentos with a quarter-note metronome marking of 80, while Qhantati performed them on the average around 72. Huata played the ligero genre around 92, and Qhantati uses an average tempo of 84. In regard to the tuning of tropas, Huata used a single consort for an entire year with the lowest arca (malta, or ankuta) tube sounding an E^{b4}. On the other hand, Qhantati takes pride in changing tropa tunings from one fiesta to the next. For the three occasions considered here, the tropas were tuned so that the lowest pitch on the arca malta was (1) slightly below E^4, (2) E^4, and (3) slightly below E^{b4}.

Conimeños stressed that Huata and Qhantati had extremely different performance styles, but did not elaborate beyond the two features mentioned above. I can add only a few other observations. Huata tended to play in a more staccato fashion, in contrast to the smoother style of Qhantati when the group was at its best. The two groups tended to use slightly different strong-stroke, weak-stroke drum patterns. In addition, Huata used less differentiation between strong and weak drum strokes, with strong strokes being played more consistently. The members of Qhantati made a conscious effort to vary their cadence formulas for the ligero genre in order to distinguish their style.

According to Jaime Montaño, a Peruvian colleague and siku player who has studied in Conima, the sikuri groups from Huata and Qhantati Ururi are also recognized by the players themselves for being better at certain genres:

> When various members of Khene [Q'keni, the sikuri group of Huata] were asked independently about which group plays the best, their answers were very similar, "Qhantati plays *calmados* [*lentos, sikuris* 'slow pieces'] the best . . . but in the performance of ligeros [fast pieces], they do not equal us." Similarly, when anyone in Qhantati is asked [this question] they respond that "Khene has a special *gusto* [flavor, quality, ability] for ligeros, but there is no one else like Qhantati for lentos." (Montaño, personal communication, August 1990)

This distinction regarding genres makes sense given Qhantati's generally smoother style of playing (particularly important for lentos) and the slower tempos that they favor for all genres, just as Huata's forceful drumming and more staccato blowing style would contribute to a perceived excellence in ligero performance. Conimeños in general tend to compare and discuss Qhantati and Q'keni Sankayo of Huata more than other ensembles, since they are considered the best in the district.

Other community sikuri ensembles differ from Huata and Qhantati more fundamentally in terms of the sound they produce. For example, Sikuris de Cambria (Ayllu Checasaya) used the same parallel harmonic configuration as the other groups, but in the performances I heard they tended to have more players on the contra voices, which emphasized the open fifths. I was not able to determine whether this was purposeful or whether the different balance of voices resulted from the ad hoc nature of the group (i.e., simply that more contra players showed up for these particular occasions). This varying balance of the voices, however, was not generally recognized by Conimeños as a stylistic distinction as much as a mark of the lesser quality of the group. Indeed, I never saw them attract a crowd in the plaza during fiestas.

Originality and Innovation

Conimeños' emphasis on originality is the basic reason that Qhantati changes its tropa size from one fiesta to the next. When I asked Filiberto about this, he replied that if the group plays with the same tropa for every fiesta, the people become bored with its sound, and hence it will not be able to attract large crowds. Also, he said, since Qhantati was a leader in the sikuri tradition, the other groups were always copying its tropa sizes. Therefore, Qhantati must keep changing its tropas to maintain its distinctive sound.

In addition to stressing Qhantati's unique musical identity, the constant changing of tropa sizes is perceived by group members as an illustration of their greater competence in all aspects of the tradition. They are proud that they have a maker who does not need to copy other groups but can continually come up with his own tropa sizes. Qhantati members were frequently reminded not to lend their instruments or lose them where they might be found by people from other groups, out of fear that their special tropa sizes would be imitated.[8]

The importance of changing tropas for Qhantati was burned into my memory during lengthy discussions held to reach consensus about the tropa size that should be used for an upcoming festival. On one occasion after the decision had been reached, a member of the group commented, "We will kill them with this one." What kinds of pitch differences are involved between one tropa capable of "killing them" and another? In this case, the core musicians decided to change the tropa so that the pitch differed slightly less than a semitone. Typical for many aspects of music making in Conima, variations that seemed rather subtle by my standards seemed to make major differences to Conimeños.

During my visits with him, however, Filiberto repeatedly expressed a desire to initiate much larger innovations in his sikuri ensemble. For example, he said that he would like to experiment with totally new types of harmonic voicing. Filiberto felt that the novelty of such a change would make the group particularly popular in Conima and would enhance their competitive edge. Since the other Conimeño, and many non-Conimeño, ensembles were now playing in the same harmonic style (part 2), he favored a total change of voicing to distinguish his ensemble and maintain its position of leadership within the sikuri tradition. He explained, however, that trial and error was the only way he could experiment with new voice relationships, and he lamented that the amount of cane needed was beyond his economic means.

Filiberto's desire to create a totally new voicing arrangement for his sikuri ensemble mirrors the attitude that drives musical creativity and originality in Conima generally. This innovative spirit differs sharply from popular notions of "traditional" peasant musicians and practices as static and inflexible. In Conima, the values of innovation and uniqueness are tied to the importance of music for expressing collective identity in situations of competition among communities of basically equal social power.

This offers a striking contrast to the Conimeño residents in Lima, who were, and still are, under different kinds of pressures—to disassociate themselves with markers of their past and to imitate the cultural style of city dwellers. The residents have developed much more conservative attitudes about musical innovation precisely because of the distinct nature and meaning of Conimeño identity in the capital. As a partial result of the character of musical competition in Lima (formal contests), the residents have also arrived at conceptions of musical performance that are different from the notions of their relatives in the ayllus.

Along with the spirit of competition, the basic dispositions shaping musical practices in Conima relate to the ethics of egalitarian relations and collective participation. Conimeños' resistance to any sort of hierarchical musical organization in the ayllus is underlined by the story of Putina's tarka guía who was temporarily deposed during the 1986 Carnival. I have also tried to illustrate how ideas about musical sound and community are complexly intertwined, and how both the collective and competitive aspects of musical performance require tradeoffs between (or balancing of) different types of ethical-aesthetic values and motivations. These themes continue to be important in the following chapter about musical rehearsals, ensemble repertories, and processes of composition.

T H R E E

Making the Music: Rehearsals, Composition, and Musical Style

MY FIRST REAL entrance into musical life in Conima took place the night before Carnival in 1985, during the rehearsal of Tarkas de Putina. I had recently come from Puno with a letter of introduction from one of the member's sons, who was working in the city as a teacher. After a long and uncomfortable conversation—small talk about his son, the beauty of Conima, and the purpose of my visit—he reluctantly mentioned the evening's rehearsal. He told me that I could come, pointing vaguely to a hillside to indicate where it would be held. From the coolness of the invitation, I did not get a sense that I was particularly welcome.

Following the general direction, the advice of a few people who were out, and, finally, the sounds of muffled tarkas, I finally arrived and was admitted into the one-room adobe house of the fiesta sponsor. Inside, a single oil lamp burned and ten men sat in a close circle playing tarkas, seemingly a variety of different tunes and parts of tunes simultaneously, softly to themselves. No one paid much attention to me for some time; perhaps I should I say that I was studiously ignored, although the shot glass of alcohol and the bag of coca were always offered to me by the host in turn. Finally after about thirty minutes, the man who had invited me mumbled, "I said he could come." A few men nodded to me, some men glanced up, but basically they continued playing different motives and sections of tunes softly to themselves without speaking.

After what seemed like a long time, with nothing being said, the musicians gradually took up the phrase one man had been playing and began performing it together—each musician playing at a volume just above a whisper. Ever so often they stopped and went back to experimenting individually with the section before taking it up again as a group. Later another phrase was added, and still another. The musicians continued playing what was by

72

then a completed piece. At different intervals they would stop and some of the men would simultaneously play with, or alter, a given section softly to themselves. After they had played the completed piece for some time, Filiberto handed me a tarka and said, "Play if you can." With the short tune planted firmly in my ear, I joined in with the musicians with whom I would continue to play during the next year and a half.

Over the span of several hours, a new tarka piece had been composed jointly, without discussion, through a process that was as automatic to the musicians as it was miraculous to me. We immediately began brainstorming ideas for a second tune. The men had seemed surprised and pleased that I could play at all, and I was encouraged along with the others to offer musical ideas upon which a new tune could be based. While I was to have greater success in subsequent composition sessions, the ideas I produced during that first evening inspired smiles and a kind of superior, and yet not unkind, laughter. By around one in the morning, we had finished composing the three pieces we would need for the fiesta, and we could play them passably well. We went outside and, for the first time, played the new pieces at full volume with the booming accompaniment of the bass drum. Carnival 1985 had begun for Ayllu Sulcata.

Before we broke up to go home at around two A.M., Jorge and Leo invited me to perform with them at Carnival; they told me to meet them at the sponsor's house around nine that morning. Of course, I arrived well before any of the other musicians and sat and waited as the fiesta sponsor, his wife, and several helpers raced around preparing for the day ahead. When we arrived at the plaza after midday, the presence of a gringo playing with Tarkas de Putina generated a great deal of attention and amusement among the spectators. Although I did not realize it at the time, the musicians from Putina understood immediately that I would be a great boon in the musical competition. In the beginning this was clearly the reason for my continued acceptance in the group: I was entertaining and I fulfilled a valued function of providing novelty.[1]

REHEARSALS

Composition and rehearsals are the fountainheads of the whole creative chain of musical performance. In Conima, rehearsing and communal composition take place simultaneously one or two nights before a given fiesta. I participated in eight rehearsal-composition sessions with Putina, with the men of Sulcata in Qhantati Ururi, and with the pitu group from Cambria of Ayllu Checasaya. The proceedings in each case were very similar.

Rehearsals are special occasions that mark the actual beginning of a fiesta for the core musicians. These sessions serve as a warm-up period for people who may not have played the particular instrument or genres since the same event the year before. The rehearsals are usually scheduled for late afternoon or early evening and often conclude in the early morning.

The fiesta sponsor cleans and arranges the largest room of his house, or his patio, with benches lining the perimeter. The invited musicians begin to appear one or two hours after the appointed time. As each musician enters, he touches hands with those already seated and takes a seat himself. After four or five men have come, the sponsor moves around the circle offering coca to the musicians, who place the leaves in their *chuspas* (coca bags), in their pockets, or on their ponchos. In the dimly lit room, the men begin to chew the leaves while their host serves alcohol. Beginning with the guía or the oldest man present, the sponsor pours a shot and offers it to the musician. He receives it in his left hand and holds out his right beside the right hand of the host who faces him. Both men simultaneously whisper words to Pachamama, the achachilas, and the ancestors; they then wish each other and the rest of the group health, prosperity, and a good day. The musician pours drops of alcohol on the ground before drinking; afterward, he hands the shot glass back to the sponsor, who then repeats the ceremony with everyone else. After this first offering, each new arrival is given coca and alcohol as well, so that all receive an equal share. The men sit around for some time, conversing quietly, while waiting for everyone to come.

When enough musicians have arrived, the guía, who is usually one of the first to appear, signals the sponsor to begin the rehearsal officially. This is done by preparing a *t'inka* in the center of the floor. Coca leaves, cigarettes, and two cups of alcohol are placed on a woven cloth by the sponsor. The guía and oldest musicians place leaves in the cups first; they are followed by the younger men. During the rehearsal for Carnival in 1986, the contents of the first pair of cups (for Condor Mamani and the cabildo) were tossed by the sponsor on the outside wall of his house. The coca and alcohol in the second pair of cups were thrown outside by the eldest musician in Tarkas de Putina, in the direction of the achachila of Sulcata and into the air for the aviadores. For the third repetition, the guía hurled the cup for the ancestors outside, while the wife of the sponsor, the only woman present, took the cup for Pachamama and poured it on the ground in a special place dedicated to her.[2] Following the t'inka, the musicians took coca and cigarettes from the woven cloth in two waves, according to age.

If a new tropa has been purchased, the sponsor or the guía will hand out the instruments after the t'inka. For all but pinkillu tropas (all flutes of the same size), the guía often distributes the instruments, since he knows the voice that each musician likes to play or should play. For panpipe performance, for example, the largest voices are usually distributed to younger men, because they have more strength and their mistakes on the longer, softer instruments will not be so readily heard. The piercing suli voices will be given to older, more experienced players, since greater skill and control are required to blend them with the ensemble. The bajo voices go to musicians who are used to playing them, since the parallel-thirds melody sounds distinct from the others and is considered more difficult to play. The guía and other men recognized as musical leaders will usually play the ankuta voice so that the main melody will be firmly established, and those with the least experience will also be given ankutas: the prominence of this part and its medium size makes it the easiest to play.

If a new tropa is not forthcoming, the guía takes out one of several instruments that he brought with him and begins to blow it tentatively, inviting the others to find instruments that match. In any event, the core musicians usually bring several instruments already in their possession to rehearsals. It is usually known in advance if a new tropa has been purchased. When a new tropa is not forthcoming, the core musicians usually decide ahead of time which sikuri tropa size they will play; pitu, tarka, and pinkillu sizes are fairly standard. For sikuri composition sessions, musicians who have them will bring both an arca and an ira row so they can experiment with complete phrases. If they do not have both rows, during composition people will borrow the one they lack if they have a musical idea that they want to try.

The musical part of the evening begins as the guía calls pieces that he remembers from former years. Other musicians also suggest old favorites that they might play. The first several renditions of a piece will be played very softly, at the level of a whisper, so that people outside the rehearsal do not hear an inadequate performance as the group gets its bearings. The musicians then stop and begin the piece in earnest. An hour or more is dedicated to running through some of the group's old repertory. The pieces are rehearsed merely by playing through them a number of times. No comments or corrections are made, and, in fact, very little is said. After each piece, the sponsor (who does not play) offers his formal thanks to the musicians and occasionally serves coca and alcohol.

Following this warm-up period, the sponsor and his wife serve a hot supper of soup, coffee, and bread; coca is passed around during the subsequent conversation. Wealthier sponsors may serve a meat dish during supper, and beer and cigarettes after the meal. These items are highly valued by the musicians and indicate that the fiesta will be a good one. This is, in part, a strategic move on the sponsor's part, since he is aware that word will get out quickly and will inspire heightened attendance and participation at his fiesta on the important opening day. The sponsor's standing in the community will be affected if he does not meet what everyone knows to be his financial potential, but many people are not able to serve luxury items such as meat and beer at rehearsals—they must save their resources for more important public displays of generosity. If the offerings at the rehearsal are particularly good, it bodes well for the festival as a whole.

COMPOSITION

After the rehearsal supper, the guía takes up his instrument, suggesting that it is time to begin composing. The fact that it is almost halfway through the evening and several pieces must be created before the musicians can go home creates an atmosphere of seriousness and tension.

Both the number of pieces required and the emphasis placed on composition itself depend on the particular fiesta. Conimeños particularly stress new compositions for the larger fiestas celebrated in the town plaza, where musical competition is most pronounced. For Tarkas de Putina, two new tarkiadas and at least one faster dance piece are considered a minimum for Carnival performance. Pinkillu groups usually come up with at least two new pieces for Carnival. Typically, the main time for composing sikuri choclo and ligero pieces is before the Easter fiesta, and each group usually creates at least two new pieces and perhaps a new entrance march. Groups about to perform for costumed dances, such as satiri or imillani with sikus, or achachk'umu with pitus, may create a new dance piece, but often only a new entrance march is composed, because the repertories for the different sections of the dance are in the public domain (not belonging to any one community) and are relatively fixed. In such cases, the entrance marches become all the more important as identity emblems for the community ensembles.

As in most performance contexts, the musicians involved in composing sit roughly in a circle. When the guía indicates that it is time to begin, the musicians who are able to do so start to offer musical ideas, usually two or three complete motives that can serve as the A section of the piece (the vast majority of musical genres have an AA BB CC form). When a musician has an idea, he will try it out, repeating it softly to himself on his instrument. At times five or more people may be playing their own phrases or motives simultaneously. There may also be periods of silence to which the guía or other musicians might respond with verbal encouragement.

This initial brainstorming phase is often rather lengthy. If the men are not interested in certain material that is being offered, they will simply ignore it rather than directly rejecting it, just as they do with inappropriate ideas offered in decision-making meetings in Conima. After a period of time, if a musician gets no reaction to the phrase or motives he is playing, he will drop them and try something else or simply fall silent. When an idea is found promising, however, others will gradually take notice, stop what they are doing, and join in softly on their instruments until everyone has taken it up. Once the musicians have learned the A section through multiple repetitions, they begin brainstorming the subsequent B section, and then the C section. This occurs in the same manner, with the latter sections based heavily on A motives.

When all three sections are completed, the group plays through the entire composition. The compositional process then enters a new phase as the musicians begin to alter or correct the parts. Individuals simultaneously brainstorm ideas for changes or corrections softly on their instruments until a promising alteration is taken up by the group. The corrected section will be played first by itself, and then in the context of the entire piece—at which time the alteration may or may not be found acceptable. The musicians may enter into a discussion on this matter. More commonly, though, if people are not satisfied with a change they simply return to brainstorming new possibilities for improving the piece, thereby indicating their disapproval indirectly.

This correctional phase continues until no one can offer further acceptable changes and the piece is considered "perfect." Sometimes, after the ensemble members run out of ideas for improvement and the piece is still not acceptable, the entire composition will be abandoned and the musicians will begin to compose another piece from scratch. In other cases, the original material may not need much correction, and a general consensus can be reached rapidly regarding its acceptability. It should be stressed, however, that at each phase an implicit consensus is required and that, in keeping with the Conimeños' general style of social interaction, people's ideas are not directly rejected but rather are passively ignored. Moreover, as in decision-making meetings where the idea or issue on the floor is gradually shaped by interested parties in turn, once a musical idea is offered it is considered communal property; anyone is welcome to suggest changes of any scope without offense to the originator.

For pieces created in this communal manner, the ensemble as a whole is considered to be the composer, and individual input is not generally recog-. nized. In actuality, however, certain musicians take more initiative, and others largely follow their lead. In the matter of consensus—signaled by musicians' taking up the idea or alteration—people join in playing once a substantial group has done so, and this is often initiated by the most respected musician-composers of the group.

In another common type of compositional process, entire pieces are created by individuals before they come to the rehearsal. When this happens, during the initial musical brainstorming period the composer will play his completed piece softly to himself. If it is appealing to other musicians, they will begin playing it with him; if not, his tune will be ignored. Once the melody is taken up, it is subjected to the same group correction process for a final acceptance or rejection, and during this phase the tune is considered group material available for shaping.

If the original composition is finally accepted in a highly altered form, the group is considered to be the composer. If few changes are made, the ensemble members will proclaim the individual as composer, although in public he will usually maintain that it is the ensemble's creation—again, highlighting the fact that individuals do not like to draw attention to themselves. Regardless of who receives credit for the composition, the piece *belongs* to the ensemble, and, once it is in the repertory, the individual composer has no special rights over it.

Musical Sources for Composition

There are a variety of sources for the musical ideas that serve as the basis for new compositions. Conimeños are most proud of music whose basic material was originally created by someone in their own group. Only certain people have the ability to compose new pieces or the germ motives used for group composition, and these men are highly valued. Some of these composers say that entire pieces come to them at night while sleeping. Such people typically work out tunes or motives on their instruments at home before coming to rehearsals.

A second major source of musical ideas for new compositions is borrowed material—phrases and motives from preexisting pieces of any genre or instrumental medium. People borrow parts of mestizo waynos played by brass bands or string groups heard over the radio, as well as the music of communities outside the district. Frequently musical ideas will be shifted among different instrumental traditions within the same community. A repertory that is considered public domain also exists for each instrument type, since the age of the pieces makes ownership unverifiable. Tunes within these repertories are available both for anyone to perform and as sources for composition. Borrowing between communities within the district may take place, but I never heard anyone admit to having done so—although people frequently claimed that others had stolen from them.

Conimeños seem to feel no contradiction between their emphasis on group originality and the practice of borrowing musical material from outside the community. A tune resulting from only slight alterations of a preexisting piece is still considered new and original. Although this may be related to the fact that small contrasts mark major differences in Conima, what seems important to Conimeños is that the musicians put their community stamp on the material through the process of collective "composition" or alteration. Finally, what is particularly significant is that the resulting piece be new to the public in Conima, thereby attracting attention and admiration during fiesta competition.

The common practice of borrowing, along with the closely defined parameters of the musical genres, results in collections of tunes that are extremely similar both within and across community repertories. Although the direct source for borrowing is acknowledged if it hails from within the community or outside the district, Conimeños do not conceptualize groups of pieces in terms of "tune families." The similarities between the compositions of different communities within the district may be the result of "stealing" material or may simply result from the fact that pieces in the public domain served as a common basis.

Complaints of stealing are not made formally, but the real issue, in any event, seems to be the community's self-aggrandizement resulting from such accusations. Conimeños' distinctions between the legitimate use of preexisting material and "stealing" illustrates the situationally relative nature of their social identities. Most basically, material shared between individuals or across instrumental genres within the same community is considered legitimate. Since the music is owned by the group, it may be used in multiple ways within the community. Between social units in conflict or competition within the district, borrowing is not legitimate, since it negates the identity-marking function that music fundamentally serves.

People outside of Conima are, in most cases, of little concern to community identity in the context of district fiestas. Therefore, from the Conimeño point of view, outsiders' musical material once again becomes fair game. As we shall see in parts II and III, however, Conimeños—both older people in the ayllus and the residents in Lima—feel that non-Conimeño ensembles should not use their compositions and sikuri harmonic style. For older musicians in the district, this became an issue only after young people in the cities with no connection to Conima began to play their music. Once again, this is considered stealing, and the threat to their identity—this time as Conimeños at a broader regional level—remains the issue.

MUSICAL STYLE

Almost like pouring liquid into a somewhat flexible mold, the original or borrowed ideas that serve as the basis for new compositions are made to adhere to the parameters that define specific musical types, as well as to general features of Conimeño musical style.

Conimeños classify the different *genres* ("musical type"—e.g., waltz versus polka) according to one or more criteria. Most commonly, genre names refer to the associated dance, fiesta context, or instrument, although in certain instances (such as ligeros and lentos) the genre titles are musically descriptive terms. With the exception of three five-hole pinkillu genres, which are differentiated only by context (carnavales, todos los santos, and wifalas are considered different genres but sound the same), every musical genre in Conima is distinguished stylistically. The style markers that differentiate genres include specific formulas, introductions, and conclusions; scale types; phrase lengths; melodic shape; rhythmic motion; tempo; and the percussion used. In the atypical case of the choclo and ligero sikuri genres, in which the same tunes are used interchangeably, the same piece will be defined as one or the other depending on the type of drum accompaniment used (bombos with ligeros versus snare and bass drums with choclos).

There are also stylistic features that cut across all the different genre categories, unifying Conimeño musical style as a whole. With the exception of a few pieces, all music in Conima is in a standard AA BB CC form. Usually, the A section is created first, and its motives serve as material for the B and C sections, which are composed in sequence. Typically, motives from the A section are repeated literally, in new juxtapositions, or in slightly altered form in the B and C sections, with perhaps only one or two short motives distinguishing the subsequent sections (see the musical examples in appendix 3). One or two motives leading up to section cadences are almost always repeated in all three sections. While the specific musical types have distinguishing formulas, the placement of these formulas is basically the same for all genres: in introductions and conclusions; leading up to and at section cadences, and leading into the C section.

Another feature that crosscuts the different genres in Conima is the use of duple meter and syncopated rhythmic figures. It is important to emphasize that a variety of scales are used in Conima. Despite the typical characterization of Andean music as pentatonic, however, five-note scales are a minority, and six- and seven-tone scales (often with a flatted seventh degree) are the mainstay. In fact, tarka music (a recent arrival in the 1930s) is the only tradition featuring pentatonic scales most prominently—with a six-tone scale second in frequency.

The musical "materials," or resources, available for the process of composition consist of these general structures and features as well as the aspects that define the individual genres. Without an attempt to be comprehensive, it is worth illustrating these aspects by comparing and contrasting a few major genres in detail.

Sikuri Genres
Lentos and Ligeros

The two most important sikuri genres, lentos (slow pieces, also called sikuris or *calmados*) and ligeros (fast pieces),[3] are alternated for social dancing in a variety of fiesta contexts. (The use of ligeros in this way may be a relatively recent development, as is discussed in chapter 5.) These genres share two equally prominent scale formations: a six-tone scale with a flatted third and seventh (e.g., F, G, Ab, Bb, C, Eb), and the natural minor scale (e.g., F, G, Ab, Bb, C, Db, Eb). An undulating-descending melodic shape is also found in both genres, with a "semi-arch" melodic contour (that is, beginning medium range, rising, and then cadencing below the initial pitch) being the most commonly found alternative. A hallmark of the Conimeño sikuri style is the frequent practice of holding pitches across beats marked by the bombos or bass drum. This characteristic may be related to the ideal of stressing group blend and the meshing of the arca and ira parts. That is, the practice of slightly extending the ira pitch over the arca's entrance, and vice versa, may have developed into the practice of playing pitches across the beat. This interpretation is supported by the less frequent performance of "tied" pitches in the other instrumental traditions in Conima.

As the genre names imply, a major feature distinguishing lentos from ligeros is tempo. Ligeros are usually played between the quarter-note metronome values of 80 and 96, depending on the ensemble and occasion, whereas lentos vary between 66 and 82. Lentos are also distinguished from ligeros by the use of a long-held chord played on the finals of each voice part. This genre formula is used for the introduction, for the conclusion, and at section cadences (see appendix 3, example A.1). By way of contrast, the ligero (and choclo) genre is marked by a formula known as *chuta chuta*[4] which also appears in the introduction, in the conclusion, and at section cadences (except between B and C, and between the C sections). The chuta chuta is a figure that alternates evenly and rapidly between the arca and ira players (see examples A.3, A.4). The feeling of animation and excitement produced by this formula contrasts fundamentally with the feeling of calm and repose resulting from the use of the long-held chord in the lento genre.

Conimeños generally consider the lentos to be the most emotionally profound ('full of sentiment') sikuri genre, while the ligero and choclo genres are considered lighter and more upbeat. The common use of scales with minor thirds in Andean music and the conventional meaning associated with this scale within the European tradition have led coastal criollos and foreigners alike to stereotype highland music as melancholy. For Conimeños, and people in southern Peru generally, the minor scale does not seem to index any particular emotional state, whereas in Conima, tempo and perhaps tessitura are recognized as expressing different emotional qualities.[5]

Ligeros invariably end with what is known as the *fuga* section. In Conima, the term *fuga* refers to a faster repetition of the same piece to bring the music and dance to a climax (e.g., quarter note = 100 versus 92).[6] Lentos, consistent with their character, do not include a fuga section. Therefore, the difference in tempos, the character of genre-specific formulas, and the presence or absence of the fuga differentiate the ligero and lento sikuri genres and underscore differences of meaning ascribed to them.

Drumming

In both lentos and ligeros, the core musicians play a constant series of eighth notes on the bombos; the strokes fall on the "back side" of (slightly behind) the beat. Drum patterns, molded to specific melodies, are created by varying a range of strong and weak strokes. Jaime Montaño describes the arm motions of the drummers, and the various heights to which the sticks are raised away from the heads, as being so "perfectly uniform that it seemed a single arm was moving them" (personal communication, August 1990). While there are set drum patterns for given pieces, in my experience the patterns can be varied in a flexible manner during performances. The drummers, including the guías, act like the conductors of the group and may change the intensity of drum strokes to guide the animation and spirit of a given performance.

In lentos, the difference between stronger and weaker strokes tends to be more highly marked and controlled; in ligeros, as a performance becomes more animated, the drummers may drive the ensemble with stronger strokes more consistently, inspiring even greater animation. Approaches to and precision in drumming, however, vary among different ensembles.

Satiri and Imillani

Two sikuri genres that are related to each other but differ from lentos and ligeros are *satiri* (planter of tubers, danced May 15) and *imillani* (coming out of young girls, May 3). These genres are most clearly distinguished from lentos and ligeros by the use of a seven-tone diatonic major scale (most prominent), or a six-tone major scale without the seventh (examples A.5 through A.7). They are also distinct from the other sikuri genres in that their A section melodies are usually arch-shaped. When performed for the traditional dance, imillani music is accompanied by cajas (large indigenous snare drums), although this music is sometimes played for generalized social dancing with bombos. Satiri music is accompanied by bombos.

The satiri genre is characterized by prolonged introductory and final chords (about two beats). Like most Conimeño genres, it has a series of stock formulas, such as the opening sixteenth-note ascending motive in examples A.5 and A.6. Another formula that specifically distinguishes satiri pieces is found at the sustained section cadence pitch where the malta players split, some moving down to the lower final and some performing pitched slides to the final an octave above (example A.6, beat 7).[7] The opening motive in the first two beats of the c section in example A.6 is another standard formula for this genre.

The imillani genre is most clearly marked by its driving rhythm and, when performed traditionally, by the use of cajas rather than bombos. In contrast to the accented/unaccented eighth-note drum patterns found in satiri, lentos, and ligeros, imillani pieces are characterized by the consistent performance of strong strokes. Imillani pieces are less syncopated than most other sikuri genres. A rhythmic figure consisting of an eighth and two sixteenth notes followed by two eighths is used for this genre's distinguishing introduction. This rhythmic motive is also a stock formula at section cadences, played by the ira and arca rows in octaves on the final pitch of the phrase. The opening motive (first two beats) of section c in example A.7 is a standard formula for this genre. In addition, however, opening c-section formulas like the one noted for satiri pieces are sometimes used in imillani.

Chapter Three

Five-Hole Pinkillu Music

The three major genres for the five-hole pinkillu (carnavales or pandillada, todos los santos, and wifala) represent the only case in which the musical categories identified by Conimeños are not marked musically; all three will be considered here together (examples A.8, A.9).[8] At least five scale formations are used in five-hole pinkillu music (starting pitch is relative, and the tuning variances discussed in chapter 1 are prominent): B♭, C, D♭, E♭, F, A♭, most common; B♭, C, D♭, E♭, F, G, commonly used; and B♭, C, D, E♭, F, G, A; B♭, D♭, E♭, F, A♭; B♭, C, D♭, E♭, F, less frequent. The melodic contours commonly have an undulating-descending shape, and the melodies consistently fall within the range of an octave. A typical pattern for five-hole pinkillu composition is to begin by stressing the fifth degree of the scale, with movement up to the highest pitch of the piece early in the A section. The climax pitch is often not repeated again in the B and C sections. A rolling ostinato figure (falling between an eighth-note triplet and an eighth and two sixteenths) played by the cajas is basic to this genre. The tempo for this music falls around a quarter-note metronome marking of 88, and as with ligeros, a fuga section is added. Like all Conimeño music, there is a great deal of motivic repetition among the three major sections. Schemes like the following are typical:

Example A.8	*Example A.9*
A = a, b, c, d	A = a, b, c
B = c, e, c, d	B = d, b, c
C = f, b′,c, d (g)	C = e, c (f)

As in the other Conimeño genres, certain motives and formulas are used to mark the pinkillu music. Most prominent is the two-eighths/quarter note figure found at section cadences (example A.8). As a hallmark of the pinkillu genres, the cadence of the second repetition of the C section systematically slides (or leaps) from the final to the fifth scale degree (example A.8, motive *g*; example A.9, motive *f*). Other standard formulas are used commonly for the lead-in to C sections (example A.8, motive *f*; example A.9, motive *e*).

The Use of Formulas and Repetition in Composition

By comparing pieces that are related through borrowed material, we can arrive at a clearer appreciation of the compositional process and how a limited number of resources—the repeated motives and stock formulas—are used. In the tarka piece shown in example 3.1, motives *a* and *b* are the extent of the originally composed material. The *c* motive that serves as the

Example 3.1. Tarkiada Genre, "Brisas de Hingachi," by Tarkas de Putina

Example 3.2. Sikuri Choclo/Ligero Genre by Qhantati Ururi
(Filiberto Calderón)

cadence in all sections is a stock formula for the tarkiada genre. Section B consists of nothing more than a twofold repetition of *b*, and the cadence formula *c*. Section C opens with another tarkiada-genre formula (*d*), which again is followed by motives *b* and *c*. Note, then, that between the repetition of the same motives and the use of preexisting formulas, a minimal amount of new material is required to complete the piece.

The sikuri ligero/choclo piece by Filiberto Calderón shown in example 3.2 is a composition that was based on this tarka tune (borrowed from within the same ayllu). In the panpipe piece, motive *a* is the extent of the borrowed

Example 3.3. Tarkiada Genre, "Qhantati," by Tarkas de Putina

material; the rhythm is altered to fit the characteristics of the sikuri genre. Motive *c* and the chuta chuta figure are stock formulas for ligeros. Due to the set melodic shape of ligero phrases, requiring that the melody descend to the lower final before the chuta chuta formula, however, motive *b* is little more than a transitional descending motive that is formulaic in function and melodic direction, if not in the exact rhythmic motives and pitches used. Hence, the entire A section consists of borrowed and formulaic material. It would have been totally acceptable for the composer to construct the B section with material almost entirely generated from A, as was done in the original tarka piece and as is often the case. Here, however, two new motives, *d* and *e*, are provided in B for a novel effect. The *f* motive leading into section c is a formula of the ligero genre which precedes the repetition of motives *b*, *c*, and the chuta chuta figure. As with the tarka example and most music in Conima, then, a minimum of new material is needed for the creation of what is considered an entirely new composition.

In the next pair of compositions to be considered (examples 3.3 and 3.4), the direction of borrowing (again from within the same ayllu) is reversed. In this case, the tarka piece titled "Qhantati" by Tarkas de Putina was based on a preexisting ligero composition by Filiberto and Qhantati Ururi. For the

Example 3.4. Sikuri Choclo/Ligero Genre by Qhantati Ururi
(Filiberto Calderón)

88

tarka piece through beat 9, the composers incorporated almost identical material from the ligero (motives *a, b,* and the first beat of *c*). Due to the shorter section length prescribed by the tarkiada genre, the A section of the ligero piece was cut short, and the standard tarkiada cadence formula (*d*) was simply inserted after a short descending motive (*c*). In section B, the composers begin with a new motive (*e*) leading into the previously used *c* motive and cadence formula (*d*). The *f* motive is another stock tarkiada formula for leading into c sections. In this tarkiada piece, section c consists of *f* followed by a repetition of *c* and *d*. Again, between the use of borrowed material, genre formulas, and the use of repetition in prescribed ways, the composers were required to create very little new material for what was considered a completely new piece.

Repetition and Contrast

From my perspective, Conimeños use, and recognize, a rather subtle scale of contrasts to mark meaningful differences: between ensembles' performance styles, between compositions, and between the sections of a piece. The aesthetic appreciation of small contrasts in musical practice has parallels in other spheres of life in the ayllus. In the culinary style, for example, the same type of food, prepared in much the same way, is consumed day in and day out during particular seasons. Dishes that are alike in all but one ingredient, spice, or detail of preparation (and that to my palate taste the same) are considered distinct and given different names. In culinary style and musical style, as with the sense of time in daily life, small variations are highlighted in a context of extended repetition.

In a detailed discussion of Andean weaving practices in Cusco, Ed and Chris Franquemont and Billie Jean Isbell discuss how the repetition and variation of a relatively small amount of information (for example, picks and patterns in weaving) enable Andean weavers to produce highly complex designs. They conclude, "Doubtless many other Andean social, physical, and conceptual phenomena also employ the principle of a small body of information that is repeated rhythmically and symmetrically to fill time and/ or space" (n.d.:19). The intense repetition of musical motives and formulas within compositions shows the same economy of information mentioned by these authors. Although the principles of repetition and economy are fundamental characteristics of Andean music generally, in Conima they are partially related to the collective nature of musical practice, and the way music is learned.

PARAMETERS OF MUSICAL COMPOSITION

The process of composing collectively, and the fact that Conimeños often must create several pieces within a limited number of hours, favors well-delineated musical structures and an economy of means. The emphasis on repetition and stock resources for musical creation, however, cannot be attributed solely to time constraints and processes of communal composition. In fact, Filiberto seems to have followed basically the same type of procedures for his ligero discussed above (example 3.2), a piece composed individually under no particular time limitations. A more important factor in the compositional process and repertory selection is the way music is learned in Conima.

Within the district, few people practice music by themselves, and individuals are generally not taught to play by other, more experienced musicians.[9] For beginners and ad hoc players, instrumental technique and new pieces are learned by watching and doing during actual fiesta performances. The formulas and the motives repeated at the cadences of each section of a piece serve as points of entry; people pick up and join in on these first since they are already known or are repeated constantly. With each repetition of the tune, they gradually begin to learn the new material presented by the piece until they can play the entire melody.

This method of learning music, and the fact that novices and ad hoc ensemble members do not rehearse new compositions before performances, puts constraints on what some of the more advanced players-composers can, and in some cases would like to, compose during rehearsals. If composers do not follow the tight, repetitive genre structures and formulas, or if they provide too much new material in any given piece, ad hoc and less experienced players will not be able to pick up the tune quickly enough during performance. Instead of excluding these people, Conimeños tend to drop tunes from the repertory if the pieces do not prove readily accessible.

For Carnival 1986, a particularly unusual composition—one heavily based on a Bolivian brass-band piece learned from the radio—was created by Tarkas de Putina. Indeed, the tune underwent only minor alterations, resulting in a reduction of the usual stock formulas used by Conimeños, and much less motivic repetition between sections. In Conima, borrowed material is usually used as the basis of the A section of a new composition, and the B and C sections are generated from this material by repeating motives. In this tarka piece, all the sections of the Bolivian tune were borrowed, so that the possibilities of altering the foreign material according to Conimeño procedures and form were limited.

The guía and core musicians of Putina chose this unusual tarka tune for their first entrance into the plaza on the fiesta's opening day. Before our entrance, we stood in an outlying street and began to practice the tune, shoring it up for its debut. By this time, the number of ad hoc musicians, who had not attended the rehearsal the night before, was about equal to the number of core musicians. As we warmed up, it became clear that those who had not rehearsed the tune would not be able to master it quickly enough for the entrance. We then changed to another of the new pieces which fit the typical tarkiada structure, and it was easily learned by everyone.

The original piece selected for the entrance was not attempted again during the fiesta. While people own cassette recorders in Conima, I never saw one being used as an aid for rehearsing or recalling repertory.[10] Since memory is the primary musical archive, requiring repeated performances of a piece during the year of its composition, I can assume with relative confidence that the difficult tarka piece was permanently excluded from Putina's repertory. This incident, then, illustrates how the open, nonspecialist character of the ensembles determines the selection of repertory as well as the degree of innovation available to composers.

The fact that the guía and core musicians of Putina initially chose their most distinctive new composition for the ensemble's first entrance, however, brings up another fundamental parameter of musical creation. To compete effectively with other groups in the plaza, an ensemble's music, and especially the tune selected for the entrance-emblem piece, should be as distinctive as possible, to catch the attention and admiration of the spectators. Putina's unusual tarka piece was initially selected because, if we had been able to execute it successfully, it would have demonstrated a high degree of competence and originality, serving us well in the competition. This strategy failed, but in general, within the tight formulaic genre structures that foster accessibility, the goal is to compose pieces in which new turns of creativity and originality shine through.

For example, Conimeños considered Filiberto's ligero piece discussed above (example 3.2) to be particularly fresh and innovative. I believe that this was, in part, because of the addition of a substantial amount of new and interesting material in section B, a place where it might not normally be expected. In many societies, playing with expectations and conventions is a typical way of producing aesthetic pleasure and excitement. Filiberto's creative move succeeded, however, because the piece also contained enough that was familiar—the borrowed material from the tarka piece had been played by many of the same musicians only months before during Carnival, and the composition also contained the expected formulas.

Balancing Creativity and Tradition

The experience of having a piece that I composed accepted by Tarkas de Putina illustrates the same point, although the dynamics were certainly different. After a year of doing transcription and analysis, I was approaching the understanding of Conimeño musical genres that I have presented here. For the 1986 Carnival I composed a piece using the stock resources, formulas, and style of repetition characteristic of the tarkiada genre, in an effort to create a piece that would sound as if it were from Conima. When I presented it in whisper fashion during the rehearsal, I was surprised to find that it met with general approval and was accepted with only minor changes in rhythm so that it would "sound like a tarkiada." The piece (entitled "Texas" after my alma mater) was a hit during the festival—it became Putina's emblem piece for that year. I was pleased that I had been able to compose a piece that could pass as Conimeño, or so I thought at the time.

When I listened to a recording of the composition months later with Conimeño residents in Lima, they remarked what a weird (*extraño*) tarka piece it was. Hearing it with hindsight and the rush of creativity gone, I could only agree. I do not think that the piece's acceptance in Conima was out of deference to me; the musicians had been only too happy to ignore my less successful efforts. Rather, my attempt to copy the Conima style as exactly as I could, in combination with my own foreign musical ideas, led to the creation of a piece that was, for Conimeños, extremely familiar and easy to grasp, while at the same time very strange. I believe it was precisely this combination of novelty and accessibility that led to the composition's success.

The balancing of new ideas with stock resources occurs in musical creation universally. What differs according to particular cultural situations is the specific nature of the balance and the reasons that one side might be granted more importance than the other. Conimeños' open, communal orientation to musical performance—in a society where many people do not have the desire to become specialists or rehearse diligently before a performance—tips the balance away from innovations that fall too far outside the traditions. Simultaneously, the competitive nature of Conimeño musical life, as well as the emphasis on originality for distinguishing community identity and competence, demands creativity and uniqueness.

All things totaled, in Conima the balance is slanted toward the use of stock resources. For the relatively few men who put their whole heart into composition, this is a source of frustration; for the many who are able to join in without much preparation, it is important to keep the balance as it is. In Conima, music and dance are a special type of public activity in which the creation of overt distinctions among community members is specifically avoided.

Beyond this, music and dance help people get into sync: moving together, and sounding together, they discover and rediscover an explicit way of being together. When things are right, the depth of such moments moves within and beyond the beauty and power of the sound and movement. Such moments cannot be rehearsed or prepared in specialized musical or choreographic terms alone, but rather—like musical practice itself—they are part of a much broader preparation for life.

FOUR

Three Fiestas

DAILY LIFE IN CONIMA is often solitary. People may work in their fields by themselves, or with one or two family members, for days on end. The evenings are cold and dark, and most people stay in their houses. Fiestas change all of this; they are times when communities come together, when the public places are filled with people and the silence is broken.

Fiestas in Conima differ substantially in length, purpose, and intensity (see appendix 1). The larger district-wide festivals are at least partially centered in the town plaza, where various communities celebrate simultaneously; other fiestas take place primarily within specific ayllus or communities and have a different dynamic. In either event, the same fiesta may differ radically in quality from one year to the next, depending on many factors, particularly the weather, economic conditions, the generosity of the sponsors, and the level of participation. In this chapter I describe three different fiestas, and I investigate certain special qualities inherent in music and dance that make these arts particularly powerful media for creating heightened moments of community unity and identity, and for expressing the complexities of social experience. Through music and dance, and within the festival frame as a whole, Conimeños articulate some of the most important things that they have to communicate about themselves and their particular views of the world.

FIESTA DE LA CRUZ, MAY 3, 1986

At midday on May 2, 1986, the *víspera* (eve of the principal day) of the Fiesta de la Cruz, I stood with the ten pitu musicians, the two drummers, and people from Ayllu Checasaya at the home of the fiesta sponsor. This house, like almost all places in Checasaya, stands below and in clear sight of the mountain known as Muyuni; the *achachila* (mountain divinity, 'place') of the ayllu. The musicians had rehearsed during the two previous evenings but now stood silently, while others joked and talked together quietly. As afternoon came on, newcomers joined us, and people kept glancing up at Muyuni; I followed their eyes but saw nothing unusual. Around one o'clock we began to hear eerie laughter and strange voices coming down from above. Suddenly, clouds of smoke erupted from the outcrop of Muyuni, and distant figures emerged from the mountain.

For what seemed like hours, the voices and laughter kept getting louder as the *achachk'umus* (hunchbacked old men) moved down Muyuni toward the house. Children raced to the base of the mountain to await their arrival; finally, those of us who remained at the house could see them clearly as they moved onto the road. The achachk'umus chased the children and, in high-pitched, raspy voices, hurled jokes and abuses at everyone they met.[1] Children unlucky enough to get caught received beatings. Still, they swarmed around the achachk'umus like gadflies, frightened neither by this rough treatment nor by the bizarre appearance of these creatures who come out of the mountain each year to dance among the people for the Fiesta de la Cruz.

The achachk'umus had goat faces with long, coarse hair hanging from their chins. The fur on their hands and feet also made them seem like animals, and yet they stood like men, at times leaning over their heavy walking sticks as if too old to move, at others times relentlessly chasing the children. Their backs were terribly hunched and deformed beneath the homespun jackets and above the knee-length pants that represented those of colonial Spaniards. In addition, they wore white, broad-brimmed, European-style hats made of papier-mâché.

When the achachk'umus arrived at the sponsor's house, they moved into formation and began to dance, accompanied by the pitu ensemble. The choreography for the main portion of the dance had a number of figures that resembled a European-based *contradanza,* but it was performed in a body position and style of movement appropriate for the achachk' umus' old age and deformity. In the first dance figure the eighteen achachk'umus stood in two lines, contrasting to the circular formation more commonly used for dancing in Conima. The lines faced each other with their sticks placed in the center. They hopped in place for one statement of the musical form and then, at the cadence, spun around and repeated the same movement facing outward. After a number of repetitions of this dance, they walked erect in a circle with their sticks held out in front of them. They then started another series of line dances.

In 1986, only this one dance ensemble took part in the Fiesta de la Cruz, and it was a rather atypical group in that musicians and dancers from outside of Checasaya participated. The dancers were high school boys and middle-aged men, whereas the pitu musicians were, with the exception of one man in his twenties, all older people. The fiesta as a whole was considered a poor one due to the lack of ensembles and general participation, and the sponsor's limited resources. At the time, the district was almost depopulated. Most of the people living in nearby cities or who were working on the eastern slopes of the Andes did not come back for the fiesta. The paucity of available dancers and musicians from Checasaya inspired the sponsor and ensemble *guía* to invite the participation of performers from other communities.[2]

Although the sikuri ensemble from Huata had performed the imillani dance for the fiesta the year before, in 1986 they were away in Bolivia, playing on contract for a mestizo fiesta. Having been told that the community of Japisi might play chokelas (vertical end-notched flutes), I walked over the mountain to the community to inquire if and when they would play. People there told me, "Everyone has gone," explaining that there were not enough men left in the village who remembered or could play the chokela music. The direct impact of emigration on musical practices is evident here. It is striking that people from Sulcata told me that Japisi might play chokelas even though they had not done so for years, as if their descriptions of the festival were locked in a memory of how the fiesta used to be.

It was late afternoon by the time the achachk'umus had finished dancing next to the sponsor's house. The sponsor and members of his family then served a meal to the people who had come, in the order of their importance: the musicians, the dancers, the older men, and then everyone else. The musicians were served as a separate group inside the house, a place of honor. The dancers, too, formed their own circle and ate outside; as usual, the men and women of the community ate separately. The meal was followed by a t'inka ritual and beer.

In the evening, the achachk'umus danced to the home of the mestizo *teniente gobernador* (lieutenant governor) of the district and were served beer after performing for him and his family. The tradition of having peasant groups dance to the mestizo official's house during fiestas originally may have been one way for the vecinos to link the ayllus ritually to the central district government (Schaedel, personal communication; see Buechler 1980:149).

Upon leaving the district official's home in town, the dancers, pitu musicians, and other fiesta participants moved up Calvario (Calvary), the sacred hill and achachila of the entire district.[3] Here they performed briefly in front of a small cross that had been erected for the occasion in the center of the sacred place, about twenty feet away from an earth shrine where different types of rituals, including the burning of offerings for the achachila, are conducted.

The complexity of local Andean religious beliefs and festivals, resulting from the combination or juxtaposition of Catholic divinities and feasts with indigenous ones, is evident in this celebration. The tremendous energy expended by the Peruvian colonial state to convert Andeans to Christianity is well known, and it played an important role in strategies of political domination (see Dillon and Abercrombie 1988:50; Abercrombie 1991; Silverblatt 1988:182–83).[4] According to an article of the First Lima Church Council of 1551, local shrines and idols of the indigenous people were to be destroyed and replaced by churches, or at least crosses, depending on the importance of the site (Vargas 1951).

The Second Lima Council of 1567 (article 104) demanded "rigorous punishment" for the performance of Andean songs in agricultural rituals and for the ancestors (Vargas 1951:253–54). The "extirpation of idolatry" campaign, directed by church officials from Lima, included the destruction of indigenous musical instruments and dance costumes associated with Andean religion in different parts of the highlands (Arriaga 1920; Kubler 1946:400). Even during this period, however, allowing indigenous music and dances in Catholic celebrations was seen as an important means of involving Andeans in the European religion (see Turino 1991a). The achachk'umu dancing up on Calvario—an achachila—before the small, temporarily erected cross is somehow related to this history, although I do not know how the particular strands came together in Conima.[5] What is apparent, however, is the long-standing impact of the Lima-centered state on rural highland musical practices and occasions—a topic I take up later specifically for the twentieth century. As with the dancing at the teniente gobernador's home, the origin of various fiesta customs cannot be divorced from the broader webs of political relations.

After leaving Calvario, the performers and entourage danced through the central plaza and back to the home of the fiesta sponsor before retiring for the night. On the following day, the dancing, eating, drinking, and performance of t'inka rituals continued at the sponsor's house and on Calvario, although a good deal of time was spent performing in the central plaza, where the horseplay between the achachk'umu dancers and spectators became even wilder than it had been during their initial entrance. New choreographic figures were introduced in the plaza during the afternoon, such as *chara chara* (leg between leg) and *pirqa* (wall), which are particularly entertaining since they include mock fights and a great deal of clowning. The fiesta finally broke up early in the evening; the next day the achachk'umus were gone. The rest of the people also scattered, back to their homes and separate tasks.

The Meanings of Achachk'umu

Many of the people of the ayllus had definite ideas about the meaning of the achachk'umu dance. Initially, people's explanations, in combination with my own observations, only complicated my attempts at understanding. In response to my questions about what the achachk'umu dancers represented, some people told me, "They are our ancestors," and others stated directly that this was a serious dance in which the performers represented the achachilas—the sacred 'places' of the mountains. This much was consistent with the dancers' original emergence and descent from Muyuni, and the fact that the sacred places are often described as "ancestors" and as old men. The dancers' decrepit movements and the bearded goat-face masks depicted old age; even the combined animal/human imagery of the costumes could be understood as an attempt to represent beings from another plane. But what about the colonial Spanish garb, the atypical use of the contradanza choreography (an index of European or foreign culture), and the clownish, sometimes obscene, antics throughout the fiesta? Other people, when asked about the meaning of the dance, answered straightaway that it was a comical satire of the Spanish—without, or before, mentioning the achachilas.

After receiving these different types of interpretation during the course of the fiesta, I finally turned to one of the older pitu musicians and asked him two leading questions: "Is the dance a serious one in which the performers represent the achachilas?" and "Is the dance a funny one mocking the Spanish?" He replied yes to both in rapid succession, without blinking an eye. In exasperation, I asked him how the dance could simultaneously represent both—the most sacred 'place' defining the very heart of the ayllu, and Spaniards who are thought of locally as foreign and negative—and how it could be at once serious, sacred, comical, and grotesque. By this point his patience was clearly wearing thin with questions that he seemed to take as the height of foolishness. He replied once more: "It has to be that way; a dance has to have a number of meanings, it cannot have just one." Then he changed the subject.

Within the fiesta as a whole, the same complex combinations of meaning emerge. For example, it seems fitting that a satire of the Spanish be performed for their present-day analogues at the mestizo governor's house. It is also striking that performers representing the achachilas should dance for the cross on top of the achachila of the district. The temporary placement of the cross on Calvario and the use of the name Calvary itself for the most powerful achachila in the district provide other instances that we might understand as the result of campaigns for Christian conversion, but which Conimeños might simply regard as another fusion of meaning within a realm that must have multiple meanings.[6]

Music, dance, and drama are especially apt media for *simultaneously* articulating and uniting widely divergent and even conflicting images and meanings. The achachk'umu dancers, for example, represent figures of power who are at once local, sacred, foreign, positive, human, negative, divine, animal, serious, and comical through a performance that is both lightly entertaining and deeply meaningful. How could Conimeños' relations with their divinities—which have been affected by a long history of harsh political relations with "Spaniards"—be expressed simply?

Even more than the unorthodox syntax and unusual semantic combinations possible in poetry—as opposed to propositional speech—music, choreography, and costuming all have a heightened potential for simultaneously combining many signs with varied and even conflicting significance into a single sign complex, enabling the fusion and creative play of diverse images and meanings within a unified whole. These artistic practices open the possibility for transcending "rationalist" discourse and unifying *difference;* the various fusions and creative visions become real insofar as they can be seen, heard, danced to, and enjoyed. For Conimeños, and people in many places, dance dramas, musical performance, and most other aspects of life have multiple and varied layers of meaning, not just one. The complex imagery within Conimeño performing arts and festivals articulates—perhaps more accurately than other semiotic practices, such as everyday speech—the complexity and tensions of history and of life itself. One of the main values of art in Conima, and in many places, is its potential to do this kind of semiotic work.

THE FIESTA OF CANDELARIA, FEBRUARY 2

Unlike the May 3 fiesta, which actually incorporates the image of the Catholic cross, some fiestas in Conima are given European or Catholic-derived names but have little to do with Christianity. One example is the Fiesta of the Virgen de la Candelaria (February 2) as celebrated in Japisi and in other communities on the Tilali side of the district. In Conima this festival is called Candelaria, but just as frequently it is referred to as the "festival for the first products"; Jorge, a man from Putina, called Candelaria the "birthday of the potato." It is a festival to celebrate the ripening of plants and romantic relationships among young people. It is a rainy-season festival that expresses hopes for well-being and abundance.

On the morning of the víspera (February 1) in Japisi, the spiritual leader of the community went to the fields with his wife to collect the largest agricultural products of each type grown by the community. These first products were placed on a black woven cloth, and the man, ritually dressed in black, conducted a ch'alla for the female earth and first products.[7] The man and woman took the bundle of products to the home of the fiesta sponsor and laid the cloth out on the floor of his house. Two other couples of elders from the community did the same. From morning until midafternoon, when they emerged from the house to join the rest of the community, the ritual specialist, his wife, and other elders of the community prepared the first products in a variety of ceremonies.[8] Meanwhile, another part of the fiesta, involving music and dance, was taking place outside the sponsor's house.

It had been decided by the musicians at their rehearsal the evening before that they should arrive promptly at nine in the morning to get the fiesta under way early. They began showing up at a leisurely pace between ten and twelve. As each musician arrived, he was offered coca and alcohol by the fiesta sponsor. This offering was accompanied by a ch'alla and words to the earth and the achachilas; words of greeting were also exchanged between the sponsor and musicians. After enough players had come, they formed a circle in an open place next to the house and began to play a wifala tune that they had composed for the occasion; the music drew other people to the fiesta from their homes and work. Eight older or middle-aged men, dressed in the local-style red and black striped ponchos, played pinkillus accompanied by five caja players.

A number of young people came to dance, as did a few older couples who led the performance of the wifala dance. The women wore multiple skirts of deep greens and blues, while the men wore their best slacks and suit coats or sweaters. The men also wore shoes, as they usually do in fiesta dances when costumes are not required.[9] The hats of dancers and musicians were decorated with flowers. A little after midday, the dance began. Playing the five-hole pinkillus, the musicians repeated each wifala tune for twenty minutes or more as the dancers formed a wide circle in the field below them. In single file and with forward-moving, shuffling steps, the boys and girls, men and women, created alternating threads of a single strand. As in most Andean dancing, the upper part of their bodies remained relatively straight and motionless, the main action being in the legs, feet, and arms. The men carried *huichi huichis* (multicolored pompoms made of yarn on a string two feet long). They were swung in time to the music and were held in both hands over the head for a 360-degree turn at the end of each repetition of the piece. The dancers always moved counterclock-wise.

After the circling dancers and cyclical tune had gone on for a long time, the musicians increased the tempo for two or three final repetitions of the piece—the fuga section—and dancers broke into couples for the more animated part of the dance. After each piece the male dancers moved off by themselves to drink and rest, while the women did the same, both groups remaining separate from the musicians. Other men and women from the community stood or sat in small groups with members of their own sex; dancing is one of the few ways men and women interact directly in public fiestas. After ten or fifteen minutes of rest, the musicians launched into another wifala piece on their five-hole pinkillus, and the dancers once again formed their circle; this piece was followed by another rest period.

Forming another large circle with rows of two or usually three people across—alternating rows of men and women—the dancers performed an unaccompanied antiphonal song at around three o'clock. This was one of the rare times in Conima that vocal music was a prominent aspect of an ayllu fiesta celebration. The song, like many heard elsewhere in southern Peru during the Carnival season and for courting occasions, took the form of a romantic dialogue as well as a song duel between the sexes (Turino 1983; see Buechler 1980:97). Parts of it were sung, and one long section was shouted (in a speaking-chanting voice) back and forth between the young men and women as they walked in the circle.

As is typical of courting songs in southern Peru, the text was filled with sexual metaphors as well as fairly direct statements. In the wifala song, imagery of ripening and fertility is suggested by the repeated word *verbena*, a flower native to Peru, which ends each line. Olivia Harris has suggested that flowers are the most common symbol of fertility in the Andes (1982:48). Just as they were a central motif in this courting song, flowers adorned the musicians' and dancers' hats and were used to decorate plants in the fields during Candelaria. The poetic device of repeating *verbena* at the end of each line parallels the way the same motives are repeated at the end of each musical phrase in almost all Conimeño music. The song performance lasted for about thirty minutes, but a small portion of the text (translated by J. Apaza) will provide a taste of the song's flavor:

WOMEN: My little flower is my flower verbena,
And my flower garden of gold is verbena.
In the world there is occasion, verbena,
We shall mount a horse, verbena,
Such is my desire, verbena,
For us to be in love, verbena.

MEN: Whom are you going to tell, verbena,
That you have dressed for the dance, verbena.
What I have is as it is, verbena,
You should have told me before, verbena,
An old dog is this verbena.

WOMEN: My little flower is my flower verbena,
My flower garden of gold is verbena.
We shall be dancing, verbena.
With whom are they dancing, verbena?
On horseback one can ride, verbena,
Although it is I you shall mount, verbena.

MEN: Small mouth of a baby, verbena,
With me you are skipping, verbena,
Tiny feet of a baby, verbena,
With mine your legs can entwine, verbena.

Even this small portion of the text illustrates the flexible nature of strophic form typical of indigenous songs in southern Peru: these stanzas have four, five, and six lines. Among the Quechua speakers in southern Peru, Carnival and courting song texts are often improvised in a formulaic fashion—that is, recombining preexisting lines or combining them with new lines to fit a given situation. Usually the couplet is the basic unit for text formulas, but as in the five-line stanza here, singers do not necessarily feel restricted to even-numbered strophes. Especially when the singing between young men and women becomes a heated song-duel, I have heard singers extend stanzas to eight lines or more, to get the last word. The image of mounting a horse in the Candelaria text is also part of Carnival and courting songs in the Province of Canas in southern Cusco, indicating the wide diffusion of this and other imagery.

When the singing was finished, the five-hole pinkillus were played once more for a wifala dance, boys and girls alternating in the circle as before. Shortly thereafter, the musicians changed to the six-hole pinkillus and began playing a "candelaria" piece as the elders emerged from the sponsor's house, carrying the sacred first products in woven cloths on their backs. Illustrating the specificity with which Conimeños associate their musical instruments with given uses and occasions, during this festival the six-hole pinkillus were reserved for times referred to as "ch'alla" (in this context, ceremonies conducted by the elders for the first products, the Earth, and the achachilas).[10]

Upon leaving the house, the elders entered the community gathering outside with great dignity and solemnity. The ritual specialist led the men to an "earthen table"[11] on which the first products were placed, while necklaces of bread, onions, and potatoes were hung around the necks of the ritual specialist and his wife. Once the men were seated, the sponsor and his family served a meal to those present in order of their importance in the event: the ritual specialist and male elders at the earthen table; their wives, who had joined the separate female circle; the musicians' circle; the dancers; and then other community members, who ate in separate male and female circles. Before eating, the elder or the guía of each separate group said words over the food. This was the only time that I heard the Virgen de la Candelaria's name invoked along with the names of the Earth and local places of power.

After the meal, a complete t'inka with cups of alcohol was performed by the male elders at the earthen table, while the other circles were provided only with woven cloths covered with coca and cigarettes. After the formal t'inka was completed, the members of each circle took cigarettes and coca for themselves. As a typical part of the t'inka, members of the different circles repeatedly selected three perfect leaves and, placing them together, offered them to other members of their group. The use of coca in the t'inka, then, not only serves as the medium for maintaining bonds with the local divinities and ancestors but is also a form of social communion (Allen 1988). Following the t'inka, alcohol was served all around.

After drinking, the musicians began to perform a candelaria piece on the six-hole pinkillus, and the elders alone got up to dance. Led by the ritual specialist with a man on each arm, followed by his wife with a woman on each of her arms, five rows of three dancers each moved in a wide circle, with the black cloths containing the sacred products tied to their backs. The choreography, with its alternation of male and female rows of three dancers each, resembled that of the young people during their song. In the elders' dance, the most important person was in the center of each row (the ritual specialist, his wife, the most important elders, and their wives). After a number of turns in a wide circle, the ritual specialist led this party away from the sponsor's house to a path that went up the mountain. The musicians followed in the procession, playing six-hole pinkillus in rows of three across, with the men in the center playing the melody a parallel fifth below. The rest of the community joined to the rear.

Halfway up the valley that leads out of Japisi, below the pass over the mountain of Cambrapi, there is a small hill crowned with a rectangular flat place surrounded by stones. This is the ritual place of power of Japisi. When they arrived, the musicians continued playing on top of the hill, while the entire community joined hands and danced around its base, almost embracing it. During the dance some men and women sang vocables along with the flute melody, although this practice is unusual for Conima in my experience. When the dance ended, everyone ascended the small hill; before a rock shrine, the ritual specialist spoke to the Achachila and Pachamama. The elders then moved to the flat place surrounded by stone seats and laid the cloths with the sacred products in the center. The elders took products from their bundles and offered them to each other while words were said; afterward another t'inka was performed.

The activities on the hilltop were private. The musicians, dancers, and the rest of the community walked down to an open field below and began to perform another wifala dance while the elders conducted their rituals above. I stayed briefly to watch the beginning of the exchange of products and the preparation for the t'inka, but then it became apparent that I should leave too. Later, a friend explained the rituals for the first products to me and paraphrased the nature of the words spoken. Although his imagined version of what was said on the hilltop should not be taken literally, the theme of his text clarifies the meaning of the festival for Conimeños, and thus seems worth quoting:

> First Corn,
> Bring us an abundance of corn.
> Call the corn from the north, from the south,
> From the east and west,
> From here and from there.
> Draw out the corn from the chakras,
> Call them to us.
> Bring so many that they fill our houses,
> So that there is abundance for everyone.

First Potato,
Bring us an abundance of potatoes.
Call the potatoes from the north and south,
from east and west,
From here and from there.
Draw out the potatoes from the chakras.
Bring so many that they fill our houses,
So that there is abundance of potatoes for everyone.

More rituals for the sacred products, the Earth, and the achachilas were conducted by the elders the following day, and the young people continued their courting dance and song. The use of the different flutes and genres helped to frame the separateness of the two types of activities and to define where community attention should be focused at any given time. The close juxtaposition of young people's courting songs and dances and the elders' rituals for the ripening of plants suggests a metaphoric relationship between the activities. The metaphor is made explicit in the verses sung by the girls, who compare their sexuality to flower gardens of gold.

Students of Andean societies have frequently observed the juxtaposition of courting activities and rituals for agricultural and animal fertility within Carnival and other rainy-season festivals. Writing of Carnival in Ayacucho, Peru, Vásquez and Vergara suggest that "the most fundamental [meaning of] carnival fiestas is, without doubt, the relation between young men and women, *conceived as an expression of fertility*. In conception and practice within Quechua culture, human fertility is integrated with the fertility of nature: of the land and of animals" (1988:40, my stress).

Judging from Candelaria and a variety of festivals that I have attended in southern Peru, this seems to be a valid interpretation at one level, yet it is far removed from the spirit of courting activities. Although weddings in North America may be interpreted as celebrations of an institution that ensures the continuity of the species, few newlyweds are probably thinking about this on their wedding night. Likewise, for the young people in southern Peru *involved* in courting activities and lovemaking, I doubt that "fertility" is the image uppermost in their minds. It is important to keep such things in mind when writing and reading ethnographic descriptions; the alternative is a potential violence—ranging from misunderstanding to military action—rendered possible through the objectification of other people.[12]

CARNIVAL

In Conima, given individuals enjoy certain fiestas more than others. For Filiberto, who likes sikus more than any other instrument, playing panpipes all night during the Easter festival is unsurpassed. For my compadre Jorge and his brother Leo, who are particularly fond of tarkas, Carnival is the favorite. Since Checasaya's panpipe and pinkillu ensembles rarely gain distinction in the larger fiestas, people from that ayllu suggested that May 3, when they dance achachk'umu, is most enjoyable. The three-day community wedding fiestas, where a sikuri ensemble performs lentos and ligeros, are also a favorite with many people who are not especially involved in musical performance. One reason is that, since several weddings may be held around other major festivals, they extend a given fiesta period for a number of days, and Conimeños appreciate long fiestas.

There is a general consensus, however, that Todos los Santos (November 1 and 2; see chapter 9) and Carnival are the most important festivals in Conima.[13] All communities participate in these two occasions (as opposed to Candelaria, the Fiesta de la Cruz, and many other festivals in which only certain communities take part). Todos los Santos involves maintaining relationships with the ancestors and the recent dead, whereas Carnival is more strictly tied up with the agricultural cycle and with the rainy season itself. In spite of their European names, Candelaria, Carnival, and the Easter celebration are actually conceptualized and celebrated as part of the agricultural cycle in Conima. This is demonstrated by Conimeños in a dance called satiri (planter of potatoes), performed on May 15 to the accompaniment of sikuris.

Satiri is a costumed dance in which different communities (Central Sulcata, Putina, Huata, Checasaya) perform a dramatization of their entire agricultural cycle: from the clearing of the fields through planting and harvest. Within this dance drama, Conimeños enact the performances of Candelaria and Carnival; the dancers bring out pinkillus to do a parody of their own dances for these festivals. At the proper place in the agricultural-cycle sequence during satiri, the sikuri ensembles that accompany the dancers break into a choclo piece, a genre that is associated with the Easter fiesta. Since satiri is clearly a story Conimeños tell about themselves and their own conception of the agricultural cycle, the reference to these three fiestas in the drama is good evidence that they are actually considered part of the agricultural cycle: Candelaria and Carnival as ripening/fertility festivals and Easter as a harvest celebration (in the dance drama, Easter is parodied directly before the harvest is enacted).

Carnival itself is a week-long fiesta.[14] The two opening days (Sunday and Monday before Carnival) and the closing days a week later (Sunday, "Tentacíon," and Monday, "Kachapari") are celebrated in the town plazas

106

of Conima and Tilali by the ayllus of the two sides. During these days, competition among the different villages' musical and dance ensembles mounts to a head. Each ensemble is accompanied in the plaza by people from the same community who come to dance, drink, and celebrate.

A fiesta sponsor from each community is responsible for organizing the musical ensemble as well as ensuring that between roughly twenty-four and thirty-six dancers participate. The formally invited dancers—dressed in their best clothes and decorated with streamers—circle their tarka ensemble, holding hands in pairs and doing a short, rhythmic shuffle step known as tarkiada or carnavales. The simple, forward-moving step resembles steps used in most other noncostumed social dancing in Conima. As a fiesta day progresses, more and more people join in, and the dancing gets wilder. Sometimes all the dancers join hands and, forming a ring around the tarka musicians, move faster and faster until, people actually fall down. This is most apt to happen during the rapid, concluding fuga section.

Some communities, such as several from Ayllu Checasaya, use five-hole pinkillus instead of tarkas during Carnival. The dance done to pinkillu music (pinkillada) uses the same shuffle step, but the dancers form a single-file circle around the ensemble, and the alternating men and women swing huichi huichis (pompoms on a string) in time with the music. At each completion of the musical form, the dancers hold their huichi huichis between their hands above their heads and make a 360-degree turn, as was described for the wifala dance. Also consistent with wifala choreography, the pinkillada dancers break into couples, who dance holding hands during the fuga.

During Carnival, some of the young girls of marriageable age take special pains to dress in fine embroidered shawls and skirts, some making a display of changing festive clothing several times within a given day. Even more than other fiestas, the Carnival days in the plaza are a time for public display, courting, and secret lovemaking, and often a rash of weddings follows during the fiestas of Easter, May 3, and San Isidro (May 15).

One of the belles of the ball from Sulcata in the 1986 Carnival was everywhere to be seen. A special aura glowed around her that cannot be described, only recognized. She danced with many men during the festival, but I would guess that her fate was sealed long before the music started. Her beautiful clothing and aura may have been as much a farewell as a sign of welcome to the field of suitors. She was married during the following year.

Carnival days in the plaza are also a time of heavy drinking. As in other celebrations, heated arguments, fistfights, and even rock-throwing bouts pepper the fiesta. Fiestas become occasions to settle scores or vent tensions that have been brewing between people for months with no other means of resolution, but sometimes people get abusive just for fun.

Late in the afternoon on the second day of the 1986 Carnival, an older man from another community, who was very drunk, decided to take on one of the members of our tarka ensemble from Putina while we were playing. There was no particular cause for the feud except that the attention we had been receiving got his attention as well. Others in our group intervened as did the ayllu *teniente* (leader), who is responsible for keeping peace among his community. The man broke away from those restraining him, kicked in our drum, and then ran off, at which time the teniente insisted, along with others in our group, that it was time to go home. Some of our musicians were angry about having to find another drum, and some wanted the offender to find one for us, but most people just shrugged it off as if this were a normal part of the fiesta—with apparently no major grudges held.

Many people in Conima told me about brawls that had broken out between musical ensembles during festivals, especially when groups from Conima were performing in fiestas in other towns, but I never witnessed this.[15] Because I was a gringo and a source of general entertainment during fiestas, people sometimes wanted to fight with me. Luckily, I would get only as far as taking off my jacket or poncho and returning an insult or two before the members of my group would intervene, physically surrounding me and assuring me that no one was going to touch me as long as *they* were around.

Fighting, lovemaking, drinking, blowing flutes until your mouth is sore, dancing until you fall down, and being deeply and expressively part of your community are all reasons that fiestas, particularly the longer ones like Carnival, make life worth living for the people of Conima.

While the celebrations in the plaza are the wildest and most exciting, it is the two central days, referred to as Martes and Miercoles de Ch'alla or *ch'allada*, that constitute the fiesta's ceremonial core. On these days each ayllu, or different combinations of ayllu units, celebrates independently in its own community with tarka or five-hole pinkillu music, dance, and a series of t'inka and ch'alla rituals for the homes and fields of community members.

On these days in 1985 and 1986, Putina from Lower Sulcata celebrated with Central Sulcata, and their cooperation as well as their separate identities were articulated in various ways during the fiesta. For example, each ayllu unit supplied its own sponsor, each with different roles, for the joint festivities. The first part of Tuesday was celebrated in Central Sulcata and the first part of Wednesday in Putina. A single tarka ensemble with members from both communities performed together throughout Carnival. In the late afternoon on both Tuesday and Wednesday, however, the tarka ensemble split into two groups. The members of the two communities also separated and, accompanied by their half of the ensemble, walked to the place where the late-afternoon dance was to be held, on the border between Lower and Central Sulcata. When the second community group and ensemble arrived, the two halves of the musical ensemble stood next to each other and began to perform in open competition—trying to play longer and louder. Shortly thereafter, however, the musicians came back together and played as one for a single community of dancers that circled the tarka players.

Illustrating the relative and rather fluid nature of community and "ayllu" identity, this ensemble and the people who accompanied it created a united front when performing in the town plaza. When left to themselves, however, the members of each ayllu subdivision celebrated both their cooperative relationship and their distinctiveness. As usual, this was clearly realized through musical competition, in this case between the two halves of the ensemble. In addition, the Tuesday and Wednesday celebrations were split spatially between the two communities, but each day's festivities ended in the neutral center between them.

For the Tuesday of Ch'allada in Central Sulcata, the musicians met in the morning at the home of the fiesta sponsor. They then began visiting a series of homes in the community where they had been invited. They also made an obligatory penultimate visit at the ayllu teniente's house, and a final visit at the home of the sponsor before moving off to the late-afternoon dance. While walking from one house to the next, the ensemble always continued playing, even as they moved up fairly steep slopes. Upon entering each home, they performed one or two pieces before being served a full meal— soup and a second course followed by beer. After the meal, the ensemble leader and the musicians officiated a special t'inka for the host and his family; the significance of the visit centered on this act.

While an individual can hold a private t'inka at any time to uphold the reciprocity with the ancestors, the earth, and achachilas, to do so on the days of Ch'allada makes it more powerful. The cost and effort entailed in providing food, drink, and coca for the musicians and one's compadres and neighbors is one basis for the heightened significance within the community (that is, the offering is greater). The other is that the presence of the musicians, and the music itself, creates a special festive atmosphere that publicly frames the event and adds importance to the ritual.

During these days of celebration, the focus was on interayllu relations and on maintaining relationships with the forces of the world that affect the life of the community. After several days of rest (Thursday through Saturday), the people of Putina and Central Sulcata returned to dance together in the plaza for the fiesta's finale.

THE ART OF FESTIVAL

Conimeños particularly seem to enjoy long fiestas such as Carnival. Sustaining the celebration over many days is crucial for reaching a high level of intensity, and for opening the way to various types of special experiences. Anthropological writings on ritual and festival often stress how rituals invert or alter everyday reality: the world turned upside-down, the creation of *communitas*, the creation of a special reality (for example, Turner 1969; Abrahams 1977; Smith 1975). "The everyday" often refers to a public social reality. Festivals also allow for the private thoughts, desires, feelings, and strategies of individuals—which are just as real and "everyday," albeit usually hidden—to become public and to be acted out in a variety of ways (drunken fistfights, lovemaking and elopement, the donning of special clothing to become belle of the ball).

These special possibilities and the interruption of the everyday are still not the whole story, because fiesta behavior is also modeled on, and is often an intensified version of, patterns of everyday social style, relationships, and beliefs (Abrahams, 1977). Fiesta activities such as the satiri dance are stories Conimeños tell about themselves and their daily routines, blending humorous caricature with a literal dramatization. Community, family, and coparent relationships, which are important in daily life, become intensified as well as tested and perhaps altered during festivals. During fiestas, individuals play out, communicate about, and manipulate "everyday" social positions and roles; fiestas are public occasions to enhance, cement, or diminish prestige, to fulfill or fail in one's duty to the community (Buechler 1980). A person's successes and failures during fiestas affect his or her social position after the festival is over.

Factionalism within an ayllu or formalized community is articulated publicly through the choices people make about who they want to celebrate with during festivals. Because of the voluntary character of musical performance, the actual unity of a social group determines musical ensemble formation, regardless of formal ayllu and sub-ayllu divisions. For example, Lower Sulcata, comprising the villages of Huata and Putina, is a formal political unit. Huata and Putina share a school and must do joint work projects for its upkeep; they have the same political officials and religious practitioners, requiring cooperation in certain rituals and activities. In the 1985 and 1986 Carnivals, however, Putina joined with Central Sulcata, whereas Huata celebrated independently. During my stay, Putina and Huata never celebrated a major fiesta together, and each ensemble was engaged in particularly intense musical competition with the other. The complexities and tensions of other political relations—parodying Spaniards for the mestizo teniente gobernador during the Fiesta de la Cruz, achachilas dancing for the cross—are also played out during fiestas.

For celebrating fiestas, people join with those whom they actually identify as being of the same community, based on feelings of trust or some type of genuine affinity. Extended musical repetition and long periods of dancing during fiestas are particularly powerful means for bringing people together and allowing for heightened social union.

In his discussion of culturally specific styles of movement, Edward Hall emphasizes how synchrony of movement between individuals becomes an extremely important medium for social bonding beginning soon after birth. Moving together and sounding together—*being in sync*—are fundamental to being together, and are crucial to feelings of belonging within a social situation. Hall describes how this largely unconscious type of human communication takes place throughout life: people walking in step in airports, the choreography of gesture and stance during conversations, children moving in rhythm on the playground, feeling clumsy or out of step in a foreign society (see Hall 1977). The imagery and concomitant feelings of unity created through syncing is also often consciously used: pledging allegiance to the flag, military marching in step, the use of music to coordinate working in factories.

Music and dance bring the state of being in sync—of being together—to a heightened level of explicitness. With each repetition of a piece in Conima, the possibility of "being in sync" is extended and the social union is intensified, contributing to an affective intensity. In such contexts, extended repetition does not lead to boredom; it is the basis of aesthetic power. Not unlike making love, music and dance open the possibility for deeper physical and spiritual connections between community members. During special moments, culturally specific rhythms and forms of movement are not merely semiotic expressions of community and identity; rather, *they become their actual realization*. In this regard, it seems to me that Hall's work opens important theoretical avenues for ethnomusicologists who study music and dance in relation to the construction and realization of social participation and identities.

The importance of music within processes of social syncing has been discussed in a different way by Charles Keil in his paper "Participatory Discrepancies and the Power of Music" (1987). Keil writes:

> The power of music is in its participatory discrepancies, and these are basically of two kinds: processual and textural. Music, to be personally involving and socially valuable, must be "out of time" and "out of tune."
>
> For "participatory discrepancies" one could substitute "inflection," "articulation," "creative tensions," "relaxed dynamisms," "semiconscious or unconscious slightly out of syncnesses." For "process" one could substitute "beat," "drive," "groove," "swing," "push," etc., and for "texture" one could substitute "timbre," "sound," "tone qualities," "as arranged by," and so forth. (1987:275)

Keil provides a valuable framework for what should be a central issue in comparative musicological work—the study of how musical sound and movement (dance) heighten the potential for social participation, union, and extraordinary experience.

Initially I had difficulty with the term "discrepancies" because it seemed to priviledge a reified musical standard against which the processual, textural aspects that Keil was calling attention to would be judged. When things are right, Conimeño music is not "out of time," "out of tune," or "slightly out of sync" according to local standards of variance. If a certain type of deep, bodily, community participation is a primary purpose of performance, then the "slightly out of syncness" Keil mentions can only be defined as being "in sync" when the purpose is realized (realization being the standard, not abstract sonic characteristics).

More importantly, Keil suggests a whole range of musical qualities that aptly describe Conimeño music—relaxed dynamism, dense timbres, wide and variable intonation, and an emphasis on making the music 'run' or groove. As he points out, similar qualities are found frequently in musical styles that are related to creating community participation and unification (I have already emphasized extensive repetition, long performances, and loud volume for Conima in this regard).

Further research and thinking are required to understand why these processual and textural features often correlate with participatory music. Along the way, the notion of "discrepancies," vis-à-vis musical conventions and standard cultural movement, may be worth reinserting. The strictly conventional (deeply rooted) signs of habit provide comfort, but hardly require notice and cannot distinguish one special moment from another or one performer or group from others. It is the play around the edges of convention that wakes us from habit and calls our attention to the moment, to each other, and to the festival or enactment that make special relations possible (Abrahams 1977).

Also during festivals, relationships with the forces that affect Conimeños' daily lives—the earth, the achachilas, the ancestors—are brought into stronger relief and are celebrated through rituals such as t'inka. Older Conimeños seem to place great importance on tradition itself as a means of maintaining relationships with their ancestors and the past. This is accomplished through what people perceive to be a similarity between past and present: a repetition of practices and the enactment of customs "the way our ancestors did them" (see Bruner 1986a:12).

Like the achachk'umu dance, fiestas in Conima allow people to fuse many levels of personal and collective meaning, different purposes, and a wide range of experiences. The power of festivals is, in part, made possible through the special *frames* created around and by these events (Bateson 1972; Goffman 1974). Roger Abrahams writes,

> Surely there is a difference between the way we interpret everyday experiences and those that jump out at us as being significant. This difference is carried, in part, by the interpretive apparatus we use to discuss any experience. Somehow and somewhere between experience and the Big Experience we impose a frame on the activity by calling attention to its extraordinary character. This attention commonly is elicited by the self-conscious stylization of the activity and through developing some kind of preparation for it, through rehearsal, warming up, or simply through special kinds of anticipatory behavior. (1986:62)

Yet in the same paper Abrahams seems to suggest that both the notions of intensification and inversion of the "everyday" that often surround discussions of ritual, festival, and art are problematic because they depend on the idea of some paramount reality that can be cleanly separated from these other types of experiences (1986:67). Things that occur during festivals, as well as at other times, vary in terms of intensity, extraordinariness, and the degree of heightened awareness and formal framing, so that it is difficult to maintain a rigid dichotomy between "celebrations" ("rituals," "festivals") and "the everyday" (see Seeger 1987).

Fiestas are a frequently recurring part of the annual routine in Conima.

They have been institutionalized within the "daily life" cycle, reflecting an understanding of people's regular need for play, communion, catharsis, for reaching further within, and getting further outside, themselves. Festivals are routinized occasions for recognizing routine, habitual moments for awaking from habit.

Through the performance of music and dance, communal meals, t'inka rituals, drinking, and community presence and participation, fiestas provide a framework that enhances the potential for extraordinary experiences, although festivals do not guarantee them. Against the quietude of Conima and the almost total absence of musical performance on other days, the sound of community ensembles is key to invoking the festival frame that, in turn, conventionally signals the potential (social expectation) for unconventional experiences. Music does more than help cue the festival frame, however. Inseparable from dance, it is the primary medium for getting in sync and, through prolonged repetition, staying in sync—for making a deep cultural synchrony explicit.

The originality of the ensembles' emblem pieces for a given fiesta marks community identity. But the pieces, like the particular quirks and surprises of specific performances—Keil's "participatory discrepancies"—also become indices of the particular moment and hence bring the people who participated into a special relationship based on "being there." Each year a piece is played, every time a distinctive musical device is used, it collects a new level of indexical meaning and adds time depth—"still there," "still together"—which is one important meaning and purpose of Tradition.

Fiestas and the performance of music and dance do not guarantee extraordinary experiences. Nonetheless, Conimeños savor these times for what they can, and often do, become. Understandably, many older people express regret when sponsors or enough musicians and dancers cannot be found—an occurrence that is increasingly common because of migratory movement away from Conima.

PART TWO
The Local, the National, and the
Youth of Conima

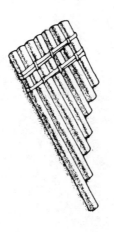

F I V E

Qhantati Ururi of Conima

On MAY 3, 1985, AT the same time that the small Fiesta de la Cruz was taking place in Conima, a much larger mestizo celebration was under way in the provincial capital of Huancané, some forty miles away.[1] For many years it has been customary for the First Alferado (the most important mestizo sponsor) of the fiesta to contract the sikuri ensemble Qhantati Ururi of Conima to accompany his entourage during the festival.

For the 1985 Fiesta de la Cruz, other alferados in Huancané also hired sikuri ensembles from various districts in the province, including Moho, Rosaspata, and the District of Huancané. Whereas in an earlier era town mestizos would have distanced themselves from actually performing sikuri music, by 1985, many of the ensembles in Huancané consisted of young town mestizos and urban-oriented youths from the ayllus. Although older people of the ayllus throughout Huancané's various districts pride themselves on maintaining their own distinct musical traditions, most of these young sikuri groups played in the harmonic style specifically associated with Conima.

That other groups were playing in their style and even using their repertory irritated the Conimeños of Qhantati. These troubles were compounded by personnel problems within the ensemble that jeopardized their performance during this fiesta in 1985, and thus their prominent reputation in the region. The conflict emerged along generational lines, between the older peasant musicians and a group of young Conimeños, most now living in the city of Puno, who were needed for the performance. The young Puno faction refused to participate, leaving Qhantati seriously shorthanded for the musical competition with its own imitators in the Huancané festival; in the end, Qhantati Ururi did not do very well in the musical competition.

When Conimeños perform for fiestas in their own communities, they are considered important people; they receive warm thanks and steady offerings of drinks, coca, and food. When the peasant musicians are working for a

117

vecino alferado and his mestizo guests in contracted situations, they are treated like servants. In the 1985 Huancané fiesta, Qhantati was hired to accompany the alferado and his party in the religious processions for the cross, as well as to supply music for noncostumed social dancing, both in the streets and at the alferado's home. They had to perform all day for five days, and sometimes late into the night. The sponsor and his guests continually told the musicians when, where, and what to play. The vecinos complained loudly if they thought the ensemble was resting too often, drinking too much, or not playing long or powerfully enough. Wearing suits and formal dresses, the alferado and his guests ate and drank at elaborately set tables inside the house, while the musicians were fed outside on the patio, sometimes with the food placed on woven cloths on the ground.

The Conimeños outwardly accepted the treatment they received, but as might be expected, they complained or made sarcastic remarks about the vecinos among themselves. Given their avoidance of mestizos in Conima and the pride they show in themselves and their heritage when at home, it seems strange that they would want to perform in Huancané at all. Their reason may be the money, no matter how minuscule (about a dollar a day per musician), and the prestige gained at home from receiving invitations to perform outside the district. Equally important, the fiesta in Huancané is an important site for interdistrict musical competition. Conimeños felt that it was important to uphold their position as the performers for the First Alferado.

I played with Qhantati throughout the Fiesta de la Cruz in 1985, and my presence caused difficulty for the alferado. Highland vecinos are, in my experience, extremely hospitable and kind with visitors, and with most people who are perceived to be of a similar or higher social position. The alferado did not want me eating with the musicians, and during the first days, he graciously and repeatedly invited me inside to celebrate with the guests. My explanations and refusals became less polite as I observed their treatment of the musicians, just as the invitations became less frequent—although my food continued to be served on a plate accompanied by silverware. At one point, with patience gone on both sides, the alferado and I came to harsh words over a rude remark and a strident demand that he had leveled at the weary musicians.

After that we avoided each other. I had certainly been insensitive to his position, feelings, and customs of hospitality, all of which were genuine and proper from his point of view. It was, after all, his house and his party. His attitudes toward and treatment of the 'Indians' were deeply rooted in habit and were normal from his perspective. But in such situations in highland Peru, neutrality, or crossing social lines with the idea of crossing back, is simply not an option. The Conimeños who had observed our dispute seemed to take no notice and never mentioned it later, but my relationships with many of the musicians in Qhantati were noticeably closer after the Fiesta de la Cruz was over.

The distance, barriers, and sites of conflict between the peasants of Qhantati and the Huancané vecinos, between the different generations of Conimeños, and between the alferado and myself were made very clear to me during the Huancané festival. Any comprehension of these different subject positions—a major objective of the following chapters—must be grounded in a relatively detailed discussion of Peruvian history, politics, and ethnic/class relations at various local, regional, and national levels.

Qhantati Ururi's traditional role in the Huancané festival, as well as the creation and initial diffusion of the Conimeño panpipe style itself, can be traced to the influence of an urban-based intellectual movement of the early twentieth century, known as *indigenismo*. Qhantati's prominent place in the Huancané fiesta is matched by its position of honor in the history of the urban panpipe movement that emerged among migrant and university groups in Lima and other cities in the 1970s. The activities of these urban panpipe players subsequently raised the prestige of sikuri music, and particularly the Conimeño style, among young peasants and mestizo town dwellers in Conima and throughout the Province of Huancané—explaining the presence of Qhantati's young imitators in the Fiesta de la Cruz in 1985.

Part I of this book emphasized the local character of musical practices in Conima. In part II, we move outward to a consideration of the links between the local and the national during two particular historical conjunctures—the *indigenista* period circa the 1920s and the Velasco and post-Velasco era after 1968. The Conimeño sikuri tradition, the Fiesta de la Cruz in Huancané, and the histories of two important musical institutions, Qhantati Ururi de Conima and Asociación Juvenil Puno (chapter 6), serve as important reference points for understanding Conimeño musical life in its broader contexts.

THE STATE, THE NATION, AND NATIONALISM IN PERU

Peru became an independent state in 1821, but it has never been a single "nation" in the sense of a group of people who recognize a common heritage, bonds of unity, and shared goals for the future. The overt oppression and marginalization of rural peasants (often identified as 'Indians') has hindered any sense of their belonging to the nation. For instance, after the War of the Pacific (1879–83), when the Chilean victors sought to collect tribute from a group of indigenous communities in the department of Lima, the villagers refused on the grounds that "they had nothing to do with Peru" (Cotler 1978:117).

As another example, Hernando de Soto describes how "In the 1946 legislature, the senator for Junín, Manuel Faura, presented a bill that would have prohibited people from the provinces, particularly from the mountains, from entering Lima. In the next legislature, Representative Salomón Sánchez Burga submitted a request, with the House's approval, which would have required people wishing to enter the capital from the provinces to carry an entry *passport*" (1989:10, my emphasis). While these measures were not passed, they give a sense of the social attitudes that surely discouraged feelings of nationalism among highland peasants. The desire to maintain a social distance from Andean peasants, neatly symbolized by the passport, marks the vecinos in Huancané as well as senators and representatives in Lima.

The Peruvian situation cannot be described simply as several nations (such as indigenous versus criollo, highland versus coastal, or dominant versus subordinate) contained within the Peruvian territory. Quechua and Aymara speakers in the rural highlands frequently perceive their identity concretely in terms of their localized community, ayllu, and region; this is the case among people of the ayllus in Conima. Conimeños sometimes put up a Peruvian flag outside the sponsor's house in the ayllus during fiestas; the men are drafted into the army, and the children attend state schools in gray uniforms. They are certainly aware of their links to the state and its effects on their lives, but the older people's feelings of nationalism seem vague and tangential to their daily experience.

The localized purview among the older generations of rural Andeans is matched by the factionalism among elite groups in Peru since the colonial period. The social unit defined in cultural and class terms as *criollo*, which has directed state operations since the birth of the republic, must be understood in terms of a complex web of competing factions and shifting alliances along lines of economic interest. There is no single "dominant group" in Peru, although from an indigenous person's perspective it may appear this way.

The Republican State

The republican state during the nineteenth century was characterized by competing conservative and liberal factions (Palmer 1980:36; Cotler 1978:75). Military leaders tied to traditional land-based elites held sway during the first fifty years of the republic, but in response to heightened international capitalist penetration (1870–1930), rising commercial and agro-exporting factions located on the coast began to challenge the military *caudillos.*

The former ruling group did little to alter the colonial patterns of domination of Andean peasants; it was not in the interests of highland elites, whose wealth was based on land control and indigenous labor. The members of the rising factions, who stressed the need for a modernized national infrastructure to facilitate production and transportation for export markets, likewise did not alter the economically dominated and politically marginalized position of Andean peasants. Rather, as coastal middlemen supporting the advance of international capitalist enterprises into the sierra (the English wool trade in Puno is a prominent example; see Tamayo 1982:86–101), they were among the powerful new forces that entered the competitive arena for Andean peasants' land. The more powerful coastal entrepreneurs also posed a threat to the economic position of local elites in the southern rural sierra, thus exacerbating the coast-highland schism.

Nationalism

During the nineteenth century and the first decades of the twentieth, the Peruvian upper classes continued to look to European cultural models, and as Iturriaga and Estenssoro observe, the Peruvian aristocracy in Lima preferred to import European composers and musicians as a matter of prestige, rather than use the home-grown variety (1985:115). During this period, Andean music and other cultural forms were largely disparaged or ignored by the local and national criollo elites, just as the well-being of the indigenous population remained largely outside the purview of governmental concern. Following independence, a type of musical nationalism emerged, marked by the production of patriotic or military marches, hymns, and songs in a European idiom. "This satisfied the needs of the aristocracy who saw themselves as a nation in an international context without having to distinguish themselves as unique [from Europeans]" (Iturriaga and Estenssoro 1985:116).

In the period after the War of the Pacific with Chile (1879–83), however, a new nationalistic discourse arose that focused increased attention on Peru's indigenous Andean peoples and planted seeds for an alternative vision to the former European-centered orthodoxy (Tamayo 1980:162). Peru's defeat led Manuel González Prada, among others, to tie Peru's "national problem"—the lack of sociopolitical, cultural, and economic integration—to the

"Indian problem" in a new way. In his famous speech of 1888, he suggested that Peru was not a unified nation and hence could not defend itself as one. González accurately related the indigenous population's lack of national consciousness, as well as their poverty, to systematic oppression and marginalization rather than to racial inferiority, an earlier stock explanation for the "Indian problem" (Francke 1978: 116–17).

González and other thinkers of the second half of the nineteenth century were forerunners of a series of intellectual and political positions that became known collectively as indigenismo. As the centerpiece of a growing liberal-nationalistic discourse, indigenismo began to have profound affects on Andean cultural practice in such isolated rural corners of the country as Conima, as well as in the very heart of Lima by the 1920s.

Indigenismo

Indigenismo refers to a group of discourses and debates that revolved around a heightened concern for, or interest in, native Peruvians, indigenous culture, and the political and economic difficulties faced by peasant communities. Indigenista sentiments grew up among middle- and upper-class intellectuals, artists, political thinkers, and teachers in urban centers—Cusco, Puno, and Lima, among others—between 1900 and the 1940s.

Indigenismo was not a unified ideology or movement, nor was it always fueled by the same motivations. For some, indigenista activities resulted from deeply felt humanitarian concerns about the oppression of indigenous Andeans; for others, it involved issues of regional or national identity—paralleling romantic-nationalist movements elsewhere in the Americas and Europe. Writers such as José Carlos Mariátegui (founder of the Communist Party in Peru) saw the struggle to liberate the 'Indian' as part of a broader struggle for socialist revolution. All the various currents of indigenismo were complexly lodged within a series of conflicts over political and economic power during the first decades of the twentieth century.

A number of organizations, many centered in universities and producing their own periodicals, served as the basis for diffusing indigenista ideas—largely to people of the same classes. Usually, indigenous people were not directly involved in indigenista activities themselves but rather were the focus of interest, concern, and legal and moral support. By some accounts, however, indigenismo helped to inspire peasant activism (Tamayo 1982:229–43; Rénique 1987:22, 1991:77).

One early organization, Asociación Pro Indígena, was active in the University of San Marcos in Lima during the first decades of the century. The objectives of the organization included coming to the aid of indigenous communities in cases of legal complaints and land recovery, assigning free lawyers to defend them, and developing research teams to undertake a study of the "condition of the Indian" in every province in the nation. The organization sent delegates to carry out this work in many parts of the country. Alberto Flores notes that many of the members—students, lawyers, and other professionals among them—were inspired to join the organization because of the dismal situation of the Indian in Peru. He goes on to say, "Their messengers [workers in the provinces] were a testimony to the courage of a young generation to move toward a meeting with the peasant world and to organize moral indignation against *gamonalismo* [an oppressive system of peasant domination by large landowners]" (Flores 1988:323–24). While other activist groups were to follow the Asociación Pro Indígena, the majority of indigenista organizations confined themselves to academic and artistic activities in the spirit of romantic nationalism or regionalism.

Like many regionalistic and nationalistic movements, indigenismo and the concern with the "Indian problem" may be interpreted as rising out of a perceived threat, although the precise definition of the menace depended on the political and class positions, as well as the region of different intellectuals. For certain writers, the perceived threat was simply anything that stood in the way of progress and economic development—either at the national or at the regional level. Indians were considered to be among the obstacles, and some writers of this ilk suggested the forceful cultural assimilation of Andean peasants into the "national society" as a way of solving the "Indian problem" (Francke 1978:149). One basis for indigenista sentiments among those toward the left was a growing apprehension about U.S. and European economic domination. In the southern sierra, coastal entrepreneurs' increasing stake in the highlands and their collusion with international capital led indigenistas or *serranistas* to react against coastal as well as foreign imperialism.

Leguía and Indigenismo

It is no mere coincidence that indigenismo flowered during the eleven year rule of President Augusto B. Leguía (1919–30), who had an important role in fortifying Peru's dependent position in international capitalist relations. Through his efforts to "modernize" the country, he became particularly involved with U.S. capital and interests, spurring a heightened concern about foreign imperialism. Also high on Leguía's agenda was the strengthening of the Lima-based state and the centralization of power. This was seen as a threat by local elites and intellectuals in the southern sierra.

Describing the situation in Cusco, José Luis Rénique notes that

> more than being the beginning of a revolutionary alliance between intellectuals and Indians, "serranismo" and "indigenismo" expressed the eruption of regionalism. [It was] a defensive attitude against a centralist integration that threatened the interior of the country with a uniformity not only economic, but also spiritual. In the best of cases, the type of political action that can be inferred from "serranista" writing is of a popular coalition whose ultimate objective was the recognition of the intellectuals as a regional political class, in other words, their incorporation into the state as administrators of the region. (1991:110)

The regionalistic fervor that flowered as a result of Leguía's centralist politics often included a heightened interest in the local indigenous culture and the use of distinguishing Andean identity emblems (ponchos, music, coca chewing) among indigenistas.[2]

As part of Leguía's attempt to consolidate a centralized state, he also articulated populist, pro-Indian positions in opposition to regional power blocs—the traditional landed elites. Rénique writes that Leguía generated more "indigenista legislation" between 1919 and 1924 than had been produced throughout the previous century (1987:22). For example, article 58 of the 1920 constitution states that "the state will protect the indigenous race and dictate laws especially for its development and culture in harmony with its necessities. The Nation recognizes the legal existence of the indigenous communities" (quoted in Basadre 1968:44).

In 1920, the government established the Comisión Pro-Indígena made up of well-known indigenistas from Cusco and Puno who were to investigate ways of resolving the "Indian problem." In 1921, the government proclaimed June 24 as a national holiday, "Día del Indio," and the Section for Indigenous Affairs was created under the direction of the indigenista Hildebrado Castro. The Patronato de la Raza Indígena was established in 1922 for the legal protection of Andean peasants' rights. In the same year the use of free indigenous labor, traditionally obligated by local authorities, was outlawed. Strikingly, the central government had already instituted a law that obliged indigenous peasants to work without pay on the construction of national roads (Cotler 1978:188–89). While seemingly contradictory, the two laws pertaining to free indigenous labor underline Leguía's primary concern with weakening local elites and strengthening the central government's control.

Leguía's relation to the indigenista movement thus had a curious double aspect. His moves to consolidate the power of a centralized state inspired resistance in the form of regionalism, which, in turn, generated interest in local indigenous cultures. At the same time, his "indigenista legislation" added legitimacy and support to pro-Indian sentiments and created a common ground where prominent highland indigenistas could be incorporated in state activities and institutions.

It has been noted by many writers, and by Leguía himself (see Basadre 1968:309), that the pro-Indian legislation of this period proved to be largely ineffectual. Indigenismo did have long-term ideological ramifications, however, in subsequent struggles for civil rights. Cracks in the former orthodoxy about the inferiority of 'Indians' had been initiated by important intellectuals, and by the state itself.

Indigenismo and Andean Musical Practice

In most regionalistic, nationalistic, and nativistic movements, people choose identity emblems that most clearly mark the unique character of the group (Linton 1943:231). Emblems from indigenous Andean culture clearly distinguished Peru—as an Andean nation—from Europe and the United States, just as indigenistas in the southern sierra appropriated the same types of emblems to differentiate themselves from coastal Lima. In their choice of emblems, indigenistas also frequently stressed ancient Inca "high" culture, both as a romantic allusion to Peru's glorious past and as a reference to the long history of European domination. Stressing the Inca past may also have helped mestizo and criollo indigenistas negotiate their own residual prejudices regarding the contemporary indigenous peasantry.

In the spirit of romantic nationalism, artistic and academic activities were the *raison d'être* for a large number of indigenista groups. Anthropological and folkloristic studies were initiated. Writers began to publish Quechua poetry, and Andean subjects were presented in novels and paintings. Perhaps because music and dance were both central Andean art forms, and recognizable as such from a European-criollo perspective (as opposed to weaving, for example, at that time), these domains were granted special attention in the indigenistas' quest for nationalistic or regionalistic emblems.

Urban-academic composers in Lima, Cusco, Puno, and other Peruvian cities created interpretations of Andean musical genres and themes in what was basically a European romantic idiom (Lloréns 1983; Rozas 1985; Tamayo 1982:352–54; Turino 1988:131–32). Highland mestizo institutions and ensembles were formed for the study, preservation, and diffusion of indigenous Andean performing arts—Centro Qosqo de Arte Nativo in Cusco (1924); Conjunto Musical y Folklorista Victor Masias, Ork'opata, and Centro Vernacular Los Intimos, in Puno, beginning in the early 1920s; and the Estudiantina Duncker (1928) in Puno (Gonzáles Ríos 1982:19–20).[3]

These institutions featured urban mestizos performing stylized, costumed versions of rural Andean dances on stage. The mestizo-indigenista musicians blended instruments associated with the Andean peasantry, such as the kena and charango, with guitars, mandolins, violins, and (somewhat later) accordion, in an ensemble type known as *estudiantina*. The musical repertory consisted of indigenous melodies that were stylized and arranged, sometimes using closed forms;[4] new compositions based on Andean music; and mestizo genres such as the *wayno, yaravi, pasacalle,* and *marinera.* This smooth style of performance featured a melody played or sung in unison or parallel thirds with a triadic, homophonic accompaniment and an active bass line. Estudiantinas usually balanced higher-pitched instruments such as the mandolin with instruments in the bass and middle ranges, making this music less strident overall than indigenous musical style.

These indigenista musical organizations did not primarily serve the stated functions of preserving and diffusing indigenous music and dance. The estudiantinas, and the dance troupes that they accompanied, were but one example of how indigenismo inspired the creation of new musical and choreographic styles through the combination of local-indigenous and criollo elements and sensibilities.[5] It was mestizo rather than indigenous identity that was at stake within indigenista circles, and the musical styles that resulted from their activities articulated this.

In addition to creating their own syncretic musical styles, indigenistas had an impact on indigenous musical and cultural practices in specific locations, Conima among them. The climate fostered by the urban-based indigenista movement led mestizos of local rural elites to become actively and creatively involved with the local peasants' arts in a more direct way than before. The local mestizos' ability to influence and alter cultural practices in the ayllus was based on their greater social power, allowing them to bring different types of social and economic incentives to bear on indigenous activities. Most crucially, the values and outlook of mestizo indigenistas were largely grounded in a Western-criollo orientation. Hence, in spite of their symbolic identification with indigenous society, their input into local musical life was strongly colored by their own criollo-mestizo aesthetics and social values. These dynamics are evident in the history of Natalio Calderón's involvement with the most famous musical ensemble from Conima: Qhantati Ururi.

A History of Qhantati Ururi[6]

Natalio Calderón was a *vecino* (mestizo town dweller) and a landowner in Conima. He was also involved with the indigenista movement and was sympathetic to the Huancaneño peasants' dramatic struggle against vecino oppression during the 1920s. During the first half of the decade, there was a peasant movement throughout the Province of Huancané which had been aided by a Lima-based indigenista organization, Comité Pro-Derecho Indígena Tahuantinsuyo (Pro-Indian Rights Committee Tahuantinsuyo; founded 1920). In 1922, two peasant leaders from Huancané traveled to Lima and gained an interview with President Augusto B. Leguía himself. They received his support for a project to create a new town in Huancané in which land, local markets, and peasant labor would be independent of vecino control; the town would also have its own school. In spite of the president's verbal encouragement, the project of creating a "free zone" in Huancané was blocked by vecino landowners and officials in the province, who feared the erosion of their power. Their continuing abuses of peasant communities resulted in the violent indigenous rebellion of Wancho-Lima (December 1923–January 1924).

In this uprising, the peasants from a number of districts in Huancané allegedly attacked haciendas and towns, although Conimeños say that they did not take part in violent activities. The vecinos armed themselves, and government troops were called in from Puno; the rebellion was quickly and violently crushed. In the backlash, vecino landowners stepped up their oppression of indigenous people throughout the province, confiscating more lands and animals from the ayllus (see Tamayo 1982:229–43).

Augusto Calderón recounted how his father, Natalio, was against the atrocities perpetuated by the vecinos and how, because of this attitude, he was ostracized by the other vecinos in Conima, even his own relatives. While Natalio apparently did not take an activist role in the peasants' struggle before or after the rebellion, his indigenista sentiments are clear.

There appear to have been active connections among people involved with indigenismo in the cities of Puno and Juliaca and the provincial and district capitals of the department. Augusto said that Natalio was personally associated with the well-known Puneño indigenista Manuel Quiroga (see Tamayo 1982:323), and with other indigenista intellectuals such as Vicente Mendoza of the provincial capital of Huancané. Although Natalio completed only a primary education, Augusto recalled that his father read pamplets by Marx and Engels and by Puneño indigenistas. It was specifically mentioned that Natalio read *Boletín Titikaka,* a publication produced by Ork'opata.

The best-known indigenista group in the region, Ork'opata, had been active in the city of Puno during the 1920s. The Peruvian historian José Tamayo notes that Ork'opata was a cultural organization whose activities were primarily "literary and theoretical" (1982:264). During their gatherings on Saturdays and Sundays, these urban artists and intellectuals "drank *chicha* [Andean corn beer] and liquor, chewed coca, wore *chullus* [Andean knit hats associated with the peasantry], and sang songs in Quechua and Aymara" (1982:265), but Tamayo underlines the fact that Ork'opata was "not an institution for the political agitation of the peasantry" (1982:264).

In line with this style of symbolic indigenista activity, and against the stormy backdrop of the Wancho-Lima rebellion, Natalio Calderón became closely involved with Conimeño musicians from the ayllus. According to various local accounts, in April of 1928 (or 1929—oral sources differ), when Vicente Mendoza was visiting Conima, he and Natalio Calderón decided to organize a sikuri ensemble composed of indigenous players from the different ayllus of the district. According to another account given by Natalio's son Lucio Calderón, Natalio simply became involved with a peasant group that already existed; he assumed the role of 'president,' directed the ensemble, and, at a later point, gave it the name Qhantati Ururi.[7]

Natalio's son Augusto maintains that his father organized the group, and stated that his interest in this ensemble and its music involved a defensive position:

> To defend their land they also had to stand up for the *zampoñas* [panpipes], and, for them, the *zampoñas* were their homeland. They were defending their homeland, because according to my father, to defend your music is to defend your homeland. [There was also] the idea that one should not allow the use of metal [brass band] musical instruments—which were starting to be used at that time. He said, "We should not buy even one metal instrument because to do so was to fill the pockets of the rich with money."[8]

This description of Natalio Calderón's attitudes includes typical indigenista sentiments such as glorification of the indigenous panpipe (versus "foreign" brass-band instruments) as an emblem of the homeland, and the need to defend one's home against the imperialism of outsiders ("the pockets of the rich"). These comments should probably be interpreted in a regionalistic rather than a nationalistic light. Indigenismo in Puno had a strong localist orientation; Puneño intellectuals traced the severe economic problems in the region to the centralism emanating from Lima (Tamayo 1982:322).

The musical ensemble that became known as Qhantati Ururi (morning star in the dawn; star that comes up in the dawn) differed in many ways from the community ensembles described in the first part of this book. According to various local sources, Natalio chose the best indigenous players from the different ayllus in order to form a group of superior quality. Not only did this modus operandi single out particular individuals within the communities, but it contrasted fundamentally with the normal mode of community-specific ensemble organization; and it projected the image of ensemble identity at the level of the district rather than in terms of individual communities. The ensemble structure, with formal offices of president, vice president, secretary, and treasurer, was also unusual for ayllu musicians. Natalio served as Qhantati's president for many years; he was also referred to as the 'director' of the ensemble. People in the ayllu asserted that Natalio did not actually perform with the group; his son Augusto suggested that he did. In any event, his role was clearly distinct from that of a typical ayllu guía.

Under Natalio's leadership, the voluntary, ad hoc structure of ayllu ensembles was replaced by relatively fixed personnel. Toribio, the oldest living member of the group, stressed that when Qhantati received an invitation to perform somewhere, everyone had to go—indicating that some type of pressure was brought to bear on participation. The heightened stability of personnel changed the quality of performance, since the musicians became a well-rehearsed unit. Moreover, the ensemble rehearsed more often than usually occurs (that is, only one or two nights before a given event). During rehearsals under Natalio's direction, musicians were made to play alone or in pairs in order to check performance quality; people who did not come up to standard during these 'examinations' were not allowed to stay with the group.

The singling out and testing of individual players, restrictions on participation, and mandatory attendance at performances all ran counter to the basic style of Conimeño ensemble organization. From my point of view, the most dramatic change was that all aspects of ensemble organization were directed toward ensuring a good quality of sound, abstracted from the quality of social participation and interaction. This style of organization depended on hierarchical relations within the group. Stated simply, only a mestizo could

129

get away with such behavior in Conima, and only because certain types of incentives and social pressures were used. The story in chapter 2 of the Putina tarka guía's unusual behavior during Carnival 1986 illustrates the more typical response to attempts at hierarchical control in Conima when relations of asymmetrical power are not involved.

A man who joined Qhantati in 1931 stated that, to organize the group and to maintain stable participation and discipline, economic incentives were offered to the musicians; these included preferential access to land. Natalio's son Augusto stated that *compadrazgo* (coparent) ties between his father and various peasants were involved in organizing the ensemble. The vecinos' greater wealth enables them to form large networks of *compadres,* which are used to elicit services from the people in the ayllus in return for aid or protection. While more specific information is unavailable, it is apparent that Natalio used economic incentives and his higher social position to organize this rather atypical group and to direct its course. It also seems possible that Natalio's sympathy for, and positive relations with, the people in the ayllus aided him in organizing the ensemble.

The Creation of the Conimeño Panpipe Style

Natalio Calderón's input into the local musical culture was not limited to the organization of Qhantati Ururi. According to various local sources, he was also involved in the creation of the Conimeño sikuris harmony using parallel thirds. The story has it that Natalio was a harp player who used to perform duets with a church organist (apparently string music was not always absent in Conima). Inspired by the organ's sound and based on his knowledge of harmony from harp performance, he thought of placing the *octavin* or *bajo* voices a third below the major melody-carrying voices (the suli, malta, and sanja) so that a sikuri ensemble "would sound like an organ." Under Natalio's direction, Mariano Villasante, the man who 'cut' the panpipes for Qhantati, began to make the style of tropa with nine voices in parallel thirds. By some accounts, Villasante was an active collaborator in this innovation.

Although there is not complete unanimity regarding Natalio's creation of the Conimeño harmonic style, people both within and outside the district identify Conima as the place of its origin.[9] It is also generally agreed that the local community ensembles performed in parallel octaves, or with fourths, fifths, and octaves, at the beginning of this century. Because tertian harmony is so strongly linked to mestizo/criollo tradition in Peru and occurs in none of the other Peruvian panpipe styles or Conimeño flute traditions, the cited oral history provides the most likely explanation for the harmonic innovation. Other issues suggest that a mestizo with some knowledge of Western harmony was involved. As I noted in chapter 2, the best panpipe maker in Conima said that he was unable to create new harmonic voicing except through the economically prohibitive practice of trial and error; moreover, the musicians in the ayllus generally do not think about harmonic intervals in abstract theoretical terms.

With a sikuri ensemble under his direction, Natalio Calderón had both the knowledge and the medium through which to realize a new siku-tropa voicing. Interviews yielded no information about other individuals who were in such a position, and no other explanations for the creation of the Conimeño sikuri style were forthcoming during my investigation. The bajo voice was in place by 1931, according to Toribio, who joined Qhantati in that year. Filiberto told me that when he was a boy, this was the only group that "played with all the voices complete." All statements indicate that Natalio's ensemble was responsible for diffusing the style.

Under vecino direction, Qhantati performed in fiestas both in Conima, and, through Vincente Mendoza's promotion, in Huancané, thereby initiating the tradition of performing for the First Alferado in the Fiesta de la Cruz in Huancané. With mestizo initiative and sponsorship, the ensemble traveled to Lima in 1939 to perform in the Fiesta de Amancaes on the Día del Indio, the holiday instituted by Leguía. Through these activities, Qhantati began to gain some recognition outside the district and heightened prestige within it. The trips and the group's recognition probably served as an additional incentive for peasant musicians to belong to the ensemble.

Qhantati in Lima, 1965

When Natalio passed away, his son Lucio assumed the directorship and presidency of the group, and by all accounts (see chapter 10), it remained a disciplined performing ensemble. As before, the repertory included the "best" dances and musical genres that the different ayllus had to offer. The ensemble maintained the local practice of playing all the different Conimeño wind instruments (pitus, chokelas, tarkas, sikus, kallamachus). For 'folkloric' festival and stage performances, however, various costumed dances (associated with different times of year) were performed sequentially to add variety to the stage show.

In 1965, Qhantati returned to Lima. Lucio Calderón, a schoolteacher in the city of Puno, helped organize the trip with funds from a departmental-government development agency and from the district government. The purpose of the trip was to petition the Belaunde government to put a road through to Conima, build schools, and put in a potable water system. Lucio, his wife, and other vecinos who made the trip were invited to the governmental palace, where the petitions were presented to the president and Qhantati played in his honor.

A series of photos taken at the governmental palace, one including President Fernando Belaunde Terry himself, indicates that twenty men and seven women from the ayllus made the journey.[10] Filiberto, and other current Qhantati members who went, suggested that the ensemble was taken along to make an impression on the president. (The petitions were granted.) The relationship between the Aymara musicians of Qhantati and the vecinos is illustrated in the photos taken at the governmental palace. The musicians were dressed in a particularly elaborate indigenous sikuri costume, while the mestizo director, his wife, and several other vecinos stood in front and to one side wearing formal suits, ties, and dresses. In these and other photographs taken during various performances in Lima, it is evident that Lucio did not perform with the group in the capital and that, through clothing style, he maintained a marked distinction between himself and the peasant performers.

Housed with Conimeño residents in Lima, Qhantati stayed three weeks and performed in a number of locations, including the prestigious Teatro Municipal in downtown Lima. In the newspaper the ensemble was billed as ''El Grupo de Arte y Danzas Folklóricas, QHANTATI.'' Also during this sojourn they recorded an LP record with the Odeón company; the instruments and dances on the recording were the same as those used for the stage performances, as far as I can ascertain from photographs. Due to the scarcity of sikuri recordings, Qhantati's record, along with its relatively wide exposure, ensured major recognition and a place of honor for the group when interest in panpipe music began to mount among young people in Lima after 1970. Being the earliest recording of Qhantati or Conimeño music that I have access to, its contents are worth considering in some detail.

Qhantati's 1965 Recording

The record included seven siku performances, two pitu dances, one chokela performance, one kallamachu panpipe performance, and one tarkiada. The sikus were used for two sikuris (or lentos) played with bombos and were probably performed on stage with the ornate *traje de gala* worn at the governmental palace (see plate 14). The three fast sikuri pieces were played in choclo style with snare and bass drum. These were probably used for the dance *soldado pallapalla* in the stage performances, as documented in photographs taken during the trip. Soldado pallapalla is a dance with costumes representing republican soldiers; it is still performed during the Easter fiesta in Conima. A soldado pallapalla march was recorded with sikus, snare drum, and bass drum as well. An imillani piece on sikus accompanied by two cajas was included, and it was in this dance that the young women participated during the stage presentations in Lima.

Given the prominence of sikuri ligeros (with bombos) in contemporary Conimeño performance, it is curious that this genre was not included on the record. Since the older name for the lento genre is simply "sikuri," it is probable that this may have been the original, and primary, genre for the panpipe tradition and dance of that name. The current practice of alternating lentos and ligeros for social dancing in Conima, within what is now conceptualized as the sikuri tradition, may be of more recent origin. The ligero genre (with bombos) may simply have been an adaptation of the choclo music played during the Easter fiesta. This would explain why the same tunes are used for both styles of performance, and why the Easter festival is the main occasion for ligero composition.

Conimeño sikuri groups have done the same thing with the imillani music in contemporary practice; they have adapted it for social dancing within the sikuri tradition, accompanied by bombos instead of the cajas used for the actual imillani dance (for example, by Huata in the Fiesta de la Cruz, 1985). The contents of Qhantati's record suggest that each contemporary genre was originally associated with a specific dance, and basically considered a separate tradition, as is still the case in Bolivian Aymara-speaking communities. It is likely that the number of genres considered to be part of the sikuri tradition has been expanded in recent years.

All the performances on the record are extremely tight, supporting contemporary contentions that under vecino direction Qhantati was a highly disciplined ensemble. In the tarka and pitu performances the musicians play in parallel polyphony, with little hint of the individual variations and looser approach that occur in spirited contemporary fiesta performances. The siku pieces are not in strict parallel polyphony. Various voices overlap in different ways (for example, lower voices holding pitches longer than the maltas; see chapter 1). These devices occur uniformly throughout a performance, however, indicating that they were carefully arranged rather than being the product of individual variation, as is typical in contemporary festival

133

performance. The tuning of the siku, pitu, and tarka tropas sounds much as it does today when new consorts have been purchased or made; the mestizo director apparently did not alter the use of wide variances in intonation.

The sikuri costumes worn by Qhantati in the photos at the governmental palace and on the 1965 record jacket resemble those worn by sikuri ensembles elsewhere (such as in Copacabana, Bolivia; Verger 1945). The costume included a feathered headdress worn above the *chullu* (knit hat with earflaps), a short red poncho, black pants, a white ankle-length skirt opened in the front, and ojotas (tire sandals). This costume, known presently as traje de gala, has not been used in fiestas within Conima in current memory. According to one older member of Qhantati, it was worn on the trip to Lima, and before that, only much earlier in the century.

The use of this costume, then, may have been considered important by Lucio to accentuate the group's 'folkloric' character. The young women who performed as dancers in Lima appear with bare feet in the photos at the palace. Since people from the ayllus prefer to wear their best shoes, jackets, and dresses in fiestas in the plaza of Conima, I would speculate that it was not their idea to wear ojotas or to go barefoot while visiting the hall of state. The members of the Conimeño clubs in Lima still use the 1965 record jacket photo as a model when making their costumes for important performances in the city (chapter 6).

The Current Phase of Qhantati

Qhantati's opportunities to travel to Lima and to record were dependent on the vecinos' sponsorship. It is also probable that Qhantati's acceptance by audiences outside Conima—including vecinos in Huancané and people in urban centers—was probably aided by the fact that their playing style was shaped by mestizo conceptions of polished performance, as well as by the folkloric packaging. The growing acceptance of, or at least interest in, indigenous Andean music within urban contexts must be attributed in part to changing attitudes influenced by indigenismo. It is significant that Qhantati played at the Fiesta de Amancaes during its 1939 trip to Lima. Leguía himself was directly involved in initiating highland musical performance during this event in the capital in 1927 (Turino 1988:132).

Lucio's death in 1979 marked the end of mestizo direction and sponsorship for Qhantati. With Filiberto as guía, the ensemble has changed in major ways. Rehearsals are held only immediately before performance events, and the 'examinations' have been dropped. During rehearsals and performances, the local custom of not commenting on other people's playing has been reinstated among the older players. Another major change has taken place in regard to personnel. Between the 1970s and 1986, the group included young vecinos from Conima and young people from various ayllus who now live in nearby cities. The older peasant members no longer hail from all over the district but are primarily from Sulcata (upper, central, and Putina), the guía's home, or nearby. Moreover, for fiestas in Conima, anyone from these communities is welcome to play. Thus, within district fiestas that require panpipes, Qhantati has basically come to represent these communities (although the young town mestizos add an extra element); in keeping with the typical organization of ayllu groups, it has become an ad hoc ensemble.

Some of the older members of Qhantati, who were particularly fond of Lucio and who enjoyed their former success, expressed regret at the loss of their dedicated president and sponsor. It was usually vecino critics, however, who claimed that since the passing of Lucio, the discipline of Qhantati has decreased, and with it the quality of performance. In my estimation, what has happened is that the group has returned to functioning primarily as a traditional community ensemble for performances within the district. With this transformation its sound has changed as well due to the priorities of egalitarian relations and collective participation within the ensemble, and a conception of musical sound that is not abstracted from the ethics of this way of behaving.

This return to a more typical mode of ayllu ensemble organization raises important issues. The innovations in the group under vecino direction were instituted largely through external incentives. The changes in values and modus operandi, however, were not internalized or internally generated by Qhantati members, but depended on the hierarchical relations made possible by vecino participation. Once this disappeared, so did the mestizo innovations that conflicted with the basic style of communal relations in the ayllu.

Significantly, the innovation of the harmonic style not only was maintained but had spread to all the Conimeño community ensembles by 1984. Filiberto, who currently makes the panpipes for Qhantati, learned to do so from, and uses the measuring sticks of, his predecessor, who made the tropa with parallel thirds. Filiberto told me that this is the only way he knows. Important to the style's diffusion within the district, Qhantati's fame and popularity outside Conima raised the prestige of this type of tropa. It therefore began to be adopted by other groups in Conima, until it became associated with the district as a whole.

Such sound changes are easier to institute in Conima than are innovations that require changing basic styles of social behavior. In fact, Filiberto told me that he potentially favors radical sound changes (such as the creation of totally new sikuri voicing) because such innovations would make his ensemble distinct (chapter 2). On the other hand, if an Aymara guía attempted to give 'examinations,' restrict participation for fiestas within the district, or tell individual players what to do, the musicians would probably simply begin to ignore him and he would, thus, forfeit his leadership role.

Although the tropa with nine voices is relatively recent, people throughout the district regard it as the 'traditional' Conimeño style. Like the tarka that allegedly came into Conima in the 1930s, the history of the Conimeño sikuri style illustrates the dynamism of rural Andean musical practices—in contrast to common notions about the "ancient," static character of such traditions. These examples, among many, underline the methodological importance of studying rural musical traditions, and the notion of "tradition" itself, in relation to specific historical conjunctures and lines of development (see Rice 1987:474; C. Waterman 1990b; Blum, Bohlman, and Neuman 1991).

The history of Qhantati and of the innovations described provides various points of contestation and different ranges of meaning for Conimeños, often according to their ethnic/class position. The people most apt to reject Natalio Calderón as the creator of the Conimeño consort type were rural peasants who usually attributed the fundamental aspects of their musical practices to their ancestors, because of the importance of music as an identity emblem and the antagonism they felt toward mestizos. Peasant musicians not affiliated with Qhantati were especially likely to deny Natalio's role. Conversely, those who had the most investment in stories about the vecinos' responsibility for Qhantati's former glory and quality of performance were from the mestizo faction—the obvious implication being that for something of worth to be established, vecino leadership would have to be involved. Whether or not one accepts Natalio as the actual innovator of the consort with nine voices, it seems clear that he had an important role in the organization of Qhantati Ururi and the diffusion of the style.

CONTRACTED PERFORMANCE SITUATIONS IN MESTIZO FIESTAS

Qhantati remains distinct from the typical village ensembles in Conima because it maintains its formal name, rather than simply being referred to by the village and instrument used on a particular occasion: Tarkas de Putina, Sikuris de Checasaya, Pinkillus de Checasaya. Along with its name, Qhantati has *name recognition* outside Conima. It is also atypical in that it accepts contracts to perform on a semiprofessional basis in other towns, although within most district festivals it performs on the same collaborative basis as other groups.

Two other sikuri ensembles in Conima perform outside Conima for contracted engagements: Q'keni Sankayo of Huata and Juventud Conima, composed of town dwellers. Juventud was formed relatively recently in response to the popularity of sikuri music generated by the urban panpipe movement in the 1970s. Augusto Calderón told me that Q'keni Sankayo was founded by his wife around 1940, although the people in Huata say that they had always had a sikuri ensemble and that Mrs. Calderón merely gave it a name.

Huata was one of three small haciendas in the district of Conima before the Velasco land reform, and Augusto's wife was the daughter of its owners. After her marriage, and her parents' death, the hacienda came to her and Augusto. Perhaps inspired by the growing success and reputation of Qhantati Ururi, Mrs. Calderón decided to become involved with a sikuri ensemble among her peasants and to give it a name.

Such activities among hacienda owners in Puno were not unusual. Filiberto told me that in the 1950s he had been hired by several mestizo landowners from other districts in Huancané to spend a couple of weeks on their haciendas in order to cut a siku tropa and create a Conimeño-style ensemble among their *colonos* (peasants tied to a hacienda). Much as Southerners in the United States used slave musicians to provide entertainment at white parties and gatherings on their plantations (Epstein 1977), hacienda owners apparently felt that it would be useful to have their own sikuri ensembles. Conimeños told me that this was one way different sikuri styles were diffused to regions where they had not been performed previously.

The use of indigenous musicians and dancers to enliven vecino-controlled Catholic fiestas is widespread in southern Peru.[11] This practice predates the indigenista movement; it can be traced to the activities of colonial clergy who consciously included, or simply allowed, Andean performing arts during Catholic fiestas to aid the conversion process (chapter 4). This represents the primary exception, albeit an important one, to my generalization about the marginalization or ignoring of Andean arts by mestizos and criollos during much of Peru's history. Indeed, Catholic fiestas were the main contexts for the creation of new musical fusions in Peru before the indigenistas took over during the twentieth century (Turino 1991a).

Arrangements and Personnel Selection for Contracts

Qhantati, Q'keni, and Juventud receive contracts only to perform sikuris; this suggests that it is the most popular of all the local instrumental traditions among mestizos in the region. This fact also explains why, at present, these ensembles' names are primarily associated with panpipe performance, even within the district. When the people from Sulcata in Qhantati, or the Huateños, perform during Carnival, they simply go under the more informal community titles, such as Tarkas de Putina.

Qhantati travels most years to perform for the Fiesta de la Cruz in Huancané. Like Q'keni and the less popular Juventud, they also travel to district-capital towns in Huancané province and as far as La Paz, Bolivia, to perform for patronal fiestas sponsored by mestizo alferados. There is usually a written contract between the vecino alferado and the ensemble, with stipulations for transportation, cane for a new tropa of sikus, meals and lodging during the fiesta, and some minimal payment for the musicians.

For Qhantati's contracted performances, participation is ideally limited to around twenty-four players—an arrangement that balances the desire for complete voicing with that of splitting the money among as few people as possible. Particular musicians are selected for a performance by the person who holds the formal position of president, with input from the guía and other core musicians. Leo and other younger members of Qhantati told me that the presidency is now an elected position, but there do not seem to be any formal mechanisms or schedules for holding elections. Aldemir, a town mestizo and schoolteacher from Conima, has been president for some time.

The older players do not seem to take much interest in holding the formal offices themselves (if Filiberto, Juan, or another core player wanted to be president, he probably would receive support). Perhaps they feel that the young town mestizos are better equipped, as Natalio and Lucio had been, to make contracts with people from outside the district. It is also quite probable that the older players actually avoid the presidency so that they do not have to take responsibility for personnel selections and the tensions that might result. In any event, because of personnel shortages in 1985 and 1986 the problem was not so much who to leave out of a contract as it was to find enough players to complete the ensemble.

Personnel problems in Qhantati came to a head for the Fiesta de la Cruz in Huancané in 1985 and 1986. A conflict emerged between the older players from the ayllu and younger players who lived in town or in nearby cities. This incident, described in the following chapter, illustrates the character of relations between the generations in Conima, the nature of young people's involvement with the music, and the impact of the urban panpipe movement in Huancané.

SIX

The Urban Panpipe Movement and
the Youth of Conima

UNTIL THE 1970s, the Conimeño tropa style remained localized within the district among musicians from the ayllus, while the performance of sikuri music was a rarity in cities—especially in Lima. By the mid-1980s, however, university and Puneño-migrant groups were playing in this style, frequently using Qhantati repertory, on a weekly basis in the cities of Lima, Arequipa, Cusco, Juliaca, and Puno. Ensembles of young town mestizos played in this style in various districts of Huancané, as well as in other rural (Quechua) areas of Puno such as Lampa. Within the District of Conima, young men from town as well as from the ayllus showed a great interest in sikuri performance; with the exception of a few individuals, however, young people were not participating in the other local instrumental traditions. All these phenomena emerged out of a complex historical conjuncture involving the cultural policies of President Juan Velasco Alvarado (1968–75), urban migration, and struggles to legitimize Andean identity among highland migrants in the cities.

Two periods stand out in the history of the Peruvian Republic when the state made pronounced attempts to forge links with the peasantry: Augusto Leguía's eleven-year rule (1919–30) and the Velasco era. It was during these periods that local Andean musical and cultural practices were most dramatically and directly affected by, and included within, broader networks of intellectual and political discourse. Using the same terms, both presidents publicly declared their intention to create a "new country" in which the various sectors would be incorporated into the state. During these periods, pathways were opened to rural Andeans and their marginalization was reduced, in relation to the state.

Of the two governments, Velasco's policies and symbolic gestures in support of Andean culture were the more convincing among the peasantry. During the 1920s, for example, the strategy among peasants in Huancané had been to increase their isolation and independence from local vecinos and government officials by creating an Indian "free zone" within the province (chapter 5). Although the Huancaneño peasant leaders had (mistakenly) counted on Leguía's support for their project, the plan itself did not indicate a desire to integrate themselves within the broader society. In contrast, since the Velasco period young peasants have increasingly attempted to move into the national society, inspired by promises that social mobility was indeed possible.[1] Velasco's goal of assimilating indigenous Andean people into "the national," as part of a larger hegemonic strategy, was thus partially success- ful. At the same time, his policies, in combination with the activities of Andean migrants in the cities, led to a greater acceptance of certain aspects of highland culture among urban dwellers and rural youth. The urban panpipe movement was a part of this process.

THE VELASCO ERA

Velasco's "Revolutionary Government of the Armed Forces" (RGAF) emerged in reaction to a series of crises within the Peruvian state during the 1950s and 1960s, including peasant uprisings over land control, increasing militancy among urban labor, foreign (primarily U.S.) economic control within the country, and corruption in the civilian government (Handelman 1975; North 1983). Proclaiming an anti-imperialistic, anti-oligarchic, and fervently nationalistic ideology, the RGAF emphasized nationalizing foreign- held companies (such as the International Petroleum Company), moderniza- tion and increased worker control within the industrial sector, and an agrar- ian reform that began in 1969.

A relatively large and critical literature exists analyzing the contradictions and failures of the Velasco "experiment" (e.g., McClintock and Lowenthal 1983; Chaplin 1976; Palmer 1980). Central among these was the contradic- tion between the government's rhetorical stressing of popular participation in the creation of a "new society" and the top-down corporatist control structure, which often had to revert to coercion.[2] Little attention, however, has been granted to the Velasco regime's profound impact on state-peasant relations and on social and cultural practices in rural communities. In this regard, Velasco's agrarian, educational, and media reforms were particularly significant, as was his law making Quechua an official national language.

With the clear understanding that the revolution could not take place without popular support for state leadership, a concerted effort was made to establish hegemony in Gramscian terms simultaneously on a number of political, economic, and cultural fronts (Velasco 1972:65). The agrarian re- form, more than any other single act by the Velasco government, redefined the position of the state in the minds of rural Andeans. The reform was strategically proclaimed on June 24, 1969, "Día del Indio," a holiday established by Leguía in the 1920s and renamed "Día del Campesino" (Peasants' Day) by the RGAF because indio carried negative connotations. The government's plan involved the redistribution of all large haciendas by 1975. Velasco explicitly stated the goals of integrating Andeans into the economy and, by raising rural incomes, creating a larger consumer market for national industry (1971:48). Regardless of the reform's failings and underlying agendas, Velasco was, and still is, viewed by many peasants ás a liberator from the landowners (e.g., Neira Samanez 1974:105–19); this can be truly comprehended only in light of the profound hatred peasants harbored against the local landed elites.

Under the rubric of educational reform, new policies articulated Velasco's pro-Andean position; they were also designed to diffuse an ideology of national integration. In a speech made in February 1971, Velasco maintained that the educational system had previously upheld the discriminatory social structure, but that:

> the educational reform of the revolution aspires to create an educational system that satisfies the necessities of the entire nation; that will reach the great masses of [indigenous] peasants, always exploited and always deliberately kept in ignorance; that will create a new consciousness among all Peruvians of the basic problems of our country; and that will contribute to *forging a new type of man within a new social morality.* (Velasco 1972:63, emphasis added)

Whereas for much of Peru's history indigenous peasants had been denied access to education, during the Velasco period rural education expanded, and figures show that rural illiteracy was markedly reduced between 1972 and 1981 (Consejo Nacional de Población 1984:102). Mestizo schoolteachers, sent to work in indigenous communities, have had a central role in involving rural children with the world outside their communities, both by teaching about it and by providing tools (Spanish, literacy, styles of behavior) that increase peasants' chances of successfully operating within it.[3] By helping to decrease the marginality of younger generations of rural Andeans, education has made the choice to move away from their local communities both more desirable and more possible.

Although the use of native languages for teaching had been prohibited since the 1780s (after the Tupac Amaru rebellion),[4] the use of Amerindian languages was reinstituted as a part of Velasco's educational reform in 1975. More dramatic, another law (21156) was created making Quechua an official national language on par with Spanish. The law stated that after April 1976 the teaching of Quechua would be obligatory at all educational levels, and after 1 January 1977 all legal proceedings involving monolingual Quechua speakers would have to be conducted in Quechua (Escobar, Matos, and Alberti 1975:61–63). While the situation regarding Aymara was more ambiguous, the law now explicitly recognized the cultural plurality of Peruvian society and addressed two fundamental arenas where language had been used as a mechanism of domination: the courts and the schools.

As a part of its cultural program, the RGAF organized a series of performance contests for music and dance at the national level. Jaime Montaño explains that contests were held at the district, provincial, and state levels in the highlands. The winners of the state competitions traveled to Lima, all expenses paid by the government, to participate in an immense music and dance festival called "Inkari" (see Montoya 1987). Montaño recalls that the response in Lima was tremendously enthusiastic; by granting visibility and importance to highland performing arts, this program had an important influence on subsequent musical movements.

In 1975, the government also issued a law directing the use of mass media in accord with its nationalist position. The government's widely diffused *Inca Plan* stated that "radio and television were the pills that put the national consciousness to sleep and infiltrated it with the lifestyle from foreign countries. [The media] obeyed a structure of capitalist control and foreign ideology to orient the action of the masses and the educational criteria of the society." The 1975 law required all public and private radio stations to dedicate a minimum of 7.5 percent of their air time to "folkloric music," defined as "that which is born directly from the traditions and customs of the people and which, in particular, is the collective creation emanating from rural zones of the country" (cited in Lloréns 1983:127).

Although highland-music radio programming had already increased in Lima and highland urban centers after the 1950s as a result of urban migration and the consequent commercial market, musicians in the sierra still see Velasco's law affecting radio, as well as his other reforms, as highly significant. For example, in 1985 an older Conimeño musician in Sulcata explained the revival of interest in panpipe music among the youth of his community specifically in relation to Velasco: "The government, when Alvarado, here the president, here in Peru, this Juan Velasco Alvarado, this one, he remembered more ours, our instrument, we were not able to use foreign [instruments]. 'Let us issue the law,' [said] Juan Velasco Alvarado. After this, recently, the young people are playing here and there, the whole length of the road, with these instruments of the ancestors.''

An interview conducted in 1988 with two musicians of rural-mestizo background in Cusco illustrates a similar attitude commonly held among highlanders:

> T.T.: In earlier times were there prejudices against highland
> music in Lima?
>
> D.F.: Ah! Discrimination. Yes there was, clearly.
>
> E.V.: Yes, but this was erased, not erased, but legitimized [*val-
> orado*] a bit when Velasco Alvarado, the military president
> de facto, entered and issued a law giving, (pause) in the
> first place, making the mother tongue, Quechua, official.
> Later there came another law giving value to the wayno
> and to the national music. He required every radio station
> in the country to dedicate an hour, at least, to the pro-
> gramming of national music, including the waltz and the
> wayno. Thus, this served to give value [to the music], a
> bit perhaps. It gave it more strength, legality, so that the
> national music would be maintained and would not be
> abandoned or transformed.
>
> T.T.: And why was highland music of concern to Velasco?
>
> E.V.: Because his political position was Tupac Amarist. And Tu-
> pac Amaru was the first precursor of independence, the
> first mestizo who went out in defense of the Indian, the
> campesino. Hence, because he [Velasco] identified with
> the campesinos, it was necessary for him to give value,
> not only to the campesino himself, but also to his
> culture.[5]

In the end, Velasco did not succeed in winning the support of people within the mainstream society—the working, middle, and upper classes of the cities, and particularly intellectuals. Besides the economic threat posed to more affluent groups, people were alienated by the RGAF's too frequent reliance on force, corruption within the government, and the contradiction between an ideology of participation and the reality of state control. Student and worker demonstrations—common during this period in which the word *revolución* was part of the orthodox state discourse—were harshly dealt with by the RGAF, sparking an atmosphere of continuous rebellion and political radicalization among these groups in the cities.

Rural people in the highlands and the more conservative working-class migrants in Lima, however, remember the Velasco era as a major turning point for the acceptance of their heritage. At the same time, the RGAF's attempts to incorporate peasants into the "new nation" were partially successful among younger people. The two issues are directly connected, although on the surface the former seems to support the maintenance of distinctive rural Andean practices while the latter foreshadows a reduction of the need for cultural difference. In fact, both happened simultaneously, albeit selectively, among rural people and migrants of the Velasco generation—as the history of the urban panpipe movement illustrates.

THE URBAN PANPIPE MOVEMENT

As early as the mid-1950s, there were several lower- and working-class Puneño regional associations in Lima that played panpipes as well as tarkas, pitus, and pinkillus. One of these was Unión Progresista Conima. Although they occasionally played in public contexts framed as 'folkloric' events, for the most part these ensembles performed at their own private fiestas behind closed doors. As Jaime Montaño, an Arequipeño of Puneño parentage and an expert sikuri, put it,

> I never saw a sikuri ensemble in Lima before the 1970s, never, and I have lived here since I was a boy. . . . Like me the majority of Limeños did not even know what a siku was. Why? Because in spite of the fact that [before the 1970s] there existed two or three sikuri ensembles—I do not know exactly how many, maybe a few more—they never performed in public. While they existed, they existed only for themselves, for their reunions, for their own regional cultural and social gatherings.

In 1985, I counted sixty-nine sikuri and sikumoreno ensembles performing publicly in the capital. The count was made from radio announcements, other kinds of advertisements for performances, and groups that I encountered; it can only be partial. Fifty-seven of these groups were based in Puneño regional associations of the working and lower classes, and twelve involved middle- and working-class university students, largely non-Puneño. On practically any Sunday afternoon during 1985, there were panpipe performances in several locations around Lima. By 1985–86, panpipe ensembles had been given pride of place in a number of 'folkloric' parades and events in central Lima that had been organized by the city and national governments, and this music was becoming well known and even popular with some Limeños in the city (chapter 9).

The dramatic rise of sikuri performance, visibility, and importance in Lima between 1960 and 1985 is partially attributable to the demographic explosion of highlanders in the city and consequent changes in economic and political relations. The RGAF's policies celebrating Andean culture, as well as the radicalization of student groups during the Velasco years, were also influential. In more specific terms, the widespread public performance of panpipe music in Lima began with the activities of a particular regional organization in the capital: Asociación Juvenil Puno (Association of Puneño Youth, or AJP). By most accounts, AJP was largely responsible for the current popularity of sikuris and sikumorenos. From a broader perspective, however, the time was right for Puneños to assert their highland identity for strategic reasons, and AJP simply served as a vanguard for this movement.

Asociación Juvenil Puno

AJP began as an informal social club consisting largely of middle-class Puneño students, most of whom had come to study in Lima. Affected by "culture shock" and homesickness in the capital, the members of Centro de Estudiantes Puno began meeting in various homes in 1970 to socialize and, on occasion, to sing and play guitars. As the group evolved in 1970–71, the members chose music as a focus for their activities. One of the founders stated that they wanted to perform a type of music that would differentiate them from the mestizo string ensembles (estudiantinas) of elite Puneño clubs in Lima, such as Club Departamental Puno and Brisas del Titicaca. By one account, sikus were selected simply because there had been a pair at the home where they were meeting; panpipes were also considered particularly appropriate as an emblem connecting them with Puno and differentiating them from Club Departamental Puno and Brisas.

At first, the members of AJP knew very little about panpipe music. An early member told me that when they began they did not even know enough to perform the ira and arca parts in interlocking fashion, and that before leaving Puno he had mainly been interested in rock music. After purchasing a tropa in Puno, they began learning with a published zampoña *método* (instruction book) and commercial recordings of Puneño groups. Early in its history, AJP performed panpipes in the sikumoreno style. According to people involved, this was the style with which they were most familiar, since it was performed in the city of Puno.

During this early period, the members of AJP also continued to refine their cultural politics. Drawing on regionalistic sentiments, AJP members argued that the siku was the most appropriate identity emblem for their institution.

145

The very act of playing the siku was a demonstration of solidarity with the oppressed indigenous population, a rejection of foreign cultural imperialism, and an icon for collectivism because of the communally oriented character of highland ensembles and the interlocking technique. AJP's regionalism is partially defined by the Puneño membership; ideologically, however, the group identifies with Quechua-Aymara culture in pan-Andean terms (Montaño, personal communication, 1990). Although AJP members were responding to different conditions, their ideological positions suggest certain parallels with indigenista sentiments of the 1920s. Also like certain indigenista institutions, AJP soon developed a commitment to political-cultural activism.

On 27 June 1972, an event in the city of Puno helped to radicalize the group politically and inspired them to activity. During a rally held for the wife of Juan Velasco in Puno, a protest was staged, and Mrs. Velasco was forced to listen to accusations of political corruption leveled against her husband and his colleagues. During the rally, violence erupted, and a number of innocent people were wounded and killed by government troops. The members of AJP in Lima were scandalized by the way the event was presented in the media, and by the government's attempt to cover up the massacre. The organization, by then called Asociación Juvenil Puno, decided to take the name "Sikuris 27 de Junio" for its performing panpipe ensemble "in honor of the people of Puno and the martyrs that fell on this date" (Montaño, personal communication, 1990). Members also took it upon themselves to inform Puneños and other groups in Lima about what had taken place in Puno. Using panpipe music as a means for gaining public attention and access, the group began to perform at union meetings, in pueblos jóvenes, on the streets, and in other types of cultural events.[6] Through the activities of these young students from Puno, panpipe music began to be performed widely in public—outside the typical 'folkloric' frames—for the first time in Lima.

In 1976, eight AJP members traveled as a group to the city of Puno to perform sikumorenos in the Fiesta de la Candelaria (February 2). In 1977, AJP returned to Puno with around twenty-four players to participate in Candelaria.[7] At that time in urban Puno, only working-class people played panpipes, and only the sikumoreno, not the sikuri style, was performed. In the departmental capital there were four sikumoreno ensembles: Sikuris Juventud Obreros (Young Workers, consisting of bricklayers and municipal maintenance workers), Sikuris del Barrio Mañazo (the members were primarily butchers and other men from the Mañazo neighborhood), Sikuris

Panificadores (bakers), and Zampoñas del Altiplano (Montaño, personal communication, 1990). The last two groups had been founded only two years before AJP's first trip. César Suaña and Dante Vilca, two early AJP members, arranged for their group to play with the different Puneño sikumoreno ensembles in turn during the week-long Candelaria celebration.

The performance of sikumoreno music by the middle-class students of AJP—who enjoyed a certain prestige because they lived and studied in Lima——was a great novelty to people in the conservative departmental capital. During these trips, AJP members planted the first seeds of their 'cultural politics' in the city of Puno and raised questions about urban Puneños' prejudices against what was then considered a cultural expression of the *bajo pueblo* (low-status people). Regarding these trips Dante Vilca notes:

> We were identified [in Puno] as being from Lima, regardless of our [Puneño] origins. Through our publication *Jak'e Aru*, leaflets, and the media, we diffused the idea of the necessity of revitalizing the most genuine expression of Puno to the youth. In the years that followed, new panpipe groups appeared that consisted totally of young people, reaffirming our faith in the vitality of our people (Vilca 1982:63).

After their 1977 trip, a number of sikumoreno groups sprang up among middle-class youth and university students in the city of Puno, and more were to follow. Jaime Montaño estimates that there are currently more than twenty panpipe ensembles in the departmental capital.

Likewise during the 1975–80 period, the activities of AJP inspired the formation of panpipe ensembles among the more conservative lower- and working-class Puneño migrants in Lima. By 1970, a large number of lower- and working-class Puneño regional clubs were already in existence in Lima, but most were involved with soccer rather than musical activities; one reason was that sports did not mark them publicly as highlanders. After 1975, an increasing number of these migrant clubs began shifting their focus to music and dance, many specifically to panpipe performance. AJP had direct input into this process. When asked about the formation of his panpipe ensemble, one member of a working-class Puneño club noted: "We formed the ensemble in 1976. Well, we had seen this group of young people [AJP] playing in the streets, we saw them playing in schools, here in Lima. Well, then, we said to ourselves, 'If this group of young people who play so badly but with such enthusiasm can perform panpipes [here in Lima], why can't we who are old experienced players?' "

Following the lead of AJP after the mid-1970s, various non-Puneño university groups began forming sikumoreno ensembles. While the more conservative lower- working-class clubs tended not to adopt AJP's various ideological stances, the Limeño student groups often saw their musical activities in a regionalistic, neoindigenista, and politically progressive light. Although closer to AJP ideologically, the Limeño groups were not invited to participate in AJP's prestigious event, Encuentro de Sikuris Tupac Katari, and the hostility toward non-Puneños' playing of panpipe music began to diminish only around 1985.

The Encuentro de Sikuris Tupac Katari

In Lima, the young men of AJP consciously worked to alter the prejudicial attitudes toward Puneño heritage and music, and the feelings of inferiority affecting working-class migrants. More than merely setting an example, AJP provided major contexts for panpipe performance. In 1976 it organized the first "Festival de Música y Danzas Puneñas" in the relatively prestigious space of Campo de Marte, a park located in a middle-class area near the center of Lima. In November 1978, they organized the first event in Lima specifically dedicated to panpipe performance: the "Encuentro de Sikuris Tupac Katari," which became an annual celebration and, by 1984, was the most important occasion of the year for panpipe groups in Lima. In 1989 and 1990, AJP's Encuentro was still considered the single most important performance event and sikuri contest among the Conimeño residents.[8]

The name of the event indicates something about AJP's political position, as well as an ethnic consciousness: Tupac Katari (Julián Apasa) was the leader of a major Aymara rebellion in the early 1780s (see Albó 1987:379). Every year, the performances at the Encuentro de Sikuris Tupac Katari take place on the stage in the bandstand of Campo de Marte. Recently formed lower- and working-class migrant club ensembles from Puno such as Centro Social Conima, Sikuris Sentimiento Aymara-Inca Mamani, and 10 de Octubre de Yunguyo performed at the first Encuentro, as did older institutions such as Unión Progresista Conima. AJP members stated that several panpipe groups were formed specifically to perform in the first Encuentro, and the event inspired the formation of other Puneño resident ensembles in subsequent years.

The Encuentro de Sikuris Tupac Katari is organized around a formal performance contest with trophies, judges, and separate categories for sikuri and sikumoreno ensembles. While the contest judges at typical working-class club festivals usually hail from the regional association sponsoring the event (chapter 9), the judges for the 1985 Tupac Katari contest included some of the best-known academic folklorists and ethnomusicologists in Peru, Josafat Roel among them. The Puneño Aymara poet José Luis Ayala served as the master of ceremonies during the 1985 Encuentro. In his extremely formal, dignified style of introduction, he demanded respect, both for the performers and the music. Ayala and other speakers took special care to inform the public in Lima about the source, nature, and importance of each panpipe style being performed.

AJP makes a conscious effort to attract a large and varied audience to the Encuentro. For example, while most working-class Puneño clubs advertise their public performance events only on the highland-music radio programs directed at migrant audiences, AJP advertises the Encuentro in a wide range of media, including major newspapers aimed at the middle class and the urban population in general. Most working-class Puneño events are held in marginal neighborhoods where it is cheaper to rent a locale; typically only other Puneños attend. Holding the AJP Encuentro at Campo de Marte—a safe, accessible, and respectable place—makes it possible for people from many walks of life to attend.[9]

Through the tremendous effort and organizational abilities of AJP members, the Encuentro has become a major success. The occasion draws a substantial audience of Puneños and non-Puneños alike; I estimate that well over a thousand people attended in 1985. Lower- and working-class Puneño clubs would like to repeat this type of success, but they simply do not have the capital, contacts, and organizational structure that make it possible.[10]

The Encuentro has played a key role in AJP's struggle to legitimate Puneño culture in Lima, and to instill pride in this heritage among lower- and working-class migrants. It has proved effective in that the event inspired the formation of panpipe ensembles among some working-class clubs. Through its prestigious locale, formal framing devices (the stage, the contest, the master of ceremonies), recognized academic judges, and attraction of a large, general audience, the Encuentro has helped raise the visibility of panpipe music in Lima and has elevated the prestige of this music in the minds of Puneño residents themselves.

AJP Meets Qhantati

Besides the first Encuentro, another important event took place within AJP in 1978. In that year the group in Lima changed over from sikumorenos to the more indigenous sikuris style. After their participation in the Puno Candelaria fiesta in 1977, a number of AJP members traveled to the districts of Moho and Conima to take part in Carnival and to make contact with traditional musicians. While in Moho, they were told that Qhantati Ururi was going to play in Conima the next day; with great excitement they traveled to hear the legendary group.[11] One of the AJP members who visited Conima on this occasion recalled,

> Before then, we had had ideas about them [Qhantati Ururi] that were almost like fantasies. We had heard of them, and of the ayarachis as being the culmination and the most exuberant manifestation of our culture. It is worth emphasizing that until then the majority of us had been going through an internal transformation. I can make this clearer with the example of my case. I entered the institution [AJP] only for the music; but at that time [in the sierra] the culture became a part of my being and I a part of it. After Conima, this became more radical still. All of us wanted to turn Indian. In conversations between us we emphasized our Quechua and Aymara parentage and ancestry, and each of us wanted to be more Indian than the next person. Actually the situation moved to the point of fanaticism. Well, we traveled to Conima because we knew that a Bolivian commission [*comisión boliviana*] had arrived and had invited Qhantati Ururi [to perform]; we traveled in a truck, as was to be expected. From mid morning, when we arrived, we were in a state of rapturous amazement over Qhantati. Luckily, we met Lucio Calderón, who had seen us in Puno—he recorded [the music] for us; back then they absolutely would not allow recording.

That the members of AJP already knew about the famous Conimeño group before their visit may have been due to Qhantati's performances in Lima and Puno, and to their 1965 recording. By midafternoon, the members of AJP joined in with Qhantati and played until late in the night. Later when Dante Vilca described this trip in an article about AJP, he specifically mentioned that the delegation had gone to Conima to meet the musicians of Qhantati Ururi, "the cultivators of one of the most successful and beautiful sikuri styles of the Aymara region in Puno" (1982:63).

Certain AJP members continued to return to Conima to record, study, and perform with Qhantati and learn its style. Conimeños especially remember Jaime Montaño, who later taught AJP members in Lima and Puno to play Qhantati's style and repertory while always remaining loyal to, and respectful of, Qhantati as the masters and originators.

Through increasing familiarity with the musical traditions of rural Puno, the members of AJP came to realize that for their purposes of demonstrating solidarity with indigenous people and culture, the sikuri style was more appropriate than sikumorenos. Although some members of AJP in Lima personally preferred sikumoreno music—because of its livelier rhythm, among other factors—the ideological importance of the change took precedence over such aesthetic considerations. The AJP members' first trip to Moho and Conima made a strong impression on them; their adoption of sikuri music from this region and their subsequent activities were central to the current fame and diffusion of the Conimeño panpipe style.

AJP's Multiple Regional Bases

AJP, and its influence, expanded through the creation of a number of regional bases founded in and after 1979. There are active branches of AJP in the cities of Puno, Arequipa, Juliaca, Cusco, and La Paz, and in smaller towns including Acora, Cabanillas, Santa Lucia, and in the community of Caracoto (Montaño, personal communication, 1990). Like the original group in Lima, the membership of AJP Base Puno largely consists of young middle- and working-class students of mestizo heritage. About 40 to 50 percent of members of the bases in Arequipa, Juliaca, and Cusco are of peasant background; presently about 80 percent of the membership in Lima is of peasant heritage; the rural bases are similarly constituted or may even have a higher percentage of members from peasant families (Montaño, personal communication, 1990).

As decided in the First National Convention of AJP (and as stated in the statutes), regional bases should play panpipes in their local style. The affiliate branches of AJP located in the Province of Puno, such as the one in Acora, play panpipes in the sikumoreno style, because this is the tradition commonly performed in that province. For the urban bases comprising members from different Puneño regions, however, style and repertory tend to be more a matter of choice, and more eclectic. Various urban bases of AJP initially began playing sikuris in the Conimeño harmonic style.

When AJP in Lima changed from sikumorenos to sikuris around 1978, it used the Conimeño harmonic style and played repertory associated with Moho and Conima. As AJP Base Lima continued to develop, it added various other local sikuri traditions from Huancané and Bolivia. During 1985 and 1986, AJP Base Lima prominently performed the sikuri style of Taquile, Puno (see Valencia 1980), using Taquileño costume and choreography for stage performances. This move represents the AJP members' continuing search for increasingly indigenous types of musical expression (the Taquile style uses parallel octaves rather than thirds).

When the affiliate branch of AJP was founded in the city of Puno in 1979, it performed sikuris using Qhantati's style and repertory, along with other regional styles. AJP Base Puno also adopted a sikuris costume very similar to the one featured in the photo on Qhantati's 1965 record jacket. According to one of the members, AJP Base Puno's goal was to use the oldest, most traditional costume possible. Therefore, the members used the earliest photograph of a sikuri costume that they could find—Pierre Verger's photos (1945: nos. 38 and 39). In the manner of urban revivalists in many places, the members of AJP Base Puno place a high value on tradition and are willing to rehearse long hours each week in order to imitate a local musical style as faithfully as possible. Their decision to adopt an old style of sikuri costume, one no longer used by ayllu musicians in local fiestas in Huancané, is also indicative of AJP's orientation toward tradition.

When AJP began to emphasize sikuri music over sikumorenos, it once again acted as the vanguard for the urban panpipe movement. Following its adoption of the Conimeño sikuris style and repertory, student and migrant groups in Lima, in the city of Puno, in Juliaca, and elsewhere began to change over to sikuris and, in disproportionate numbers, to the Conimeño tropa type. Moreover, new sikuri ensembles—often incorporating the parallel thirds harmony—were formed in these cities as the popularity of this music increased. Even during my research (1984–86), sikumoreno ensembles continued to decline in visibility, while sikuri ensembles were on the increase.

AJP's mode of multibase organization was also directly imitated by other panpipe institutions. In the city of Puno, young mestizo and peasant residents from Conima have formed an ensemble using the prestigious name Qhantati Ururi Base Puno, specifically following AJP's lead. Another Conimeño club in Lima has taken the name Qhantati Ururi Base Lima. The formation of the affiliate group in Puno has proven to be a source of tension between the generations in Qhantati.

The Urban Panpipe Movement and the Youth in Rural Puno

Commonly in Peru, urban trends originating in Lima are diffused to the rural sierra through highland cities. The impact of AJP Base Lima and the urban panpipe movement on the youth in Huancané and other rural areas of the department is most directly channeled through AJP's affiliate branches in Juliaca and Puno and the other urban groups that followed their lead. In these highland cities, young people's panpipe ensembles perform in the streets during festivals and after rehearsals. They organize and participate in performance contests, some of which are aired on radio throughout the department. Several groups, including AJP Base Puno and Juventud Juliaca, have recorded long-playing records.

Many young Huancaneños—vecinos and urban-oriented youth from the ayllus—live or spend time in Puno and Juliaca. Some have been inspired by AJP and other urban student groups to form panpipe ensembles back in their hometowns. Ensembles spawned by the urban panpipe movement include Los Aymaras de Huancané from the town of Huancané, 14 de Setiembre de Moho from the district-capital town of Moho, a group from the town of Rosaspata, Juventud Conima from the district capital town of Conima, and 10 de Diciembre from the town of Lampa. These groups all play in the Conimeño sikuri style with parallel thirds, and they often use Qhantati repertory.

By way of contrast, ensembles of older players in the ayllu of these same districts continue to perform their own localized panpipe styles. One ayllu group from Moho, which I heard in the 1985 Fiesta de la Cruz in Huancané, played sikuris with open fourths, fifths, and octaves. Community groups from the District of Huancané play sikuris with fourths, fifths, and octaves, or parallel octaves, as well as chiriguano panpipes. Quechua-speaking peasant communities around Lampa continue to use ayarachi panpipes.

The adoption of the Conimeño sikuri style in these rural districts, then, is largely a phenomenon among young townsmen or Aymara youth with urban experience. Musicians in the rural ayllu of these districts continue playing a variety of flute types, according to seasonal and fiesta associations. Most young people in the cities, towns, and rural ayllus, however, do not use the other Puneño flute traditions, but specialize in sikuris or sikumorenos. This firmly indicates that they are following the lead of the urban panpipe movement, since it is only the siku that has gained popularity in the cities. On the surface it seems strange that the prestige of urban trends should lead to the renewal of interest in what was originally a rural tradition, but, in fact, this frequently occurs in cultural revitalization movements (such as "folk revivals").

Socialization by the Soundscape

As in many "folk revivals" and cultural revitalization movements, what has occurred in the urban panpipe movement is the selection of a distinctive emblem—the siku—in combination with styles and aesthetics of performance that, initially, fit most closely with the predominant musical values of the mainstream society. The softer timbre of the siku played in the Conimeño harmonic style (originally designed to "sound like an organ") certainly contrasts with the more strident and dissonant pinkillus, pitus, and tarkas. Sikumorenos and the Conimeño sikuri style are also less exotic for urban Peruvians than the ayarachi and chiriguano panpipe styles. Of all the music that I recorded in Puno, Limeño friends and acquaintances typically found the Conimeño panpipe music preferable to (or less objectionable than) the other traditions. Some lower- and working-class Puneño residents in Lima also indicated to me that they felt more comfortable performing panpipes in the city; people sometimes expressed concern that the other flute traditions would be less well received by Limeños.

In the process of their artistic and ideological development, AJP members have continually sought to overcome these attitudes through their adoption of increasingly distinct panpipe traditions (that is, styles increasingly distant from urban Peruvian music). AJP Base Lima's use of the Taquile sikuri style is one example. Through growing familarity with the original sources of musical traditions, folk revivalists in the United States and elsewhere frequently take part in a similar process of searching out the "roots" and the more distinctive styles among rural musical traditions. This is part of an educational process that involves expanding, or moving away from, one's original aesthetic position.[12]

While AJP continues to adopt ever more distinct styles of rural music, I would suggest that urban Peruvian aesthetics and values still affected their musical performance during 1985 and 1986; this is illustrated by the sound of AJP Base Puno's LP. The music on the record is flawlessly executed. Jaime Montaño stated that the members rehearsed a given style between three hundred and five hundred hours so that their performance would be as close to the original as possible—both in sound and in spirit (personal communication, 1990). The performances on the record have no rough edges, and they contain little or no individual variation from one repetition of a piece to the next. For their renditions of Conimeño music, they come as close to the ideal of "playing like a single instrument" as any ensemble I have ever heard. My students in the United States, who are relatively unfamiliar with Peruvian music, can generally distinguish AJP from Qhantati with little difficulty.

On the record (and in live performances), the sound of AJP Base Puno's ensemble is characterized by unisons, octaves, and other harmonic intervals tuned more closely in accordance with Western standards of variance. Montaño has indicated that when AJP procures a new tropa of panpipes, the members choose, by ear, the best-tuned pair of maltas, and then they use an electronic tuner to match the rest of tropa to this pair. The resulting sound of their ensemble is quite distinct from that of rural groups, who favor wider and more numerous degrees of variance among the pitches of a consort.

These observations about AJP's record are not meant as criticism— although members of AJP have taken them as such because their ultimate goal is to sound as 'authentic' as possible. Nonetheless, I think that the music on their record is beautiful. Because of the way they tune their ensemble, and because we evidently were socialized to a very similar tuning system, I find their recording more familiar than the music of many rural groups. Learning to create music using foreign systems of intonation is particularly difficult because tuning systems, like phonemic systems, are deeply ingrained through the process of socialization (see Kubik 1985). Since the members of AJP Base Puno were primarily reared in urban Peruvian society, where the Western tuning system predominated, and they learned to perform panpipes largely while living in the city, it is understandable that, in 1985, they did not yet tune, or *hear*, their tropas precisely as rural Andeans do. AJP's attitudes about rehearsing music in 1985 were also logically different from those of musicians in the ayllus; AJP members had different goals for performance, and a different social style and philosophy that aided them in approaching their goals.

AJP and other urban sikuris have set the standard in regard to tuning and ways of performing, as in other things, for many groups of young people in Puno, even those who come from rural areas. Velasco's policies, urban migration, and cultural movements, such as the one spearheaded by AJP, have led to a revaluation of rural Andean culture while simultaneously helping to diminish cultural differences between young highlanders and members of mainstream society. The intonation favored by urban sikuris is only one subtle, and yet important, example of the way musical transformations take place within, and are fostered by, cultural revitalization movements.

THE YOUTH OF CONIMA

At ten o'clock on the opening night of the 1985 Fiesta de la Cruz in Huancané, Qhantati sat on the patio of the sponsor's expansive house, waiting to be served the evening meal. We had just come down from a mountain where we had played five hours at a ceremony for the cross. On the mountain there had been speculation about why the young men who lived most of the year in Puno, and who were members of the recently formed Qhantati Ururi Base Puno, had not arrived to help with the performance. Their participation had been requested by Qhantati's president, and because of the strength young musicians add to a panpipe ensemble, it was needed. We met some of these young men on the way into the alferado's patio, and they joined us. People from the alferado's household began to serve us, placing woven cloths with potatoes and corn on the floor of the patio. The young men of the Puno contingent looked at the food on the floor and then at each other and said in disgust, "They serve us like this, without forks or spoons or anything!" They did not touch the food, though the older members, and the few younger players who had come from Conima, ate hungrily.

After supper several young men of Qhantati Ururi Base Puno began to make accusations against the Conima contingent. They claimed that the leadership in Conima had signed the contract without consulting them. The Puno group had sent a letter to Conima, saying that they were not in agreement with the usual treatment the ensemble received from the Huancané vecinos. One young man shouted, "Can't you see that they are dominating you? You signed the contract without consulting us, and yet you expect us to play under these conditions!" (pointing to the food on the floor).

As it turned out, a number of the Puno faction did not play the next day, nor for the rest of the fiesta. During the social dancing at the alferado's house, I was surprised to see that some did participate, but as dancers and guests mixing with the other vecinos.

On the streets during the fiesta, Qhantati encountered additional problems. The other ensembles of young mestizos and urban-oriented youths from the ayllus such as Rosaspata, Los Aymara de Huancané, and especially 14 de Setiembre de Moho were outplaying Qhantati in terms of volume, duration, and, from the vecinos' point of view, quality. During the fiesta, many people commented on this, and the First Alferado, his wife, and his guests complained about Qhantati frequently. A member of an urban sikuri group, who was present to record music during the Huancané fiesta, commented to me that "the imitators were doing Qhantati's repertory better than the masters."

One Competition, Two Sets of Rules

Operating basically like a community ensemble, Qhantati Ururi in Conima presently rehearses once or twice before a performance, and much of this time is spent socializing, eating, drinking, and composing. For the older Conimeños, rehearsals are part of the fiesta they are about to play. For them, rehearsing music repeatedly outside the context of a festival would be like practicing cooking and then throwing away the food. Music has use-value; it is something people dance to and enjoy. Speaking of my American fiddler friend's practicing music by himself in his room, the Conimeño musician

Mateo asked incredulously, "What would he want to do that for?" The idea of playing music separate from festival is foreign to them.

In terms of standards of performance, modes of rehearsal, and the type of sound they are striving to achieve, the young sikuri groups performing in Huancané have been influenced by AJP and other urban ensembles. Like AJP, the young sikuris who performed in the Fiesta de la Cruz rehearse intensively before a given event, because they have a different conception about what is expected of musical performance, and a different conception of what music is. Unlike AJP, but similar to Qhantati, the young men of 14 de Septiembre de Moho were very much interested in musical competition. In 1985, they were considered by many to be the best ensemble in the festival.

During the fiesta in Huancané, the aesthetics and ideas about musical performance held by Qhantati's young competitors apparently resonated with those of the alferados and their guests. For the Fiesta de la Cruz, it is these people who do the hiring and firing and who are, ultimately, the arbiters of taste. The musical competition between Qhantati and the young sikuris was no longer only a contest between panpipe ensembles. It had become, once again, a contest between different ways of understanding the world. It was a competition in which the two sides were playing by different rules, but in which only vecino rules seemed to count.

That Is How We Should Travel!

On the final afternoon of the Fiesta de la Cruz, we boarded a dump truck that the alferado had hired to transport Qhantati home. Across the street, the members of 14 de Septiembre de Moho, certain of victory, buoyantly entered the school bus hired for them. One of the younger members of Qhantati who had played during the fiesta said, "That is how *we* should travel. We travel like animals." Not that they were the only ones who noticed the school bus, but as usual it was the younger members of Qhantati who commented about such things out loud.

The personnel problems within Qhantati for the 1985 and 1986 Huancané festivals were particularly complex. Before the 1970s the musicians had been from the rural ayllus, and they, at least, shared the same game rules, the same social style. As a result of emigration, however, Qhantati lacked younger players. During the 1980s, young mestizos and peasants with urban experience from Conima wanted to join with Qhantati; they took special pride in performing with the group most revered within urban panpipe circles. Many of the members of the Puno faction within Qhantati were town dwellers' children who studied at the university or worked in Puno. Their mestizo status, their education, and their urban experience made it possible for them to join in dancing with the mestizo guests at the alferado's house in Huancané; living in the city of Puno at a time when sikuri music was in vogue made them want to participate in Qhantati.

The younger generation's social identity has thus become ambiguously constituted. In the post-Velasco period, and in the context of phenomena such as the urban panpipe movement, they have been taught to value the local indigenous culture, and as people from a rural district, they make their own identity more secure in the city by voicing this position. Yet it is not the totality of the local Aymara culture that they identify with. Rather, young Conimeños tend to become involved with the features that have been symbolically selected and given attention in the cities—sikuri music being primary among these. Back in the conservative provincial capital of Huancané, however, peasants are still looked down upon. The Puno faction of Qhantati was caught between a new and an old value system; by joining the mestizos' dance at the alferado's house, a number of them opted to emphasize their vecino status at that moment.

Age and Conflict

The situation between the generations in Conima is complicated. Several decades ago, people of all generations differentiated themselves primarily along ethnic and class lines, articulated in terms of a town/ayllu distinction. In the 1980s, however, young men of peasant background who migrated to cities rapidly ceased to identify themselves, or be identified, strictly as peasants when they returned home. Among Conimeños with urban experience below the age of thirty-five, the ethnic/class lines become blurred, and they are often ignored in social interactions among young people. Perhaps as a part of Velasco's ideological impact, and that of education itself, racism and classism within this generation have started to diminish somewhat, or are at least questioned more. After all, not only did the Puno faction of Qhantati refuse to eat food served on the ground, but they also wanted the older members of the ensemble to rebel at this treatment (even though peasants typically eat this way during Conimeño festivals).

In Conima, a new identity group is emerging in which age and degree of urbanism are offsetting the former criteria of ethnic/class heritage, although the leaders of this youth group still tend to be of vecino background. Even young men who stay in the ayllus or who work on the eastern slopes of the Andes tend to use this group with urban experience as role models—

replacing the older pattern of looking to community elders for direction and leadership. Along with the mestizo schoolteachers and the radio, then, this young urban-oriented group is most directly responsible for diffusing urban-Peruvian attitudes and styles of behavior within the district. Although still based in issues of social power and cultural difference, a new potential for factional division within the district is now forming along generational lines.

The Huancané fiesta was certainly not the only time that I witnessed disputes between the younger and older members of Qhantati. In contrast with the older players' customs of consensus decision making, conflict avoidance, and quiet social style, the younger players sometimes instigated relatively aggressive one-sided debates. Arguing is itself a break with typical social behavior within an ayllu group, and arguing with one's elders all the more so. As on the alferado's patio, the younger players often used a direct style of confrontation, speaking loudly in Spanish. Not only did this put the older Conimeños at a linguistic disadvantage, but, for me at least, it called forth a long history in which Spanish was used to cement relations of domination.

This linguistic code-switching (the young men often spoke Aymara to their elders) was part of a general cultural code-switching. If the issue at hand was not particularly important, the older members tended to react to the youths' argumentative behavior merely by turning their backs and keeping quiet. This reaction only placed additional control in the hands of the younger players, since the elders usually preferred capitulation to open conflict. Here in microcosm was the story of Indian-criollo relations in Peru—the meeting of widely divergent social styles—and the basis of the stereotype of the "passive Indian," a stereotype belied by the history of peasant revolt (Stern 1987).

The Huancané Festival, 1986

Finally, after brewing for several years, a major conflict between the generations in Qhantati did emerge, surrounding the issues of the formation of the splinter group Qhantati Ururi Base Puno and the Huancané contract for 1986. The older musicians in Conima could not understand how there could be two Qhantati Ururi ensembles, and they did not approve of the affiliate group. In 1986, Qhantati of Conima decided not to perform for the Fiesta de la Cruz in Huancané, but instead took the contract for another town, Vilquechico, where the alferado was the compadre of one of Qhantati's guías. The leadership of Qhantati counted on a number of the young Puno residents as well as young people at home to fill the ensemble's ranks.

In the meantime, the Puno faction took the contract for Huancané, using Qhantati's name. In addition, the Puno group clandestinely encouraged other young men in Conima to join them in Huancané, and a number did so—revealing their loyalties. Worse still, these players took the newly cut sikus meant for the Vilquechico performance with them. The players in Conima angrily vowed that the young people involved would never play with the 'legitimate' group again. In this incident, as in many realms of life, the young Conimeño residents in Puno provided the leadership for the youth back home. Qhantati's troubled reception the previous year in Huancané was simply another punctuation mark in the writing on the wall: the Puno faction of Qhantati represented the future in a game with new rules and new competitors, a game that the older players were simply unfamiliar with.

Not all the young players of Qhantati went to Huancané with the Puno faction. As with any social group, there is a spectrum of young men in Conima, ranging from a minority who maintain very traditional attitudes to a few who want nothing to do with their home region. Within Qhantati itself, there are several young men who consistently follow the lead of the older players and behave as a *hak'e* (human being) should rather than siding with their peers. I know of young men in the district who have had urban experience and, rejecting it, have come back to live in their communities. These men have become attentive and enthusiastic supporters of the local traditions, bringing a new appreciation of their worth. They have learned to play all the different instruments used in Conima and perform with their community ensembles. They advocate that others of their generation do the same, but as of 1986, they were a very small minority and seemed to be moving against a much stronger tide.

WHOSE MUSIC?

In Conima, the Easter fiesta is the most important occasion for panpipe ensemble competition within the district; consequently, it had been customary for Qhantati and the other sikuri groups to place the greatest emphasis on composing new pieces for this event. In 1986, however, Qhantati purposefully composed nothing for that fiesta but waited instead until May, right before the Fiesta de la Cruz. The ensemble's problems in Huancané in 1985 instigated this decision. The members explained that every year they unveiled their new compositions for Easter in Conima, and now people from the young mestizo ensembles of other districts came every year to record them. By the time Qhantati arrived in Huancané in May, all the other groups were already playing its new pieces.[13]

From the older Conimeños' perspective, this was shameless theft, and among themselves they claimed it showed that they were still the masters—"these young people can only copy, they cannot create." But, in my experience, the vecinos in Huancané do not know or care who composes the pieces; what matters is the precision with which they are played.

In February of 1986, Filiberto and I were listening to the radio at his home. The 'folkloric contest' for the Fiesta de la Virgen de la Candelaria was being broadcast from the stadium in the city of Puno. Filiberto and others of Qhantati had tried to arrange a trip to Puno so that they could participate in the contest, but most of the older players did not want to go ("Why should we?" "We would miss Carnival," "It would be too expensive").

Filiberto looked increasingly disheartened as he listened to a number of the young urban sikuri groups compete with Qhantati's pieces—several of which were his own compositions—in Conimeño style. Whereas AJP is particularly conscientious about crediting the creators of a particular piece or style, other urban groups have not followed suit. During this contest, when the origin of the music was mentioned at all on the radio, the announcer would simply say that it was "música autóctona," "música campesina," "música folklórica."

On this and other occasions, Filiberto told me that he would like to organize a totally new ensemble with a different style, repertory, and name, because now "everyone sounded like Qhantati." But, he would say, "I am too old, I do not have the energy for such things anymore." The world was moving fast around him, and the older people in the ayllus were no longer able to compete with the music that they themselves created; the music had been drawn into a new arena.

The music no longer belonged to them; it had become "traditional folklore." Within urban Peruvian society—as among many academics in the past—*folklore* is often valued for its anonymity as an index of age and distance, and for its romanticized image of people who are romantic precisely because they are invisible. For the older people of the ayllus, the appropriation of things that belong to them—this time their music—is not a new phenomenon. What is new in this instance is that young people from their own district, sometimes their own children, are perceived as having gone over to the other side.

ONE WORLD, MULTIPLE POSITIONS

Huancaneños growing up during and since the time of Velasco have learned attitudes, ideas, and forms of behavior that distinguish them from older people in the ayllus. The generation gap thus becomes a space of cultural differences, the same differences in worldview and social style that have historically marked ethnic/class distinctions. Peru is undergoing radical transformations. Although the specifics would differ, I believe that the stories I have presented here would resonate in rural communities throughout much of the southern highlands (e.g., see Allen 1988).

It is logical that younger people from the ayllus of Conima no longer want to be transported in dump trucks or to be served food on the floor; they correctly perceive that, within the broader context of Peruvian society, buses, tables, plates, spoons, and forks indicate human dignity and equality. They no longer want to associate themselves with musical styles and other social markers that block their access to these things and, more fundamentally, to better health care, higher education, and economic security.

In Peru, as elsewhere, cultural style and musical styles are integrally bound to definitions of social position and access to opportunities. In Peru the lesson is learned early that, beyond the confines of rural communities, and often even within them, people of higher social classes make the rules. When young peasants were sufficiently convinced that moving up in the society had become an option after the 1960s—through urban migration, education, and the adoption of mestizo social style—the choice to do so was so obvious that it was probably not even totally conscious; it simply became "common sense."

One day I was extolling the virtues of life in the ayllus of Conima to a young man from Putina who was bent on leaving. I told him how in other places people were desperately searching for the community he so adamantly wanted to leave behind. He turned on me and said, "OK, *you* stay here. Are you going to stay here?" My stammering reply was that Conima was not my home, nor could I ever really belong there. Since then we have both left.

I understand why he would want to exchange the dump truck for the bus, the beautifully woven cloth covered with potatoes for the plastic plate, the silence between glorious fiestas for the ubiquitous "boom-box," a society that produces no garbage for one that produces too much. What I do not understand is why particular social formations make these either/or choices—if, in contemporary Peru or the United States, they really can be considered choices.

○

In Conima and other districts in Huancané, the older people of the ayllus were already established in their style of life and livelihoods by the 1960s.

They simply grew up under different conditions and had different experiences from their children. Consequently, they have not internalized many of the ideas that are influencing the youth. Nonetheless, they must constantly react to new ideas and situations, because of the actions of young people in the region and because of the activities of people as far away as Lima (such as state officials and the members of AJP). Qhantati's refusal to compose new pieces for Easter 1986 is but one example.

Older Conimeños simultaneously express confusion, comprehension, anger, and pride about their children. But the older people regret that their adobe houses will dissolve back into the earth on the land of their grandparents. They are sorry that many of their instruments will fall silent in the absence of their children.

I believe that older Conimeños' ways of seeing the world and approaching music hold important lessons for us all. What is more fundamental is that *they* feel that their ways are beautiful and meaningful, and this makes it necessary to approach an understanding of the forces that will transform their ways of life.

○

The middle-class founders of AJP, like progressive indigenista groups before them, do not want the peasant hut, but they do not want General Motors either. Situated in the middle, they have a unique perspective on what is involved on both sides. As organic intellectuals, operating from their own distinct position, they are extremely conscious of, and relatively successful in, devising cultural strategies to approach their social goals—although, like everyone, they have their own sets of constraints. The young urban sikuris embody *tinkuy* (encounter; fusion of opposing forces to create something new; young, not fully grown) within Peruvian society.

Unlike indigenous Andeans, however, many AJP members in Puno, and elsewhere, did not grow up in a society where the concept of tinkuy and the ethics of egalitarian relations and reciprocity are fundamental to ways of living. Sikuri musicians of urban background often come to these ideas and ways of being as sincere students, sometimes with the ardor of religious converts. For me, and perhaps for others in academic disciplines such as ethnomusicology and anthropology, AJP's position is, in a way, the easiest to understand. These academic fields often involve the same romanticism, the same idealism, the same central position that skirts the necessity of committing ourselves fully to the daily struggles of a peasant's existence or the conflicts of a landlord's life. Unlike my position, however, the members of

163

AJP did take risks—of disapproval and even of repression—in places where they would have to continue to live.

○

The older vecinos, landed gentlemen, of Huancané are, like their peasant counterparts, a dying breed. Velasco's agrarian reform marked the end of an era and a way of life—a decline that had begun much earlier with industrialization and the advent of large-scale agriculture for export on the coast. With their material base of power gone, it is more essential than ever for rural vecinos to display distinguishing cultural capital, social style, and symbolic domination over the local peasantry (such as the alferado's treatment of Qhantati in Huancané). As indices of their former authority, this is largely what they have left to maintain that position. Given the attitudes of younger people, however, the disappearance of even these vestiges of former power is only a matter of time: the arena for conflict and competition has shifted to the cities.

ONE MUSICAL STYLE, MULTIPLE MEANINGS

The new ideological orthodoxy and political realities of post-Velasco Peru have set the stage for, and occasionally even require, the display of emblems such as the siku (chapter 9). In the presidential election of 1990, Alberto Fujimori's victory over Mario Vargas Llosa was attributed to support from the rural peasantry and "urban slum dwellers," many of them rural migrants (Lewis 1990). People of rural-indigenous heritage are a political, as well as economic, force that can no longer be marginalized or ignored. The potential of cultural emblems to unify groups in challenge, or conversely in support, of a particular polity explains the Leguía and Velasco states' attention to Andean cultural practices. Their strategies to incorporate rural Andeans into the state involved the attempted transformation of emblems of "Andeanness," such as sikuri music, into symbols of "nation." This, like the folklorization of Andean arts, potentially reduces the efficacy of such emblems to signify *difference* in movements to resist state hegemony. Cooption and folklorization go hand in hand.

○

At first AJP members consciously chose the siku as emblem and activity to distinguish themselves from the Puno elite. They later took up the Conimeño sikuri style, among others, in a conscious effort to identify themselves more closely with indigenous Andeans. AJP's strategies to combat racism and discrimination against Andean peasants and migrants have involved a continual process of adopting increasingly distinctive rural panpipe styles—

which they master with great fidelity. Yet the playing style and musical values of AJP Base Puno (rural bases, in particular, may differ) are still subtly influenced by its members' upbringing in urban Peruvian society; the tuning of their tropas is a primary example. Among the members of AJP Base Lima and Base Puno, attitudes about rehearsing and the emphasis on producing highly polished, 'authentic' musical performances differ from the way rural peasants in Conima approach music. Most obviously, as the original composers of the music, rural Conimeños do not have to assume the same type of self-conscious attitude about performing, nor do they have to worry about authenticity.

After reading a draft of this book, Jaime Montaño (who has been a leading member of both AJP Base Lima and AJP Base Puno) wrote to me that it was not possible or fair to compare AJP with Qhantati because their "functions, principles, goals, and objectives are very different." He wrote, "If you do not understand this, I do not believe that you can realize a good analysis of this reality." He went on to explain that AJP does not rehearse intensely in order to compete more effectively. In fact, AJP does not like competition, because it separates people. AJP strives to perform as well as possible to show the public that "native and peasant [musical] expressions are beautiful; [and that] they represent the essence of our being and our culture" (personal communication, 1990). Jaime's point, and mine as well, is that the "same" musical style may take on new meanings when adopted by different social groups for their own specific purposes. Although Jaime might not agree, I would add that within this process, other ideas about, and aspects of, practice will be distinct as well (such as attitudes about musical competition, intonation, and modes of rehearsal).

AJP's modes of rehearsing and polished performance are consistent with its goal of demonstrating the beauty and power of sikuri music to the broader Peruvian society. This, in turn, is linked to the group's important struggles against social prejudice and the feelings of inferiority among Puneño migrants. AJP's efforts have been quite successful in this regard. Its creation of a different approach to, and sound within, the sikuri tradition has been imitated by young townsmen in the Province of Huancané.

○

While young Conimeños were relatively uninterested in pinkillus, tarkas, and pitus during my period of research, the urban panpipe movement spurred a revival of interest in sikuri music among the youth throughout Huancané. Simultaneously, the urban panpipe movement has guided changes in the meaning and sound of the music among young, urban-oriented Huancaneños. For this group, playing sikus partakes of elements of the state's and AJP's discourses about the value of Andean culture, and yet the young Huancaneños' position is still distinct. When they are in the cities, involvement with the vogue of sikuri music allows them a stronger ground for identity and self-worth in terms of their own rural past. When in the more conservative towns of Huancané or Conima, however, education and urban experience allow them additional options as to how they will identify themselves. Hence, young men with urban experience have, in certain situations, decided to join the vecinos' party rather than stay with the peasant musicians outside on the patio.

○

For the older Conimeño musician quoted at the beginning of this chapter, the siku is an instrument of *his* ancestors. The style from his district is an index of "Conima," and the style and repertory of his ensemble belong to his community. From his perspective, the ancestors of AJP members are not the same as those of his family, his community, his district. According to older Conimeños, people outside these circles have no right to use their music, and this includes the state, AJP, and, in certain situations (such as the Fiesta de la Cruz in Huancané, 1986), the young people from their own district.

The Conimeño migrants in Lima have been influenced by these different constructions of meaning surrounding the Conimeño panpipe style, just as they have been affected by indigenismo, Velasco's policies, the urban panpipe movement, and the harsh hierarchical nature of Peruvian society. Because their particular experiences and needs are different from those of the groups described so far, they add yet another perspective on the meaning of Conimeño sikuri music, community, and identity, as well as on the importance of music in social life.

PART THREE
The Music of Conimeño Residents in Lima

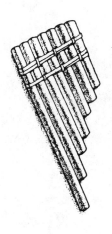

Plate 1. The town of Conima.

Plate 2. Sikuri ensemble from the community of Huata, Conima—wedding performance in Huata.

Plate 3. Filiberto Calderón Villasante making sikus.

Plate 4. Five-hole pinkillu ensemble with cajas from the community of Japisi, performing wifala during the Fiesta de la Candelaria.

Plate 5. Six-hole pinkillu ensemble with cajas.

Plate 6. Women perform a t'inka while a pitu and a sikuri ensemble perform in the background for the Fiesta de la Cruz in Conima's plaza.

Plate 7. Achachk'umu dancers during the Fiesta de la Cruz.

Plate 8. Dancing during Carnival in the Plaza of Conima.

Plate 9. Filiberto Caldéron performing tarka (tayka) during Carnival.

Plate 10. Rey Moreno, traje de luz dance, in the city of Puno during the
Fiesta de la Candelaria.

Plate 11. Sikumoreno panpipe ensemble in the city of Puno.

Plate 12. Centro Social Conima in downtown Lima.

Plate 13. Centro Social Conima warming up for a 'folkloric parade' in downtown Lima.

Plate 14. Centro Social Conima in traje de gala (costume) at Asociación
Juvenil Puno's Encuentro de Sikuris Tupac Katari.

SEVEN

Conimeños in Lima and Regional Associations

MOVING FROM CONIMA TO LIMA is not the same as going to work on the eastern slopes of the Andes, or moving to Puno, Juliaca, or even La Paz, although many of the reasons are similar. Social distance compounds the geographical distance between the highlands and the coast, between a rural ayllu and the city that was once the bastion of criollo society. Because of geographical distance—translated as time and money—Conimeño residents in Lima forsake the actual and continual involvement with home that is available to the young people in Puno, in Juliaca, and on the eastern slopes. For the residents in Lima who choose to join regional associations (themselves a special group and a minority among Conimeño migrants), "Conima" becomes a symbol, an island in the city, and the basis for creating a new community to fulfill fundamental needs. For these people, actual involvement with home gives way to, in many senses, an even more powerful involvement with a constructed, idealized "Conima."

An older resident from Moho once told me, "Puno is like our mother, and the music—well, the music is like a portrait of Mother." But more than simply a reminder or emblem of home, the performance of highland music and dance has become the primary medium for Conimeños' creation of community and alternative spaces in the city since the 1970s. These spaces are real as well as metaphorical, located in different parts of the city as well as in people's minds. In all senses, they are lodged within the larger mosaic of Lima that simultaneously defines and is defined by the myriad distinct spaces created by groups of migrants from all over the sierra, and by criollos and African, Chinese, Japanese, and other immigrant groups of different class factions.

There is an old saying that "Lima is Peru." Formerly this chauvinistically implied that everything of value was located in the capital, but now it means that a great many people from all over the country have relocated there. It is in Lima that the competition "to make room," to find and define a space for oneself and one's children, is most intense, because Lima is Peru: the anchor and microcosm of the hierarchies that ultimately influence all regions. It is in Lima that the stakes are highest and the prejudices against Andeans most pronounced. It is in Lima that the choices to join a regional association, to perform sikuri music at all, to play behind closed doors or in the street, most obviously become political decisions about the definition of alternative spaces—at once social, economic, and political—and the construction of self. Among the Conimeño residents who belong to regional clubs, the performance of music from their home district has become a central resource, and *the* central activity, in such processes.

The growing presence of highland music in Lima may be understood in three distinct phases.[1] From the 1920s through the 1940s, a kind of highly stylized Andean music was performed in the capital under the umbrella of indigenista activities (such as the estudiantinas). During this period rural indigenous performers sometimes made 'folkloric' appearances under indigenista tutelage (an example being Qhantati's 1939 trip to Lima), as did highland mestizo performers such as the Cusqueño charango virtuoso Julio Benavente in 1949. But during this period, the performance of highland music in Lima was still a novelty. The second phase in the history of highland music in the capital involved a form of commercially produced wayno music, beginning in the 1950s and 1960s, which was widely diffused by radio and on records. Professional singing stars such as Pastorita Huaracina were accompanied by regional string bands, or with an ensemble type from Junín using harp, violin, clarinets, and saxophones.[2] This trend, spurred by the growing market among highland migrants in Lima, parallels the production of "race" and "hillbilly" records in the United States during and after the 1920s. Wayno records of this type continue to be popular presently. The third phase began after 1970 with the performance of indigenous styles of music among migrants—exemplified by, but certainly not restricted to, the urban panpipe movement among Puneño residents in the capital.

The gradual rise of highland music in the city has been identified within, and used as an indicator of, a larger trend called the "Andeanization of Lima" (e.g., Altamirano 1988:65). But among the Conimeño residents, at least, the mother tongue, indigenous spiritual practices, and most other aspects of hometown social style have not remained important in their lives. Moreover, the way Conimeño residents think about, create, and perform music is certainly distinct from the ideas and practices of ayllu musicians in their home district. The migrants' impact on Lima (the "Andeanization of Lima") is not a unidirectional process. Their presence affects the timbre of the city just as they are affected by their experiences there; but in no way can the varied outcomes of this conjuncture be judged merely from the surface of cultural forms.

The Conimeños did not simply "bring their culture with them" to the city, rolling it out like an awning after moving in and setting up shop. Nor did aspects like highland musical practices, spiritual beliefs, or speaking Aymara "naturally" remain a part of their lives. On the contrary, through the 1960s, behavior and activities that would mark the Conimeños as people from a rural highland background were hidden from view or ignored by many residents. The Conimeños' relation to hometown music changed after 1970 within the context of their regional clubs and the urban panpipe movement. But other ideas and practices from Conima that, for a number of important reasons, were threatening or no longer relevant—the use of coca, Aymara, the achachilas and Pachamama, Conimeño social style—are still not part of their public or private lives. The tremendous emphasis that they place on performing music from the home region, then, is striking, but it must been seen within the context of their larger repertoire of social and cultural practices, and the *meanings* that they attach to them.

The evolution of new cultural ways of being in Lima is highly influenced by the huge variety of ideas, resources, and models for action available there. A single, stable, unified vision of the "natural" order of things is difficult to sustain in such places. Nonetheless, I think that highland residents, like people elsewhere, are constantly moving toward such a vision—like Sisyphus—through conscious acts of creation as well as unconscious processes of absorbing the life that is in and around them. People frequently have a need to search for, and create, order. For the residents in Lima, a suitable cultural order is not a given, nor is the selection and use of resources simply a matter of free choice. As Pierre Bourdieu (1977, 1984) and others have argued, cultural resources and ideas about their value are part of the hierarchies that define people's place in society. When people are no longer satisfied with their former social positions, a struggle over the use and control of cultural resources becomes part of the larger struggle for economic security and human dignity.

To locate these struggles within individual perspectives, this chapter begins with an account of two Conimeños' experiences upon moving to Lima. A more general description of the Conimeño residents follows, as does a discussion of the regional clubs, the club networks, and their musical activities. This chapter provides important background for examining the specific nature of one regional association, Centro Social Conima, and its musical practices in subsequent chapters. This chapter also illustrates how the migrant clubs and club networks become the basis of enhanced political power for highland residents in Lima. Finally, using the club-network institutions as a point of reference, I investigate the ways heterogeneous ideas and cultural resources are combined by Puneño residents to accomplish certain types of social work, given their specific goals and circumstances in the city—a topic that is central to all the chapters in part III.

MIGRATION STORIES

Tomás was born to a family of ten children in an ayllu on the Tilali side of the district of Conima in 1940.[3] When he was ten, he began to travel with his father to San Juan del Oro on the eastern slopes of the Andes. At that time there was no real road, so they would load their goods onto two mules and walk for eight days to cultivate their lower lands, while his mother and some of the children maintained their second home in Conima. Tomás completed a year of primary school before these trips began, and two more years were finished over many years during periods back in Conima.

When he was eighteen, the family was visited by an uncle who was a member of the national guard stationed in Lima. What Tomás remembered most about his uncle was his beautiful uniform with old-fashioned riding pants and high, shiny black boots. The uncle told the children about Lima, as well as other places he had seen, and Tomás asked to return with him. Rather than encountering resistance from his father, Tomás received an additional three hundred soles to augment the seven hundred that he had saved from his cash-crop work in the lowlands. As Tomás noted, "This was *money* back in those days."

At first Tomás lived with his uncle in the district of La Victoria in Lima, but soon the uncle got married and left Tomás to live alone. His original intention upon coming to Lima had been to study, but since he had no one to help support him while in school, he never realized this plan; instead he set out to find work. He told me that in 1960 there were very few Conimeños living in Lima. There was a group of vecinos and a few people who, like Tomás, were from the ayllus, but he and his peers from peasant backgrounds were shy about visiting the vecinos. There was not much of a support system among migrants back then, and Tomás remembered the first years as being extremely lonely and difficult; he described the experiences of the other early Conimeño residents from the ayllus in similar terms.

Tomás explained that, like the other Conimeños of peasant background whom he knew at the time, he had great difficulty finding work. He had come with a cushion of savings, but others were not so lucky, and they suffered a lot. Shortly after arriving, Tomás realized that he had no skills to offer and no experience to aid him in landing a job in the city. All he knew was agriculture. He began to feel fairly hopeless, but finally landed a position in a shop applying lacquer finishes to furniture. He worked his first year at this job, receiving "tips" and experience but no real pay. After two years he went to work for minimum wage for some "Chinese" in the same type of business.

During this time he had been very unhappy in Lima, and he realized that the other members of his family were making a better living back in San Juan del Oro. When I asked him why he simply did not return, he smiled and replied that he was ashamed to go back without having accomplished something in the capital, and so decided to stick it out. While working at his second job, Tomás wrote a letter home. He did not tell me what was in the letter, but the result was that his younger brother, Juan, soon came to join him. When Juan arrived, he was surprised and disappointed that Tomás was not doing better. Tomás got his brother a job for minimum wage with his Chinese employers, but both left shortly thereafter: Juan to take a salaried post as a manual worker for the military and Tomás to work free-lance in the furniture-finishing business. Both continue in these jobs today, and Tomás is doing relatively well with his own shop, which employs several other Conimeños who have come to Lima in recent years.

During a separate interview, Juan echoed his brother's story—down to the details of their uncle's shiny riding boots. He added, however, that Tomás's letter had urged that the younger brother, at that time eighteen, come to Lima. Juan said that originally he had come just to see the capital, with no intention of living or working there; laughing, he added that somehow twenty years had passed and he was still in Lima—a fact that seemed to surprise him. In Lima, Juan had married a woman who was from his ayllu, and he explained that once they had children it was next to impossible to leave. Tomás married a woman from Apurimac, a highland state next to Cusco. Both brothers have four children, all born in Lima. In telling about his own lack of education, Tomás expressed pride that his eighteen-year-old son was now studying to be an airplane mechanic in a post-high school academy. He went on to say that his own "progress" in Lima has been a disappointment, but that his children would do better.

The two families now live several doors away from each other, surrounded by other Conimeño families from the ayllus, in the pueblo jóven Mariano Melgar; both men are dedicated members and musicians in the regional institution Centro Social Conima, based in Melgar. Not having been actively involved in musical performance in the highlands, Tomás had not begun playing sikus, tarkas, and pinkillus until around 1980. Juan had gained some musical experience before leaving Conima, but his active involvement with music had begun around 1975, when Centro Social started to place a primary emphasis on musical performance. Tomás has not been back to Conima in twenty-five years, while Juan visited in 1977, 1980, and 1985.

INTRODUCTION TO THE CONIMEÑO RESIDENTS IN LIMA

These are personal stories, but in many of their details they are quite typical of the experiences and characteristics of the Conimeños with whom I worked most closely in Lima—the twenty member families of the regional club Centro Social Conima. I also got to know some members of the other three Conimeño regional associations.[4] It must be emphasized that their very involvement with the regional associations makes these Conimeños a special group. I have no way of arriving at any accurate statistics for the number of Conimeño residents in Lima who have nothing to do with the associations, but they are certainly the majority. On a questionnaire to club members, for example, I asked people to indicate how many relatives in Lima (outside their nuclear families) belonged to one of the regional associations and how many did not. Referring only to men (single or heads of households), the average number of family members in the institutions was around three, whereas most people responded that they had "many" relatives in Lima who did not belong to the associations.[5] In the discussion that follows, when I discuss "Conimeño residents" I am referring specifically to the club members unless I specify otherwise.

Of fifty-five Conimeño residents interviewed, thirty came from the rural ayllus in Conima, while twenty-five came from the town of Conima. The four Conimeño clubs divide up along peasant-vecino lines in important ways, since the tension between these two groups is carried over from the highlands. In Centro Social, only five of the twenty male members are from town, and this institution considers itself to be a 'campesino' group.

The ages of the men of the first generation (born in Conima) in the four regional clubs range from eighteen to seventy-one, with the average age being approximately forty. Only three young men of the "second generation" (born in Lima) are active performers and participants in the clubs, although all the parents encourage their children to be involved. As in Conima, then, the members of the younger generation in Lima have different interests, values, and perspectives, and must be considered separately.

Like Juan, most Conimeño residents marry women from their home district, and perhaps even their ayllu. Only five Centro Social members married women from other highland departments (none married Limeñas), and these women were fully accepted within the community. The Conimeño couples may marry after meeting again or for the first time in Lima, or they may have formed their relationship before leaving home. In 1986, a man who had been living in Lima for fifteen years announced that it was time to get married. He traveled back to Conima for several months and returned to Lima with a Conimeña bride. He was slyly unwilling to admit whether he had had anyone special in mind before embarking on his quest. Besides visits home, club social events are major occasions for meeting potential spouses and for courting.

Like Tomás, the majority of the Conimeño residents that I knew had only primary school education, and of these, many did not finish primary school. Under a third of the Conimeños had some secondary-level education, and only a couple had postsecondary schooling or training. The Conimeños work as laborers or as *empleados* (salaried workers) for the state, armed forces, and city hospitals; they work as security guards and gas station attendants. A number are self-employed in construction and in manual crafts, and some are underemployed as street vendors and shoe shiners. A few of the younger members of the associations are students, and often also hold down manual or industrial crafts jobs. The Conimeña women work as maids or, like the wives of Tomás and Juan, sell produce in the market in Mariano Melgar.

The Conimeños of vecino background tend to have more education and better jobs than people from the ayllus, but there are exceptions. The 'vecinos' in Lima take care to distinguish themselves from the Conimeño 'campesino' residents, but within the frame of Lima as a whole they remain for the most part in the same lower-working-class position. Their drive to maintain highland status distinctions within the Conimeño resident community may be all the more intense precisely because such distinctions are *not* recognized by Limeños, for whom all Conimeños are "cholos."

The Conimeños express many working-class values. They tend to be conservative both politically and socially. They value job security, and like Juan and Tomás, they tend to stay in the same jobs for a long time. They take pride in their ability to work hard and scorn members of the migrant underclass who are driven into the streets to beg. In her ethnography of highland migrants in a Lima pueblo joven, Susan Lobo writes that "upward mobility is viewed primarily in terms of attaining the material goods associated with middle-class Peruvians" (1982:66). This is partially the case for a few Conimeños who, within their financial constraints, buy televisions and cassette players even before they finish their houses. But more important, Conimeños view their own lives as vehicles for the upward mobility of their children.

As reported by Mangin (1970), Lobo (1982), and Dietz (1976) for other highland groups in Lima, the Conimeños place primary importance on their children's education and their possibilities for becoming 'professionals.' Professional status carries with it the notion of economic advancement and security. In the economic crisis of the 1980s, as more college graduates took to driving cabs for lack of other work, however, some of the residents recognized that setting up construction, craft-oriented, or commercial businesses in the informal sector can be more lucrative. In this context, the stressing of professional (that is, nonmanual) occupations seems to be influenced by criollo ideology, which associates manual labor with inferior social status. Lobo argues that highland migrants in Lima reject the typical criollo ethic that disdains manual labor (1982:67). This may be true for the first generation, since they value work as a means of getting ahead and often have no choice but to accept manual labor. But Conimeños often do not want their children to work in manual occupations and this, in the end, is probably a better indication of their true feelings.

The residence patterns among Conimeño association members must be described in the context of the clubs themselves. The members of the oldest club, Unión Progresista Conima (UPC), live in many parts of the city, including San Luis and Comas in the north; but there is a central core who live in or near La Victoria, an area that is increasingly becoming a dangerous slum. The members of the newest institution, Qhantati Ururi Base Lima, which formed as a splinter group of UPC in 1985, likewise live in these various sections of Lima.

Like Tomás and Juan, most of the Conimeños who arrived in Lima in the 1950s and 1960s first went to live with or near paisanos near downtown Lima. At the beginning of the Velasco era, however, the members of the two most active associations, Centro Social Conima and Unión Hilata, took part in the land invasions in the "southern cone." All the members of Centro Social live in a single pueblo joven, Mariano Melgar in Villa María del Triunfo. The members of Unión Hilata live in the southern pueblos jóvenes neighboring Villa María, and several live in Melgar. Since the organization of land invasions is dependent upon word of mouth, it is not surprising that groups of Conimeños who were already in close contact banded together for the invasion of Melgar. The members of Centro Social now all live in close proximity to each other, but not all Conimeños in Melgar belong to one of the regional associations.

The Conimeños' houses in the pueblo joven are at all stages of completion—ranging from straw huts within the brick wall circumscribing a family's lot to a few nearly finished two-story dwellings. Along with educating their children, the completion of their houses is a major priority for the Conimeño residents. The members of Centro Social frequently complain that since the institution is so busy performing music on Sundays (for many their only day off), they do not have enough time to work on their houses. This suggests the priority that these residents place on belonging to Centro Social, but, in fact, progress on the houses is also often slow due to a lack of money and thus materials.

The Conimeños in Melgar and their neighbors, people from all over the highlands, have worked hard to establish their community, and they are rightly proud of it. Beginning with a vacant desert, and after years of struggling with the city bureaucracy, Melgar now has water, lights, and its own school, health post, and church. By the time of my research, the people there had created a comfortable, relatively quiet neighborhood where children played safely on the streets of sand and addressed passing elders as *tío* and *tía* (uncle and aunt), terms of friendship and respect used by children in the highlands. Neighbors knew each other and visited back and forth. Melgar had its own market where food was brought from the central market in La Victoria and sold from booths reminiscent of a highland market. Walking down the street on any Sunday, one could hear music from many different highland regions, frequently performed by live groups for fiestas. The panpipe music of Centro Social and Unión Hilata was heard commonly, as were cassette players blasting out *cumbia andina,* salsa, and rock.

The Second Generation

Peruvians generally use place of birth as an important criterion for defining identity. "Conima" provides the fundamental identity base for first-generation residents in the regional associations. Since all the children of Centro Social members (and, to my knowledge, those of all the residents) were born in Lima, and many have not even visited Conima, they often considered themselves Limeños; yet the constitution of the second generation's identity is much more complex.

Once at a Centro Social function I asked an unfamiliar young man where he was from. He hesitated and then said, "My father is from Conima, my mother is from Huancayo. I do not know where I am from. . . . I guess I am

177

from Lima." He was the Lima-born son of a Centro Social—member. Other children of Centro Social members told me that they were regarded by their classmates as *provincianos* (highlanders) or Puneños, and by their parents and other first-generation residents as Limeños.

The ambiguity remains because of the social and cultural divisions between criollo coastal dwellers and people of highland heritage. Not feeling, or not allowed to feel, a part of "old Lima" or criollo society, and not being from or knowing the highlands themselves, they are caught somewhere in between. The great majority of the residents' children do not seem interested in most aspects of highland culture. They do not speak Aymara and, with a few exceptions, have nothing to do with Puneño music and the regional associations, outside of family events.

At present a substantial segment of the city's population is made up of Lima-born individuals with highland parents. These kids grow up together in the pueblos jóvenes surrounded by adults—parents, relatives, and neighbors—from all over the highlands, who themselves represent a complex amalgamation of cultural ways of being. Outside of this circle are criollo classmates, teachers, employers, fellow workers, and acquaintances, North American movies and records, Argentinean soap operas, old reruns of "Gunsmoke," ad infinitum. The variety of models for ways of thinking and acting is staggering.

The children of highland migrants are not so much assimilating into a foreign criollo society as they are involved in the construction of a new identity. The bases for identity include a pan-highland component (in contrast to their parents' emphasis on ever more discrete regions); urban ways of operating, speaking, dressing, and moving; international youth culture and rock; Latin American urban culture with cumbia and salsa; and a lower-working-class background.

The members of this emergent identity group have already begun to create their own cultural forms. Nowhere is the complex combination of outlook, aspirations, and bases for identity clearer than in a type of urban-popular music original to this group know as *chicha* or cumbia andina. Electric rock instrumentation, video-game noises, Cuban timbales, and highland nasal vocal quality are combined to create a genre that integrally fuses aspects of the highland-mestizo wayno genre (phrase structure, cadence patterns, melodic shape and movement) with the rhythm of the urban cumbia in the bass and percussion parts. The song texts are largely about love, but there are some lyrics about the class and occupational positions, as well as the problems and aspirations, of young "provincianos" in Lima (Turino 1990b).

The complex fusion of these sonic images produces an extremely accurate portrait of this group.

Although wayno melodies are quoted in, or may serve as the entire basis of, chicha pieces, and panpipe sounds are sometimes imitated by the synthesizers, the great majority of Conimeño children do not want to play waynos or panpipes themselves. Most have not yet been affected by the urban panpipe movement or the growing popularity of sikuri music among Limeño university students any more than their parents have incorporated AJP's politics. They are part of a different class faction and, perhaps, are still too close to the sting of derision—"Cholo!"—to be attracted to such things. Unlike their young cousins back in Huancané, the prestige of an urban movement privileging Huancaneño music does not necessarily impress them. They are not from Huancané, and they are surrounded by urban movements.

Finally, what do they have to do, really, with sikuri music? The resident families are, on the whole, extremely close. The children generally treat their parents with great love and respect; they are reared in a strict manner and tend to be very obedient and polite to their elders. The generational conflicts typically associated with lower-class urban families in the United States are conspicuously absent. The generational tensions found in the ayllus of Conima are not very prominent in these families, either—perhaps because the adult residents have moved closer to the emerging cultural positions of the children. But their parents' ways are still not their ways. Their life experiences have been too different.

Reasons for Moving

Among the Conimeño residents I knew, the average length of residence in Lima was approximately twenty years (in 1985), with the majority having come in the 1960s and early 1970s. This fits the profile of migration statistics for Puno as a whole.[6] Like Tomás and Juan, most of the Conimeños left home around the age of eighteen or twenty. The four major reasons given for coming to Lima were to work, to study, to visit, or simply "to look for a better life" (see Dietz 1976).

A more basic reason for moving was population growth in the highlands and an increasingly unfavorable person-land ratio after 1940. Large families like Tomás and Juan's were common in Conima, and one friend told me that, as the eldest of a family of nine, he had to leave home as a teenager because his father could not adequately feed all the children; others told similar tales. The period of the most intense Puneño migration also falls around a time of recurrent agricultural disasters. In 1956, 1957, and 1964 there were major droughts on the altiplano, and in 1960, 1962, and 1963 there were tremendous floods (Tamayo 1982:111).

Puno is one of the poorest regions of a poor country. In 1981, there were 12,717 inhabitants in the department for every doctor, and infant mortality under one year in 1979 was at the fourth highest departmental rate in the country (125 per 1,000; Moscoso and Mostajo n.d.). In 1981, the national infant mortality rate was 98 per 1,000, while in Lima it was 44 per 1,000 children (de Soto 1989:9). Only 27.5 percent of urban housing in the department of Puno had electricity and running water in 1981. Like Conima, most rural areas were without electricity.

Seeking a better, more secure life—symbolized for Tomás in his uncle's shiny black boots, beautiful uniform, and tales of Lima—is certainly understandable. Tomás and Juan, however, were not driven to Lima out of dire need. In fact, as Tomás recognizes, his family members have probably done better working in San Juan. Thus, in conjunction with the economic, educational, and health-care factors that inspired people to migrate, and which undeniably are often primary, ideological issues (for example, specific definitions of "a better life") were involved. Messages about the promise of the city were increasingly diffused to the rural areas of the highlands by returning migrants such as Tomás's uncle, as well as by the radio and mestizo schoolteachers during the 1960s and 1970s.

THE REGIONAL ASSOCIATIONS

Lima had traditionally been the city exuding the most glitter and prestige, but it also presented the greatest obstacles, such as geographical and social distance, for Puneños. Tomás's story of isolation and discouragement was typical for the 1950s and 1960s, and stories about antiprovinciano prejudices were also common. As more migrants of the lower and working classes got established, however, it became easier for newcomers, who had more possibilities for living with family members or friends from home and finding employment through paisano networks. Like Tomás, some Conimeños have been able to establish and expand their own businesses, and they typically hire other Conimeños, Puneños, or at least highlanders. As described in the introduction, by the 1980s more residents were in the position of doing hiring and firing, and reverse prejudices about criollos' laziness were frequently expressed. The advantages of being connected with a network of people from home became increasingly obvious as the number of residents grew and they became more established in the city.

But the creation of Conimeño networks, and finally communities, in Lima is not beneficial only to newcomers. Many members of Centro Social have been in Lima for twenty years, and they maintain a great dedication to the institution. Because of their growing power in numbers, and the difficulty for first-generation residents to move within criollo circles, a new strategy crystallized during the 1970s. This involved *openly* stressing regional identity as the basis for what Richard Adams (1981) calls "survival units": the primary social groups on which people depend for mutual aid and support. The regional associations became the central, formalized core for these communities, and musical performance is the glue that holds them together.

Rural-migrant regional associations are a common phenomenon throughout Latin America and Africa (e.g., Ryo Hirabayashi 1986; Little 1973). Regional clubs already existed in Lima in the 1920s and 1930s; Laos lists forty-eight regional associations in the capital for the 1928–29 period, and his list is probably not comprehensive (1929:283–90). These associations represented the district, provincial, and departmental levels, as well as total macro-regions (for example, Confederación Regional del Centro). Many of the institutions cited were formed as early as 1922. The phenomenon has grown tremendously in conjunction with highland migration and the trend of increasing regional specificity for the identity bases used by highland residents. Altamirano (1984:15) states that in 1957 there were slightly more than 200 regional clubs in Lima, whereas in 1970 Doughty identified 1,050 regional associations (1970:33), and Altamirano gives a figure of 4,000 clubs for 1977 and 6,000 for 1980 (1984:15). These institutions vary greatly in size, purpose, and mode of operation.

As is the case generally for other departments, the Puneño associations are largely divided by class status according to the regional level represented (Doughty 1970:35; Jongkind 1974; Galvez 1981). For example, the departmental association Club Departamental Puno is composed of residents from the urban highland elite. These individuals remain in the upper middle class in Lima. Puno has two other institutions that are departmental in scope: Brisas del Titicaca, also of the upper middle and middle class, and AJP of the middle and, more prominently, working class. Provincial-level clubs are also usually composed of middle-class members, whereas clubs representing the district level (such as Centro Social Conima and Unión Progresista Conima) and specific ayllus (Unión Hilata) are usually of the lower and working classes. For Puneños there is a very real social division between the departmental/provincial clubs (with the exception of AJP) and those of the district and ayllu levels. For example, in a conversation with the wife of the president of Club Departmental Puno, she stated directly and unselfconsciously that the district and ayllu clubs from Huancané were not welcome to use the departmental club's locale or participate in its activities because the Huancaneños were "of another social level."

Musical and Dance Activities within the Regional Clubs

As is suggested by scholars for the clubs of all departments, sports, religious fiestas, 'folklore' performances, social dances, barbecues, and association business meetings are the main types of social activities around which the club members unite (Doughty 1970:37; Galvez 1981; Altamirano 1984; Nuñez 1985). Given the regional and ethnic/class diversity in the Andes, however, neither the characteristics nor the activities of the clubs can be generalized any more that one can make blanket statements regarding highland communities.

Researchers usually provide rather sketchy descriptions of the musical and dance activities within the regional associations. The literature suggests, however, that while the clubs have had an increasingly major role in organizing performance events in the city since the 1960s, the club members from many departments are often not actually involved with performing themselves. On this point the district- and ayllu-level Puneño clubs differ from those of other departments. The vast majority of Puneño musical and dance ensembles in Lima are formed within the context of regional associations, whereas this is not necessarily the case for resident musicians and clubs of other highland departments.

The central importance of performing music and dance in many Puneño clubs is based in local communal patterns of musical organization in Puno. Club members from other areas exhibit different relationships to music and dance performance, again modeled on the distinct local customs of their regions of origin, and influenced by the ethnic/class position of club members. This relationship between local highland custom, social class, and club musical activities in Lima is worth illustrating with a few cases.

In July of 1985, I attended a patronal fiesta in Lima organized by the district-level resident association of Huarocondo, Cusco—Centro Social Huarocondo. The celebration of its hometown patronal saint's fiesta in the capital is the primary activity of the year for this and many regional associations (although the Conimeño clubs do *not* do this). In addition to the mass and procession of the saint—standard for rural and urban Catholic fiestas—Centro Social Huarocondo's celebration in Lima included costumed dances commonly performed in mestizo fiestas in Cusco such as the *majeños,* the *saqras,* the *k'achampas,* and the *chilenos* (Turino 1982). Having attended this same fiesta in Huarocondo, Cusco, in 1981, I observed that the traditions performed, the choreography, the costumes, and the music used in Lima closely followed the model of the highland fiesta.

Significantly, in the Lima event it was not the members of Centro Social Huarocondo who performed the music and dance. Rather, club members, most of vecino background, organized and sponsored various musical and dance groups among paisanos of campesino heritage who did not belong to the club. In most cases the musicians were paid for their performance, as were some of the dancers. In highland Huarocondo, the same type of fiesta organization occurs, with the vecinos (in Lima represented by club members) organizing and sponsoring local peasant groups for the fiesta held in the district capital town.

Nuñez (1985) reports a parallel situation for regional associations from Ayacucho, Huancavelica, and Apurimac that sponsor festivals for the performance of dansaq (the scissors dance). Here again, the performers are usually contracted from outside the club ranks. In the highlands, dansaq performers (accompanied by their own harpist and violinist) are practiced part-time professional specialists who work from a young age to perfect this extremely difficult and virtuosic dance tradition. In the rural sierra, fiesta sponsors contract the best dansaq performers available, often from outside the community and even beyond the immediate region. If we interpret the regional associations in Lima as the replacement for the highland community, as Nuñez does (1985:120), it is in keeping with highland practice that Ayacuchano associations in Lima contract the best dansaq performers from outside the club ranks. Given the specialized, esoteric nature of dansaq and the relatively small size of the ensemble, it is hardly surprising that the members of Ayacuchano clubs do not perform dansaq as their central unifying social activity.

If we imagine a continuum of highland Peruvian musical-dance traditions set out according to the degree of community participation in the performance itself, and the amount of specialization required, the rural-Aymara traditions of Conima would be diametrically opposed to dansaq. Since rural-Puneño wind performance involves large community-based ensembles, the regional clubs—which serve as a basis for community in Lima—provide the logical framework for ensemble formation. This is facilitated by the nonspecialist nature of rural Aymara music and made more significant by the fact that Aymara performing ensembles in the highlands typically function to represent their communities publicly.

The Shift from Sports to Music

The rise of Puneño musical performance in Lima is directly tied to a significant change within the district and ayllu clubs themselves. Before the mid-
1970s, all but a handful of the regional associations from Huancané were
exclusively dedicated to sports, mainly soccer, as their central unifying activity. By 1985, however, hundreds of clubs had become primarily dedicated
to the performance of music and dance.[7] Puneños explained that by the
1970s, they had reached a critical mass: the large number of paisanos lent
moral support to musical performances. Another common reason stated for
the shift was that they learned that the club could earn money with performance activities, whereas they could not really charge for sports matches.
This realization came after a vanguard of Puneño institutions, AJP primary
among them, had begun to organize performance events in Lima. Puneños
also frequently commented that many people felt *vergüenza* (shame, embarrassment) about performing highland music and dance in Lima before the
1970s; this attitude changed because of their growing numbers, changes in
economic power relations between criollos and highlanders, the effects of
Velasco's policies, and the activities of groups such as AJP.

Previously, club membership had been based on regional identity, but
people felt constrained not to express that identity in public. Soccer was not
associated with highland society or any given region, and as such was an
unmarked activity around which they could unite. In addition, the custom
of forming soccer associations had already been established in the capital by
criollo groups, and thus the highlanders were merely fitting themselves into
an established urban custom (Millones 1970).

Highland musical styles clearly indicate regional heritage. The change from
sports to musical performance, then, indicates a weakening of the constraints
that residents felt regarding the public display of their highland identity, but
this change was not necessarily reflected in other realms of practice such as
language use and religious rituals. Presently, Puneño clubs tend to be involved primarily with either sports or music and dance activities (different
networks exist for each), although some may participate in both kinds of
activities.

Types of Puneño Performing Traditions in Lima

Three types of musical traditions are performed by Puneño regional club
ensembles: estudiantina music, *trajes de luces* (costumes of light) dances with

brass band, and the indigenous wind traditions. The higher-class clubs, Brisas del Titicaca and Club Departmental Puno, use estudiantina (large string ensemble) music almost exclusively. During 1985 and 1986, Brisas hosted a weekly *peña* folklórica at its locale, where the estudiantina accompanied staged, stylized peasant and mestizo dances for a formal, seated audience of middle-class Limeños and highlanders. In this instance, the term *peña* refers to a nightclub setting; the costly entrance fee determined the class of audience. The musicians were part-time professionals, and the dancers were often middle-class students—frequently, but not exclusively, of Puneño background. The style of performance at this peña closely resembled that of other institutions, such as Centro Qosqo de Arte Nativo in Cusco, which hail back to the indigenista period.

District and ayllu clubs form either Andean wind ensembles (primarily sikuris or sikumorenos) or brass bands. Some clubs do not have musical ensembles but are organized around the performance of the urban-mestizo trajes de luces dances. The dance clubs perform in conjunction with the brass bands. The trajes de luces dances were initially diffused from Bolivia to Puneño cities and towns; these traditions have by now become popular with peasants in many regions of Puno. Along with panpipe music, ornate trajes de luces dances such as Rey Moreno and La Diablada have become most closely associated with Puno in the national imagination. It would require another study to determine why some Puneño residents choose to perform trajes de luces over playing the indigenous winds, although the spectacular quality of these mestizo dances, their fame at the national level, and highlanders' pretensions to upward social mobility may all be involved.

History of the Conimeño Regional Associations

All the regional associations representing Conima in the capital use the indigenous wind instruments from the rural district. The first Conimeño regional association in Lima, Unión Progresista Conima, was established in 1953. Several of the founders stated that at the time there were very few known Conimeños in the capital, and the group began with around eight members. They formed the club because, as one man told me, "people from other regions, from Cusco, from Huancayo, had their own institutions here in Lima, so we thought to ourselves, we should form our own club too." From the beginning they were involved in sports activities—soccer and volleyball. Atypical for lower-working-class Puneño regional associations at that time, Union Progresista became involved in musical performance almost from the start. Its musical activity seems to have been supported by interest from Arturo Jiménez Borja, a well-known scholar and collector of Andean instruments and art in Lima.

In their early days, the members of Unión Progresista played panpipes in a style that was described as being closer to the sikumoreno than to the Conimeño sikuri style, and they also played tarkas and pitus. Various people recounted that there were so few members that "someone's sister" had to play the bass drum. Most of the members of Unión Progresista had not learned to perform music in Conima before coming to Lima but rather learned from the few who had; perhaps this explains why their early panpipe style was rather undefined. As more Conimeños moved to Lima, the ensemble increased in size and musical sophistication. In 1980, with an ensemble of over twenty performers, they recorded a commercial long-playing record with Conimeño sikuri, tarka, and pinkillu music.

Unión Progresista remained the only stable Conimeño regional association in Lima until 1970, when Centro Social Conima came into being. Before this time, Unión Progresista had members from all over the district and included 'vecinos' as well as 'campesinos,' (identifications that the residents maintained). After leaving the central Lima area where Unión Progresista was based, the Conimeños who moved to Melgar—some of whom had been members of Unión Progresista—decided to form their own institution. They explained that Centro Social's cohesion was greatly enhanced by their close proximity in Melgar—facilitating communication about activities and meetings—and by the lack of vecino-campesino tensions. The majority of Centro Social members are from the ayllus, and the townspeople who do belong accept the association's self-identification as a 'campesino' institution.

Between 1970 and 1975, Centro Social was solely involved with sports activities and belonged to a sports club network. In 1975 the members formed a Conimeño-style sikuri ensemble and changed their orientation completely to music, for the reasons that have just been outlined. Some Centro Social members observed that they simply had no interest in musical performance before 1975—a fact that makes their current intense dedication to the music all the more striking. Centro Social began performing sikuris in the Conimeño style from the start, before AJP made this style fashionable in the cities.

Unión Hilata, the only Conimeño institution presently representing a specific ayllu, was also formed in 1970 among people involved in the land invasions of the southern cone.[8] In 1986 there were about twenty affiliated families. An initial reason for forming Unión Hilata was to help the ayllus

186

on the Tilali side in their attempt to split off from Conima and create their own district, the residents acting as go-betweens with the central government for the people in the ayllus.[9] Like Centro Social, Unión Hilata was involved in sports as its main social activity until after 1975 (versions differ about the exact year), when the members began playing the Conimeño wind instruments. Typical of Conimeño residents, many of the members of Unión Hilata learned to perform sikus in Lima and had not been very involved with playing music before leaving home. It was not really until around 1983 and 1984 that Unión Hilata began to concentrate seriously on musical performance; and even during my stay, its rehearsals were the most informal among all Conimeño associations.

In July of 1985, the newest Conimeño association was formed, specifically around sikuri performance. Splitting off from Unión Progresista, the members of this new group were young and middle-aged men of vecino heritage. At first they chose the name Wayna Qhantati (Young Qhantati), but quickly changed to Qhantati Ururi Base Lima, following the AJP tradition of forming multiple bases of the same group. They had also been inspired by the previously formed Qhantati Ururi Base Puno. Belonging to the family of Natalio Calderón, the leaders of this club have allegedly claimed that the famous ensemble's name, style, and repertory belong rightly to them rather than to people from the ayllus. This particular, politically motivated, construction of Conimeño music history caused great tensions within the Conimeño resident community, and at one festival in 1986, the members of Centro Social and Qhantati Ururi Base Lima almost came to blows. In 1986, the latter club only had about twelve performing members, and they had reduced Unión Progresista to about ten players, thereby diminishing the effectiveness of both groups.

Centro Social Conima continues to be the most active and successful Conimeño association in both musical and social terms. It maintains relatively strong bonds of cooperation and friendly rivalry with the 'campesinos' who make up the majority of Unión Hilata, as well as with the people who remained with Unión Progresista.

Umbrella Organizations for the Performance Clubs

Like the Puneño sports clubs, individual district and ayllu performance clubs organize themselves into formal networks. These umbrella institutions are essential for the realization of musical events. In addition, individual clubs enhance their political power by joining with others. For example, while obtaining their own locale is a primary goal for most lower- and working-class clubs, to my knowledge no individual Puneño district or ayllu institution has been able to attain this. But Central Folklórica Puno, the umbrella organization to which all the Conimeño clubs belong, was able to obtain land from the national government in 1984 for a locale to be shared by the affiliate institutions.

Since its inception in the late 1970s, Central Folklórica Puno (CFP) was dedicated to obtaining a locale for the performance clubs. Its leaders took care to foster alliances with the Instituto Nacional de Cultura (INC) by providing performers when the INC or the government needed Puneño participation (chapter 9). The leaders of CFP made the case to the central government that theirs was the institution that could best serve as representative for the Puneños of the 'popular' classes. CFP's success in convincing the government to donate land to working-class residents is a significant example of the increasing political power and organizational sophistication the Puneños had achieved by this time; it also illustrates the state's need to forge alliances with highland migrants.

The Conimeño clubs belong to a second umbrella organization specifically for sikuri and sikumoreno institutions: Federación de Sikuris y Sikumorenos de Residentes Puneños en Lima y Callao. This institution, founded in 1984, had twenty-five member clubs by 1986, largely from the provinces of Huancané, Puno, and Chucuito. The formal charter of the institution gives some idea of its ideological orientation and purpose:

PRINCIPLE OF THE FEDERATION

Our music (sikus) is the creation of our ancestors. It is a free
    and natural manifestation of community that expresses the
    living history of our Quechua and Aymara nations.

OBJECTIVES

To maintain all of the cultural values of our ancestors such as
    customs, languages, moral code, medical practices.
To maintain the relations of mutual help such as *ayni, apjata,
    minka,* among all our members.
To understand, promote, and orient the cultural values of our
    people of the Altiplano.
To unify all the sikuri and sikumoreno groups of Puneño resi-
    dents in Lima and Callao as well as non-Puneño groups.
To plan and coordinate activities among the member clubs.
To protect the rights of associated clubs, charging copyright
    fees for music and traditional costumes used by non-Puneño
    groups or non-Federation members.

> To control the filming and recording or use for television [of si-
> kuris performance], be it of the state or private.
> To obtain a locale for the Federation.

The differences between the ideas and concerns expressed in these statements and the way older Conimeños in the ayllus think about music and
themselves need little elaboration. While Filiberto would certainly be in favor
of maintaining control over his group's compositions, it has not occurred to
him to try copyrights, nor has television coverage come up for much discussion in the ayllu. The framing of identity in ethnic nationalistic terms (the
notion of "Quechua and Aymara *nations*") is foreign to most people's thinking in Conima; this conception may have been influenced by other nationalistic discourses in Peru. The charter itself certainly articulates different identity needs and problems encountered in the city, and it illustrates how
strategies from a variety of sources (such as ayni and copyrights) are adopted
to confront those problems.

Specifically, the document more closely resembles the pan-Andean discourse of AJP than it does the localist conceptions of working-class regional
institutions like Centro Social Conima and Unión Hilata. AJP is strongly
represented in the Federation and probably provided leadership in drawing
up its charter. The relationship between AJP and the Federation is a complex
and interesting one. From limited observation and gossip, I surmise that AJP
was, in principle, in favor of the broader democratic base for directing panpipe activities in Lima that the Federation represents. At the same time, I
think that some AJP members were reluctant to give up their leadership
position in urban panpipe circles. For example, there was talk of the Federation's taking over the organization of the Encuentro de Sikuris Tupac Katari
(the most important panpipe performance event in the city), but AJP was
against this.

Like the style of the Federation charter, the organizational structure and
social style exhibited in both CFP and Federation meetings have been influenced by urban-criollo ways of doing things. Each affiliate club sends two
delegates to the frequent organizational meetings, and specific committees
are formed among the delegates. The meetings are conducted in Spanish,
with Western democratic processes such as secret ballots. When presenting
a case to the assembly, delegates often adopt a forceful and formal criollo
style of speaking, in contrast to the softer, more indirect style typically used
in consensus decision making in the ayllus.

The umbrella institutions provide good examples of the ways in which Puneño residents combine different models for organization and action (for example, ayni juxtaposed to secret ballots) to solve a whole range of new problems encountered in the city: especially the organization of fiestas, gaining a locale where they can be held, and maintaining control over Puneño performance traditions. Major concerns involve highland performing arts, culture, and identity, but these concerns are voiced and handled in ways that are foreign to life in the ayllus, as indeed they must be.

As I suggested at the beginning of the chapter, the highland residents are not simply transforming ("Andeanizing") the capital, nor are they merely assimilating criollo ways; as in the examples discussed here, they often pragmatically select models for organization and action from a variety of sources, based on their complex experiences and needs in Lima. The eclectic orientation and organization of the umbrella institutions are useful for getting things done in the city. Through involvement with institutions like AJP, the Federation, CFP, and even trade unions, this type of orientation is becoming more widely diffused among working-class regional clubs like Centro Social Conima, to their advantage. CFP's land grant from the government served as a powerful example of the results that can be achieved through collective action and this pragmatic, eclectic style of organization; among working-class club members, few more convincing arguments could be made for adopting this style.

EIGHT

Centro Social Conima: Music and the Importance of Community

A Roof-Raising Fiesta

ALTHOUGH CONIMEÑOS ARE usually studiously late to social gatherings, about twenty residents in Lima, dressed in work clothes, were already at Mario's house in Melgar by ten o'clock one Sunday morning in December of 1985. Surrounded by bags of cement, empty five-gallon cans, and various tools, some stood in front of the house talking, others were drinking beer in a paisano's house-front store a block away. Meanwhile, at Benito's, a group of Conimeña women were cooking over an open fire in the roofless area that would one day be the living room.

Benito grew up in Japisi, on the Tilali side of the district; Mario is from Ayllu Sulcata. Having moved to Melgar during the original land invasion, they now live next door to each other, and both men are active members of Centro Social Conima. On this Sunday, almost twenty years after the move, some thirty Conimeño men and fifteen women came to help put the roof on Mario's home. Although the house would not really be finished for years,[1] roof raising is a celebration of its completion, as well as a major moment in the family's establishment of a place in the city. It is during events such as these that Conimeño residents articulate their depth of commitment to, and feelings for, the community that they have created. The analysis of such events and a close look at a single regional club, Centro Social Conima, will help us better understand the residents in Lima. The discussion in this chapter will also serve as the basis for comparison with highland social and musical practices.

By eleven o'clock, the hired cement mixer still had not arrived, so some of the men started mixing the cement with shovels and loading it into cans, which the others carried on their shoulders up the ramp to the roof. The pace of the work increased after the arrival of the truck around two o'clock. The men moved up and down the ramp in an unceasing chain. Mario and his wife fueled their patter with chicha and beer. Food would have to wait because, as one man pointed out, "after eating, nobody feels like working."

By evening, the roof was finished. The *padrinos* (godparents) of the roof nailed crosses decorated with flowers and champagne bottles to the wooden form containing the freshly poured cement. Everyone went into Benito's to eat: fairly drunk, very tired, and extremely happy to have been part of it.

Even at the height of musical performance, I had never felt the bonds of friendship and caring among the Conimeño residents in Lima so acutely as on this day. The motion of the work itself was like a dance, and the patter like the music that kept them moving together.[2] What they had accomplished for Mario was something that they all wanted, a goal that they all could share.

My participation in the work project drew interesting responses, especially in relation to how people in the ayllus reacted to my taking part in manual labor. When I indicated that I intended to work (this being my first roof raising in Lima), several people protested, saying that it was not necessary, that I would ruin my clothes, that I would get too tired. For the first hour friends kept trying to get me to quit, but after that they dropped the subject.

During the meal at Benito's, Fabian, the oldest and most direct member of Centro Social Conima, turned to me and said with real appreciation, "We did not know that people like you could work like that."

Wanting simply to be part of the warm feeling that had been created, I was somewhat annoyed. I asked, "What do you mean, people like me?"

He said, "You know, people like you, white people [*blancos*]."

No one in Conima ever seemed to take any special notice when I participated in manual work. I guess they had fewer preconceptions about what North Americans were supposed to do; for them, manual work is something that most people do. The residents in Lima showed a much higher awareness of, and belief in, class and ethnic stereotypes—often to their own detriment when it involved internalizing criollo attitudes about themselves.

After eating, the members of Centro Social Conima slipped away to get their sikus and bombos; upon their return, they stood in front of Mario's, playing their usual repertoire of Qhantati lentos and ligeros. When they had played a few pieces, Mario climbed onto the ramp and, although not accustomed to formal public speaking, addressed those present in his most dignified Spanish. Obviously moved, he thanked everyone for their help and friendship, and spoke about the importance of "our custom" of working together. He then introduced the padrinos of the roof, who made similar formal speeches. Flowers were used to sprinkle water for the baptism of the roof, and then the *madrinas* (godmothers) broke the champagne bottles.

Other Conimeños brought boxes of beer, the sikuris began to play, and everyone danced late into the night.

The Importance of Community

At roof-raising fiestas in Conima, the five-hole pinkillus, not sikus, are used, and a specific dance known as *achuqallu* is performed. In Conima this is done after the work has been completed, the meal has been served, and a ritual specialist has established the earth shrine (*cabildo*) and conducted important rites for Condor Mamani (the guardian of the home) and the other local divinities. The members of Centro Social do not play the pinkillus very much and do not know the achuqallu music or the dance. There is no ritual specialist among them who knows the words or rituals for Condor Mamani, or who could establish an earth shrine. Even if there were, Centro Social members do not involve themselves with such highland religious beliefs and practices—as a number of them told me. In Conima, a ch'alla and a t'inka with coca are conducted for the house; this has been replaced in Lima with a baptism and the breaking of champagne bottles. Centro Social members never use coca, which is central to highland social occasions; they seem to take the same dim view of it as most urban Peruvians do (chapter 10). Finally, older people in Conima would not normally climb onto an elevated platform to speak loudly and formally to an assembly, as Mario had done.

Nonetheless, roof raisings in both Lima and Conima are deeply similar in that they are occasions for mutual aid and the celebration of home, family, and community. Although I see the desire for community as a more generalized human need, not strictly an indigenous Andean value, Mario and the other Conimeños trace it to their highland heritage—"our custom."

Given the eclectic range of practices combined in Centro Social's roof-raising fiesta, Mario's emphasis on highland custom should not be taken simply as an expression of belief; it is also part of the discourse that constructs belief. The appeal to highland custom and tradition in many realms of the residents' lives (and certainly in relation to musical practice) helps to bring and cement the community together around the symbol and basis of their unity, "Conima." The discourse itself is a resource for unification, and the self-conscious use of such resources points to a fundamental difference in the nature of *community* and identity between the ayllus of Conima and the residents in Lima.

Community and traditions must be actively maintained both in the highlands and Lima. An obvious function of fiestas in Conima is the renewal of community. During each highland festival, the tremendous efforts to secure a sponsor for the following year, as well as the variety of strategies employed to do so, illustrate that the maintenance of tradition may not be automatic or simply the result of unconscious habit in the rural district. Yet in Lima, community, identity, and "traditional" practices must be even more actively and self-consciously *created*—a task made difficult by the size, diffuseness, dissonance, and varied nature of the social space. For the residents, the ayllu—one's social base and identity—is not "just there" because of where one was born, where one lives, and where and with whom one has always lived.

I do not want to suggest that the residents are the only ones involved in the creative invention of tradition, or that "community" simply can be taken for granted in the ayllus. The difference between the two situations is a matter of degree. It is, however, precisely this point of difference—the resident's more tentative feelings of "social security" and, consequently, their higher degree of self-consciousness about identity and tradition—that provides the crucial key to understanding a whole range of their social and musical values and practices.

The Sacred Community

The depth of commitment to their resident community and the importance that Centro Social members place on hometown identity and its musical emblems are difficult to fathom. One time when I was giving a talk in Lima, attended by a number of residents from various regions of Puno, a young man who was unknown to me aggressively attacked the study I was conducting. He said, "You can study the guitar, the accordion, or other types of music as you are doing, but you cannot study the siku in this way." Almost in Durkheimian terms, the collective has become recognizably and consciously sacred, and the emblem of the collective, its music, has taken on this sacredness.

The Conimeño residents in Lima do not take an active interest in the spiritual knowledge and practices of the older people in the ayllu. Given the importance highland Conimeños place on maintaining relations with the local divinities in the ayllu, and Centro Social members' discourse about maintaining highland culture and custom, I found this intriguing. Filomeno, a Centro Social member, pragmatically explained it this way:

> In Conima, the people depend on nature for their livelihoods,
> for their food. Here, we work for salaries, for money; therefore
> we no longer need these beliefs. Since they [people in Conima]

194

depend on nature, if one year there is no rain, they carry water up the mountain, and it always rains; or if there is a flood, they do a ceremony to stop the rain. The t'inka and the ch'alla are like prayers. But we work for salaries and no longer need these things.

This is not a statement of skepticism about these highland beliefs and practices, merely an articulation that such practices are not relevant in the residents' current circumstances. Nor do many Centro Social members go to Christian churches in Lima. Rather, they mainly use Catholic symbols and rituals on the occasions when they are moved to express that realm of being that is deeply and yet ambiguously felt as spiritual and sacred. For the Conimeño residents associated with Centro Social Conima, the community itself is frequently at the center of such spiritual moments, and the regional club and its music are the tangible focus.

CENTRO SOCIAL CONIMA: SOCIAL ORGANIZATION

Centro Social Conima can be understood as a formalized voluntary group of Conimeño families living in Mariano Melgar. When men become members, their families are automatically associated with the club. There are no single women in Centro Social who are not attached to a male member through some type of familial relationship. The wives and other female relatives are considered members, however, and can take an active role in club decision making and in organizing events; in addition, they occasionally form part of a dance ensemble that performs with the Centro Social musicians.

It is difficult to determine the exact number of member families. About thirty individuals are officially listed on the written roll of club membership, but belonging to Centro Social is more a matter of actual participation. Even if one is on the official membership list, making an appearance at only one or two club functions a year is not enough to allow one to be considered a member. Since 1975, the paramount club activity has been musical performance, and it is virtually impossible to be a club member in good standing without performing in the ensemble and taking part in the rehearsals and performances that occur almost weekly.

The musical ensemble, then, is not merely a facet of the club; musical participation actually defines membership, although reasons for belonging may not include an interest in performing per se. In fact, Centro Social's president estimated that under 50 percent of the members had any deep dedication to musical performance for itself; they played because they wanted to belong for other reasons. The number of active performers fluctuated between fourteen and twenty individuals for most occasions during 1985 and 1986, with several more joining in for the most important performances, such as AJP's Encuentro de Sikuris Tupac Katari.

Central Social Conima must also be understood as a core institution around which a larger Conimeño-resident community revolves in a less formal way. Each active member is related to other Conimeños in Melgar and elsewhere in Lima. These people, and most Conimeños, are welcome at club events, many of which may involve the entire family. Rehearsals and musical performance itself, however, are restricted to men from Conima.

Centro Social is always looking for new members, both for social reasons and to strengthen the club's musical performance. Nonmembers sometimes join in playing with the ensemble in informal situations, although participation is strictly controlled when the group is preparing for, or playing in, formal public performances.

There are a number of residents, particularly those living in and near Melgar, who have a special allegiance to Centro Social without actually having the status of full membership (indicated by the rights to hold office, participate in decision making, and play in public performances). Centro Social members explain that these "supporters" (my term) do not actually join because they do not have the time. But the boundaries of membership are fluid. People can and do pass from one type of role to another (for example, from active member to supporter), depending on the amount of time and energy invested in club activities during any given period.

Reasons for Belonging

In my experience, Centro Social is not a typical regional association in terms of the members' high level of activity, dedication, and unity. In regard to this institution, at least, there are vital reasons for belonging. At different times, for example, Centro Social has had a joint "emergency fund," the money being available to member families in times of crisis.[3] Help with home construction, child care, and the more amorphous but equally important "moral support" and feelings of belonging are ongoing benefits.

In 1987, Centro Social staked out a plot of unused land in Melgar. Although the project is still in the planning stages, the members intend to establish a community industry of furniture making and finishing. When I visited the site with friends during a visit in 1988, they remarked that the economic situation in Peru was becoming so bad that they hoped to start this communal enterprise as a source of future employment security for themselves and their children. They also had plans to purchase a community cemetery plot so that they could be buried together.

These activities, planned enterprises, and the roof raising described earlier must be understood against the backdrop of Tomás's stories of insecurity and isolation when he first arrived in Lima at the end of the 1950s (chapter 7). But they must also be seen in terms of the larger trend of migrant self-help networks created in the face of the general crisis of the Peruvian state, particularly during the 1980s.

While upward mobility within Peruvian society had always been difficult for people of rural highland background, at present the opportunity structures themselves seem to be crumbling and no longer hold out much promise generally. Unemployment in the formal sector has been estimated at 60 percent (Lewis 1990). To my knowledge, most of the Centro Social members continued in their same employment during 1990, but there was an estimated 2,000 percent inflation rate with little increase in income. During my last visit in 1988, and from letters and reports from friends since then, it is clear that the residents are having an increasingly difficult time just getting food on the table.[4]

The number of regional associations has continued to grow over the past decades along with the visibility of highland identity emblems, particularly music.[5] With the failing of the Peruvian state and economy during the 1980s, the Sendero Luminoso (Shining Path) revolutionaries and face-to-face self-help networks provide two major alternatives for reacting to the crisis. To my knowledge, Sendero has not gained acceptance among the Conimeño residents. The increasing number of clubs as well as the example of Centro Social Conima's planned economic activities suggest that grass-roots social organizations are perhaps being perceived, more and more, as the best option within a bad situation.

Members' primary stated reasons for joining Centro Social are to unite with other paisanos, to be part of a mutual aid network, and to preserve their Conimeño heritage. The members of Centro Social criticize those who have nothing to do with the associations for being ashamed of their highland heritage. The time factor was also frequently mentioned as a reason for noninvolvement. Some people suggested that the wealthier members of the Conimeño resident community were not involved because "they did not need to be"; thus they articulated the perception that the clubs are a source of actual social security for those who do choose to belong.

Decision Making and Social Style

Centro Social Conima has various offices to which people are elected on a yearly basis: president, vice president, secretary of acts, treasurer, secretary of advertising and public relations, social assistant, fiscal secretary, director of the ensemble, secretary of sports, and delegates to Central Folklórica Puno and the Federación de Sikuris and Sikumorenos. All these are held by men, with the exception of social assistant, a role that involves organizing food preparation for fiestas. In spite of the formal electoral structure, there are so many positions that they basically rotate through the membership regardless of ability. If the presidency falls to a less experienced member, he will fulfill the duties of his office but will seek advice from and defer to the opinions of older, more experienced men. Although Centro Social has a secretary of sports, during 1985 and 1986 the club never participated in athletic events.

Decision making and organizational meetings take two forms within the institution. In a more informal type of meeting referred to as 'reunions,' the men and women decide matters—such as work details for an upcoming fiesta—by implicit consensus, much as the people of the ayllus do. When more important issues have to be decided, a 'general assembly' is called. In both types of meetings Spanish is used exclusively, although the speech style differs between them.

The assemblies are extremely formal and use democratic decision-making processes such as majority voting, either by secret ballot or by a show of hands. In the assemblies, the president and secretary sit at a table at the head of the room. The president directs the meeting according to a formal written agenda, while the secretary records the minutes. The assemblies occur as often as once a week or as infrequently as once a month and must have a quorum. Only formal members are allowed to attend the assemblies, and I was able to go only after being voted in as an 'honorary member' and being given a certificate to that effect.

After the minutes are read and announcements made, issues on the agenda are introduced by the president, and concerned men and women may discuss them in turn, after being recognized. Usually the speakers will stand and address the membership, "Mr. President and distinguished members." Some members then go on to make their point using a formal, forceful speech style. This formality amazed me at first, given the close relationships among all the members and their usual relaxed ways of relating. As with Mario's words of thanks after the roof raising, however, a formal style of public speaking, resembling criollo ways of speaking, has probably been adopted to lend dignity and legitimacy to certain types of events.

On the whole, the assemblies proceed in a peaceful manner, but sometimes arguments occur, as well as direct criticism of individuals. One time, a member was harshly singled out for a misjudgment that augmented the failure of an event hosted by Centro Social. The president stepped in, saying, "The failure of the dance was everyone's responsibility, not the fault of one person. Since we all organized it, the responsibility is on all of us." The president's position was common for Centro Social and reminiscent of communal attitudes in the ayllus. But drawing public attention to individuals' faults, as well as abilities, also takes place frequently, and the residents seem more comfortable with this than their parents at home would be.

ORGANIZATION OF THE MUSICAL ENSEMBLE

The musical ensemble in Centro Social Conima has a social function, similar to that of the ayllu ensembles in Conima. It serves a unifying role and is a focal point for a community that defines itself in terms of actual bonds of unity. In the highlands, however, belonging to a community does not depend on performing music, and one cannot simply join a community by becoming a dedicated musician in its ensemble. For Centro Social, distinctions concerning insider status and rights vis-à-vis the larger resident community are maintained between actual Centro Social members and supporters based largely on musical participation. In Lima, then, musical performance has taken on even greater importance for signifying identity and social boundaries—because belonging to the association, "the community," cannot simply be assumed.

The Guía and Musical Goals

While the formal position of ensemble director rotates every year, one individual, Mario Cahuapaza, always remains the actual guía and director of the ensemble because of his knowledge and abilities; actually, the official director takes a leadership role only when Mario is not present. Mario was among the minority of residents who began performing music before leaving Conima. He states that he learned to play both in Conima and during his twenty-five years in Lima. On visits back to the district, he has made special efforts to study performance techniques and aspects of musical style so that he can lead his ensemble more effectively.

When asked why he decided to specialize in the Conimeño instruments in Lima, Mario answered succinctly, "To be directly connected [*vinculado*] to the people of Conima"; he mentioned nothing about the music or the enjoyment of playing itself. This answer, along with the ideas of 'preserving' and 'protecting' Conimeño culture, represents the orthodoxy about musical performance among Centro Social members. The use of music to link themselves with Conima requires that they reproduce the sound of hometown groups with all possible fidelity. It also requires an awareness of the aesthetic ideals of highland musical performance, and this is part of the knowledge that Mario and a few others have consciously sought through conversations and observations during visits home.

Mario is a particularly assertive, and at times dogmatic, guía who makes his will felt in most musical situations. The other members attributed much of the success that Centro Social has enjoyed to Mario's talent and strong leadership. Although people frequently become annoyed at the time, even his harsh criticisms of individual players are forgiven because the members share Mario's goal of perfecting their musical performance. His position as guía is thus the result of ability, self-assertion, and an implicit consensus that he should lead.

The explicit articulation of a hierarchy of musicianship and leadership, and the critical, dogmatic style of leadership itself, would be unacceptable in the ayllus; yet this style has proven effective in Lima. More often than not, Centro Social wins the formal sikuri performance contests that it enters in Lima. It has won first place in AJP's Tupac Katari contest a number of times in recent years. The members of Centro Social are extremely proud of their performance ability and the respect that it wins for their institution and for Conima. Since so many other non-Conimeño, and even non-Puneño, sikuris use the Conimeño repertory and style, Centro Social members feel it is particularly important that their ensemble, which actually represents Conima, be the best.

Instruments and Voicing

Besides strong leadership, other aspects of the musical organization have helped Centro Social members approach their goal of realizing the aesthetic ideals of highland performance, as they understand them. The tropas of instruments used by Centro Social belong to the institution and are kept by the president between performances. Since most people do not own instruments, Centro Social members play and practice only as a group. The institution's ownership of the tropas reduces one adverse effect of the ad hoc nature of highland ensembles; the instruments are purchased together and are consistently tuned.

In contrast to the situation in the ayllus, Centro Social's guía has complete control over ensemble voicing. At the beginning of each rehearsal or performance, Mario distributes the various voices according to the number of players, so that the group achieves the optimum balance. The residents did not make their own instruments before or during the period of my fieldwork, but rather contracted makers in Conima.[6] The members stressed the importance of using tropas made in Conima, since these were 'specially tuned' and allowed the group to reproduce the Conimeño style more faithfully.

REHEARSALS AND LEARNING MUSIC

Unlike the ayllu ensembles, which hold rehearsals only before, and as part of, a specific fiesta, Centro Social rehearses most Sundays when it does not have a public presentation scheduled (the main exception is the Christmas season, when family activities take precedence). Extra rehearsals can also be called on Friday and Saturday nights before a particularly important performance. In addition to providing opportunities to improve the members' playing, rehearsals are enjoyed as social occasions that bring people together on a regular basis. Along with festivals, they are, as one man noted, "the one time during the week that you can get together with paisanos and forget your work and your problems." The rehearsals usually take place at the home of Mario Cahuapaza. The description of a specific rehearsal follows, and should be compared with the discussion of highland rehearsals in chapter 3.[7]

On Sunday afternoon, several Centro Social members had already arrived at Mario's house by three o'clock. They sat in a circle on the chairs and benches that had been set up in the front room, which was, as yet, without a roof. Someone who had just returned from Conima had brought a cassette of sikuri music by Qhantati and Q'keni, recorded during the most recent fiesta there. Filomeno went home to get his cassette player. Tapes with the newest compositions from Conima are highly valued as the main source for Centro Social's own repertory. Having access to the most recent compositions is a point of pride for the residents; this represents a close link with hometown groups, and home.

For the next two hours, people arrived gradually and went around the circle shaking hands with those already present. As usual, only Spanish was spoken. As we waited for everyone to come, we enjoyed the new recordings.

201

Listening to Qhantati, one man exclaimed, "Qhantati is Qhantati, something special!" Others commented on the full, rich sound of the voicing and the large number of players. Another person nodded and said that Centro Social was at a big disadvantage because it usually had only around sixteen players, while many more were needed for a full ensemble. Mario commented on the improvisatory playing and identified one of the performers as Filiberto Calderón; others went on to discuss his virtuosity. As we listened, people hummed along with the newly composed tunes in order to begin memorizing them. A piece by another ensemble from Conima came on, and the group was criticized for not integrating the different voice parts very well and for the 'holes' in the performance.

The conversations about these ensembles resembled the discussions of this type that take place in Conima, suggesting that some residents are acutely aware of highland Conimeño aesthetics. These types of conversations provided an opportunity for the more knowledgeable members of Centro Social to share their understanding with less experienced players. The nature of observations made by different individuals—ranging from simple appreciatory comments to a more subtle analysis of the art of improvisation—became demonstrations of competence and a basis for authority within the group. While the group was listening to the tapes, someone went out to buy several bottles of beer. Upon his return, we drank in highland style, passing a single glass and bottle around the circle. Some of the members poured a small quantity of beer on the ground (ch'alla) before drinking, although no words were offered to the earth.

We listened to the music and socialized until around five o'clock, when someone suggested that we should play. People took the siku voices that they usually played out of the box, but because there were only fourteen members present, Mario suggested certain changes so that the ankutas and sanjas would be stressed. The group stood in a circle while Filomeno rewound the cassette and replayed a new Qhantati piece that the group had decided to learn. We listened to it several times, humming along; then, turning off the cassette player, Mario whistled the tune to the group. After a time, we began to play the entire piece, blowing softly on the panpipes. When most had learned the tune, Mario, who plays one of the two bombos, struck the drum loudly two times to indicate that we would now play the piece at full volume. At this point a blank tape was placed in the cassette machine to record our performance.

After we had played the piece, the members sat down to rest and to listen to the recording of their own performance. Mario and several others were not pleased, so the original Qhantati recording was played again in order to hear the difference. We circled up, ready to try again. Before starting, however, Mario turned to the sanja players (who were relatively experienced performers) and told them that they were playing too softly. He took up a sanja and demonstrated how it should be blown. He also cautioned a new player that the siku should not be overblown, and he turned to the other bombo player and scolded him for not striking the drum in the center, where the best sound is produced. Putting an ira and arca row together, Mario played through a difficult rhythmic section where the group had been faltering. These things said and demonstrated, the group began again.

During the next rest period, the performance just recorded was again compared with the Qhantati version; this process was repeated until the group had mastered the tune to Mario's satisfaction. One or two new pieces may be learned in this manner in a single rehearsal when new material from Conima is available. After the new tunes are learned, the guía or others in the ensemble suggest older tunes that need work or are being forgotten, and these are recorded and criticized in the same manner as is done for new material. The members sit down to relax and converse between playing the tunes, and sometimes beer is purchased for these times. During the actual rehearsing, however, people who talk or joke often receive sharp reprimands. Rehearsals usually break up around eight o'clock, although some people may linger on to listen to music, drink, and talk.

As a particularly important performance approaches, the guía drills the ensemble harder than usual, and all members are expected to show up for rehearsal. Ira-arca pairs that are found wanting are made to play individually before the rest and are then corrected by the guía, as was described for the "examinations" in the early days of Qhantati. If things are not going well, the criticisms can become quite pointed. For important performances, if newer players have not mastered their parts, Mario will ask them beforehand to play softly so as not to be heard. He also determines and rehearses the choreography they will use, such as walking in certain formations, before an important stage performance.

Although the socializing between pieces at Centro Social's rehearsals is similar in spirit to rehearsals in the ayllus, the musical activities are extremely different. In Conima, when old tunes were rehearsed, the musicians just played through their favorite pieces from past years—to warm up, and for enjoyment. There was no verbal commentary or correction of the performance, and tape recorders were certainly not used to recall pieces or assess the group's own performance.

Centro Social's rehearsals are strongly oriented toward achieving the maximum quality of performance, with emphasis on form—sound and choreography. The guía's criticisms, the 'examinations,' and the disciplined style of rehearsal are made possible by an explicit musical hierarchy operating within Centro Social, as well as by the members' shared concern with the quality of the artistic product over other considerations.

COMPOSITION

During rehearsals in the ayllus of Conima, people place a major emphasis on the composition of new pieces. Typically during rehearsals in Lima, however, the members of Centro Social do not compose music at all. Puneño residents sometimes explain their general lack of emphasis on composition in terms of insufficient musical experience and skill. A more fundamental reason suggested by some Centro Social members and other Puneño residents, however, involves the importance of music as an identity emblem and link with the home region. As one man explained, the 'ambience' in which people live greatly influences the creation process. The residents say that if they started performing too many of their own pieces, created in Lima, they would no longer "sound like Conima"—and that eventuality is something to be avoided at all costs.

Nonetheless, Centro Social members are very aware of the importance placed on composition and originality in the home region, and various musicians within the group are able to compose. In September 1985, Centro Social planned a trip back to Conima for the first time as a group, to perform in the patronal Fiesta de San Miguel (chapter 10). In the rehearsals immediately preceding this trip, Centro Social members gave primary attention to the creation and learning of their own original compositions. The flurry of creative activity was inspired by the fear that, as Centro Social members commented to each other, they would be laughed at if they returned home without any new pieces of their own.

Original sikuri pieces were indeed forthcoming. Mario composed two, and the oldest member of the group, Fabian Mamani, created a piece. During rehearsal, the composers presented their tunes to the ensemble by playing them solo. The compositions, however, did not go through the nonverbal correction process as is done in the ayllus; it appeared that the pieces were considered the individual property of the composers, rather than belonging to the group to be fashioned collectively. When several minor suggestions were tentatively made, the person addressed the composer directly and asked for his reaction. No changes were incorporated. I suppose that the members' general acceptance was necessary for the new pieces to be included in the repertory, but the pieces' acceptability was never questioned. The tunes were basically introduced and learned. With the exception of Fabian, the Centro Social members were apparently neither familiar nor comfortable with the group-creation process; they seemed largely content to leave the responsibility of composing to the few individuals who were able to do so.

Centro Social has other original pieces in its repertory; some of them were recorded on the group's own LP in the early 1980s in Lima. But these are rarely performed at important public occasions in the capital. For the Tupac Katari contest in November of 1985, for example, Centro Social specifically chose Qhantati pieces rather than the compositions that had just been created for the trip back to Conima. It is precisely for major performance occasions that ayllu ensembles in Conima place the greatest importance on original compositions. During the Encuentro Tupac Katari, however, the announcer made it clear that Centro Social was performing the music of "Qhantati Ururi de Conima"—information supplied by the residents and probably announced at their request. Thus, aside from their infrequent efforts to compose (such as for the trip home or for their record), the members of Centro Social primarily learn their repertory from tapes brought from Conima, usually of Qhantati pieces.

Centro Social members say that they specialize in Qhantati's repertory, rather than the music of other ayllu ensembles, because they prefer its compositions. The fact that Qhantati is highly revered and imitated in urban panpipe circles may also influence this choice. The fame of the hometown group strengthens the reference to "Conima" carried by Qhantati's musical style and repertory. In addition, Centro Social gains stature by linking itself, as a group of insiders, to Qhantati. Conimeño residents stated that only people from the district had the right to perform Qhantati's repertory and style. The other Conimeño clubs align themselves with Qhantati in the same way. The newest institution went as far as using Qhantati's name and claiming exclusive rights to its repertory—a point of major contention among the Conimeño clubs.

REPERTORY

Soon after my returns to Lima from the highlands, members of Centro Social, Unión Hilata, and Unión Progresista would visit to get copies of my most recent recordings from Conima, and to hear news of home.[8] During the first of these visits, I had offered to make copies of tapes recorded in other places such as Huancané and Moho, thinking that they would like to collect music from the neighboring districts as well. I was sorely mistaken. Not only did they not want copies of recordings from outside Conima (even though I usually supplied the tape), but usually they did not even want to hear them.[9]

Musicians in the ayllus of Conima feel free to adopt and shape music from many sources as the basis of their original repertory. Within the local purview, if a group such as Qhantati adapts a wayno from another region—for example, the well-known tune "Adios Pueblo de Ayacucho"—it still provides uniqueness and novelty in contrast with the other local ensembles, regardless of the fact that it is commonly performed elsewhere. The musical soundscape in Lima, however, is practically limitless, and the Conimeño residents want to "sound like Conima." It is interesting that after Qhantati started playing a version of "Adios Pueblo de Ayacucho," Centro Social began performing this piece as well, having learned it, as usual, from a Qhantati cassette recording. The members of Centro Social did not adapt waynos from other regions themselves, however, unless they had been previously sanctified by Qhantati.

The size of Centro Social's sikuri repertory is difficult to determine. The group has approximately twenty to thirty pieces ready to perform at any given time. Pieces fade in and out of the repertoire, but since Centro Social members keep collections of the original highland source recordings, a forgotten tune from years past can be relearned and reintroduced at will. Through the archiving of recordings, they have an ever-expanding body of music at their disposal. In contrast, musicians in the ayllus rely on memory to recall pieces from past years, and many tunes are forgotten over time, perhaps never to be recovered. Indeed, in spite of the common notion of the "ancient quality" of Andean music, some people in Conima described tunes as "old" if they were composed some ten years earlier; the stock forms and formulas guiding composition, however, have a greater time depth.[10]

The practice of archiving in Centro Social is analogous to the stockpiling of knowledge made possible by literacy and documentation. These mechanisms of accumulating knowledge have been a major feature of Western culture, and have been central to the creation and preservation of an artistic canon. As with the creation of a canon, Centro Social's access to cassette recordings by the 'masters' also generates a more static conception of "the piece," whereas reliance on memory in the ayllus favors continual variation and, in some senses, a greater need for constant creativity.

For Centro Social, the pieces performed most often during any given period will be the newest pieces composed by Qhantati. The residents also stress the performance of older esoteric pieces not currently in the repertories of the other Conimeño resident groups and Qhantati imitators. Thus they are concerned with distinctiveness vis-à-vis the other groups with which they interact in Lima; this concern is similar to highland attitudes. By stressing both the newest and the most obscure compositions from Conima, Centro Social is also demonstrating its strong links with home and an insider's knowledge, and this is important for expressing the group's identity as Conimeño, both publicly and for themselves.[11]

In addition to Qhantati compositions, Centro Social's sikuri repertoire includes a few pieces by Q'keni (the sikuri group from Huata), tunes from Conima's public domain, and some of its own creations. Centro Social performs the lento and ligero genres primarily, as well as a few imillani pieces for social dancing and stage performance. It also performs a version of the costumed satiri dance in formal presentations, and its repertory includes various marches, which are used for different types of processions.

Although Centro Social members put the vast majority of their energy into sikuri performance, they also perform five-hole pinkillus and tarkas— following highland custom—for Todos los Santos (pinkillus) and Carnival (tarkas and pinkillus), using the appropriate genres. For tarkas and five-hole pinkillus, tunes from any ayllu ensemble were used, and although new compositions were slightly favored, there was not the same importance placed on novelty as there was for sikuri music.

During 1986, Centro Social obtained its first tropa of pitus and, with some difficulty because of the embouchure required, began learning these instruments and the achachk'umu music. The members' lack of interest in six-hole pinkillus (as of 1986) may be related to this instrument's associations with particular religious and political occasions that are not relevant to the residents; whereas the distinctive nature of the costumed achachk'umu dance makes it particularly effective for stage presentations in Lima. Centro Social's gradual addition of musical traditions from home, the pitus most recent among them, is part of a larger trend of incorporating new and ever more distinctive elements of highland practice; the fiesta of Todos los Santos, discussed in the following chapter, is another example. This trend, like the earlier switch from sports to music among the clubs, may be understood as an index of increased self-confidence and greater value placed on highland heritage among the residents. This, in turn, is the result of changes in criollo-highlander power relations in the capital.

PERFORMANCE STYLE
Siku Playing

Centro Social's efforts to imitate Qhantati during rehearsals have resulted in a fundamental likeness between the two groups. The residents have mastered the sikuri style in terms of achieving group blend and the proper balance of voices, in techniques of blowing, and in most rhythmic and melodic aspects of the music. Centro Social sounds more like Qhantati than other ayllu ensembles within the district.

When I played my recordings of Centro Social for members of Qhantati and other people in Conima, they usually remarked with some surprise that the group had really become quite good and had mastered the style. This is all the more notable because highland Conimeños are not usually so forth-coming with compliments for other groups. Variably, people seemed to find it strange, humorous, regrettable, or some combination thereof, that Centro Social was mainly performing Qhantati compositions rather than its own music. In regard to the group's actual manner of playing, however, the general consensus in Conima was that Centro Social had developed its own unique style.

Curiously, while this was considered both normal and positive by people in Conima, Centro Social members typically interpreted differences in sound between Qhantati and their group as resulting from their failure to play well enough, or to 'capture' the piece accurately enough. Centro Social members do not always recognize the distinguishing style characteristics that would be perceived by people at home, perhaps because of less familiarity with the subtle levels of contrast used to mark style within the district. Unfortunately, people in Conima were even vaguer than usual in explaining what made Centro Social's style distinct. The usual response was simply that "they have a different way of playing" and nothing more. Based on the types of criteria and scale of contrasts used by highland Conimeños, however, some interest-ing differences are apparent when one compares Qhantati and Centro Social recordings.

Because of my stereotypic ideas of "the fast pace of the city," I had as-sumed that if there were any differences in tempo, Centro Social would perform faster. In fact, Centro Social usually performs the lento genre more slowly than Qhantati. Centro Social is fairly consistent in playing lentos between MM $\textstyle\int$ = 63 and $\textstyle\int$ = 66, as compared to Qhantati's usual range of $\textstyle\int$ = 72 to $\textstyle\int$ = 76. That Centro Social plays even slower than Qhantati, and certainly slower than Q'keni, is probably the result of the residents' emphasis on playing correctly; it seems to be an example of hypercorrection. I have heard Centro Social members criticize other groups in Lima for playing lentos from Conima too fast while noting that traditionally ayllu ensembles play pieces in this genre very slowly—the slow tempo being associated with 'profound feeling' and important to the essence of the genre. This idea, and perhaps their desire to demonstrate an insider's superior understanding of the tradition, may have led them to overcompensate. While the residents do not seem to be aware that they use slower tempos than Qhantati typically does, this is certainly a distinguishing stylistic feature that would be recognized by people in Conima (see chapter 2).

If we compare transcriptions of a single ligero composition as performed by Qhantati and Centro Social (examples 8.1 and 8.2), a few other stylistic differences emerge against a backdrop of overall likeness. First, Centro Social uses a different chuta cadence figure. This is not original to Centro Social; it is a formula that Qhantati once used. In addition, in these particular examples, Centro Social holds more pitches over the stressed beats (played on the bombos) than Qhantati does. This might be interpreted as another case of hypercorrection, based upon the residents' acute awareness of holding over the beat as a fundamental feature of the Conimeño style. Centro Social members often took pleasure in criticizing Limeño sikuris, who are less likely to do this correctly. In Centro Social's rendition of another Qhantati piece (examples 8.3 and 8.4), however, the treatment of "tied" pitches is identical; indeed, it would be difficult to hold over more pitches than Qhantati has already done.

The drumming in Centro Social's sikuri ensemble is another obvious feature that differentiates its style. In Conima, panpipe ensembles define their drum patterns with soft and hard strokes, but often the dynamic differences are not very pronounced. As fiestas move into full swing, contrasts between the loud and soft strokes become blurred further; with the rising excitement and competition, hard strokes may become the rule for the performance of ligeros. Although the patterns become relatively fixed for a given piece in Conima, they also tend to flow organically with the melody, and the volume level for different types of strokes changes throughout a given performance depending on the spirit of the guías and other drummers. In fact, for Qhantati, the drums express the emotions of the group most clearly and, in a sense, are important in shaping the level of animation for the siku players.

In Centro Social, however, drum patterns are memorized from the tapes. As a result of the residents' concern for playing correctly, the soft/hard stroke distinctions are more highly accentuated, and the group tends to use drum

Example 8.1. Sikuri Ligero Genre by Qhantati Ururi

dynamics less expressively than Qhantati. Especially in formal staged or contest presentations, when consciousness about playing correctly runs high, consistent dynamic levels for the hard and soft drum strokes are usually maintained throughout a given performance. The result is that Centro Social's bombo patterns tend to produce a stiffer, more mechanical feel, clearly differentiating its performance style from that of Qhantati.

Similarly, because of less musical experience, few residents have mastered the improvisatory *requinteando* technique (iras improvising on the arca part and vise versa). Mario and several others only occasionally attempted impro-

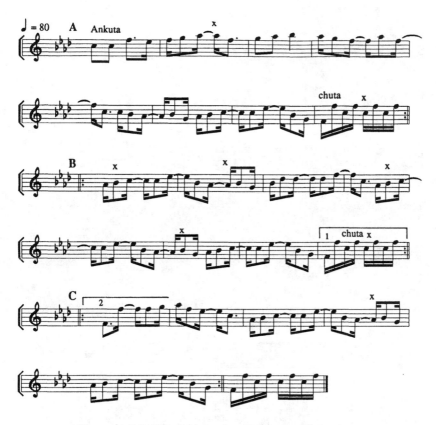

Example 8.2. Sikuri Ligero by Centro Social Conima
(x = variation from Qhantati)

vising, and it was not a prominent aspect of Centro Social's style during my period of research. Other practices that enrich Qhantati's performances—such as the simultaneous use of different chuta chuta figures, various voices' holding pitches for different lengths, and the simultaneous performance of melodic variations—were also used less frequently by Centro Social, perhaps because of the way the residents learn and think about the music. Centro Social members take fewer individual liberties within performance generally, and the attacks of the different voices coincide fairly precisely. This dearth of individual variation results in a less dense overlapping of instruments and,

Example 8.3. Sikuri Choclo by Qhantati Ururi

again, a stiffer sound. Centro Social also produces a cleaner sound; the contrast is that of a stricter parallel polyphony versus Qhantati's richer, more independent polyphony.

As the members of Centro Social themselves often comment, the smaller size of their group often hinders full voicing. Also, because of their relative shortage of personnel, Centro Social members tend to blow their panpipes harder and louder than the musicians in Qhantati in their effort to produce a powerful performance. This manner of blowing hinders the production of

Example 8.4. Sikuri Ligero Genre by Centro Social Conima
(x = variation from Qhantati)

the dense, breathy sound that characterizes large ayllu ensembles. Of course, depending on the community and occasion, the size of ensembles varies in Conima as well, and when fewer musicians are present there is a similar result.

In a comparative study of Qhantati and Centro Social performances of the same pieces, Larry Ward has observed that Qhantati "seems to prefer a brighter, higher sound, with more players on the higher voices" (personal communication, 1990). When assigning voice parts, Mario seems to stress the lower voices; in Qhantati the older, more experienced players take the higher voices.[12]

Finally, the most important distinction between the two groups is that Centro Social's playing lacks the fluidity, spontaneity, and expressive power of Qhantati at its best. While this is only my own perception, the members of Centro Social frequently say that "Qhantati is something special" and indicate that the 'masters' have some quality that is difficult to 'capture.' Indeed, the creative spark that generates improvisation and simultaneous variation is difficult to capture through imitation. In the recordings of Qhantati the details of variations are even difficult to hear, explaining why Centro Social has been slow to add this element to its performances. By the same token, given the ad hoc character of Qhantati and other ayllu groups, as well as the drinking and the spirit of Conimeño fiestas themselves, Qhantati's performances can become loose and expressive to the point of oblivion.

Again, different priorities and ideas about what musical performance is all about seem to be at the heart of the matter. What Centro Social lacks in spontaneity, numbers, and experience, it makes up for in the disciplined coordination of the ensemble. It is a highly rehearsed group that has played together, with few personnel changes, for over twelve years under the firm guidance of a conscientious guía. Its instruments are consistently tuned, blended, and balanced. Extremely self-critical, the members pay close attention to musical detail, and they carefully follow the main precepts of highland performance techniques as they understand them. Central Social members do not improvise or allow for much variation, but they also rarely get off-track in their more precise public performances. These attributes have led to a highly successful career in Lima, where others apparently share this same value orientation for musical performance.

The major differences that emerge between Centro Social and Qhantati are analogous to those between revivalists, or the faithful followers of a canon, and the original creators of a tradition; the creators have the luxury of taking a freer, less self-conscious attitude toward the music they play. The Conimeño residents are not revivalists in the sense of "reviving" a tradition, as much as they are reviving a type of music—still practiced elsewhere—in their own lives, and for very specific reasons. From their point of view, their more conservative approach to performance is necessary to create the musical-emblematic link with "Conima" that they so highly value. Finally, their emphasis on musical precision is reinforced by their participation in performance contests in Lima, where the judges and audiences share a similar orientation (see chapter 9).

Pinkillu and Tarka Playing .

Most of the comments about siku playing apply to Centro Social's performance of five-hole pinkillus and tarkas as well. These traditions do not demand the same number of performers as sikuri ensembles, so Centro Social is not put at a disadvantage in this respect. But Centro Social has not placed equal emphasis on learning and perfecting these traditions as it has on sikuris—as the members will be the first to admit. What results is a less faithful copy of the original.

In tarka performance, this is particularly evident in the rendition of the rhythm. In Conima, the syncopated rhythm of the melody is "punched out" and followed by the bass drum; at their best, Conimeño tarka ensembles "swing" in the North American sense of the word. Centro Social's tarka performance is often more tentative, as is its drumming, and the group rarely achieves this feel.

Centro Social members seem even less comfortable playing five-hole pinkillus and cajas. The two caja players in the club do not hold the rolling ♪♪ figure that makes highland Conimeño ensembles 'run' (that is, groove). Instead, their patterns tend to be uneven and uncertain, and they sometimes interject straight eighth-sixteenth note patterns that interrupt the music's flow. In the pinkillu rehearsals that I attended, no one attempted to correct the caja players. Considering this in light of the sikuri rehearsals, where all mistakes came under close scrutiny, I conclude that no one in the group was aware of, or at least able to demonstrate, the proper drum pattern.

That Centro Social members are not equally familiar with all the hometown instrumental traditions underscores the fact that most of them did not grow up playing the Conimeño traditions; the great majority learned to play later in life as a part of the club's activities. Since sikuri music became the most popular indigenous Puneño wind tradition in Lima, Centro Social simply placed more emphasis on learning about, and perfecting, panpipe performance. This is true for most other Puneño clubs that specialize in the indigenous wind instruments. Centro Social's emphasis on sikuri music over all the other hometown instrumental traditions contrasts with the situation in Conima, where, in fact, tarkas and five-hole pinkillus are considered very important because of their association with the two most popular Conimeño fiestas—Carnival and Todos los Santos.

MUSICAL CHOICES AND THE MEANING OF PERFORMANCE

In their efforts to imitate Qhantati's sikuri style and repertory faithfully, Centro Social members have made conscious choices to depart from highland musical processes and aesthetic-ethical dispositions. Their self-critical style of rehearsing with a cassette recorder, their acceptance of the guía's control and criticism, and their lack of interest in composing are but a few examples. Faithful imitation is itself a divergence from highland musical priorities. The residents are aware of these differences but see them as consistent with their own goals and situation.

This is an example of the same pragmatism that led to the decline of interest in the achachilas and Pachamama: the residents no longer need these forces because "they now work for salaries." The Centro Social members often explain their virtual abandonment of the Aymara language, even in the home, in the same terms; Spanish is simply more useful in the capital. Andean music in Lima during the 1980s, too, had become useful as its acceptance continued to increase, as networks for joining with other resident groups were developed, and as the venues for public performance expanded.

Yet not all the residents' practices hinge on pragmatic choices or strategies. It seems to me that many of the aspects of social style and musical practice that distinguish Centro Social members from people in the ayllus—different modes of speaking, interacting, and composing; the use of hierarchical organization to get things done; attitudes about the individual vis-à-vis the collective; attitudes about coca—are the result of more subtle processes of socialization. For example, I would guess that after years in Lima, Centro Social members rarely notice the hierarchical style within their musical ensemble. Being reared in a hierarchical society myself, I doubt that I would have noticed it either if I had not had the ayllu ensembles as an immediate basis for comparison. Many of the residents have lived in Lima for twenty-five years. Almost every day they are involved in situations in their workplacec and on the street where the hierarchical nature of social relations is reinforced. Over time, such experiences come to define normalcy and habit.

What is striking in the case of Centro Social is that members' ways of operating, which are the results of both conscious choice and gradual absorption, have allowed them to maintain a closer fidelity to the *sound* of hometown music than would have been possible if the values of originality and egalitarianism, as well as the ad hoc ensemble structure, had been main-

216

tained. As the Conimeño residents recognize, highland Conimeño social style and values would hinder their ability to keep strict control over the musical sound they produce. Given the varied soundscape in Lima, and the fact that many of the residents had not performed Conimeño music before joining the regional associations, hierarchical control and great effort were probably necessary if they were going to reach their primary musical goal of "sounding like Conima."

The residents' ways of operating are thus a successful adaptation, not to the city per se, but for achieving their own musical goals. These goals ultimately involve the creation and maintenance of a community and self-help network in Lima. The members of Centro Social are so adamantly "Conimeño" not just because they were born in the district; rather, they have found it useful to represent themselves in this way. Other Conimeño residents who are unaffiliated with the clubs have taken a different path.

Musical performance is very important to Centro Social members. It is a concrete activity around which they can unite, as was soccer during Centro Social's first five years as an institution. More important, the music serves as a powerful and recognizable connection with "Conima"—not the place, but the unifying symbol for the resident community. When Centro Social members say that they perform the music to preserve and protect 'Conimeño culture,' they do not mean the language, religious beliefs, social style, or agricultural techniques; actually, I think that they are talking about themselves.

NINE

The Framing of Experience: Festivals and Performance Occasions in Lima

IN LIMA, PINKILLUS and tarkas are played at festivals by Centro Social Conima and other Puneño clubs during the Carnival season and for Todos los Santos, but the residents devote their major energy to sikuri performance. Throughout most of the year, Centro Social's stature within the larger Puneño resident community is determined by the quality of its sikuri performance, which is judged almost on a weekly basis in 'folklore festival' contests organized by the regional clubs.

The popularity of sikuri music, relative to the other Puneño winds, is most immediately related to the early activities of Asociación Juvenil Puno (AJP) and the urban panpipe movement. Before the 1970s, for example, Unión Progresista Conima had apparently played the different wind instruments on a more or less equal footing, as was the case back home; but by 1985, Unión Progresista gave the same specialized attention to sikuris as the other groups did. One time, a resident from Moho told me that his sikumoreno club really should be specializing in five-hole pinkillus, since this instrument was most important in his highland community. He said the club played sikumorenos because this tradition was more accepted in Lima, and he expressed the fear that "people might laugh if we played pinkillus."

The greater acceptance of panpipe music over the other indigenous winds in the capital is partially due to the smoother, less strident sound of panpipe ensembles. Following AJP's lead, Puneños' selection of the double-row panpipe as an identity emblem is also logical because it is a particularly distinctive instrument that is specifically associated with their region in the national consciousness. (Vertical and side-blown flutes are used all over the highlands and therefore would be less useful in this regard.) Sikuri performance thus met two important criteria for selection of an identity emblem within a situation of social conflict: it represented the path of least resistance in relation to the dominant group's aesthetic dispositions while still being a distinguishing emblem. This idea is fundamental to my analysis of why AJP specialized in panpipe music in the first place, although I must emphasize that AJP members do not accept this interpretation.[1]

MUSIC, "FOLKLORIC FRAMES," AND THE REPRESENTATION OF HIGHLAND IDENTITY IN LIMA

At a more general level, the emphasis on musical performance to express highland identity in Lima must be traced back to the indigenista movement of the 1920s. The performance of highland music (albeit in a stylized form) got an early foot in the door as an acceptable public activity while other realms of practice, including indigenous languages and religion, coca chewing, and clothing styles, continued to be disparaged in everyday public contexts in cities.

The earlier acceptance of Andean musical performance in Lima may be related to the "folkloric frames" that were created around it, and to the indigenistas' constructions of Andeans that took place through performance—for example, their emphasis on 'Inca' high culture and on musical styles that were guided by criollo aesthetics. In the spirit of romantic nationalism, the images of Andean culture projected or controlled by indigenistas in urban performances (such as estudiantinas and Qhantati's trips to Lima) were appropriated to signify "nation" or "region," rather than serving as emblems of the indigenous peasantry per se. Incorporated in this way as 'national folklore,' Andean music was thus rendered less threatening as marker of cultural difference, and as a resource that could potentially challenge dominant cultural norms (see chapter 5).

The "folkloric frame" itself (involving a stage, a contest, a master of ceremonies, the very concept *folklore*) contributed significantly to the hegemonic process of incorporating highland arts into the dominant society. Both conceptual and physical, frames are metacommunicative devices that define how social action that takes place within them should be interpreted (Abrahams 1977, 1986; Bauman 1975; Bateson 1972; Goffman 1974). They thus supply the potential for social control (orthodox definition) as well as supply a circumscribed space for taking certain kinds of liberties not acceptable in "normal" practice (such as insults delivered after a wink within a joking frame, or yelling "Fire!" from the stage within a theatrical frame). Although usually less extreme, many social frames are analogous to a psychiatric ward, where patients feel freer to act "crazy" because they are expected (allowed) to, and yet are contained by walls, convention, and social definition. The walls surrounding 'folklore' festivals in Lima fulfill a similar function.

Through the use of by now traditionally established folkloric frames in

Lima, contemporary highland musicians are simultaneously rendered less threatening or objectionable to Limeño sensibilities ("it's OK, it's *only* a folklore performance") and freer to express themselves. With the exception of highland crafts production for urban and tourist markets, similar legitimating frameworks were not created around other types of highland cultural practices within the dominant society, and hence social sanctions against them (in the form of derision, for example) remained strong.

Like the Puneños' choice of the siku as an identity emblem, the migrants' emphasis on musical performance itself represented the path of least resistance in relation to dominant social attitudes, while still providing distinguishing identity markers. Dominant social attitudes in the cities that favor the use of folkloric frames for musical performance, but that still discourage other highland cultural practices such as using coca, enacting a t'inka, or speaking Aymara, seem to have deeply affected Conimeños and other Puneño residents. This is illustrated by the descriptions of Puneño performance events in Lima that follow.

FESTIVALES FOLKLÓRICOS

The most common type of Puneño performance occasion in Lima is referred to by the residents as *festival folklórico* or *desfile folklórico* (folkloric parade). These events have been fundamental for shaping the Conimeño residents' attitudes about rehearsals and musical performance. The festivals are held weekly throughout much of the year in rented walled-in vacant lots, parking lots, or school patios, although the members of Central Folklórica Puno can now use that institution's locale for performance events.

Club Networks and Festival Organization

The festivals are organized through the ayni networks of umbrella organizations such as Central Folklórica Puno (CFP) and the Federación de Sikuris and Sikumorenos; in fact, the heart of these organizations' activities is coordinating the year's festival cycle. Each member club has the right to sponsor one fiesta folklórica during the year within a given network, and the schedule is determined democratically by the member-club delegates. The sponsoring club pays the expenses, collects a cover charge from all participants (both performers and spectators), and earns money from selling food and drinks.

Ayni, a term used by the residents, is the basis for the clubs' participation. The term refers to a traditional highland system of reciprocal exchange, in which a specific type and quantity of labor must be returned in kind. In CFP, for example, there were approximately forty member clubs in 1985. Each holds a fund-raising festival within the annual cycle, with one or two festivals sponsored by CFP itself; thus, there will be forty-two festivals within a given year. Centro Social Conima might perform at the festivals of twenty member clubs, and these institutions should reciprocate by performing at Centro Social's event. The success of a given club's festival is therefore directly related to the number of ayni relations they have maintained by performing at other clubs' events. A club ensemble that performs infrequently will find an empty house on the afternoon of its festival.

Beyond the number of ayni relations established, clubs make decisions about the type and quality of other institutions' performing ensembles. Often, a club chooses the festivals in which it will participate based on the groups it wants at its own festival. Since more ayni relations are sought with the better ensembles, the degree of participation in a club's event is also affected by its ensemble's quality of performance. Finally, groups tend to maintain more ayni relations with other clubs involved in the same type of performance tradition (either the trajes de luces or panpipes); there is some crossover, however, since variety at a festival is also desired.

The Festivals

The festivals are scheduled for Sunday afternoons. The host club arrives at the locale in the morning to set up the barbecues and tables where food and drink will be sold. The performance space is swept clean, and a public address system and a table with trophies are put in place. Typically, a few guest clubs begin to arrive around midafternoon to warm up, playing panpipes or brass-band music in casual alternation with the other groups around them. The members of the guest clubs keep to themselves, drinking and playing. Cassettes or records, blaring through the loudspeaker, fill the gaps when no groups are performing.

Throughout the afternoon, during both recorded and live music, the host club's master of ceremonies talks unceasingly in Spanish over the PA system, to 'animate' the people. He welcomes groups as they arrive, identifies the names of those presently performing, narrates the contest held later in the afternoon, and makes constant small talk and jokes. As the afternoon progresses and the beer takes hold, different people take over the microphone to say whatever comes to mind, some imitating the fast speech styles and phrases used by actual radio announcers. One time a man went as far as periodically repeating a popular radio beer commercial during his stint on the mike. The overall effect is that of sportscasters at a football game. The

221

loud, constant patter is considered an important element in the sonic mix of the festivals.

At about five o'clock, the emcee announces through the scratchy PA that the formal performance contest is about to begin. The order of participation is established by the host club, which also provides the judges and trophies. Without a doubt, the majority of performers consider these contests the most important feature of the festivals; the majority of guest clubs arrive just before the contest begins, and all the performance clubs that attend participate. Panpipe performers who wear uniforms (such as *chullus, ojota* sandals, and short ponchos) and members of the trajes de luces clubs put on their costumes just for the contest. As the contest commences, the ensembles line up in the designated order and according to three categories—sikuris, sikumorenos, and trajes de luces (accompanied by brass bands).

Each group performs in turn for about ten minutes in the performance space in front of the judges' table. In some locations, such as school patios, there are bleachers for the audience to sit on; otherwise the spectators encircle the performance space or stand around and behind the judges' table. Sikuri groups enter with a march. When their entrance piece is completed, the musicians often bow to the judges and audience and then play a lento for the centerpiece of their performance and a ligero for their exit, as is prescribed. Members of the audience applaud the groups after each piece, but awareness of the performances is quite variable—some people pay close attention and attempt to judge the groups themselves, while others chat, eat, drink, and walk about as if nothing were going on. Throughout and above it all, the master of ceremonies talks on; he discusses each group and praises the wonders of Puneño 'folklore' at such a volume that it is sometimes difficult to hear the music. People whom I questioned did not mind the emcee's commentary; most people hardly seemed to notice it.

After the contest, trophies are awarded to the winners in the different categories—trajes de luces, sikuris, and sikumorenos. For Centro Social's 1985 festival contest, three aspects were considered by the judges: the quality of the music, costumes, and choreography. Comments made by the Centro Social judges later indicated that fidelity to highland style for the given tradition had also been a criterion for assessing the groups. For example, a sikuri ensemble was criticized for using choreography that was considered too slick and modern for the rural sikuri tradition. The judges said that the choreography—which used small, rapid steps and a good deal of body motion—was more in keeping with the sikumoreno tradition, which, indeed, had probably been an influence. This group was excluded from the winner's circle (first, second, and third prizes are awarded for each category).

When the contest is concluded and the trophies have been awarded, the club ensembles begin performing freely in different corners of the lot or patio, and a general social dance takes place, with couples and chains of dancers doing the wayno in Puneño style (or Carnival dances during that season) around their favorite ensemble. While the formal contest is considered the most important feature of these festivals, the playing and dancing that follow it are clearly the most spirited. During these times, the spectators become participants and the festivals allow people to let go and "forget about their problems," as residents frequently commented. It is during these times, which may last two or three hours, that the feel of the urban festivals comes closest to the spirit of highland fiestas; but this period of celebration is much too short to approach the cathartic release made possible by fiestas in the highlands, which usually last for days. Since the residents have to get up early the next morning for work or school, they begin leaving around eight or nine o'clock.

Club Organization of the 'Festivales Folklóricos'

A strong tradition since the 1970s, the 'folklore' festivals are organized for social reasons and are, allegedly, the major way that the clubs raise funds. The profits tend to be rather small, however, after money is paid out for advertising, a city tax, renting a location and a PA system, and buying trophies. The success of a given festival is gauged by the number of people who attend, and the general public is certainly welcome. During the 1984–86 period, the festivals of working-class clubs were advertised primarily on radio programs specifically directed to the Puneño resident population (such as "La Voz del Altiplano" on Radio Agricultura), on fliers, and by word of mouth. Consequently, the majority of people that came were Puneños, and they were often members of, or attached to, other participating Puneño clubs.

For their 1985 festival, Centro Social Conima wanted to attract a larger audience than usual in order to raise funds for its trip to Conima for the Fiesta de San Miguel in September (see chapter 10). Consequently, the members considered expanding their advertising campaign to various daily newspapers. When the secretary of publicity reported the cost to the members during an assembly, however, it was decided that most people who "go to these types of events" do not really read the papers, and the idea was scrapped.

223

Centro Social is not alone in this opinion. For several months in 1984–85, I surveyed two newspapers daily (*La República* and *El Comercio*), as well as the "Voz del Altiplano" radio program. During this time, the higher-class provincial- and departmental-level Puneño clubs used only the newspapers for publicity and diffusing information, while the district and community-level institutions used only AM radio. The class structure that reproduces itself in club organization and participation in club events correlates with the different types of media used for advertising (AJP's Encuentro de Sikuris Tupac Katari being a notable exception).

During my stay in Peru I attended at least thirty club-network festivals. The overall form of the festivals was amazingly identical, with one important exception: throughout most of the year the clubs that use the Puneño wind traditions play panpipes, but during the Carnival season they change to tarkas and pinkillus because, as they say, "it is customary." During the six weeks of this season, the women of the clubs and other supporters dress in highland Carnival attire and dance as the musicians perform in the festival contests. Carnival in Lima, then, uses the standard 'festival folklórico' format that I have described, with the exception of a substitution of the musical-dance traditions performed. Groups that perform brass-band music and trajes de luces dances often continue with these during Carnival. For the rest of the year, only the men perform panpipes in the festival contests, although women join in more informally during the social dancing that concludes the festivals throughout the year.

Performance Contests

The formal performance contests featured in the residents' festivals are an urban innovation. In Peru, they may be traced back at least as far as Lima's 1927 Fiesta de Amancaes as a product of the indigenista movement and President Augusto B. Leguía's cultural policies. Leguía himself was involved in organizing the first 'folklore' (highand music) festival contest at Amancaes in 1927 (Vivanco 1973:34; Turino 1988). This tradition has since been diffused throughout the highlands, even to small rural towns. In the highlands, these events are typically organized and judged by vecinos,[2] and I have witnessed various occasions where mestizo aesthetics have directly influenced indigenous performers through the opinions of the judges. In such situations, I view performance contests as an important mechanism for mestizo control over indigenous performing arts. In the highlands, they are rarely a means of "preserving" Andean arts, as is often asserted by official cultural institutions (such as the Instituto Nacional de Cultura) and the vecino organizers of such events.[3]

The case is somewhat different, however, among the lower and working-class regional clubs in Lima, which supply the judges from their own ranks. They maintain control over their performing arts and judge them according to their own aesthetic dispositions.[4] This in no way implies, however, that these dispositions represent a "continuity" with rural-highland aesthetics per se. That the Centro Social judges penalized a sikuri group for "modernizing" its choreography during the 1985 festival has more to do with the residents' conservative approach to highland arts than with the spirit of innovation typical of ayllu musicians in Conima. Within a constructed canon of "highland tradition," then, strict imitation actually enhances success in the contests, even though imitation runs counter to the values of the highland musicians being canonized.

Winning contests is quite important to the regional club musicians I know; the contests are the primary way that participating clubs gain status in the eyes of the larger Puneño resident community in Lima. In this sense the urban contests are similar to the musical competitions between communities within highland fiestas; in most other respects, however, the contests differ. In the urban competitions, the judges' decisions—not the consensus of the community—are final. The club ensembles are judged within a ten-minute span, not over the course of days. They are judged on the formal aspects of their performance alone (sound, choreography, and costumes), according to quality and canonized concepts of tradition. The manner of staging and judging the urban contests indicates, and reinforces, an abstraction of musical performance *as form* from the total gestalt of a fiesta situation.

In my view, this conception of music is *the* major difference between the Conimeño residents and the musicians in the ayllus of Conima, and it, in turn, influences many of the residents' musical practices, including their manner of rehearsing, learning, and performing music. This conception also resembles the attitudes of Qhantati's vecino directors during the group's early days, and the musical results are similar.

Puneño residents' choice to focus so much attention on the formal contests within their festivals (as opposed to, say, modeling their weekly events on highland fiestas) illustrates the lure of institutionalized urban frames for highland performing arts. The emcee, the trophies, and a stagelike performance setting (sometimes for a sit-down audience) are framing devices that may be valued by the residents precisely because they link their perfor-

225

mances to other established urban venues. The residents' acceptance of the term 'folklore' for their own cultural practices—derived from indigenista, state, and international academic discourse—serves a similar framing, legitimating function. In contrast to AJP and Limeño-student panpipe groups, lower- and working-class Puneños are frequently uncomfortable performing on the streets of Lima outside of sanctioned performance frames. This observation, as well as the state's role in constructing its own images of highland performing arts, is illustrated in the following descriptions of government-sponsored performance events in Lima.

GOVERNMENT-SPONSORED FOLKLORIC' EVENTS

At different times, and for historically specific reasons, the Peruvian government has taken an interest in Andean performing arts as part of its efforts to forge hegemonic links with the peasantry and highland migrants. Leguía was directly involved in developing showcases in Lima for highland music and dance in 1927 and 1928 (at the Fiesta de Amancaes); President Juan Velasco's Inkari festival falls within this same tradition (see chapter 6). There were also a number of government-sponsored highland music events in the capital during the second half of the 1980s, reflecting politicians' recognition of the migrant population as a potent political force after democracy returned in 1980.

Between January 1985 and June 1986, four major government-sponsored performance occasions were held; Centro Social Conima participated in two of these. The Conimeño club was enlisted by the Instituto Nacional de Cultura (INC), through Central Folklórica Puno, to participate in two 'folkloric parades' through the streets of downtown Lima. One of these was held in the context of the INC's National Congress of Folklore. Regional clubs from all over the country and Limeño student groups performed regional music and dances for an enthusiastic crowd that lined the streets. Centro Social performed sikuris, and some of the members wore satiri costumes. They did not actually perform the satiri dance drama, portraying Conima's agricultural cycle, however; the costumes were worn primarily to make Centro Social's ensemble distinctive.

Centro Social participated in a similar parade through the streets of downtown Lima during President Alan García's "Week for the Integration of Latin American Culture" (SICLA) in April of 1986. This event, to foster Latin American unity, involved well-known artists, musicians, and writers from Caribbean and other Latin American countries. Performances of the Chilean/pan-Latin American *nueva canción* and the Cuban *nueva trova* musical traditions were featured prominently; concerts of contemporary and classical academic music were also originally scheduled as part of the event. Musicians of rural-popular and indigenous traditions, however, were glaringly absent from the original SICLA program.

As an afterthought, perhaps in response to criticism, García scheduled a 'folkloric parade' of highland Peruvian music and dance as part of the SICLA festivities. The INC officials had to scramble to secure regional club participation at the last moment, and they offered various inducements to the clubs—promises that were not kept. To the members of Centro Social, the SICLA festivities were indicative of the government's attitude toward the resident communities and their culture. Several voiced the opinion that they had been treated like second class citizens and that the government favored 'commercial' (specialized, professional) music over theirs. The government's use of and attitudes toward highland arts and migrant performers were equally clear in another official event, "The Anniversary of Lima."

THE ANNIVERSARY OF LIMA

On the evenings of January 17 and 18, 1985, the Izquierda Unida (United Left) municipal government sponsored two nights of music in celebration of the 450th anniversary of the founding of Lima. The main events took place in the Plaza de Armas, the administrative and symbolic center of "Old Lima."

On the first night, a stage was set up on the steps of the governmental palace in the plaza, and a program of *música criolla* was televised. The *vals* (waltz) *criollo*, performed with Spanish guitar, *cajón* (wooden box played as a drum), and rich, powerful voices, filled the square. Once the music of working-class neighborhoods and bars in the capital, the vals criollo has become the nostalgic emblem of "Old Lima"—Lima before the highland invasion (Lloréns 1983). It is a nationalistic emblem for those Limeños who still wish to see Lima as the nation.

The second evening's program, labeled a desfile folklórico (folkloric parade), was the United Left Party's tribute to the large portion of the capital's population that now hails from all over the highlands. For this evening's celebration two stages were built. One, in the nearby Plaza San Martín, was dedicated to performers of the professionalized wayno style created during the 1950s and 1960s. Here country stars such as the Princesita de Yungay performed between 9:00 P.M. and 1:00 A.M., backed by professional string bands and Junín-style orquestas.

The center of the action was located in the Plaza de Armas. A huge stage for the "música y danzas folklóricas" was set up across the square from the

227

governmental palace steps where música criolla had been performed the night before. The participants for the stage performance in the Plaza de Armas had been enlisted by the government in two ways. Well-known artists were contracted through the INC. In addition, two weeks before the event an ad had been run in the newspaper, *La República* as an open invitation for artists and regional club ensembles to take part. Interested parties were to send a representative to city hall to fill out a data sheet on their group; a week later, ensemble representatives were to return to city hall for instructions and to draw lots determining the order of performance. According to an acquaintance who attended the meeting, around thirty-four ensembles were represented.

Crowds surrounded the stage in the Plaza de Armas to watch the performance and, perhaps equally important, the filming of the televised portion entitled "Perú canta en Lima" (Peru Sings in Lima). The TV cameras and lights not only framed the event for the viewers at home but also indicated to those of us in the plaza where our attention should be cast. The televised portion of the program privileged certain performing groups: the order determined by lots at the city hall meeting was not honored, and apparently the groups contracted for the event were given pride of place.[5]

Thirteen acts were filmed for television:

1. A police band performing a mestizo wayno in the Junín *orquesta típica* style (harp, violin, saxophones, clarinets);

2. Baile Folklórico Nacional, performing a couples' social dance, the *marinera limeña* (contracted professionals);

3. Máximo Damián and his scissors dance ensemble performing *dansaq* (Ayacuchano residents, contracted professionals);

4. A Limeño student group enacting a peasant dance from Canchis, Cusco;

5. Unidentified ensemble performing a dance from Piura on the north coast;

6. Baile Folklórico Nacional performing the costumed "Danza de los Incas" (same performers as number 2);

7. Limeño student group performing the Puneño costumed dance "Los Tucumanos" (a representation of Argentine mule drivers);

8. Brisas del Titicaca performing "La Diablada," the most famous Puneño *trajes de luces* dance, accompanied by a sikumoreno ensemble (contracted semiprofessionals);

9. Todos los Sangres, a Limeño-student sikumoreno ensemble performing in the Tacna style;

10. A group of children doing a children's dance from the north coast;

11. Balseros del Titicaca (a lower- and working-class Puneño regional club) performing "La Diablada" accompanied by brass band (same dance as numer 8);

12. A children's dance group performing "Los Chunchitos" (costumed dance representing jungle Indians);

13. A Limeño university ensemble performing a dramatic representation of an Ayacuchano agricultural dance.

Balseros de Titicaca was the only working-class regional club to perform on the TV program. Along with Máximo Damián, and perhaps some of the police and university students, they were the only participants of rural high-land background. The rest of the performers presenting stylized versions of Andean arts in, and for, the national view were children, high school and university students from Lima, and contracted professionals. The performance of the student groups could be likened to U.S. high school students dressing up as Plains Indians and doing a version of a war dance.

In Peru, this type of staged 'folklore' performance dates back to the days of indigenismo, but remains current in schools and mestizo cultural institutions throughout the country. It is particularly striking that the Baile Nacional Folklórico performed twice before the cameras, while many grass-roots regional clubs waited in the wings. Like the students' performances, the Baile Folklórico's choice to present the indigenista-style "Danza de los Incas" indicates the persistence of romantic-nationalist images of Andean culture within the mainstream society. In the end, the television program was not "Peru singing in Lima" as much as it was a certain official segment of Lima singing its version of the highlands and of Peru.

Street Performance during the Anniversary Celebration

After the TV cameras were turned off, the attention of the crowd in the plaza became divided between the continuing stage presentations and the action on the opposite side of the plaza, where two sikumoreno and three sikuri ensembles were performing freely for large, excited groups of dancers in the street. The street playing was not part of the programmed event, but it was certainly more lively than the staged enactments. While three working-class sikumoreno clubs from Yunguyu, Puno, waited patiently for access to the stage, the ensembles involved in the street performance were all Limeño-student ensembles who had chosen not to participate in the official Anniversary activities.

Members of one of the middle-class Limeño groups explained with pride that their performance for street dancing was more in keeping with highland custom than playing on stage. Speaking with members of one of the working-class Yunguyu clubs from Chucuito, Puno, waiting to get on stage, I was told that they had aspirations to make a record and to become well known in Lima. Perhaps they saw the TV broadcast as a good way to get publicity. Even when it became clear that they would not get on the broadcast, however, they did not move from the lineup, and after playing on stage they did not join the street performers; instead they packed up and went home.

The Urban Panpipe Movement Revisited

Ten sikumoreno and sikuri ensembles performed during the Anniversary celebration. Although traditions from many highland and coastal regions were represented in the Plaza de Armas, large-ensemble panpipe groups outnumbered any other single tradition five or ten to one—indicating the strength of the urban panpipe movement at that time. Only three of the panpipe groups were known district-level clubs (Yunguyu). Brisas used a fourth unidentified Puneño sikumoreno group on stage. The remaining six ensembles were Limeño groups, only one of which (Todos los Sangres) chose to perform on stage; none of the highland club ensembles performed in the street.

Regardless of the makeup of the different ensembles, the presence of ensembles playing "Indian" music for street dancing in the Plaza de Armas of Lima represents an astounding change over what could have occurred there even two decades earlier. Puneño residents often point to the performance of panpipe music in the capital as a significant indicator of social change. As one man from Moho remarked, "We Puneños, through the regional clubs, have begun to change the culture in Lima. We have begun to influence Limeño-criollo culture. It used to be that we provincianos and our culture were not accepted in Lima, but now there are even sikuri ensembles performing in the *center of Lima, in the streets!* We Puneños have made Lima change even more than the people of the central highlands."

Panpipes were indeed being played in central Lima. During the Anniversary, as in most instances that I observed, however, it was Limeños, not Puneños, who were doing the performing in the streets outside of officially sanctioned performance frames—AJP being the oldest and most notable exception. Puneños have changed Lima; the fact that some young Limeños want to play panpipes at all supports this. Puneño residents' reluctance to express themselves outside of officially sanctioned performance events, however, suggests that the constraints created by racist and classist prejudice are still at work.

'Folkloric' Frames

When left to themselves to organize their own public 'folkloric festivals,' the Puneño clubs reproduce the same legitimating devices provided by the government (the stage, the emcee, the label 'folklore'). While it is true that these frames provide a kind of safety, allowing Puneños to express their identity and heritage in Lima, reliance on them (that is, reluctance to perform without them) reduces the potential of using such expressions to contest their subordinate social and political position. In this case, 'folkloric' performance frames are as much mechanisms of control as they are liberating.

The members of AJP have long recognized the importance of playing panpipes outside of sanctioned contexts. In keeping with the comments quoted above about "changing Lima" through panpipe performance, some of AJP's activities have been culturally revolutionary; the members have asserted the right to express their Puneño identity openly and freely. The middle-class Limeño sikuris have not had to face ethnic and class prejudice on a daily basis; hence, they too are freer to perform when and where they like.

Lower- and working-class Puneños have, understandably, been slower to follow suit. While they no longer perform only among themselves behind closed doors, as was the case before the 1970s, they are still constrained by criollo prejudice. After having changed from sports to music, shedding the need for 'folkloric' frames is simply the next door in a long series that lower-class residents will have to pass through to achieve social equality. An important aspect of this struggle involves transcending their own attitudes that represent forms of "internalized domination."

The Anniversary of Lima celebration is a good illustration of how the state attempts to construct and control images of highland Peruvians and to articulate displays of cultural difference to the state, thereby projecting the idea of national unity. As Stuart Hall has suggested, hegemony does not imply the disappearance or destruction of cultural difference; it is the construction of a collective will through (by incorporating) difference (1991b:58). The lower- and working-class Puneños' reliance on sanctioned performance frames illustrates the potency of this strategy. Imagery production flows from both the uncontested "commonsense" view of things and, in some cases (such as advertising and particular political discourses), a

231

conscious manipulation of imagery to influence how people perceive reality and see themselves. This, in turn, shapes behavior as well as what *can* be thought, done, said, and contested, and hence is fundamental to political control (Gramsci 1971; Bourdieu 1977:15).

The orthodox images (and marginality) of Andeans that were projected during the official Anniversary of Lima celebration are reinforced daily by the schools, the state bureaucracy, and the media. Yet, given the social and economic crisis that enveloped Peru during the 1980s, the ideological positions of the ruling elites were unsure and conciliatory, and they were increasingly being contested by lower-class groups. AJP boycotted the Anniversary. The members of the Conimeño, Moheño, and other Huancaneño clubs with whom I spoke simply had no interest in attending. On other occasions when there was some incentive, all these groups have participated in government-sponsored events. For the Anniversary celebration, however, there was apparently not enough incentive—and this includes perceptions of a link with the United Left Party or with Lima itself.[6] By way of contrast, in 1985 members of Centro Social Conima went to tremendous effort and expense to travel back to Conima to perform in the patronal festival of San Miguel, which, by coincidence, was referred to by the residents as "The Anniversary of Conima" (see chapter 10).

CENTRO SOCIAL CONIMA: LIFE-CYCLE FIESTAS

In addition to performing at club festivals and government-sponsored events, Centro Social's ensemble provides the mainstay of music at life-cycle celebrations within the associated Conimeño resident community. For these occasions—including roof-raising fiestas, weddings, first haircutting ceremonies, and, occasionally, birthday parties and funerals—only sikuri music is performed, and for some of these events playing panpipes represents a new tradition. For example, when the beloved founder of Unión Progresista Conima, Hugo Saravia, died, he was carried to the grave in a procession with sikuri music and buried with a pair of panpipes. In Conima, music is not used for funerals or birthday celebrations in the ayllus; and pinkillus, not sikus, are used for roof raisings.

The first haircutting celebration, a welcoming of children into the community, is a pre-Columbian Andean ritual that is carried over from the highlands and is reproduced in Lima in a very traditional fashion, including the use of sikuri performance. In contrast, weddings among the residents in Lima do not incorporate the elaborate wedding rituals used in the ayllus (Turino 1987:339–44). Instead, they follow the criollo-Occidental style of wedding, even including the first dance to a recording of the "Blue Danube" waltz. The use of panpipe music—lentos and ligeros for dancing—at Centro Social weddings is the only point of resemblance with weddings in the ayllus.

Todos los Santos

With the exception of first haircutting ceremonies, Todos los Santos (All Saints' Day) is the only fiesta among Conimeño residents in Lima that is primarily modeled on the corresponding highland festival. Both in the highlands and among Conimeño residents in Lima, family and close friends hold a special celebration for a person three years after his or her death. As in Conima, the residents hold the festival in a public cemetery as well as in the home of the deceased.

Although there had been a number of deaths in the Centro Social community before 1983, until that time the residents had celebrated Todos los Santos, as one member put it, "only by lighting candles and laying flowers on the graves like everybody else." In 1983 one of the founders of Centro Social passed away. In that year the residents began celebrating the fiesta in a manner based on highland Conimeño tradition: placing food and decorations on the grave and accompanying the celebration with five-hole pinkillu music. When I asked Centro Social members why they had not celebrated Todos los Santos in this way before 1983, some said that the death of this particular friend inspired a deep collective emotion that led to the more elaborate fiesta. Others told me that as more Conimeños, and Puneños in general, moved to Lima, they lost their shyness about practicing such customs openly in the cemetery.

Along with Carnival, Todos los Santos is usually cited as the most important fiesta of the year by the people of the ayllus in Conima. Marking the beginning of the rainy season, the celebration is traditionally accompanied by five-hole pinkillu music "to cheer up the family of the deceased." Although relationships with the ancestors are maintained throughout the year by the performance of t'inka rituals in the ayllus of Conima, the coca and food placed on the grave during Todos los Santos are especially important for providing sustenance for the spirit in transition within the three-year period after death. A few people in Conima told me that coca is the only thing the spirits consume.

The importance of the three-year fiesta cycle, and the significance of feeding the spirit during Todos los Santos, is widely recognized in the altiplano region. According to Bastien, the people of the nearby Charazani area of Bolivia divide their universe into *junaq pacha* (the heavens), *kay pacha* (this world), and *ura pacha* (the netherworld). In the three-year journey from the netherworld to the heavens, the new spirits are most closely associated with the living during the middle year (Bastien 1978:171). Similarly, Hickman has observed that Aymara speakers of Chucuito, Puno, feel it is important to give more food to the spirit during the central year of the three-year fiesta cycle (1975:66).

Among the residents in Lima, coca and t'inka ceremonies over the grave and at the home of the deceased have been replaced with Catholic prayers and the recitation of Ave Marias. This is a significant change, since the t'inka rituals and feeding the spirit with coca are central to the meaning of the fiesta in Conima. The residents' substitution of rituals is understandable given their aversion to coca use and their lack of involvement with highland religious ritual and beliefs.

In all other major respects, however, the residents followed highland custom in their Todos los Santos celebration. They placed abundant amounts of food, including fruit, sweets, and bread (fashioned in the shapes of people, animals, and other things), as well as a high arch made of cane, over the grave. As in Conima, guests at the celebration in Lima carried some of the food away in bags brought for this purpose, reminding me of the custom of trick-or-treating in the United States. During Todos los Santos in 1985, the final year of the three-year cycle, Centro Social played five-hole pinkillus and cajas while walking around the grave of the club founder. Later in the afternoon we went to different parts of the cemetery to honor the graves of other friends and relatives with music. Centro Social, along with Unión Hilata, was among a handful of ensembles (including a third Huancaneño pinkillu group and two orquestas from Junín) in the immense cemetery of Nueva Esperanza (New Hope).

Located on the margins of the pueblos jóvenes in the southern cone of Lima, Nueva Esperanza is a huge region of barren sand and stone, stretching up into the foothills of even more barren mountains. Nothing green grows there. It is dotted with thousands of grave markers: piled stones, simple wooden crosses, and more elaborate white cement tombs. As we first entered the cemetery in 1985, a depression seemed to fall over our group, and I heard several Centro Social members mutter softly: "This is the cemetery of Peru's poor," "I want to die in Conima," "I do not want to be buried in this paupers' graveyard," and "We will all end up here."

Once safely inside the cemetery gates, Centro Social began to play, and the pinkillus and drums reverberated strongly against the gray mountains and the damp morning fog. As we walked to different parts of the cemetery to play over other Conimeño graves, strangers from different highland regions begged us to come and play over the grave of their loved one. They requested songs from their highland home which we either did not know or were unable to play on pinkillus. They were grateful for the music that we did provide, but sometimes seemed disappointed that we could not create the musical bond with their homeland—a bond that they wanted and, perhaps, needed at that moment.

During Todos los Santos, as at other times, the residents' use of highland music and custom had less to do with the specific meanings of those practices in Conima than with their power to draw the community together in Lima and to celebrate its special character. Particularly in the vast setting of Nueva Esperanza, where families from all over the nation came to honor their dead silently, anonymously, and alone, the presence of the Centro Social community and the sound of the pinkillu music seemed to soften the Conimeño residents' thoughts of the inevitable future and to make the present time and place seem more like home.

T E N

From Lima to Conima:
The Residents Return Home

PERHAPS WITHOUT BEING fully aware of it, I had developed different public personas and styles for interacting with the residents in Lima and the people in Conima. In the highlands I felt greater latitude to shape the roles I would play, since people there simply had fewer ideas about how and who I should be. Because the rural Conimeños recognized that the place that I came from must be very different indeed, they accepted a greater degree of naiveté. This facilitated taking the role of student and neophyte, which, in fact, was what I was, and that role in turn made research easier.

During my first trips to Conima, I rented a room in town and ate at the home of a woman who cooked for the schoolteachers, the police, and other people who were not from the district. On one occasion this woman took a trip, and, by coincidence, the stores in town that sold canned food were also closed for a few days. Unprepared for this, I went for a day and a half without eating. Getting up my courage, I went to Filiberto's home and, after some initial small talk, told him that I was hungry. On the following day he helped me move my belongings into his home, where I stayed for the rest of my time in Conima. My need on this occasion brought an important barrier down. This was the beginning of a deeper stage of our friendship, which depended, among other things, on the *possibility* of maintaining a reciprocal relationship.

The people I became close to in Conima seemed secure as individuals and as members of a community. They were on their home ground, and they were the majority. At first they ignored me, but when it became apparent that I would be around for a while, they began treating me as a *h'ake* should treat others. Mainly this involved reciprocity, but also the expectation that I would chew coca, do manual work, miss home and family, feel the cold, take a drink, enjoy playing music and dancing, like to eat, and get angry but not show it. If I made mistakes or was a nuisance at times, I was also enjoyed for the novelty that I provided.

In Lima, things were quite different. Even after a twenty-year residence, the Conimeños there were not on their home turf. While there were a huge number of highlanders in Lima, they were still excluded in many ways from the "majority" society. They had developed defensive ideas and prejudices about *blancos* (white people) and members of the upper classes, and, understandably, they placed me in these categories. Through sustained training they had been taught how to interact with me—with formality and distance. For a long time they called me Señor Tomás and were uncomfortable inviting me into their homes. I got beyond such barriers with friends in Lima, but it took longer, and vestiges of formality were more difficult to break down than in the highlands.

Whereas my novelty wore off among people in Conima as time passed, I became a novelty among the residents only after they got to know me personally. In contrast to their ideas about blancos, I could work hard in roof raisings, I was dedicated to learning their music, but most important, I kept coming back—to rehearsals, to performances, to weddings and first-haircutting ceremonies, and simply to talk and share experiences. I participated constantly in a community that was defined by participation. Nonetheless, the tension produced by a feeling that I had to continually prove myself never left me because of the stereotypes held by some Centro Social members. Members of minorities must feel a similar, though much more intense, tension on a daily basis when living within racist societies.

In Lima, many things revolve around money, and in all our minds there was no doubt that I would always have more than the members of Centro Social. Unlike my experience in Conima when I went without eating, in Lima I was never in material need. The basis of reciprocity in the highlands—to address an equal humanity—is much more difficult to establish or maintain in cross-class relationships in Lima, because the differences in wealth are so startling. Among people of the lower classes, reciprocity with people of higher stations is replaced by accentuated public respect, and private tactics to see what can be gained from any particular interaction. These types of attitudes have evolved over centuries within the context of the paternalism fostered by members of elite groups, especially large landowners, bureaucrats, the clergy, and local officials. These attitudes colored my relations with some of the Conimeño residents as well.

Although the Conimeño residents did not know the details about *etnomusicólogos*, they were sure that I was expert at something; yet I continued to ask them questions. Their ambiguity about my level of understanding and, hence, how I should be understood was compounded by the fact that I was also studying with the 'masters' back in Conima. This gave me a certain prestige in Centro Social and made me valuable in various ways (for example, my carrying of information, tapes, and goods back and forth). While my performing with ensembles in Conima was an asset for attracting spectators in the district fiestas, the members of Centro Social were sometimes criticized by other resident groups for letting a gringo join them. As it turned out, for the more important public performances I was not invited to play with Centro Social, whereas the members of Qhantati always welcomed me, even in the contracted performance in Huancané.

The emphasis in North American society on being an individual and "being one's own person" obscures the degree to which other people's perceptions and expectations of us—within larger patterns of social determinations—shape our personal style and self-view within specific situations. I was different, just as my relationships differed in the two major locations of research, and all of this influenced the way I perceived things.

Traveling back and forth between Lima and Conima, I kept the two experiences, the two sets of loyalties, and my two personas largely separate. This remained possible until September of 1985, when fourteen members of Centro Social decided to travel back to Conima for the first time as a group to perform in the patronal Fiesta de San Miguel. I did not travel with Centro Social to Conima, but had gone ahead of them a few weeks earlier. Perhaps only semiconsciously, I did this to create some kind of autonomous space for myself within a social situation where people usually had to align themselves unambiguously with one group or another. During San Miguel, the two groups I was affiliated with came together in a dramatic and telling way.

The Fiesta de San Miguel

San Miguel (September 29), the mestizo patronal fiesta of the district, is celebrated in the town of Conima. Like mestizo patronal fiestas all over the highlands, it included a major market, a mass, and a procession for the patron saint. Conimeño resident groups from highland cities—Puno and Juliaca—returned to perform trajes de luces dances, including the elaborate "Rey Moreno." Four brass bands performed during the fiesta in 1985.[1] In Conima, as elsewhere in highland Peru, the patronal fiesta was organized and sponsored by town mestizos, and the local people of the ayllus took part, if at all, in auxiliary roles under the direction of vecinos. As in the Fiesta de la Cruz in Huancané (chapter 5), the vecino sponsor in Conima traditionally contracts a sikuri group to accompany his entourage; in 1985 the sponsor passed over Qhantati Ururi for Q'keni Sankayo of Huata, allegedly because of ties between his wife and Huata.

In other mestizo patronal fiestas in southern Peru, a great deal of emphasis is placed on the religious significance of the celebration. This was not so in Conima. While a mass and procession of the saint took place, even the Conimeño vecinos in town stressed that the fiesta was basically for fun as well as being good for business. The members of Centro Social referred to the fiesta as the "Anniversary of Conima" more frequently than they mentioned San Miguel. For them, it seemed to involve a kind of religious celebration of place—of home—more than of the Catholic saint.

For this festival in Conima, it is typical for resident groups from nearby highland cities to return to perform, and even for a few residents from Lima to visit as individuals. But the return of Centro Social Conima as a group for the first time was the cause of excitement. In the weeks before the fiesta, people in Conima commented frequently that "los limeños" were going to return—for so the residents were called by the people in Conima. One reason for excitement was that Centro Social members had sent messages ahead that they would present a number of gifts to the town and ayllus, although they did not specify what the gifts would be.

THE RESIDENTS IN CONIMA

The members of Centro Social looked exhausted from the trip when they first arrived; they were warmly greeted by family and friends in the plaza. I could not help noticing that they also looked unusually affluent, a remark that appears a number of times in my field notes. This impression may have been created relative to local dress, but the residents also looked different from how they typically appeared in Lima. They stepped off the bus sporting new clothes, and several men wore expensive leather jackets. I was reminded of Tomás's story about being inspired to travel to Lima by his visiting uncle's shiny black riding boots (chapter 7), and of the image of relative affluence that returning migrants often project in their home communities.

As I spoke with one of the Centro Social members shortly after their arrival, he noted that although he had not been back to Conima for ten years (among the group that came, this varied between five and twenty years), he felt no strangeness in being there. The strangeness that Centro Social members and I felt about being back in Conima together began the following day when we attended a wedding fiesta in Huata.[2]

I had gone to the wedding fiesta with a friend from Putina, and five members of Centro Social showed up later on their own. During weddings, a special t'inka ceremony is held for the bride and groom with coca, cigarettes, and alcohol, and during the last part of the ritual the coca and cigarettes are shared among the guests. By this time, people in Conima were used to the fact that I enjoyed chewing coca, but I remember feeling distinctly uncomfortable accepting the leaves as the members of Centro Social looked on. Standing some distance away, they laughed and spoke among themselves as they watched me, and then it was their turn. Visibly embarrassed, the Centro Social members, too, consumed the leaves, but after they had been left to themselves and I had joined them, they continued to tease each other, and me, about chewing coca.

The sharing and enjoyment of coca is fundamental to being considered a socialized adult in the ayllus, and it is an important indicator of indigenous identity in Conima, as elsewhere in the Andes (Allen 1988). It is also one of the indigenous practices that come under the most severe criticism from mestizos and criollos, especially in cities. Although I understood the residents' avoidance of coca in Lima, during the wedding, with no mestizos present, I was struck by how deeply they had internalized criollo and mestizo attitudes about coca chewing. This, of course, should have come as no surprise. I had known the residents less than a year, yet my self-consciousness about chewing coca in their presence showed how rapidly I had been influenced by the attitudes and expectations of others whose opinions I valued and whose help I needed. How much more profoundly must they have internalized Limeño attitudes toward coca chewing, and toward so many other things, after living in the capital twenty years?

The residents' reaction to coca chewing simply points to the subtle ways that dominant ideologies are absorbed and how they affect self-identification and social practice. It also underscores the complex nature of the residents' own discourse about respecting and maintaining Conimeño indigenous culture, a discourse that underpins and is selectively articulated through their musical activities in the capital.

THE GIFTS

On the following day, September 27, Centro Social sponsored—through the purchase of trophies—a girls' volleyball championship in the morning and a soccer match between the Conima and Tilali high schools in the afternoon. Both events drew big crowds and were major successes for Centro Social Conima. Around midday, Centro Social made a formal presentation of a Peruvian flag to the primary school in town—one of the gifts that had been promised for Conima.[3] The presentation ceremony was attended by the mayor, school officials, officers of the police force, and other vecinos. The Centro Social members sat formally in a line and were honored with speeches. After a formal, prepared speech by one of the Centro Social members, two women from the club presented the flag to a group of school-children. The children then recited poetry and performed a version of "La Diablada" traje de luz dance for the visitors. Although the majority of the residents had been born in the ayllus, on this occasion they dressed, behaved, and were treated as vecinos *by* vecinos in Conima. In Lima, the members of Centro Social identify themselves as campesinos (indigenous peasants).

On the morning of the opening day of the fiesta (September 28, the *vísperas*), the members of Centro Social, with about eight members of Qhantati, walked to the small town hall in the plaza playing panpipes. They had come to make their major presentation to the town, the gift of a clock. They continued playing inside the town hall for several hours while they waited for the usual battalion of officials and vecinos to arrive for the ceremony. The local dignitaries were late. The official presentation consisted of the same type of formal, flowery speeches that had occurred the day before for the presentation of the flag at the school. Afterward, the ensemble, under the banner of Centro Social Conima, continued to play lentos and ligeros primarily belonging to Qhantati. More Qhantati members joined in as the residents grew tired or became involved in conversations with the dignitaries and in other types of celebrating.

Around three o'clock, the Fiesta de San Miguel began in earnest as the participating dance groups entered the plaza. Accompanying the fiesta sponsor's entourage, Q'keni Sankayo also entered the plaza playing sikus. The members of Centro Social and Qhantati went outside the town hall to watch, but did not play since they were without an official role in the opening procession to the church.

Meeting around ten o'clock the next morning (September 29, the principal day of the fiesta), the residents of Centro Social and the collaborating members of Qhantati took a turn around the plaza performing sikuri music and then waited at the town hall, where another presentation to the town— a Peruvian flag—was to be made. It seems that the residents had tried to organize too many ceremonies, for this time not even the mayor showed up. When the mayor finally did come, two hours late, he said that he could not find the keys to the town hall, and the presentation ceremony was not held.

The residents were hurt and annoyed. They had looked forward to, and talked about, these gift-giving ceremonies with great anticipation before and during their trip; this moment of triumph had been taken from them. I suspect that the vecinos in Conima were particularly busy on this, the principal day, of San Miguel, and moreover, that they had hoped that more than flags and a clock would be offered. It was a disappointing moment for everyone involved. Further disappointments awaited the residents on the following day during a formal meeting that they had organized with Qhantati Ururi.

CENTRO SOCIAL MEETS QHANTATI URURI

Over the years, the name Qhantati Ururi had achieved a kind of mythic significance within urban panpipe circles. Members of AJP described their journey to Conima and their meeting with Qhantati in 1977 as if it were a pilgrimage back to the sacred source of their music and their evolving identities (chapter 6). Following AJP's lead, members of young Limeño, Puneño, and Huancañeno sikuri groups traveled to Conima to record Qhantati and other ensembles during Easter fiestas. Conimeño resident groups in the cities of Puno and Lima had taken the name Qhantati Ururi to express their close link with the 'masters,' and to enhance their prestige among urban sikuris. For many years during their rehearsals, the members of Centro Social had lived and breathed recordings of Qhantati. These cassettes were the model and inspiration for Centro Social's repertory and style, and the music on these recordings provided a tangible bond with home.

Many urban sikuri groups looked to Qhantati as the 'legitimate' creators of the music that had become such an important part of their lives. The members of various non-Conimeño groups (AJP included) knew, however, that they did not have Qhantati's sanction to perform the music.

On the morning of the last day of the Fiesta de San Miguel, September 30, the members of Centro Social requested a special meeting with Qhantati Ururi at the home of a Qhantati member, to strengthen and formalize their relations with the famous hometown group and to pay them homage. In this meeting, perhaps more than at any other time during the residents' visit, major differences in social style and ideological orientation between Centro Social members and the older people of the ayllus became apparent.

A Multiplicity of Styles

The Centro Social members came to the meeting as a group. The Qhantati members who arrived early were primarily older men, as well as several middle-aged and younger members from Ayllu Sulcata. After waiting quite a while for other Qhantati members to appear, Mario, the guía of Centro Social Conima, finally stood up and initiated the meeting by delivering a composed speech in formal Spanish. He began by giving a ceremonious greeting to Qhantati Ururi from the members of his institution, and he stated that there were four points he, as representative of Centro Social, wanted to discuss.

First, Mario informed them that Centro Social was primarily performing Qhantati compositions and wanted to know whether his group had permission to do so. Second, he told the members of Qhantati that a new club in Lima was using their name, and Centro Social members wanted to know if this was acceptable. He explained that they in Centro Social Conima had never even considered taking the name because they placed it in such high regard and that, indeed, Qhantati Ururi was the "patrimonio de Conima" (patrimony of Conima). Next, Mario told them that certain non-Conimeño groups in Lima had actually recorded Qhantati pieces on LPs without giving credit.

The final issue on the agenda was that the members of Centro Social were concerned because Qhantati had been dormant for too long; the residents wanted the famous ensemble to become more active again. Since the members of his club lived in Lima, Mario told Qhantati, Centro Social could act as the "bridge between [the people] in the countryside and the government," and he explicitly mentioned the Instituto Nacional de Cultura. Mario concluded by saying that Centro Social members wanted to help Qhantati in any way they could, and then asked Qhantati members to respond to the issues raised.

After Mario sat down, an awkward silence fell. The older Qhantati members looked at the ground. After what seemed like a long time, another Centro Social member asked permission to speak and was recognized by Mario. This man stood up and told the assembly that Centro Social was dedicated to performing the music of Conima and diffusing it more widely. As the "sons and grandsons of Qhantati," he said, they had the right and duty to do this, but others had no such right, and he specifically mentioned AJP. Mario then asked Filiberto, as the 'director' of Qhantati, if he would reply to the statements that they had made. The other Qhantati members nodded in agreement that Filiberto should speak—they certainly did not want to.

From his seat, speaking in a soft voice as he looked at the ground, Filiberto greeted the residents in Spanish but then immediately switched into Aymara. He said that Qhantati was not in agreement with other groups' using its name, and also that the Conimeños in Lima were welcome to play Qhantati's music. After this brief response, an uneasy silence returned.

Shortly thereafter, however, Aldemir and Eugenio, two younger vecino members of Qhantati who held the posts of president and secretary, arrived. Mario seemed relieved, and to my great surprise, he stood up and began the meeting all over again, as if nothing had been said. As he got up to speak, he asked everyone else to stand with him so that they might begin formally. The older Qhantati members, somewhat mystified, half rose and then sat back down. Both Centro Social members who had spoken previously repeated their words almost verbatim. Then without coaxing, Qhantati's president, Aldemir, rose and spoke at length in Spanish.

He thanked the members of Centro Social for their kind words and for their respect for Qhantati. Broaching the subject of Qhantati's recent inactivity first, Aldemir observed that Lucio Calderón had been president of Qhantati for many years and had been successful in keeping the group both active and disciplined. Since Lucio's death, he said, Qhantati's presidents had not been able to do much for the group because of a lack of funds; he noted that any support the residents could provide would be greatly appreciated.

Aldemir then turned to the issue of other groups' using Qhantati's name. Because the members of the different regional clubs in Lima were related to various members of Qhantati (significantly, his own brother was a founder of Qhantati Ururi Base Lima), Aldemir hoped that the different Limeño clubs would band together to help Qhantati and not feud among themselves, since this might cause tension in Conima. Aldemir said that his group was aware that resident ensembles in different cities were using the name Qhantati, but, contradicting Filiberto, he felt that having different bases of the same institution could be a source of strength. He specifically mentioned that AJP's multiple bases had given that group broader financial support.

Aldemir announced that, with the "junta directiva" of the ensemble, he would create a series of rules that Conimeño resident groups would have to follow if they wished to use the name Qhantati Ururi. He added that Centro Social was welcome to perform Qhantati music, but then launched into a discussion about how non-Conimeño groups should not record Qhantati's material. Aldemir told the gathering that he planned to register copyrights with the Instituto Nacional de Cultura in Puno—an idea similar to that stated in the Federación de Sikuris charter (see chapter 7).

A Multiplicity of Agendas

The meeting then became a dialogue between Qhantati's two young vecino members and Centro Social Conima. The older Qhantati members remained silent, clearly uncomfortable in the situation, and perhaps relieved that they would no longer be called upon to speak. Before Aldemir and Eugenio arrived, a few younger men from the ayllu were already present, but they had not presumed to speak before their elders. The young vecinos felt no such compunction—nor did they ask for confirmation from the older men, as they usually did when talking at private Qhantati gatherings. Given the protocol established by Mario, Aldemir and Eugenio were in their element; they simply took the leadership role as a matter of course.

Knowing that some of the older members of Qhantati regarded AJP as a rival, I was struck that Aldemir mentioned that group as a model for having multiple institutional bases. Filiberto and older Qhantati members never fully understood why other groups would even want to use their name, repertory, and style. To older musicians who have a localist purview and feel that imitation demonstrates a lack of integrity, the argument that Conimeños should form multiple bases of the same institution at the national level—in imitation of AJP!—must have seemed like strange reasoning indeed.

That Aldemir cited AJP as a model, however, illustrates rural vecinos' distinct attitudes regarding the vanguard of the urban panpipe movement (see chapter 6). Like Aldemir's plan to register copyrights with INC, his interest in institutional affiliates at the national level suggests a familarity with the style of political-cultural organization developed by highland residents in cities.[4] Indeed, Aldemir may be correct in his assessment of the types of strategies needed for cultural and social institutions to remain viable in contemporary Peru, as social life at the local-rural level becomes more diffuse.

While Aldemir accepted AJP as a role model, the Centro Social member who spoke second in the meeting criticized AJP's use of Conimeño style and repertory. This was not a condemnation of borrowing other groups' material per se—after all, Centro Social had been playing Qhantati compositions for years, and this meeting was the first time the group had asked permission to do so. Rather, this man's comment points to a specific competition over Conimeño music, as an identity emblem, within urban panpipe circles in Lima. Centro Social had called this meeting to stake a claim to an insider position with Qhantati vis-à-vis both non-Conimeño groups and Qhantati

Ururi Base Lima; the latter group had allegedly asserted that the Qhantati legacy was its alone. Centro Social members had hoped to be enlisted as the avenging angels for the illicit use of the sacred name but were disappointed when Aldemir made it clear that Qhantati would handle it.

An intriguing feature of Mario's speech was the mention of Qhantati's recent inactivity. Qhantati had been playing steadily in hometown fiestas, in Huancané, in La Paz, and in other highland towns on contract for vecino fiesta sponsors (see chapter 5); apparently the residents had some other type of activity in mind. Mario's suggestion that Centro Social could create links between Qhantati and the INC in Lima indicates a desire to enhance Qhantati's diffusion and fame at the national level, especially in Lima. This in turn, would boost Centro Social's own prestige, as a Conimeño group, in urban panpipe circles. That a group of outsiders, "los limeños," had criticized Qhantati members to their face by saying that they had been inactive, however, certainly must have seemed out of line to the older musicians.

Whereas Filiberto simply ignored the comment (a typical way of dealing with problems in the ayllus), Aldemir agreed with the observation. Like other vecinos in Conima, he explained Qhantati's "recent inactivity" and declining discipline by the death of Lucio, Qhantati's former vecino president, thereby linking the group's earlier success to mestizo sponsorship and to its 'folkloric' performances in certain types of sanctioned contexts. Aldemir also saw the residents' concern about Qhantati's inactivity as a means of soliciting outside financial support for his own program for the ensemble: a return to the vecino-directed glory days.

Filiberto and the other core musicians were not averse to recognition and fame in urban panpipe circles, but by the time of this meeting, too many people were using Qhantati's music and name to serve too many agendas that simply did not fit with the older musicians' own goals for musical and dance performance. Filiberto told me at various times that he would like to create a totally new sikuri style and start a new ensemble with a different name because "now everybody sounds like Qhantati." The use of the music had somehow moved beyond the older musicians' community identity, beyond the relations with their ancestors, beyond their way of doing things, and beyond their control.

CONCEPTIONS OF MUSIC

The older musicians of the ayllu ensembles might echo Karl Marx's observation that one cannot legitimately own something that one did not create—be it artifacts, art, or a style of life. As the composers of the music, they feel

246

that, essentially, it belongs to them and their communities.[5] Through the music they are able to demonstrate their cultural competence and originality and, by extension, the special quality of the community that they represent during musical competitions in the town plaza. The music is also important because it is accessible and all the men of a community can join in. When a panpipe or tarka piece is repeated for a long time, it concretely unites *their* community by helping people get into "sync" through synchronized movement and sound (see chapter 4). The music and dances have been at the center of festivals that, in turn, have provided continuity in the lives of rural Conimeños, and fiestas have provided some of the most joyous and meaningful moments of those lives. I suspect that from the older musicians' point of view, these deeper levels of meaning attached to music and dance are not relative, and they cannot be transferred or borrowed.

The members of Centro Social Conima, AJP, and other urban sikuri groups, however, take a different view. They have been able to use Qhantati's style and repertory successfully for their own purposes, and they have attached new levels of meaning to their musical practices in Lima. Throughout the first part of this book I emphasized that in the ayllus of Conima "the sound object" may not be the most important thing about music, and it cannot be abstracted from the ethics, processes, and occasions of communal life. For the Conimeño residents in Lima, however, musical sound *is* most important: "to sound like Conima," and to sound "good" in the 'folkloric' contests and festivals where sound, along with other formal components (costume and choreography), is abstracted and judged against an established canon of a vibrant as well as an imagined tradition. I have suggested that this abstracted conception of music represents the most fundamental difference between Conimeño musicians in Lima and those in the ayllus, and many of the other differences in their musical practices and styles flow from this (chapter 8).

Equally important to musical sound among Conimeños in Lima is the verbal discourse about social identity and community within which "sounding like Conima" is embedded. Qhantati's music has been abstracted from the "whole way of life" of the ayllus and inserted into new ways of life in the city. In spite of the relatively close similarity in sound between a Qhantati and a Centro Social sikuri performance, their distinct processes of creation and contrasting musical conceptions lead me to ask whether the two groups are, in fact, even playing the same music. I believe that the residents would answer this question adamantly in the affirmative; the response of older musicians from the ayllus might be a more tentative "Well, yes and no."

The Location of Culture and Identity

In terms of both styles of interaction and the issues raised, the meeting between Centro Social and Qhantati was a "cross-cultural experience"; it was also a meeting that was often at cross-purposes because of the complex nature of the social identities involved. People from the ayllus considered Centro Social members—"los limeños"—to be outsiders in the context of Conima. The older Qhantati members' reluctance to talk during the meeting mirrored their general aversion to speaking openly during interactions with mestizos and with people from outside their community. Although the meeting had been called to strengthen bonds with Qhantati, the use of Spanish by the residents and their formal style of presentation reinforced the cultural distance from the 'masters' whom they had emulated so long.

During the meeting, however, Filiberto gave Centro Social permission to play Qhantati's music in Lima; perhaps this was done out of graciousness, but it was also because some of the residents were from Sulcata.[6] Likewise, when I carried recordings back to Lima from Conima, Qhantati members pointedly mentioned that I might share them with the Conimeño clubs, but no one else. While Qhantati members considered the residents to be outsiders in Conima, they were clearly perceived as insiders relative to non-Conimeño sikuri groups in Lima.

As in this instance, social identities and the boundaries of specific groups are often complexly constituted, and they are always fluid and dependent on context. Aldemir is a member of Qhantati but not of an ayllu; Centro Social members are self-identified as Conimeño 'peasants' in Lima, but they sought to associate themselves with vecinos, and behaved more like vecinos than peasants, during their visit to Conima. Like social identity, the uses, 'legitimate ownership,' and meanings of sikuri music and other identity emblems are constantly being redefined and contested relative to specific situations and according to the goals and strategies of the particular actors involved.

The fluidity and multiplicity of cultural positions articulated during Centro Social's meeting with Qhantati, as in so many of the situations described in this book, makes it difficult to think about "culture" and social identity in fixed, essentialist terms. At the same time, older people in the ayllus do share some deeply rooted sensibilities about the nature of life, and as I have tried to describe, these dispositions tend to create conformity and coherence in their cultural practices. Similarly, the residents in Lima, their children, and

AJP members are all involved in the process of constructing new sensibilities and equally coherent ways of life that fit their specific goals, needs, and constraints in the capital. Although the cultural resources available in Lima are more heterogeneous than those in Conima, this does not necessarily imply a situation of "cultural rupture" or a "postmodern" condition among the residents.

The consistency of the migrant-club festivals, rehearsals, and decision-making meetings that I witnessed in Lima indicates that, indeed, highly formalized, coherent traditions, practices, and institutions have been created by the residents in Lima. But they were just that: recent creations that incorporated elements from a variety of sources and in novel ways. The results are neither essentially Andean nor Western. The situation among the Conimeño residents, as I understand it, does not fit standard concepts such as the "Andeanization of Lima" or the "Westernization" of Andean culture, precisely because the residents are neither Andean nor Western; culturally and socially they are something new, and they must be understood on their own terms.

In this book, I have tried to locate "culture" at a point of balance between individual experience and broader patterns of social experience within specific historical conjunctures. I have conceptualized cultural ideas, practices, and forms as resources for living and for accomplishing specific types of social and political work. I have used a notion of "ethnographic context" that expands outward from specific times and places to ever broader instances of social motivations, determinations, and constraints across time and space. Thus, it is my belief that one cannot fully understand why rural Conimeños play panpipes as they do without comprehending the politics of Leguía, Velasco, indigenista intellectuals, and the vanguard of the urban panpipe movement, and without grasping how class and ethnic relations influence all realms of life in Peru. Many of these same strands came together in Centro Social's meeting with Qhantati.

THE CONCLUSION OF THE FIESTA

At the end of the meeting between the two ensembles, Mario presented Qhantati with a diploma accompanied by a formal speech of praise; the diploma was received by Qhantati's young vecino president with equally eloquent words. Beer was purchased, hands were shaken, and the formal meeting was concluded. While they were drinking, some of the older members of Qhantati finally spoke up and proposed that they join with Centro

Social to perform in the plaza on this, the final day of the Fiesta de San Miguel. To my continuing surprise, Mario answered that his group had lost their panpipes and performing together would not be possible. Since Centro Social's instruments miraculously reappeared the next day, I can only assume that with their ceremonies in town completed, and perhaps because of certain disappointments that emerged during the meeting, they no longer wished to play in the fiesta or with Qhantati.

Later, I walked with several members of Qhantati to the plaza, where the fiesta was still in full swing. The brass bands and trajes de luces dance groups were performing. As usual, the main sponsor's entourage, sikuri band, and vecino guests remained in their private locale, celebrating separately and making only occasional forays into the plaza. After we had been drinking a while, we met a couple of other Qhantati members who by now also wanted to play. Finding enough sikus to go around, we took to the streets with only ten musicians. Just before we began to perform, I saw some of the members of Centro Social Conima standing in a corner of the plaza. I went over and asked them to come and play: "Qhantati needs you." One of them just smiled and said, "There are no panpipes," and the conversation was closed.

When the main fiesta sponsor of San Miguel contracted Q'keni Sankayo rather than Qhantati, it had been a blow to Qhantati's pride. Filiberto had tried to raise a group to play for the *altareros* (ayllu leaders who officiate t'inkas at four altars set up in the corners of the plaza during the main days of the fiesta). He had suggested to his colleagues that playing for the altareros was preferable anyway, because they were more generous with beer and coca, and were not as demanding as mestizo sponsors. This greater freedom during the fiesta would enable Qhantati to have a better time. Filiberto's argument, however, was not convincing enough to members whose pride had been hurt or who did not want to perform for other reasons. For many Qhantati members it was better not to play at all than to play second fiddle to Q'keni, their chief rival.

The eight or nine Qhantati members who did want to perform during the festival had joined with Centro Social Conima for its ceremonies in town during the preceding days—not out of any particular loyalty to the residents, but because they wanted to play sikus. Now they wanted to continue playing but desperately needed more people to make a good showing. Why Centro Social refused to reciprocate with Qhantati, especially after what had just been said in that morning's meeting about "doing anything they could to help them," remains a mystery to me.

What I do know, however, is that for Filiberto, Leo, Juan, and the others who wanted to perform, a fiesta simply isn't a fiesta unless they are playing music. And we did play, until evening, among the brass bands, and the drunks, and the spectators, and the merchants, and the dancers that filled the square. For Filiberto and the others, this would be the last opportunity to play panpipes until Easter. For this core group, at least, it was not an opportunity to be missed—regardless of blows to their pride, and the poor showing that they might make with so few people.

Moving Away from Silence

My strongest memory of the residents' visit home comes from the final day of their stay in Conima, actually the day after the Fiesta de San Miguel had ended. The residents and I were riding in the back of a truck through the ayllus. They had brought gifts—Peruvian flags—for the primary schools in the various members' ayllus, and we rode from one school and one elaborate presentation ceremony to the next.[7]

It was a beautiful sunny day, and the ten men and four women of Centro Social stood in the back of the truck greatly enjoying the view and waving and shouting to people as we passed—for me, combining the images of people on holiday and returning heroes. They had me in tow, like a professional photographer hired for the occasion, to document the flag presentations, as well as the drinking and elaborate meals offered by the communities in return. The people of Ayllu Mililaya had built an arch of greens, and streamers were strung along the entrance to the schoolyard through which Centro Social Conima walked triumphantly, playing panpipes. It was a proud day. It may have even approached the residents' expectations for reception, and their images of some ideal relationship with their home communities that they had maintained in Lima over so many years. On this day, the residents had finally arrived.

Like the gift-giving ceremonies so carefully planned by Centro Social Conima members for their visit home, their own musical activities in Lima were part of a process of searching for and creating some kind of space for living: to participate, to be recognized, and to enjoy. For the Qhantati members who wanted to play panpipes on the last day of the Fiesta de San Miguel, performing was a matter of moving away—as in that morning's meeting—from all the things that could not be said, and of making one's mark on the soundscape. For both the residents and the musicians of the ayllus, music was an antidote to silence and to being alone: the silence between highland fiestas; the silence of rush hour in downtown Lima; the silence of one's children moving away from Conima; the silence of the cemetery of Nueva Esperanza in Lima; the silence of an adobe house going back to the earth; the silence of unemployment and monstrous inflation; the silence separating the ancestors from the living; the silence of voices silenced by racism; the silence of my headphones on the plane going home.

APPENDIX ONE

Calendar of Musical Occasions

in Conima

(* = discontinued)

I. ANNUAL FIESTAS

Año Nuevo (January 1)

a. Six-hole pinkillus with cajas and bass drum for the genre/dance año nuevo. Performed by the majority of ayllus and sub-ayllu divisions at the homes of the community leaders passing out of office, with the main performance in the towns of Conima and Tilali. This event is part of the political cycle.

Virgen de la Candelaria (February 1 and 2)

a. Five-hole pinkillus with cajas and vocal music for the genre/dance wifala.
b. Six-hole pinkillus with cajas for the genre/dance candelaria. Both traditions are performed in the communities on the Tilali side of the district. The event is linked to the agricultural cycle.

Carnavales (movable date in February or March)

a. Tarkas with snare and bass drums for the genres/dances tarkiada (or carnavales) and wayno.
b. Five-holed pinkillus with cajas for the genre/dance pinkillada (or carnavales or pandillada). Most community units participate in the performance of music and dance, which takes place both in the individual communities and in the towns of Conima and Tilali. The event is linked to the agricultural cycle.

Pascuas (Easter, movable date in March or April)

a. Sikus with snare and bass drum to perform choclos and marchas for the dance soldado palapalla (Qhantati, Juventud), or for general uncostumed dancing (Cambria, Huata) in the plaza of Conima.
b. Drums, various percussion instruments, and vocals for the genre/dance tundiqui (or los negritos, Chilqapata, and a mestizo town group). Performed in the plaza of Conima.

c. *Lokepallapalla panpipe for the genre/dance lokepallapalla. This tradition has been discontinued for several years. The fiesta is linked to the Catholic calendar and to the harvest.

Santa Cruz (May 3)

a. Pitus with snare and bass drums to perform the genre/dance achachk'umu (or auki auki) by a single ensemble made up of people from Ayllu Checasaya and several other communities (1986). Performed in the town of Conima.
b. Sikus with cajas for the genre/dance imillani. Performed (1985 but not 1986) by Huata in the ayllu and in the town plaza.
c. *Chokelas with cajas for the genre/dance chokela. Traditionally performed by Japisi and other communities on the Tilali side of the district, it has recently been discontinued.
The fiesta is linked to both the local and Catholic religions.

San Isidro (May 14 and 15)

a. Sikus and bombos for the genre/dance satiri and marchas. Performed by Qhantati Ururi with dancers from Ayllu Sulcata, also by Huata, and Cambria in the town of Conima and in these communities. The fiesta is linked to the agricultural cycle and the Catholic calendar.

*Corpus Cristi (Thursday after Trinity Sunday in June)

a. *Chokelas with cajas for the genre/dance chokela. Traditionally performed by Cambria and other communities in the ayllu and in the town. The fiesta has been discontinued; it was part of the Catholic calendar.

Nuestra Señora de la Asunción (August 14, 15, and 16)

a. Sikus with bombos to perform ligeros, lentos, and marchas for the mestizo alferado in the town by Qhantati Ururi (1985).
b. *Kallamachu panpipes for the genre/dance kallamachu. Traditionally performed by Cambria in the ayllu and in the town, but it has been discontinued for at least twenty years.
c. Pitus with snare and bass drums for the genres/dances *chunchos, *turcos, and *cullawara. Traditionally performed by Huata and other communities, but these traditions have been discontinued.
The fiesta is part of the Catholic calendar.

San Miguel (September 28, 29, and 30, patronal fiesta of the town)

a. Sikus and bombos to perform ligeros, lentos, and marchas in the town by Qhantati Ururi and Q'Keni Sankayo (1985).

b. Brass bands for the music of various trajes de luces ensembles as well as religious marches and hymns. Performed in the town by professional and resident groups from outside of Conima as well as by an ensemble from Cambria (1985).

Todos los Santos (November 1 and 2)

a. Five-hole pinkillus with cajas for the genre Todos los Santos. Performed by community ensembles all over the district in the cemeteries and at the homes of recently bereaved families. The fiesta is linked to the local religion and the Catholic calendar.

Navidad (Christmas)

a. Pitus (ankutas only) with snare and bass drums for the dance piece pastorcitos. Performed by a single ensemble from the town, around the town of Conima and in the plaza. The fiesta is part of the Catholic calendar.

II. VARIABLE (LIFE-CYCLE) FIESTAS
Weddings (any time of year, but frequently around the time of other fiestas)

a. Sikus with bombos for lentos, ligeros, and marchas.
b. *Pitus with snare and bass drums to perform a processional. This tradition has been discontinued for a number of years.
c. Brass bands to play marchas and social-dance music in the community of Japisi and Checasaya.

Roof-Raising Fiestas (any time of year)

a. Five-hole pinkillus with cajas to perform the dance piece achuqallu.

First Hair Cutting Ceremonies (any time of year, but often timed with other fiestas)

a. Sikus with bombos to perform ligeros and lentos for social dancing. The use of music for this occasion depends on the wishes of the family.

Historical Background of the Musical Instruments

THE SIKU: DOUBLE-ROW PANPIPE

Archaeologists have found panpipes dating back thousands of years on the arid Peruvian coast. These instruments have been studied recently by various scholars (Bolaños 1985, 1988; Stevenson 1968; Rossel 1977; Haeberli 1979; Valencia 1982), but there is little agreement among them beyond the observations that single-row panpipes were used, and that they were sometimes played in consorts with two different sizes of instruments tuned an octave apart. These studies of pre-Incaic coastal instruments also generally indicate that high tessitura was favored. The panpipes that have been measured usually ranged from the F below middle C into the third octave above, and many have had starting pitches well above this F (Bolaños 1985; Rossel 1977; Stevenson 1968).

There is some iconographic evidence that double-row panpipes may have been played in interlocking fashion during pre-Hispanic times on the Peruvian coast. But Bolaños argues that in his research of archaeological instruments, he has found none to corroborate this (1988:19, 41). Representations on ceramics from Moche culture depicting two panpipe players whose instruments are connected by a cord do not necessarily imply that a single scale alternated between the two panpipes or that the musicians were interlocking their parts. Although Valencia (1982:36) and others have used these representations as evidence of double-row interlocking panpipes, he admits that no such instruments have been found. Stevenson mentions archaeological examples of double-row panpipes (1968:249–51), but since he notes that they came from a "scattering of excavations" there is doubt whether the double-row instruments he discusses were actually played as such. Stevenson (1968:251) also mentions a double-row panpipe in Arturo Jiménez Borja's private collection that was taken from a gravesite just outside Lima, but the instrument is not dated in Stevenson's account.

Alberto Rossel (1977:247, 249, 254) discusses a group of five coastal Nasca panpipes that he believes formed a consort. Each of these single-row ceramic panpipes contained twelve tubes. According to Rossel, the consort comprised panpipes of two different sizes tuned in octaves as well as a middle-sized instrument that, if corresponding tubes were blown simultaneously, would have produced a variety of harmonic intervals. This, at least, casts doubt on the use of the type of parallel polyphony heard today. Bolaños is rather critical of the accuracy of Rossel's work generally (e.g., 1988:62) and also questions the way Rossel has grouped some instruments into consorts (1988:68), although not specifically the ones of concern to us here. When they studied the same instruments, however, often their pitch measurements generally corresponded.

Bolaños suggests that he may have identified several consorts of Nasca panpipes with different sized instruments tuned in octaves as well as panpipes with corresponding ("unison") tubes tuned roughly a quarter tone apart (1988:105–6). He gives cents measurements demonstrating pitch variations between the instruments' corresponding tubes, and these closely resemble what I described for Conima.

As of yet, there is little information regarding archaeological instruments from highland Peruvian cultures; our sketchy knowledge of pre-Columbian and early colonial music in the sierra is largely derived from historical sources and iconography of the sixteenth century.

For the early colonial period in the Peruvian highlands, the chronicler Garcilaso de la Vega ([1609] 1973:127) gives a description of "los indios Collas" playing double-row panpipes in interlocking fashion on the altiplano. Garcilaso's reference to different voice parts (tiple, tenor, contralto, contrabajo) in Colla panpipe performance may suggest some type of polyphony. His mention of the Collas, "or [people] of their district," specifically identifies the region in question as being around Lake Titicaca in present-day Peru and Bolivia.

Garcilaso, born to a Peruvian mother and a Spanish father, grew up in the city of Cusco during the period right after the conquest. The way he writes about the double-row panpipe, associating it specifically with the foreign Collas, suggests that it was localized farther south from the former Inca capital in what remains its current center of diffusion. Garcilaso's text is as follows:

> Tañan los indios Collas, o de su distrito, en unos instrumentos hechos de cañutos de caña, cuatro o cinco cañutos atados a la par; cada cañuto tenia un punto mas alto que el otro, a manera de organos. Estos cañutos atados eran cuatro, diferentes unos de otros. Uno dellos andaba en puntos bajos y otro en mas altos y otro en mas y mas, como las cuatro voces naturales: tiple, tenor, contralto, y contrabajo. Cuando un indio tocaba un cañuto, respondia el otro en consonancia de quinta o de otra culquiera, y luego el otro en otra consonancia y el otro en otra . . . siempre en compas. (1973:127).

257

In accounts of highland societies from the early colonial period, panpipes were called *antara* (e.g., Guaman Poma 1980), and the term *siku* (*sico*) may also be found in Bertonio's Aymara dictionary of 1612 (1956).

PITUS: SIDE-BLOWN FLUTES

In Conima, the transverse flute is known as *pitu, falawatu* (*falawita, falawata*), or simply *flauta*. Robert Stevenson has suggested that side-blown flutes were used in the pre-Columbian period on the Peruvian coast: "During the Chimu period, last before the Incas subjugated the north coast, cross flutes came into vogue" (1968:255–56). He mentions recovered flutes and Chimu iconography as evidence. Dale Olsen also reports seeing an archaeological example of a pre-Columbian transverse flute from the Peruvian coast (personal communication 1991).

PINKILLUS: DUCT FLUTES

Although the word *pinkullu* (Quechua variant, also *pincollo, pingollo*) is a pre-Columbian term that seems to have referred generically to vertical flutes (see Guaman Poma 1980; Stevenson 1968:254, 259), I know of no firm evidence pointing to the existence of vertical duct flutes in the central Andes before the conquest (Bellenger 1980, 1981). The term may have denoted pre-Columbian end-notched vertical flutes that resemble the contemporary *kena* and *chokela*. End-notched flutes, whistles, and ocarinas are contained in the archaeological record, but vertical duct flutes are conspicuously absent. The chronicles and dictionaries written close to the time of conquest do not specify the types of mouthpieces used for vertical flutes. The presence of pre-Columbian clay whistles and ocarinas indicates that the technology for duct mouthpieces existed, but we must assume that vertical flutes of this type were a colonial innovation until evidence emerges suggesting otherwise.

APPENDIX THREE

Musical Examples

Example A.1. Sikuri Lento Genre, "Camacho" (public domain), performed by Qhantati Ururi

Example A.2. Sikuri Lento Genre, "Manuelita," by Qhantati Ururi

Example A.3. Sikuri Choclo Genre by Qhantati Ururi

Example A.4. Sikuri Ligero Genre by Q'keni Sankayo of Huata

Example A.5. Sikuri Satiri Genre, "Siembra" (public domain), performed by Ayllu Sulcata

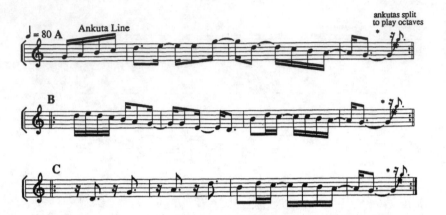

Example A.6. Sikuri Satiri Genre, "Cosecha" (public domain), performed by Ayllu Sulcata

Example A.7. Sikuri Imillani Genre (public domain), performed by
Qhantati Ururi

Example A.8. Five-hole Pinkillus Wifala Genre, Community of Japisi

Example A.9. Five-hole Pinkillus Carnival Genre, Community of Cambria

Example A.10. Pitus Achachk'umu Genre, Community of Cambria

N O T E S

1. All translations are mine unless it is indicated otherwise.

2. Here and throughout the book, I use the term "ideology" in a layperson's sense as it might be defined in a standard dictionary—i.e., as the doctrines, opinions, or ways of thinking of an individual or social group. In my usage it does not necessarily carry the negative connotations of "false consciousness" or "the ways in which meaning (or signification) serves to sustain relations of domination" (Thompson 1984:4; Giddens 1979:6), although these aspects may pertain in certain cases. The term has been theorized in so many ways that it has become bankrupt as a theoretical concept, hence my return to common usage. The term "discourse" refers to both the style and the content of the articulation of ideas and internalized dispositions in the full range of semiotic codes available (speech, music, gesture, etc.); it is not restricted to language.

3. From Durkheim and Saussure through Kroeber, cultural traditions, practices, and domains like language and religion, as well as social systems and structures, have often been described as superindividual. Language is used as a common example. Individuals learn to speak a given language that existed before, and that will exist after, their lives as speakers; hence, it is argued, the language exists independently of any specific speakers. From the analytical-methodological perspective taken here, however, a child's process of learning the language and styles of speaking is dependent on actual interaction with his or her parents and other individuals in the environment. The importance of this shift in emphasis for ethnographic work is that it focuses attention on how, where, why, and among whom social and cultural resources, practices, and systems are reproduced, created, or transformed within the actual processes of living (see A. Seeger 1980).

4. A similar statement is made by Christopher Waterman: "From this perspective, it is clear that an adequate analysis of 'the music itself'—a classic example of scholarly animism—must be informed by an equally detailed understanding of the historically situated human subjects that perceive,

learn, interpret, evaluate, produce, and respond to musical patterns. Musics do not have selves; people do" (1990a:6).

5. "Essentialism," in this sense, refers to the idea that if one is born in a given place, or is of a particular ethnic group or class, then one will have a certain essence, i.e., will "naturally" be a specific type of person, will hold a specific set of beliefs, will behave in prescribed ways, etc.

6. Poststructuralist critiques of essentialism in anthropological work should not confuse the analyst's essentialist tendencies with the views people hold regarding themselves and their own ways of life. Conimeños, both in the highlands and in Lima, frequently do not view their beliefs, identities, and practices in relativist terms; to do so would be counterproductive to the social and political work that they are attempting to accomplish.

7. Puno is a *department*, which is like a state in the United States. Puno is also the name of the city that serves as the capital of the department. In Peru, provinces are the next smallest political subdivision (like large U.S. counties), and districts are further subdivisions of these.

8. The six ayllus in Conima include Ayllu Checasaya, and Ayllu Sulcata, Ayllu Malcu, Ayllu Cupisaya, Ayllu Hilata, Ayllu Huatasani.

9. This information was given to me by the commanding officer stationed in Conima. I have no way of judging the accuracy of this figure, nor how it relates to temporary migrants. Furthermore, no breakdown was provided for the division between town mestizos and ayllu dwellers.

10. The use of mestizo-style clothing by the older people of the ayllus in Conima and throughout Huancané is notable given their maintenance of distinctive local practices and social style in most other realms of life (agriculture, music, language, spiritual beliefs, and decision making, among others). Weaving, one of the central Andean arts, is of little importance in Conima. Men in the ayllus throughout Huancané use a red and black striped poncho, but this is the only piece of clothing in either male or female dress that distinguishes a local style. This contrasts with the situation in the Cusco area, where, as Franquemont (1986:85–86) and Allen (1988:215–16) have observed, clothing and weaving styles are important emblems that distinguish the people of the ayllus from mestizos.

11. Two detailed discussions of Andean conceptions in the spiritual realm may be found in Allen (1988) and Bastien (1978).

12. Harry Tschopik (1946:539) also stresses the community basis for social identity as well as competition between communities: "Today, the Aymara have no of feeling of national unity in spite of a common language and similar customs. . . . the Aymara of one village look upon the people of all others as outsiders. This lack of national feeling is manifest by fights during fiestas and frequent arguments among the Indians of adjacent towns over grazing land."

13. Statements about "egalitarian" social relations in the Andes do not usually take into account the position of women or the complex nature of gender relations. In Conima, women did not have equal access to a variety of social roles; for example, they were excluded from political leadership roles and from the playing of musical instruments. (The few times I asked women if they would like to play musical instruments, they simply replied that women do not do such things.) My own understanding of the position and attitudes of women in Conima is not well developed, since I worked almost strictly with male musicians, and women tend to keep a distance from men. Catherine Allen's (1988) ethnography of a Quechua community in Cusco offers the best description I know of gender and issues of inequality in highland Peru.

14. In many regions of Peru, the wealthier people of the rural highlands often maintained a second residence in local cities. Pressed by the accelerating invasion of international and coastal capital into the southern highlands around the turn of the century (Tamayo 1982), and lured by possibilities of economic improvement, the members of local elites were often the first to migrate permanently to highland and coastal cities (Schaedel, Escobar, and Rodríguez 1959:13). Vecinos were more economically capable of making the move and of reestablishing themselves elsewhere. They were also better prepared to make the move, both culturally and in terms of education, in comparison with rural peasants.

15. As a similar case, before the Civil War in the United States, free blacks remained an oppressed group because of the social hierarchy and attitudes of prejudice that the slave system generated (Jacobs 1987).

CHAPTER 1

1. In Conima, women take part in fiestas primarily as dancers; on the rare occasions when vocal music is performed, they join with the men as singers. With the exception of a small hand-held drum (*tinya*) in departments further north, musical instruments are played exclusively by men in indigenous communities of the Peruvian highlands. (Women played drums in the Andes in pre-Columbian times, according to the early Peruvian chronicler Guaman Poma de Ayala [1980].) In contemporary Puno, Cusco, and Ayacucho, and elsewhere in Peru, women (especially young women) are the preferred singers due to a general indigenous Andean predilection for high tessitura (Vásquez and Vergara 1988).

2. Usually panpipe ensembles range from sixteen to twenty-four musicians, while the other ensemble types typically have between twelve and twenty players. The only time I witnessed a large ensemble of approximately fifty players in Conima was a sikuri performance during the Easter fiesta in 1985. In that event Qhantati Ururi (see chapter 5) had fifty-two players.

3. As reported by Buechler, the seasonal associations with certain instruments have community-specific meanings. For example, among Aymara speakers in Compi, on the Bolvian side of Lake Titicaca, he suggests that

> between the end of the dry and the beginning of the wet seasons, a period during which rain falls irregularly, the tarka, a hoarse-sounding wooden flute, was strictly prohibited, for its sound could harm the freshly sown crops. . . .
>
> In the neighboring Chua, panpipe dances . . . were expected to assure a good harvest and were played between carnival and Rosario (first Sunday in October). An elderly informant assured me that when the brass bands replace the panpipes, production decreased, only to regain its original level when the pipes were recently reintroduced. (Buechler 1980:41).

In another community south of La Paz, Buechler writes, the hoarse sound of the tarka was thought to attract dry spells, whereas the clearer sound of pinkillus was relied upon to attract rain (1980:358).

People in Conima, however, do not seem to attribute such meanings to instrument use. Only one man, out of many questioned on the matter, associated sikus specifically with the harvest. The use of five-hole pinkillus for All Saints' Day and Carnival was typically explained in terms of the instrument's happy, lively sound being appropriate for these festivals. The most common responses to my questions about the association of given instruments with their contexts were "it is our custom," "that is how it is," "that is the way we do it," and "that is how our ancestors did it."

4. These and the Conimeño styles discussed in this chapter may be heard on the compact disccassette reissue of *Mountain Music of Peru, Vol. 2* on Folkways.

5. The pitches were measured on a Peterson audio/visual tuner, model 520. I blew the tubes as consistently as possible, as loudly as I could without overblowing. One can produce substantial pitch variations on a single tube simply by changing the angle of the panpipe and the intensity of blowing. These measurements, then, are meant to give only some approximation of the tuning variances common within Conimeño panpipe tropas.

6. This more staccato manner of playing sikus is typical of certain rural Bolivian styles and in urban-revivalist solo performance, where the ira and arca rows are played by a single person.

7. The 1612 Aymara dictionary of Bertonio translates *tayka* as "mother." A more recent Aymara dictionary produced for Puno (Apaza et al. 1984) translates *tayka* as (1) "mother [person]," (2) "old woman, ancient woman," (3) "old *hembra* [female also, for animals]." *Ankuta* is translated as "young *hembra* [female, also refers to animals]." Bertonio translates *malta* as "in the middle, neither large nor small." The term *sankha* is translated by Apaza et

al. as "brecha de tierra" (hole, gap in? the ground), although I do not know if this relates to the voice name. *Suli* seems to be a term specific to the highest panpipe voice, and was translated by Conimeños as "ultimate." These same terms are also used to refer to the different pitu and tarka voices used.

8. In Peru, the term *wayno* (a highland spelling; also *huayno, wayñu, huayño*) must be understood in terms of specific ethnograpic contexts. It refers to the most widespread mestizo song-dance genre of highland Peru and Bolivia. In this instance the term may be understood as a genre rubric, although the style of mestizo waynos differs regionally. For people in the ayllus of Conima, and indigenous peasants elsewhere, however, the term wayno is used almost synonymously with "song" or "music" in the broadest sense. For example, one time when I was playing a Shona mbira piece in the home where I lived in Conima, Filiberto commented, "Oh, you are composing a new wayno?" Indigenous Andean people use the word to refer to any type of music, including their own music for which they have more specific generic categories. This has led to great misunderstanding among scholars, who have interpreted the indigenous use of the term as a reference to a specific genre. In the case of the tarka genre mentioned here, the term wayno seems to be used only to differentiate the faster type of dance music from the tarkiada genre—that is, the faster tarka music did not have a specific name, so they simply called it wayno.

9. All evidence indicates that there were no stringed instruments during the pre-Columbian period in the Andean highlands. The violin and diatonic harp, which are extremely important to Quechua (Quichua) speakers in Peru and Ecuador, were largely diffused by Spanish missionaries (see Schechter 1991). The *charango* (usually a small, guitar-shaped instrument with ten or twelve strings [Turino 1983, 1984]), is an Andean innovation of the colonial period. It is played in indigenous communities in Peru in the Department of Huancavelica and to the south through Bolivia. The *bandurria* (shaped like a mandolin with sixteen to twenty strings in four courses) is largely localized in Cusco. In some places, such as the island of Taquile, Puno, in Lake Titicaca, the guitar and mandolin have been adopted by Quechua-speaking musicians, but these instruments tend to be more closely associated with mestizo music.

10. *Estudiantinas* are large mestizo ensembles consisting of several guitars that have a bass and harmonic function, violins and mandolins, charango, accordion, and occasionally *kenas* (Andean end-notched flutes). Frequently performing in stage and chamber settings in highland cities and towns, they became an important tradition since the indigenista period (see chapter 5). A typical estudiantina repertory includes mestizo genres (waynos, marineras, pasodobles, and waltzes) as well as arrangements of indigenous wind music (see Gonzáles Ríos 1982). There are various estudiantinas in district capital

towns in Huancané, including a rather informal one in Moho, the district next to Conima.

11. As in Huancané, wind music is paramount in the Aymara-speaking Province of Chucuito, and in Aymara communities in the Province of Puno. In Acora, Puno province, however, I have witnessed the performance of *kh'ajhelos* (a courting song-dance accompanied by charango) in rural communities (see Paniagua 1982), and I have seen women singing vocables in unison and octaves with male flute performance during Carnival celebrations. I have not done extensive fieldwork in Puno and Chucuito, so there may be additional singing traditions there of which I am unaware. Nonetheless, it is clear that vocal music is less prominent among Aymara speakers generally than in the Quechua regions that I know.

12. Older men in ayllu Sulcata still had these different panpipes and chokelas tucked away in their storerooms, and I was able to solicit recordings of some of the old tunes privately. The kallamachu music was recorded by Qhantati Ururi of Conima (see chapter 5) in 1965.

13. I define aesthetics as a set of internalized dispositions affecting the creation and evaluation of things and experiences associated with the affective and artful realms of life. Following Stephen Blum (personal communication), John Chernoff (1979), and others, however, I am arguing that the distinction between aesthetics and ethics is basically an artificial one. I continue to use the term aesthetics because it is part of public discourse about music and the affective realms of life. Moreover, for political reasons I do not want to abandon the concept to those who argue that aesthetics is primarily a Western elite phenomenon (e.g., Merriam 1964), or to those in the Kantian tradition who oppose "aesthetics" and "functionality," since they are simply defining the general concept ethnocentrically in terms of one specific aesthetic position (see McAllester 1954; Bourdieu 1984).

14. Similarly, John Chernoff has suggested that the way the aesthetics of music work "to establish a framework for communal integrity, offers a superb approach to understanding Africans' attitudes about what their relationship to each other is and should be" (1979:36). Other ethnomusicologists have suggested the unity of aesthetics and ethics as well (e.g., see McAllester 1954:5; Blum 1977:41; Feld 1988).

Chapter 2

1. In Canas, Cusco, some boys walk to work in the fields playing charango regularly. In rural Cusco, Ayacucho, and parts of Puno, I have heard shepherds playing kena and other instruments to entertain themselves, as well as people playing alone in other contexts.

2. Hans Buechler notes that in the Aymara community of Compi on Lake Titicaca in Bolivia, the guías play the largest panpipes. This may suggest

another kind of ranking for the different panpipe voices in that community (1980:53).

3. In other Andean regions there are formal systems indicating the order (according to importance of the fiesta) in which the sponsorship roles must be taken, leading to higher political offices (e.g., Carter 1967:61; Buechler 1980:44).

4. Grebe (1980), among others, has noted that the physical placement of indigenous Andean ensembles within a performance space is iconically related to the political and spatial relations of the communities that they represent. In the town of Conima, some of the ensembles' stable performance locales in the plaza roughly corresponded to the relative locations of the communities on the Conima side of the district although this was not systematically the case. For example, while ensembles from Checasaya usually stood in the corner of the plaza closest to their ayllu, during one Carnival celebration a second Checasaya community group performed on the opposite side of the plaza. Perhaps related to the proximity of Huata and Putina, as well as their political bonds, their ensembles invariably stood next to each other, but it was not on the side of the plaza that, by my reckoning, would have placed them closest to their communities' locations.

5. The timing of the first entrance into the plaza seemed to be of great concern to the guía and core musicians in the group I played with, Tarkas de Putina. They clearly did not want to be among the first to arrive, but did not want to let too much of the afternoon pass without joining the fiesta. Our group was about fourth to enter.

6. There are exceptions, however, such as when the tarka ensemble of Central Sulcata and Putina divided into two groups and then briefly engaged in musical competition during the central days of Carnival (see chapter 4).

7. Because informal musical competition is a feature of fiestas throughout the Peruvian Andes, the pragmatic importance of volume has contributed to the popularity of brass bands in some regions. Perhaps it is the more specialized (exclusive) nature of the brass instruments that has favored the continuity of the local instrumental traditions in the ayllus of Conima.

8. Although the members of the best groups are sure that others copy their instruments, I have no way of knowing whether this takes place, or if it is only part of the one-upmanship discourse produced by competition between communities.

CHAPTER 3

1. Throughout the day, and the next, and even during later fiestas, men from other groups clandestinely invited me to come and play with them. I was tempted, because this seemed a good way of broadening my base of contacts, but for some reason I stayed with Putina. From hindsight it is clear

that if I had switched groups, no one would have trusted me. If I had not shown dedication to a single group over time, I would not have belonged anywhere. In Conima, to attempt neutrality is to remain outside of everything.

2. If women are not present for a t'inka, or are participating in a separate circle away from the men, as is often the case at fiestas, a man will offer the cup to Pachamama. Nonetheless, it is significant that, in this event, the sponsor's wife made the offering to the female divinity—illustrating ideas about the separation of the genders. The act was also a tribute to this woman, who, along with her husband, was making tremendous sacrifices to sponsor the fiesta.

3. In this discussion, choclos (referring to corn on the cob), performed with snare and bass drums for the Easter fiesta, will be considered synonymous with the ligeros, since the same tunes are used and only the percussion accompaniment changes to mark the genre distinction. Lentos (also called calmados and sometimes sikuris) and ligeros are often called *waynos lentos* and *waynos ligeros*. In this context, as is frequently the case among Andean peasants, the term *wayno* basically becomes a broad generic category almost synonymous with "piece," "song," or "tune."

4. In a study exploring the concept of *chuta* in the department of Cusco, Gary Urton discusses the term as the flexible (negotiable) dividing of physical space pertaining to communal work projects (1984). Citing a variety of ethnographic cases in which the term is used, he illustrates how sections of the plaza in need of cleaning, roads and walls in need of repair, and agricultural rows are divided into segments known as chutas, each becoming the responsibility of a given community unit or individual. The early Aymara dictionary of Bertonio (1612) also defines chuta in terms of measurements of space (cited in Urton 1984:16). Citing Gonzáles Holguin's (1608) Quechua dictionary, Urton (1984:28) notes that all the definitions refer to expansion or stretching out. In a metaphorical sense, the chuta chuta figure might be seen as extending the sections of a piece. As a cadence formula, it might be interpreted as marking the boundaries of a given section. As a figure that rapidly alternates between the ira and arca players, it may serve as a delineation of "melodic responsibility." Unfortunately, I can only speculate if and how the term relates to the broader Andean concept of chuta, because I did not pursue its meaning in any depth while in Conima. I asked one musician about its meaning and was told that it was an onomatopoeic term referring to the fast, even interchange of the ira and arca parts (chuta-chuta-chuta-chuta). This explanation seemed logical at the time; hence I did not investigate it further.

5. Fast tempos are considered happier, more upbeat. The issue of tessitura is less clear and is based only on the comparison of the higher (happier)

five-hole pinkillu verses the deeper ('more sentimental') six-hole instrument in Conima and a few observations in other Peruvian regions. The six-hole pinkillu music tends to be slower than the five-hole genres, and of course the association of emotional qualities with the two pinkillus may just as well have resulted from the tempos of the music and their associations with particular, serious, performance occasions. The association of lower tessituras with 'more sentimental' music, however, is worth probing further in future research in the Andes. For scale types, however, it is certain that both mestizos and indigenous people in southern Peru use minor scales for happy, funny, serious, and sad songs and pieces, the scale itself being a neutral vehicle for them.

6. The term *fuga* is used throughout Peru to refer to a concluding or coda section of dance pieces. In the context of mestizo waynos, and in string music among Quechua musicians in other departments, the fuga usually consists of a different tune and text played at the same tempo or only slightly faster. In Cusco and elsewhere, slower mestizo genres such as the marinera and yaravi will often be coupled with a faster concluding mestizo wayno, referred to in this instance as a 'fuga de wayno.' In Puno, among both mestizo string players and indigenous wind ensembles, the term *fuga* usually refers to a faster repetition of the same piece.

7. In this formula, the ira and arca ankuta players play octaves, but which group moves up to the final and which groups moves down depends on the given cadence pitch of a particular phrase.

8. The only other type of music currently played on the five-hole pinkillu is a single piece, *Achuqallu,* used to accompany a dance during roof-raising fiestas. This piece is musically distinct.

9. An exception is a father's casual guidance of his young son's musical beginnings. Nonetheless, formal music lessons and a pedagogical tradition do not exist in Conima. Indeed, autodidacticism and learning by watching and doing seem to be the rule among Andean peasants, with the exception of certain specialist traditions such as *dansaq* (scissors dance) in Ayacucho, Apurimac, and Huancavelica.

10. People who have cassette machines usually record the music of a fiesta to enjoy and remember it in the weeks afterward, but then use the same tapes to record the next festival.

CHAPTER 4

1. The achachk'umus, and costumed dancers at other fiestas in Conima, often become involved in horseplay with young and older spectators alike. Sometimes they can become quite rough as well as insulting. Jaime Montaño, who has studied with musicians in Conima, suggests that the horseplay has two functions. First, it is entertaining, but Montaño feels that it is also

a way of involving people directly in the fiesta drama and of "recognizing individual participants and creating links between them" (personal communication, 1990).

2. In a recently published paper (Turino 1990), I discuss the atypical features of this ensemble and of the fiesta as a whole in detail.

3. Conimeños associate different-sized political-geographical units (ayllu, district, province) with specific achachilas, whose power increases with the size of the associated region. Simultaneously, Conimenos expend more energy maintaining relationships with achachilas closer to home than with others that might be more powerful but farther away. Frank Salomon (1987:158–59) has observed that

> most students of Andean religion agree that within any local belief system Andean deities can be considered as points in a system of segmenting oppositions that ramify downward from the most cosmic or pan-Andean numina through regional gods (volcanos, etc.), to origin-shrines representing self-defined collectivities at descending levels of inclusiveness. . . .
>
> Cock and Doyle (1979) and others have observed that the upper parts of the system suffered greater erosion in colonial times than the lower ones, and after the major 'extirpation' [of 'idolatry'] campaigns apical cults almost cease to figure.

4. Abercrombie points out that the concern for conversion directly involved overturning the indigenous political system, in which rulers' legitimacy was bonded by their relation to ancestor divinities (1991).

5. Elaine Silverblatt's (1988) caution that we should not view conversion efforts simply as a unidirectional process should be taken seriously. She talks about "Andeanized" Saint Santiagos and the "Hispanified mountain gods" and notes that "divine Spanish and native images of power sputteringly fused as colonized Quechua created a new Andean religion inseparable from the political realities in which it was spawned" (1988:183).

6. Silverblatt discusses how mountain divinities were fused with the image of the Catholic saint Santiago as a result of Andeans' response to colonial domination and their attempt to reinterpret their world in terms of the colonial order of political relations (1988). Her discussion of changes in religious meaning in light of changed relations of social power adds new depth to discussions of religious syncretism. It is frequently suggested, however, that male saints, not just Santiago, have frequently become fused with Andean spiritual concepts associated with the masculine principle, just as female saints have been linked with feminine Andean concepts such as Pachamama (e.g., Allen 1988).

7. A friend in Sulcata told me that traditionally each family in his ayllu on the Conima side of the district used to "ch'alla la papa" during Candela-

ria. This included the ch'alla for the first products and the earth, as described for the religious leader in Japisi. In addition, however, the people used to decorate the largest plants of each type in their fields with flowers out of their gardens. After decorating the plants, they would dig up the largest products of each type, place them in a manta on their backs, and dance in the chakra to pinkillu music and song. But this is no longer done; now it is usually only the woman of the house who goes to the chakra to conduct the ch'alla.

8. I glanced in the door several times, and the procedures were described to me, but no one besides the elders was allowed in the room. The events that took place inside the house were not for public knowledge.

9. Women's clothing at fiestas is the same in style as their everyday garments, contrasting only in terms of quality. Men usually wear Western-style clothing and sandals (*ojotas*) made from car tires. Men's clothing at fiestas is also consistent with daily wear, except that it is distinguished by newness or quality. The wearing of shoes—reserved for festivals or trips to the city—is a clear mark of the specialness of the occasion.

10. Conimeños explain that the six-hole pinkillu is reserved for more serious moments in the fiesta because it is more emotionally powerful, whereas the five-hole type is considered a 'happier' instrument that is better for wifala and Carnival dancing. It is equally probable, however, that association with given contexts has formed Conimeños' attitudes about the instruments.

11. A trough two feet deep and two feet wide was dug in a rectangular shape. The male elders sat with their feet in the trough, and the ground in the middle served as the table.

12. In the writing and reading of ethnographic descriptions, I have developed something I call the "neighbors test"; that is, would I feel comfortable describing myself and my own neighbors in the same terms I use for discussing Peruvians or the people in other societies? Later, I came upon a discussion by Renato Rosaldo regarding ethnographic representation that expressed a very similar idea (1989:46–54).

13. Buechler offers a contrasting case for a community on the Bolivian side of Lake Titicaca, where Carnival is relatively unimportant and the major celebrations take place in the dry season (1980:39).

14. As I have already suggested, Carnival is a European term that seems to have been superimposed over a series of preexisting celebrations for the earth and rituals for agricultural and human fertility and productivity (see Allen 1988:182–83).

15. In many places in the Andes, the rainy months, and Carnival in particular, are a time for formalized ritual battles between different communities. Slings, stones, and whips are used, and serious wounds and death sometimes

result. This is not a tradition in Conima or in the Huancané region as far as I know, although spontaneous fights between individuals are fairly common during fiestas, and fights allegedly take place between musical ensembles in Huancané.

CHAPTER 5

1. I was present at the Huancane Fiesta de la Cruz in 1985, and participated in this same fiesta in Conima the following year.

2. At the same time, other writers involved in indigenista debates such as José Carlos Mariátegui, founder of Peru's Communist Party, opposed the regionalistic and romantic currents of indigenismo. For Mariátegui, regional and ethnic divisions were obstacles to the clear definition of class struggle and the move toward a socialist revolution in Peru.

3. According to Gonzáles Rios, the Estudiantina Dunker recorded the first "Puneño record" in 1936 with RCA Victor (1982:20).

4. By "closed forms" I mean set arrangements such as verse-refrain structures where the number of verses and refrains is predetermined. This contrasts with the open forms that characterize Andean peasant performance, where a given piece can be repeated indefinitely.

5. In an early article, I described the evolution of the urban-mestizo charango tradition in southern Peru (Turino 1984). I would suggest that the development of this tradition in many ways paralleled the development of the indigenista estudiantinas.

6. The history of Qhantati Ururi has been pieced together through a variety of interviews with the founder's family members, a peasant musician who has played with the group since 1931, and other people in Conima, as well as photographs and documents regarding the group's excursions to Lima. With the exception of information regarding the Lima trips, the dates given represent a consensus, but even these must be taken with a grain of salt. The information presented in this chapter was previously published in a shorter form (Turino 1991b). Several errors in that article have been corrected here, thanks to information kindly offered by Jaime Montaño.

7. The interview with Lucio Calderon, who died in 1979, was conducted by members of Asociación Juvenil Puno. I would like to express my thanks to Jaime Montaño for sharing this information with me (personal communication, August 1990). Auugusto Calderón stated that the ensemble had several other names before Natalio finally settled on the title Qhantati Ururi around 1937.

8. I would like to thank Leo Casas for sharing this interview tape with me.

9. The fact that this harmonic style originated in Conima is supported by the fact that groups from other regions, who later adopted it, cite Conima

as the source. Given the degree of regional chauvinism in the sierra and the usual custom of claiming important innovations as coming from any given speaker's home, Conima's claim to the sikuris harmony with parallel thirds seems relatively sure.

10. These photographs are in the possession of an early member of Qhantati in Conima.

11. Beyond the Huancané example discussed in this chapter, I have investigated or witnessed a variety of occasions in Cusco when mestizo sponsors contracted or organized local peasants to perform dances and/or music for their religious fiestas—including events in Paucartambo, Huarocondo (Anta Province), Tinta (Canchis Province), and San Sebastián, near the city of Cusco. Peasant musicians also perform for the mestizo-controlled patronal fiesta of San Miguel (September 28–30) in Conima, as discussed in chapter 10. The practice seems to be generalized throughout the Peruvian sierra.

Chapter 6

1. The impact of Velasco's assimilationist policies on the cultural outlook of rural Andeans cannot be separated from the results of the migration process or the causes of migration. These issues will be taken up in part III.

2. David Chaplin (1976:19), for example, has suggested that SINAMOS (the National System of Support for Social Mobilization) was established to appear as if it were fostering popular participation, while in actuality it was creating a system of vertical segmentation controlled from the top. He goes on to note that the cooperative model of the Industrial Community Program had as a major goal the elimination of trade unions and the threat that they posed. That popular support was not forthcoming from the labor force is indicated by the fact that more and larger strikes occurred during each of the years 1973–75 than for any other year in the 1965–76 period (Palmer 1980:114).

3. Various friends who worked as rural schoolteachers in Cusco during the Velasco years described the excitement and feeling of mission that was created by the educational reform. More widely, however, there were reports of absenteeism and lack of commitment on the part of many mestizo teachers, who felt that they were being banished to a hard life in the rural areas.

4. Tupac Amaru was the leader of a large indigenous uprising in the 1780s in southern Peru.

5. Velasco consciously used Tupac Amaru as a symbol of nationalist, populist revolution (e.g., Velasco 1972:178), a symbol that was particularly potent among highlanders in southern Peru.

6. AJP never charged for performances, and during this early period, the group even paid its own transportation costs.

7. According to Jaime Montaño, who joined AJP in 1975, there were

about fourteen regular members around this time, although for certain important events, between twenty and twenty-four participants might materialize.

8. In letters I received from friends in the Conimeño clubs during 1989 and 1990, they typically mentioned how they had done in the Encuentro Tupac Katari contest as the major indicator of how their ensemble was doing.

9. Tickets to the Encuentro in 1985 cost about fifty cents; the money goes to covering the expenses of the event.

10. For example, the Conimeño clubs have found that "only certain kinds of people" come to their events and that these people do not read newspapers. Hence, they found that it was not cost-effective to pay for the expensive newspaper ads. They simply could not afford to rent more prestigious locales.

11. Qhantati had received a special invitation to perform sikuris during this occasion because some visitors from Bolivia were in town. Under normal circumstances they would not have been playing panpipes during Carnival.

12. Learning to enjoy Gary Davis's version of "If I Had My Way" after being introduced to it by Peter, Paul, and Mary and searching out recordings of South African music after hearing Paul Simon's *Graceland* are examples of this process.

13. Actually, urban sikuris from as far away as Lima make the trip to Conima for this fiesta to scoop the new compositions.

CHAPTER 7

1. For more detail on the history of highland music in Lima the reader may consult José Antonio Lloréns (1983), Romero (1985), and an earlier article of mine (1988).

2. This style of music may be heard on John Cohen's classic recording *Mountain Music of Peru* (Folkways FE 453), side 1, "Music from Tent Show, 'Coliseo National,'" and it is also featured in Cohen's film *Mountain Music of Peru*. The best source available is Cohen's compact disc, *Huayno Music of Peru* (Arhoolie CD 320). This publication contains reissues of pieces performed by some of the major stars of the commercial wayno style, including Pastorita Huaracina.

3. The two names used here, Tomás and Juan, are pseudonyms.

4. I got to know and interview the twenty men of Central Social Conima, and some thirty-five Conimeño men who belonged to the other three Conimeño associations. I received twenty-six responses to a questionnaire from this group of fifty-five people; ten responses were from members of the other institutions. I also had opportunities to speak with a few Conimeño residents who did not officially belong to any of the associations.

5. This differs dramatically from Altamirano's findings among Aymara

speakers in Lima from the District of Vilquechico, Huancané (1988). Out of a sample of 130 adults interviewed, 117 said they belonged to one of the twenty-two regional associations pertaining to Vilquechico in Lima. These figures, and the number of regional clubs itself, are striking—Conima only has four active institutions. I have no way of accounting for these and other differences between Altamirano's data and mine. For instance, he writes that "all the peasant communities have festivals for their patron saints that are celebrated in a parallel fashion in the communities and in Lima (organized by the associations)" (1988:75). Not one of the four Conimeño regional associations celebrated or hosted a celebration for the patron saint of Conima (San Miguel) or any other saint in Lima during my research, nor had they ever done so before, according to club members.

6. In 1961 there were 14,881 (first-generation) Puneños living in Lima; in 1972 there were 41,482; and in 1981 there were 55,424 (Instituto Nacional del Estadística 1985:30; Henríquez 1980: anexo cuadro 2). These figures show that the largest wave of migration was in the 1960s and remained substantial but leveled off during the 1970s. During the 1960s and early 1970s, Puno had the eleventh largest migrant flow of the twenty-two departments.

7. The large number of clubs involved with musical performance can be determined by those mentioned on the "Voz del Altiplano" radio program in Lima, the primary medium through which Puneño sports and musical events are publicized.

8. There have been brief attempts at forming other ayllu level institutions among Conimeños, but none of them lasted.

9. This factionalist movement within the District of Conima is discussed in the introduction; see the section "Political and Economic Organization in Conima."

CHAPTER 8

1. I visited Mario's house again in 1988, and the inside remained far from finished.

2. As discussed in chapter 4, moving together in dance is one way the Conimeños realize their ideal of "being as one." The same could be said for moving together, synchronized by the verbal patter, during the construction of Mario's roof.

3. This fund dried up during my stay in Peru because, with the increasing economic crisis, there was no surplus to support it. With the help of outside sources, it was reestablished during 1990.

4. I have neither the expertise nor the space to assess the complex causes for Peru's current economic crisis. It hardly needs to be pointed out, however, that the country's dependent position in relation to international capital

is one root cause—the García state's struggle with the International Monetary Fund being a concrete articulation of this. Important for the present study, however, is the notion that the "ethnographic context" of Conimeño residents includes the actions of the IMF as well as the contexts that led banks to want, and need, to lend to the nations of Latin America in the first place.

5. By counting the number of AM radio hours dedicated to highland music (not including chicha) in Lima over a number of years, José Antonio Lloréns has documented a continued increase in this music's presence and popularity in the capital since 1986 (personal communication, 1989).

6. A friend, Nancy Van Deusen, visited with the members of Centro Social during the summer of 1990. She returned from Lima with a tropa of panpipes that they had sent as a gift for me. The members of Centro Social told Nancy that they had made the tropa, indicating that they have, since the time of my fieldwork, gained this ability.

7. The rehearsal I describe here is typical of the many that I participated in during 1985 and 1986. On a visit during 1988 I attended a rehearsal and found things very much the same.

8. Friends from other institutions would visit for the same reason, but I had been carefully instructed by musicians in Conima not to give recordings to people from other regions.

9. This is not to say, of course, that the members of Centro Social do not hear a wide range of music in Lima. In fact, there are several types of music that the Conimeño residents tend to favor in addition to their own music. This is indicated by the recordings that they play at private Centro Social fiestas (weddings, roof raisings, first haircutting ceremonies) in Melgar when their own ensemble is resting. In order of frequency, the records and tapes usually heard during these times were Colombian cumbias, chicha, commercially produced waynos from other highland departments, and occasionally Puneño brass-band music. Their favorite wayno music, mestizo in style, was either performed by *orquestas* from Junín (featuring saxophones, clarinets, violins, and harp), or by string bands from Ancash, Cusco, and Ayacucho. When waynos from other departments were played, many of the Conimeños changed their style of dancing to that of the region in question, displaying a familiarity that comes out of their Lima experience. Sometimes when the teenagers took control of the record player during the club ensemble's breaks, they put on more "modern" music such as salsa and rock; but it is striking that Puneño estudiantina music was conspicuously absent. I also never heard Conimeños play recordings of traditions that resembled their own—sikuris, tarkas, pitus, or pinkillus—from other Puneño regions during their private club fiestas, although they would sometimes play the records of Qhantati or Unión Progresista, or their own LP.

10. The age of the stock forms and formulas for Qhantati can be traced with certainty only to its 1965 recording, the earliest sound document that I have for Conimeño music. In terms of general characteristics, however, this music is identical to contemporary compositions.

11. During the 1980s, members of middle-class Limeño sikuris ensembles traveled to Conima to record the newest compositions in Pascuas and other important fiestas. On several occasions during my stay in Peru, the Limeño ensembles "scooped" the Conimeño clubs, bringing out new Conimeño tunes first at public performances. This was quite irksome to the residents as well as to the highland musicians, who feel that their music and style should be restricted to Conimeños.

12. In previous comparative research on charango styles in southern Peru (Turino 1983, 1984), I noticed that there were various continua of preferences between mestizo and peasant players. One of these involved density, with mestizos preferring a cleaner, more precise quality of sound—realized through the use of nylon instead of the more vibrant thin metal strings, as well as by the use of a plucking technique in place of the peasants' continuous strumming. Another spectrum of difference emerged in regard to tessitura, with peasant charango players favoring higher-pitched tunings, smaller instruments, and the absence of the low octave (E) string usually found in the middle course on mestizo instruments. Strikingly, these differences are suggested in the Qhantati-Centro Social comparison, although pragmatic reasons such as fewer players with experience may be involved rather than, or in addition to, aesthetic preferences.

CHAPTER 9

1. The idea that subaltern groups select distinguishing identity emblems that represent the path of least (aesthetic) resistance in relation to the dominant group also informs one of the oldest and most widely accepted theories of "musical acculturation" in ethnomusicology. Richard Waterman and Alan Merriam have suggested that in situations of "culture contact," "musical acculturation" occurs most readily between musical styles that share similar characteristics (Waterman 1952; Merriam 1955; see Nettl 1983:347). There is a basic problem with this formulation as it has come to be used (although perhaps not as it was intended to be used, especially by Waterman). Ethnomusicologists basing analyses on this idea often conceptualize the "musics" in contact as reified, almost animate, systems with lives of their own. The similarity of the musical styles is used as the basic cause of syncretism, while the agency of musicians and their goals, constraints, and dispositions are usually left out of the equation.

In contrast, what I am suggesting in relation to AJP and other working-class Puneños is that they initially selected a distinguishing musical style from the resources available to them, but that their choice was constrained by the aesthetics of the dominant society. Criollo dispositions had an effect in this case through their internalization by AJP members and other Puneños, as well as more directly through negative reactions to highland performing arts by people in the cities. The musical identity emblem selected by the working-class Puneños, then, was the one that provided the best fit with (was most similar to) criollo music, but that would still be able to signify ethnic and class position—a fundamental objective of the actors involved. As with the creation of parallel thirds harmony for the panpipes, rather than for any other instrumental tradition in Conima, the "like musics" theory of acculturation seems to pertain to the Puneño residents' situation. I would emphasize, however, that this theory should be informed by a deeper type of conjunctural analysis with emphasis on specific actors and issues of social power, political situations, motivations, and constraints.

2. For one such contest in a town in Canchis, Cusco, in 1982, I, as a "foreign expert," was asked by the vecinos to serve as one of the judges.

3. A contest for 'autochthonous dances' performed by groups from surrounding indigenous communities is organized by the Instituto Nacional de Cultura (INC) and other cultural institutions in the stadium of the city of Puno each year during the major fiesta for the Virgen de la Candelaria (February 2). The director of the INC in Puno explained that this contest was created in 1977 for the purpose of preserving local indigenous traditions that were being abandoned because of the growing popularity of brass bands and mestizo dances among the peasantry. He recognized that plucking the indigenous dances out of their original contexts was disadvantageous, but he noted that because of resource limitations, the creation of a centralized event in the city was the only practical way to preserve peasant performing arts. As is usually the case for highland contests, the judges were urban mestizos, often people with an interest in Andean arts. The use of mestizo judges and the presence of an urban audience clearly influences the form of performance. In order to win, community groups shape their performances according to what they think the judges and audience want.

The most dramatic case of stylization of a rural performance tradition that I witnessed in the Candelaria *concurso* of 1985 involved the k'hajelo, an Aymara courting dance in which the male dancers simultaneously supply charango accompaniment. The original dance was traditionally localized in the Puneño provinces of Puno and Chucuito, but it has long been stylized and performed on urban stages by mestizo indigenista-type dance groups accompanied by estudiantinas. The mestizo stylization has become standardized and widely diffused, as has the single tune used (in rural Puno, the k'hajelo is an entire song genre). I have seen the mestizo version done on stage in basically the same form by groups in the cities of Lima, Cusco, and Puno, accompanied by estudiantinas. The mestizo version includes a caricature of Andean courting, and stereotypes of Andeans generally, including clownish or silly behavior, feigned drunkenness, and struggles between the courting partners (some of the women lasso their henpecked, "drunken" partners, dragging them off at the end of the performance). The result is hardly flattering to Andeans' dignity.

I was surprised during the 1985 Candelaria contest in Puno, then, to watch an Aymara community ensemble from Acora, Puno, perform its own k'hajelo tradition in imitation of the mestizo stylization. The group was accompanied by a separate string band (rather than the men accompanying themselves on charango). This rendition even included the caricature of drunkenness and the staged antics between the partners, with some women leading their men away with ropes at the conclusion!

4. Strikingly, within urban panpipe circles, AJP is the only institution I know that uses outsiders for judges. At its prestigious Tupac Katari contest in Campo de Marte in 1985, the judges were primarily academics: anthropologists, ethnomusicologists, and folklorists.

5. When I spoke with the representative of the group, Todos los Sangres, that performed ninth in the program, she indicated that their lottery number had been two.

6. Michael Herzfeld's notion of *disemia* is useful here. Herzfeld defines disemia as the expressive play of opposition that subsists in all the varied codes through which collective self-display and self-recognition can be balanced against each other (1987:114). He goes on to say, "Disemia is thus not merely a symbolic opposition between interior and external perspectives. It is also, and much more significantly, a battle between intimate social knowledge and official cultural form. As such it occurs at all levels at which people recognize certain social alignments as relevant to their lives. This is significant in itself: it makes nonsense of the state's self-proclaimed right to generalize cultural orthodoxy as 'national character' " (1987:159).

CHAPTER 10

1. All these features, including the return of people who have migrated away, are very typical of mestizo patronal fiestas all over the Peruvian highlands.

2. Because many people come back to Conima for major fiestas, weddings and life-cycle celebrations are often held at such times.

3. In the literature and academic discourse surrounding regional associations in Lima, there is the notion that a major reason for the existence of these clubs is to provide economic aid for the development of the home communities. The name "Unión Progresista Conima" reflects this, and during its early period this club had indeed been concerned with helping Co-

nima. The members of Centro Social were aware that it was customary for regional associations to make contributions to the development of their home communities, but the gifts that they brought on this trip represented their first attempt to do so.

4. Aldemir and Eugenio have been residents in Puno and La Paz, Bolivia, respectively, and Aldemir has visited Lima.

5. The residents partially shared this view, since they wanted Qhantati's sanction for performing the music. Nonetheless, they had been playing Qhantati compositions for years without the group's permission. Their request for permission at this time was also linked to other issues, such as their competition with Qhantati Ururi Base Lima.

6. Mario's own brother was from Sulcata and sometimes played with Qhantati; he was present at the meeting.

7. Flags were chosen as gifts because they were affordable, and, as the Centro Social members noted, they did not really know what the schools needed. Nonetheless, for me, their choice to carry the emblem of the nation from Lima back to their rural communities was striking.

GLOSSARY

Achachila, Aymara: place. Divinity associated with a specific mountain in the local Aymara religion.

AJP (Asociación Juvenil Puno). A regional association of Puneños with branches in various Peruvian cities and towns, including Lima, Arequipa, Puno, and Cusco.

Alferado. The (mestizo) sponsor of a mestizo fiesta.

Alma, Spanish: soul; spirit of a human. In Conima the term is used to refer to the ancestors, or persons who have died.

Ambulante. Street vendor. In Lima, the term implies that the person is part of the "informal sector."

Ankuta, Aymara: youth, young female, young female plants and animals. The medium-sized instrumental voice in Conimeño ensembles, a synonym for "malta."

Arca, the one that follows. The larger row of the double-row panpipe usually having seven (or eight) tubes versus the six (or seven) tubes on the *ira*.

Aviadores. Divinities in the local Aymara religion akin to achachila but not linked to place.

Ayarachi. A pre-Columbian panpipe tradition performed presently by the Quechua in Puno in three parallel octaves.

Ayllu. A rural, indigenous geographical, political, religious social unit; like community, but sometimes comprising smaller communities.

Bajoankuta (bajosuli, bajosanja, bajomalta, etc.). Refers to the panpipe voice a minor third below the major voice of the voice group (suli, sanja, malta, ankuta, etc.). Also called the *octavin* voice.

Barriada. A squatter settlement, a synonym for "pueblo joven."

Bombo. Large double-headed drum played by sikuris. The term is sometimes used to refer to the Western-style bass drum.

Cabildo. Earth shrine.

Caja. A large, double-headed indigenous snare drum, played with heads perpendicular to the ground with one or two padded mallets.

Campesino, Spanish: peasant. The term refers to all peasants, but especially to peasants of indigenous heritage. Since the Velasco era, it has become a euphemism to replace the term "indio." It is now often used by indigenous people to refer to themselves in relation to outsiders.

CFP (Central Folklórica Puno). A Puneño club umbrella network.

Ch'alla. A ritual for various divinities, including Pachamama, in which alcohol is offered.

Chicha. An indigenous Peruvian drink made from corn or certain types of fruit. The term has been borrowed to refer to an urban-popular musical style also known as "cumbia andina."

Chiriguanos. A panpipe tradition using three parallel octave voices and no percussion. Performed specifically on May 3 in Huancané.

Chokela [choquela]. A large end-notched vertical cane flute played in large ensemble. In Conima, chokelas are sometimes found as duct flutes. The term also refers to the specific dance and musical genre performed.

Cholo. A word that is used relatively to refer to people in social transition from indigenous to mestizo identity. It is sometimes used to refer to rural highlanders in cities; it can be a term of disparagement when used by people of the upper classes to refer to highlanders.

Chuta chuta. A fast ornamental formula found at section cadences in the choclo and ligero sikuri genres.

Compadrazgo [compadre, comadre]. Refers to "coparenthood" or "godparenthood."

Condor Mamani. Divinity of the house in the local Aymara religion in Conima, as well as in other Peruvian and Bolivian communities.

Contraankuta (contramalta, contrasuli, contrasanja, etc.). The panpipe voice a fifth below the principal panpipe of the voice group (ankuta, suli, sanja).

Concurso. Contest.

Criollo. A person of Spanish heritage born in the New World. In Peru, the term has a number of situationally defined meanings, but as used in this study, it refers to the dominant, Western-oriented social group.

Cumbia andina. An urban-popular musical form that fuses aspects of highland music with the cumbia, also known as "chicha."

Dansaq. Also called the *danza de las tijeras* (scissors dance), a peasant performance tradition from the departments of Ayacucho, Huancavelica, and Apurimac; it is accompanied by a harp and violin duo.

Estudiantina. An urban-mestizo musical ensemble type usually composed of guitars, mandolins, violins, charangos, accordion, and sometimes kenas.

Federación de Sikuris y Sikumorenos de Residentes Puneños en Lima y Callao. A regional club umbrella organization for panpipe ensembles in Lima.

Fuga. A contrasting final section or piece coupled with the main piece of a performance. A marinera dance, for example, is often completed with a "fuga de wayno" in highland performance. In Conima, fuga sections consist of the same piece played at a more rapid tempo.

Guía Spanish: guide. The leader of a musical ensemble.

Huancané. The Aymara province in Puno in which the district of Conima is located; the name also refers to the provincial capital town, and a district in the province of the same name.

INC (Instituto Nacional de Cultura). The official agency of the Peruvian government dedicated to cultural affairs.

Indigenismo. An ideological and political movement during the first half of the twentieth century in which mestizos and criollos became symbolically involved with indigenous society and culture.

Ira, the one that leads. The smaller row of the double-row panpipe having six (or seven) tubes.

Kallamachu. Single-row panpipe tradition of Conima played in three parallel octaves (suli, ankuta, sanja) accompanied by cajas. The term refers to the panpipe, the musical genre, and the dance.

Loke pallapalla. Single-course panpipe tradition of Conima traditionally used by young boys in learning panpipe performance. The term refers to the instrument, the musical genre, and the dance.

Madrina. Godmother.

Maestro, Spanish: master, teacher, person of skill. In Conima the term is used in the musical realm to refer to musicians recognized for their skill.

Malta. Middle instrumental voice size, synonymous with "ankuta."

Marani. A rotating religious office in the ayllus of Conima.

Marinera. A mestizo song-dance genre in 6/8 meter related historically and stylistically to the *cueca* of Bolivia and the *cueca chilena.* In Peru, different variants exist: the marinera serrana, the marinera limeña, and the marinera norteña. In all cases it is a social couples' dance.

Mestizaje. The process of becoming mestizo.

Mestizo. Literally, a person of mixed Spanish and Indian blood. As it is used in Peru, however, the term refers to a sociocultural group defined by cultural and economic traits (such as bilingualism, clothing and speech styles, life-style, relative wealth, and occupation) rather than actual heritage.

Moho. The district in the Province of Huancané bordering Conima.

Pachamama, Quechua, Aymara: Earthmother. The pre-Columbian concept of the earth as a sacred, living female entity.

Padrino. Godfather.

Peña. As found presently, an urban, nightclublike musical performance context. "Peña folklórica" refers to a place where highland or urban-revivalist Andean music is performed, in contrast to a "peña criolla."

Pinkillu (Quechua: *pinkullu*). Vertical duct flute.

Pitu (also *falowata, falawita*). Transverse cane flute.

Provinciano. Person from the provinces. The term is largely used in Lima to refer to people of the highland departments, or non-Limeño Peruvians.

Pueblo joven. Squatter settlement often formed on the outskirts of cities by land invasions.

Qhantati Ururi Base Lima. Conimeño regional club in Lima.

Requinto. The resonating row on panpipes.

Requinteando. A technique in panpipe performance in which the arca player improvises an accompaniment for the ira part and the arca player improvises on the ira part.

Resident. A person who lives outside his or her place of birth. A Conimeño living in Lima is still a Conimeño but is also a "residente" of Lima.

Sanja. For pitu and tarka ensembles, it refers to the largest instrument type in the ensemble. In sikuris, it is the voice an octave below the ankuta (or malta).

Serrano. A highlander.

Siku. A generic term for the double-row panpipe, synonymous with the Spanish term "zampoña."

Sikumoreno. A double-course (ira/arca) panpipe tradition performed in two or three parallel octaves accompanied by bass and snare drums and often cymbals. As performed in, and diffused from, the city of Puno, it is associated with the mestizo trajes de luz tradition because of the ornate costumes often worn. The tunes are played relatively rapidly with a syncopated rhythm, and the blowing technique is generally more staccato than the technique of the Conimeño panpipe style. The cadence figure (termed "chuta chuta" in Conima) is a hallmark of the sikumoreno style.

Sikuris. A term that refers to a specific double-row panpipe tradition, to a specific panpipe genre (synonym for lento), and to the ensemble and the musicians who perform in this style.

Suli. The smallest, highest voice in pitu, tarka, and panpipe ensembles.

Tabla (siku). A rectangular-shaped panpipe in which the stops are caused by natural joints in the cane at different places in the tubes, but the tubes themselves are all cut to the same length.

Tarka. A carved wooden vertical duct flute.

Tayka, Aymara: mother, old woman. In pitu and tarka ensembles, the largest instrumental voice; in sikuris, the voice an octave below the ankuta (or malta). The term is used interchangeably with "sanja."

T'inka. In Conima, a ritual in which coca and cups of alcohol are offered to the divinities of the local Aymara religion. The same term is used elsewhere in Peru for rituals that differ somewhat in form.

Traje de luz, Spanish: costume of light. In Peru, this term refers generically to a variety of mestizo costumed dance and dance-drama traditions which utilize ornate costumes and are most frequently accompanied by estudiantina for mestizo stage performance, or more rarely by siku-morenos. For street festival dancing, and among the residents in Lima, these dances are usually accompanied by brass bands. This tradition is said to have come to Puno from Bolivia. "La Diablada" and the "Rey Moreno" are the most famous dances of this type in Peru.

Tropa. A tuned consort of a given instrument type, as in "a tropa of pitus."

Unión Hilata. A Conimeño regional association in Lima representing the single ayllu of Hilata.

Unión Progresista Conima. The first Conimeño regional association in Lima.

Vals criollo. A Peruvian waltz genre identified with the coast, and particularly with Lima.

Vecino. Town mestizo. The term implies a certain elite status; hence campesinos who have moved into town would not be referred to as vecinos.

Wayno (wayño or huayno). This term is situationally defined. It refers to the most ubiquitous mestizo song-dance genre of the highlands, as well as to specific musical genres and dances as defined by given indigenous communities. It is also often used almost synonymously with "song" or "music" by indigenous peasants in Conima. The mestizo genre is characterized by duple meter and sung stanzas in Spanish, Quechua, or Aymara, or Spanish mixed with an indigenous language. The mestizo dance is done by couples; in indigenous communities the dance can be done by couples or in groups. The exact choreography and dance step vary widely according to region.

Yaraví. A slow, lyrical mestizo song genre, largely associated with the city of Arequipa.

Yatiri, one who knows. In the ayllus of Conima, the term refers to spiritual leaders and healers.

Zampoña, Spanish: panpipe. The term is used generically for double-row panpipes, synonymous with siku.

BIBLIOGRAPHY

Abercrombie, Thomas
1991 "To Be Indian, to Be Bolivian: Ambivalence and Ambiguity in the Construction of Ethnic and National Identities in Bolivia," in *Nation-State and Indian in Latin America*, edited by Joel Sherzer and Greg Urban. Austin: University of Texas Press.
Abrahams, Roger D.
1977 "Towards an Enactment-Centered Theory of Folklore," in *Frontiers of Folklore*, edited by William R. Bascom. Boulder, Colo.: Westview Press.
1986 "Ordinary and Extraordinary Experience," in *The Anthropology of Experience*, edited by Victor Turner and Edward M. Bruner. Urbana: University of Illinois Press,.
Adams, Richard N.
1975 *Energy and Structure: A Theory of Social Power.* Austin: University of Texas Press.
1981 "The Dynamics of Societal Diversity: Notes from Nicaragua for a Sociology of Survival." *American Ethnologist* 8(1):1–19.
Alberti, Giorgio, and Enrique Mayer, eds.
1974 *Reciprocidad e intercambio en los Andes Peruanos.* Lima: Instituto de Estudios Peruanos.
Albó, Javier
1966 "Jesuitas y culturas indígenas: Perú 1568–1605 (segunda parte)." *América Indígena* 26(4):395–445.
1974 "La paradoja aymara: Solidaridad y faccionalismo." *Estudios Andinos* 4(2):67–110.
1986 "Khitipxtansa? Quienes somos? Identidad localista, étnica, y clasista en los aymaras de hoy," in *Identidades andinas y lógicas del campesinado.* Lima: Mosca Azul Editores.
1987 "From MNRistas to Kataristas to Katari," in *Resistance, Rebellion, and Consciousness in the Andean Peasant World, 18th to 20th Centuries*, edited by Steve J. Stern. Madison: University of Wisconsin Press.
Allen, Catherine J.
1988 *The Hold Life Has: Coca and Cultural Identity in an Andean Community.* Washington, D.C.: Smithsonian Institution Press.

Allen, Guillermo, and Javier Albó
1972 "Costumbres y ritos aymaras en la zona rural de Achacachi (Bolivia)." *Allpanchis* 4:43–68.

Altamirano, Teófilo
1984 *Presencia andina en Lima metropolitana: Un estudio sobre migrantes y clubes de provincianos.* Lima: Pontificia Universidad Católica del Perú.
1988 *Cultura andina y pobreza urbana: Aymaras en Lima metropolitana.* Lima: Pontificia Universidad Católica del Perú, Fondo Editorial.

Ames, David W.
1973 "Igbo and Hausa Musicians: A Comparative Examination." *Ethnomusicology* 17(2):250–78.

Ampuero, Fernando
1984 "El tsunami de la chicha." *Caretas* 831:64–67.

Ansion, Juan
1986 *Anhelos y sinsabores: Dos décadas de políticas culturales del estado Peruano.* Lima: Grupo de Estudios para el Desarrollo.

Apaza, N., K. Komarek, D. Llanque, and V. Ochoa
1984 *Diccionario aymara-castellano.* Puno, Peru: Proyecto Experimental de Educación Bilingüe.

Aranguren, Angélica
1975 "Las creencias y ritos mágicos religiosos de los pastores puneños." *Allpanchis* 8:103–32.

Arguedas José María
1977 *Formación de una cultura nacional indoamericana.* Mexico: Siglo Veintiuno Editores S.A.
1985 *Indios, mestizos, y señores.* Lima: Editorial Horizonte.

Armstrong, Robert Plant
1971 *The Affecting Presence: An Essay in Humanistic Anthropology.* Urbana: University of Illinois Press.

Arriaga, José
1920 *Extirpación de la idolatría en el Perú.* Lima: Colección de Libros y Documentos Relativos a Historia del Perú.

Basadre, Jorge
1968 *Historia de la república.* Vol. 13. Lima: Editorial Universo.

Bastien, Joseph W.
1976 "Relación comentada sobre los aymara." *América Indígena* 36(3): 587–616.
1978 *Mountain of the Condor: Metaphor and Ritual in an Andean Ayllu.* St. Paul, Minn.: West Publishing.
1983 "Los aymara: Notas bibliográficas." *Revista Andina* 1(2):545–78.

Bateson, Gregory
1972 "A Theory of Play and Fantasy," in *Steps to an Ecology of Mind.* San Francisco: Chandler Publishing.

Bauman, Richard
1975 "Verbal Art as Performance." *American Anthropologist* 77(2):290–311.

Baumann, Max Peter

1979 "Música andina de Bolivia" (notes). Lauro Records Internacional LPLI/S-062.

1981 "Music, Dance, and Song of the Chipayas (Bolivia)." *Latin American Music Review* 2(2):171–222.

1982a "Music in the Andean Highlands/Bolivia" (notes). Museum Collection Berlin MC 14.

1982b "Music of the Indios in Bolivia's Andean Highlands (Survey)." *The World of Music* 25(2):80–98.

1985 "The Kantu Ensemble of the Kallawaya at Charazani (Bolivia)." *Yearbook for Traditional Music* 17:146–65.

Becker, Judith, and Alton Becker

1981 "A Musical Icon: Power and Meaning in Javanese Gamelan Music," in *The Sign in Music and Literature*, edited by Wendy Steiner. Austin: University of Texas Press.

Béhague, Gerard

1979 *Music in Latin America: An Introduction.* Englewood Cliffs, N.J.: Prentice-Hall.

1984 *Performance Practice:* Ethnomusicological Perspectives. Westport, Conn.: Greenwood Press.

Bellenger, Xavier

1980 "Les instruments de musique dans les pays andins: Première partie." *Bulletin de l'Institut Français d'Études Andines* 9(3/4):108–49.

1981 "Les instruments de musique dans les pays andins: Deuxième partie." *Bulletin de l'Institut Français d'Études Andines* 10(1/2):23–50.

1983 *Peru: Ayarachi and Chiriguano,* (phonodisc and notes). UNESCO MTC 1.

Bertonio, Ludovico

1956 *Vocabulario de la lengua aymara.* La Paz, Bolivia: Editorial del Minis-
(1612) terio de Asuntos Campesinos.

Blacking, John

1967 *Venda Children's Songs: A Study in Ethnomusicological Analysis.* Johannesburg: Witwatersrand University Press.

1978 "Some Problems of Theory and Method in the Study of Musical Change." *Yearbook of the International Folk Music Council* 9:1–26.

Blum, Stephen

1977 "An Ethnomusicolgist's Reflections on 'Complexity' and 'Participation' in Music." *College Music Symposium* 17(2):25–41.

1990 "Response to the Symposium Papers: Commentary." *Ethnomusicology* 34(3):413–21.

1991 "Prologue: Ethnomusicologists and Modern Music History," in *Ethnomusicology and Modern Music History*, edited by Stephen Blum, Philip Bohlman, and Daniel Neuman. Urbana: University of Illinois Press.

Blum, Stephen, Philip Bohlman, and Daniel Neuman, eds.

1991 *Ethnomusicology and Modern Music History.* Urbana: University of Illinois Press.

Bolaños, César
1985   "La música en el antigüo Perú," in *La Música en el Perú*. Lima: Patronato Popular y Porvenir Pro Música Clásica.
1988   *Las Antaras Nasca: Historia y análisis*. Lima: Programa de Arqueomusicología del Instituto Andino de Estudios Arqueológicos (INDEA).
Bolton, Ralph
1973   "Aggression and Hypoglycemia among the Qolla." *Ethnology* 12: 227–57.
Bourdieu, Pierre
1977   *Outline of a Theory of Practice*. Cambridge, U.K.: Cambridge University Press.
1984   *Distiction: A Social Critique of a Judgement of Taste*. Cambridge, Mass.: Harvard University Press.
1985   "The Social Space and the Genesis of Groups." *Theory and Society* 14:723–44.
Bourricaud, François
1967   *Cambios en Puno*. Mexico: Instituto Indigenista Interamericano.
Briggs, Lucy T., and Domingo Llanque
1982   "El humor en el cuento aymara," in *Identidades andinas y lógicas del campesinado*. Lima: Mosca Azul Editores.
Bruner, Edward M.
1986a   "Experience and Its Expressions," in *The Anthropology of Experience*, edited by Victor Turner and Edward M. Bruner. Urbana: University of Illinois Press.
1986b   "Ethnography as Narrative," in *The Anthropology of Experience*, edited by Victor W. Turner and Edward M. Bruner. Urbana: University of Illinois Press.
Buechler, Hans C.
1980   *The Masked Media: Aymara Fiestas and Social Interaction in the Bolivian Highlands*. The Hague: Mouton Publishers.
Buechler, Hans C., and J. M. Buechler
1971   *The Bolivian Aymara*. New York: Holt, Rinehart and Winston.
Cadorette, Raimundo
1977   "Perspectivas mitológicas del mundo aymara." *Allpanchis* 10:115–36.
Caretas
1983   "Quienes son? Los electores." *Caretas* 772:B, D, 25–31.
1986   *Caretas* 900.
Carter, William E.
1967   *Comunidades aymaras y reforma agraria en Bolivia*. Mexico: Instituto Indigenista Interamericano.
Casaverde, Juvenal
1970   "El mundo sobrenatural en una comunidad." *Allpanchis* 2:121–245.
Centro Pernano de Estudios Sociales
1983   *Radio y sectores populares en el Perú*. Lima: Author.

Certeau, Michel de
1984   *The Practice of Everyday Life*. Berkeley: University of California Press.
Céspedes, Gilka Wara
1984   "New Currents in 'Música Folklórica' in La Paz, Bolivia." *Latin American Music Review* 5(2):217–42.
Chaplin, David
1976   *Peruvian Nationalism: A Corporatist Revolution*. New Brunswick, N.J.: Transaction Books.
Chernoff, John
1979   *African Rhythm and African Sensibility*. Chicago: University of Chicago Press.
Clifford, James, and George E. Marcus
1986   *Writing Culture: The Poetics and Politics of Ethnography*. Berkeley: University of California Press.
Cobo, Bernabé
1893   *Historia del nuevo mundo*. Vol. 4. Sevilla: Imprenta de E. Rasco, Bustos Tavera.
Cock, Guillermo, and Mary Eileen Doyle
1979   "Del culto solar a la clandestinidad de Inti y Punchao." *Historia y Cultura* 12:51–73.
Collier, David
1973   "Los pueblos jóvenes y la adaptación de los migrantes al ambiente urbano limeño." *Estudios Andinos* 9(3):25–49.
1978   *Barriadas y elites de Odria a Velasco*. Lima: Instituto de Estudios Peruanos.
Comaroff, Jean
1985   *Body of Power, Spirit of Resistance: The Culture and History of a South African People*. Chicago: University of Chicago Press.
Consejo Nacional de Población
1984   *Perú: Hechos y cifras demográficas*. Lima: Author.
Coplan, David B.
1985   *In Township Tonight: South Africa's Black City Music and Theater*. London: Longman.
Cornejo, Jorge
1986   "La administración cultural en el Perú: Una mirada sobre el pasado." *El Comercio*, 1 June, "Dominical" section, pp. 7, 14.
Cotler, Julio
1975   "Crisis política y populismo militar," in *Perú hoy*. Mexico: Siglo Veintiuno Editores S.A.
1978   *Clases, estado, y nación en el Perú*. Lima: Instituto de Estudios Per-
(1985) uanos.
1983   "La mecánica de la dominación interna y del cambio social en el Perú," in *Perú Problema*, edited by Jose Matos. Lima: Instituto de Estudios Peruanos.

Cuentas, Enrique A.
1982a "El ayarachi: Expresión musical de un rito autóctono." *Boletín de Lima* 4(20):81–91.
1982b "La danza 'choqela' y su contenido mágico-religioso." *Boletín de Lima* 4(19):54–70.
1983 "La wiphala, danza del departamento de Puno." *Boletín de Lima* 5(29):45–55.

Daniel, E. Valentine
1984 *Fluid Signs: Being a Person the Tamil Way.* Berkeley: University of California Press.

Degregori, Carlos Iván
1981 "El otro ranking: De música 'folklórica' a música nacional." *La Revista* 4:34–39.
1984 "Huayno, 'chicha': El nuevo rostro de la música peruana." *Cultura Popular* 13/14:187–92.

De Soto, Hernando
1989 *The Other Path: The Invisible Revolution in the Third World.* New York: Harper & Row Publishers.

Dietz, Henry
1976 *Who, How, and Why: Rural Migration to Lima.* Cambridge, Mass.: MIT Center for International Studies.

Dillon, Mary, and Thomas Abercrombie
1988 "Destroying Christ: An Aymara Myth of Conquest," in *Rethinking History and Myth: Indigenous South American Perspectives on the Past,* edited by Jonathan D. Hill. Urbana: University of Illinois Press.

Doughty, Paul L.
1970 "Behind the Back of the City: 'Provincial' Life in Lima, Peru," in *Peasants in Cities,* edited by William Mangin. Boston: Houghton Mifflin.
1972 "Peruvian Migrant Identity in the Urban Milieu," in *The Anthropology of Urban Environments,* edited by Thomas Weaver. Washington, D.C.: The Society for Applied Anthropology.

Elbourne, Roger
1975 "The Study of Change in Traditional Music." *Folklore* 86(2):181–89.

Epstein, Dena J.
1977 *Sinful Tunes and Spirituals: Black Folk Music to the Civil War.* Urbana: University of Illinois Press.

Erlmann, Veit
1990 "Migration and Performance: Zulu Migrant Workers' *Isicathamiya* Performance in South Africa, 1890–1950." *Ethnomusicology* 34(2): 199–220.
1991 *African Stars: Studies in Black South African Performance.* Chicago: University of Chicago Press.

Escobar, Alberto
1975 "El problema universitario o el vacío ideológico," in *Perú hoy.* Mexico: Siglo Veintiuno Editores S.A.

Escobar, Alberto, José Matos, and Giorgio Alberti
1975   *Perú: País bilingüe?* Lima: Instituto de Estudios Peruanos.
Escobar, Gabriel
1969   "The Role of Sports in the Penetration of Urban Culture to the Rural Areas of Peru." *Kroeber Anthropological Society Papers* 40:72–81.
Feld, Steven
1982   *Sound and Sentiment: Birds, Weeping, Poetics, and Song in Kaluli Expression.* Philadelphia: University of Pennsylvania Press.
1984   "Sound Structure as Social Structure." *Ethnomusicology* 28(3):383–410.
1988   "Aesthetics as Iconicity of Style, or 'Lift-Up-Over Sounding': Getting into the Kaluli Groove." *Yearbook for Traditional Music* 20:74–113.
Flores Galindo, Alberto
1988   *Buscando un Inca: Identidad y utopia en los Andes.* Lima: Editorial Horizonte.
Francke, Marfil
1978   "El movimiento indigenista en el Cusco," in *Indigenismo, clases sociales, y problema nacional,* edited by Carlos Iván Degregori. Lima: Ediciones Celats.
Franquemont, E. M.
1986   "Threads of Time: Andean Cloth and Costume," in *Costume as Communication,* edited by Margot Blum Schevill. Providence, R.I.: Brown University, Haffenreffer Museum of Anthropology.
1987   "Cloth, the Andean Art." Ithaca, N.Y.: AWASQA. Typescript.
Franquemont, E. M., B. J. Isbell, and C. R. Franquemont
n.d.   "Awaq Ñawin: The Weaver's Eye," in *An Andean Kaleideoscope,* edited by B. J. Isbell. Forthcoming.
Fried, Jacob
1959   "Acculturation and Mental Health among Indian Migrants in Peru," in *Culture and Mental Health,* edited by Marvin Opler. New York: Macmillan.
1961   "The Indian and Mestizaje in Peru." *Human Organization* 10:23–26.
Fukumoto, Mary
1976   "Relaciones raciales en un tugurio de Lima: El caso de Huerta Perdida." Master's thesis, Pontificia Universidad Católica del Perú, Lima.
Galvez, Bertha
1981?   "Etre aymara aujourd'hui: Migration et clubs regionaux." Ph.D. diss., Université de Toulouse le Mirail, Toulouse, France.
Garcilaso de la Vega, Inca
1973   *Comentarios reales de los incas.* Lima: Biblioteca Peruana, Promoción
(1609) Editorial Inca S.A.
Giddents, Anthony
1979   *Central Problems in Social Theory: Action, Structure, and Contradiction in Social Analysis.* Berkeley: University of California Press.
Goffman, Erving
1974   *Frame Analysis: An Essay on the Organization of Experience.* New York: Harper Colophon.

Gonzáles, José Luís, and Teresa María van Ronzelen
1983   *Religiosidad popular en el Perú: Bibliografía antropología, historia, socio-logía, y pastoral.* Lima: Centro de Estudios y Publicaciones.

Gonzáles Holguin, Diego
1608   *Vocabulario de la lengua general de todo el Perú llamada lengua Qquichua o del Inca.* Lima: Francisco del Canto.

Gonzáles Ríos, José
1982   *La música popular de Puno.* Cusco, Peru: Centro de Estudios Kuntur.

Gramsci, Antonio
1971   *Selections from the Prison Notebooks of Antonio Gramsci.* Translated and edited by Q. Hoare and G. Nowell Smith. New York: International Publishers.

1988   *An Antonio Gramsci Reader: Selected Writings 1916–1935.* Edited by David Forgacs. New York: Schocken Books.

Grebe, María Ester
1980   "Generative Models, Symbolic Structures, and Acculturation in the Panpipe Music of the Aimara of Tarapaca, Chile." Ph.D. diss., The Queen's University of Belfast.

Grossberg, Lawrence
1988   *It's a Sin: Essays on Postmodernism, Politics, and Culture.* Sydney: Power Publications.

1992   *We Gotta Get Out of This Place: Popular Conservatism and Postmodern Culture.* New York: Routledge Press.

Guaman Poma de Ayala, Felipe
1980   *El primer nueva corónica y buen gobierno.* Mexico: Siglo Veintiuno Editores S.A.

Guillermoprieto, Alma
1990   "Letter from Lima." *The New Yorker,* October, pp. 116–29.

Haeberli, Joerg
1979   "Twelve Nasca Panpipes: A Study." *Ethnomusicology* 23(1):57–73.

Hall, Edward
1977   *Beyond Culture.* Garden City, N.Y.: Anchor Books.

Hall, Stuart
1974   "Marx's Notes on Method: A 'Reading' of the '1857 Introduction.'" *Working Papers in Cultural Studies* 6:132–69.

1980   "Cultural Studies: Two Paradigms." *Media, Culture, and Society* 2: 57–72.

1985   "Signification, Representation, Ideology: Althusser and the Post-Structuralist Debates." *Critical Studies in Mass Communication* 2(2): 91–114.

1986a   "On Postmodernism and Articulation." Interview by Lawrence Grossberg. *Journal of Communication Inquiry* 10:45–60.

1986b   "Gramsci's Relevance for the Study of Race and Ethnicity." *Journal of Communication Inquiry* 10:5–27.

1991a   "The Local and the Global: Globalization and Ethnicity," in *Culture,*

Globalization and the World System, edited by Anthony B. King. Binghamton, N.Y.: State University of New York Press.

1991b "Old and New Identities, Old and New Ethnicities," in *Culture, Globalization, and the World System,* edited by Anthony B. King. Binghamton, N.Y.: State University of New York Press.

Handelman, Howard
1975 *Struggle in the Andes.* Austin: University of Texas Press.

Harcourt, Raoul d', and Marguerite d' Harcourt
1925 *La musique des Incas et ses survivances.* Paris: Lib. Orientaliste Paul Geuthner.
1959 *La musique des Aymara sur les hauts plateaux boliviens.* Paris: Sociétè des Américanistes.

Harris, Marvin
1973 "The Highland Heritage," in *Peoples and Cultures of Native South America,* edited by Daniel R. Gross. Garden City, New York: Doubleday and Natural History Press.

Harris, Olivia
1982 "The Dead and the Devils among the Bolivian Laymi," in *Death and the Regeneration of Life,* edited by Maurice Bloch and Jonathan Parry. Cambridge, U.K.: Cambridge University Press.

Hebdige, Dick
1979 *Subculture: The Meaning of Style.* London: Methuen Publishers.

Henríquez, Narda
1980 *Migraciones y estructura productiva regional.* Lima: Pontificia Universidad Católica del Perú.

Henríquez, Narda, José Blanes, and Sandra Vallenas
1979 *Migraciones internas, estructura urbana, y estructura productiva.* Lima: Pontificia Universidad Católica del Perú.

Henríquez, Narda, E. Henry, José Blanes, and Sandra Vallenas
1978 *Características demográficas y sociales de la migración interna en el Perú, 1961–72.* Lima: Pontificia Universidad Católica del Perú.

Henríquez, Narda, Ana Ponce, Sandra Vallenas, José María García, Carlos Wendorff, and Victoria Ponce
1985 *Lima: Población, trabajo, y política.* Lima: Pontificia Universidad Católica del Peru.

Herzfeld, Michael
1987 *Anthropology through the Looking Glass: Critical Ethnography in the Margins of Europe.* Cambridge, U.K.: Cambridge University Press.

Hickman, John M.
1974 "Control social y la adaptación de los aymaras urbanos y rurales en la zona de Chucuito (Perú)." *Estudios Andinos* 4(2):111–30.
1975 *Los aymara de Chinchera, Perú.* Mexico: Instituto Indigenista Interamericano.

Hill, Jonathan D., ed.
1988 *Rethinking History and Myth: Indigenous South American Perspectives on the Past.* Urbana: University of Illinois Press.

Hobsbawn, Eric
1990 *Nations and Nationalism since 1780: Programme, Myth, Reality.* Cambridge, U.K.: Cambridge University Press.
Hobsbawn, Eric, and Terrence Ranger
1983 *The Invention of Tradition.* Cambridge, U.K.: Cambridge University Press.
Hodge, Robert, and Gunther Kress
1988 *Social Semiotics.* Ithaca, N.Y.: Cornell University Press.
Hornberger, Esteban S., and Nancy H. Hornberger
1978 *Diccionario tri-lingüe: Quechua de Cusco/English/Spanish.* Cusco, Peru: Quechua Community Ministry.
Hornbostel, Erich Muritz von
1975 "The Problems of Comparative Musicology" [1905], in *Hornbostel Opera Omnia,* Vol. 1, edited by Klaus P. Wachsmann, Hans-Peter Reinecke, and Dieter Christensen. The Hague: Martinus Nijhoff.
Instituto Nacional de Cultura
1978 *Mapa de los instrumentos musicales de uso popular en el Perú.* Lima: Instituto Nacional de Cultura, Oficina de Música y Danza.
Instituto Nacional del Estadística
1985 *Peru: Compendio estadístico 1984.* Lima: Author.
Isbell, Billie Jean
1973 "La influencia de los inmigrantes en los conceptos sociales y políticos tradicionales: Estudio de un caso peruano." *Estudios Andinos* 3(3): 81–104.
1978 *To Defend Ourselves: Ecology and Ritual in an Andean Village.* Austin: University of Texas Press.
Iturriaga, Enrique, and Juan Carlos Estenssoro
1985 "Emancipación y república: Siglo XIX," in *La Música en el Perú.* Lima: Patronato Popular y Porvenir Pro Música Clásica.
Izikowitz, Karl G.
1970 *Musical and Other Sound Instruments of the South American Indians.* Yorkshire, U.K.: S. R. Publishers.
Jacobs, Harriet (Linda Brent)
1987 "Incidents in the Life of a Slave Girl," in *Classic Slave Narratives,* edited by Henry Louis Gates, Jr. New York: Mentor Books.
Jameson, Fredric
1981 *The Political Unconscious: Narrative as a Socially Symbolic Act.* Ithaca, N.Y.: Cornell University Press.
Jiménez, Arturo
1951 "Instrumentos musicales peruanos." *Revista del Museo Nacional* 19/20:37–190.
Jongkind, Fred
1974 "A Reappraisal of the Role of the Regional Associations in Lima, Peru." *Comparative Studies in Society and History* 14:471–82.
Kaeppler, Adrienne L.
1978 "Melody, Drone, and Decoration: Underlying Structures and Surface

Manifestation in Tongan Art and Society," in *Art in Society,* edited by Michael Greenhalgh and Vincent Megaw. London: Duckworth.

Karp, Ivan
1986 "Agency and Social Theory: A Review of Anthony Giddens." *American Ethnologist* 13(1):131–37.

Kartomi, Margaret J.
1981 "The Processes and Results of Musical Culture Contact: A Discussion of Terminology and Concepts." *Ethnomusicology* 25(2):227–50.

Keil, Charles
1979 *Tiv Song.* Chicago: University of Chicago Press.
1985 "People's Music Comparatively: Style and Stereotype, Class and Hegemony." *Dialectical Anthropology* 10:119–30.
1987 "Participatory Discrepancies and the Power of Music." *Cultural Anthropology* 2(3):275–83.

Kilson, Martin
1975 "Blacks and Neo-Ethnicity in American Political Life," in *Ethnicity: Theory and Experience,* edited by Nathan Glazer and Daniel P. Moynihan. Cambridge, Mass.: Harvard University Press.

Kleymeyer, Charles D.
1982 *Poder y dependencia entre quechuas y criollos.* Lima: Centro de Investigaciones Socioeconómicas.

Kubik, Gerhard
1985 "African Tone-Stystems—A Reassessment." *Yearbook for Traditional Music* 17:31–63.

Kubler, George
1946 "The Quechua in the Colonial World," in *Handbook of South American Indians,* Vol. 2, *The Andean Civilizations,* edited by Julian H. Steward. Washington, D.C.: Government Printing Office.

Laos, Cipriano A.
1929 *Lima: La ciudad de los virreyes.* Lima: Touring Club Peruano and Editorial Peru.

Lewis, Paul
1990 "New Peru Leader in Accord on Debt." *The New York Times,* 1 July, pp. A1, A9.

Leppert, Richard, and Susan McClary
1987 *Music and Society: The Politics of Composition, Performance, and Reception.* Cambridge, U.K.: Cambridge University Press.

Linton, Ralph
1943 "Nativistic Movements." *American Anthropologist* 45:230–40.

Little, Kenneth
1973 "Urbanization and Regional Associations: Paradoxical Function," in *Urban Anthropology,* edited by Aidan Southall. New York: Oxford University Press.

Llanque, Domingo
1969 "Los valores culturales de los aymaras." *Allpanchis* 1:123–33.
1973 "El trato social entre los aymaras." *Allpanchis* 5:19–32.

Lloréns, José Antonio

1983   *Música popular en Lima: Criollos y andinos.* Lima: Instituto de Estudios Peruanos.

1985   "Los 'programs folklóricos' en la radiodifusion limeña," in *Materiales para la comunicación popular.* Lima: Centro de Estudios sobre Cultura Transnacional.

1986   "Migrantes andinos y radiodifusión: El caso de los 'programas folclóricos.' " B.A. thesis, Pontificia Universidad Católica del Perú, Lima.

Lobo, Susan

1982   *A House of My Own: Social Organization in Squatter Settlements in Lima, Peru.* Tucson: University of Arizona Press.

Lomax, Alan

1968   *Folk Song Style and Culture.* Washington, D.C.: American Association for the Advancement of Science.

Long, Norman

1973   "The Role of Regional Associations in Peru," in *Urbanization.* London: Open University Press.

Luna la Rosa, Lizandro

1975   *Zampoñas del Kollao.* Puno, Peru: Editorial Los Andes.

McAllester, David P.

1954   *Enemy Way Music: A Study of Social and Esthetic Values As Seen in Navaho Music.* Cambridge, Mass.: Harvard University, Peabody Museum.

McClintock, Cynthia, and Abraham F. Lowenthal, eds.

1983   *El gobierno militar: Una experiencia peruana, 1968–1980.* Lima: Instituto de Estudios Peruanos.

Mangin, William

1959   "The Role of Regional Associations in the Adaptation of Rural Populations in Peru." *Sociologus* 9:23–35.

1967   "Squatter Settlements." *Scientific America* 217(4):21–29.

1970   "Similarities and Differences between Two Types of Peruvian Communities," in *Peasants in Cities,* edited by William Mangin. Boston: Houghton Mifflin.

1973   "Sociological, Cultural, and Political Characteristics of Some Urban Migrants in Peru," in *Urban Anthropology,* edited by Aidan Southall. New York: Oxford University Press.

Mannheim, Bruce

1986a   "The Language of Reciprocity in Southern Peruvian Quechua." *Anthropological Linguistics* 28:267–73.

1986b   "Popular Song and Popular Grammar: Poetry and Metalanguage." *Word* 37:45–75.

Martínez, Hector

1980   *Migraciones internas en el Perú: Aproximación crítica y bibliografía.* Lima: Instituto de Estudios Peruanos.

Matos, José

1961   "Migration and Urbanization, the 'Barriadas' of Lima: An Example of Integration into Urban Life," in *Urbanization in Latin America*, edited by Philip M. Hauser. New York: International Documents Service.

1967 "Las haciendas en el valle de Chancay," in *Les problemes agraires des Ameriques Latines*, Paris: Editions du Centre Nacional de la Recherche Scientifique.

1968 *Urbanización y barriadas en América del Sur: Recopilación de estudios realizados entre 1956 y 1966*. Lima: Instituto de Estudios Peruanos.

1984 *Desborde popular y crisis del estado*. Lima: Instituto de Estudios Peruanos.

Meintjes, Louise

1990 "Paul Simon's *Graceland*, South Africa, and the Mediation of Musical Meaning." *Ethnomusicology* 34:37–73.

Merriam, Alan P.

1955 "The Use of Music in the Study of a Problem of Acculturation." *American Anthropologist* 57:28–34.

1963 "The Purposes of Ethnomusicology: An Anthropological View." *Ethnomusicology* 7(2):206–13.

1964 *The Anthropology of Music*. Evanston, Ill.: Northwestern University Press.

1977 "Definitions of 'Comparative Musicology' and 'Ethnomusicology': An Historical-Theoretical Perspective." 21(2):189–204.

Michaud, A.

1970 "La religiosidad en Qollana." *Allpanchis* 2:7–18.

Millones, Luis

1970 "Deporte y alienación en el Perú: El fútbol en los barrios limeños." *Estudios Andinos* 1(2):87–95.

1978 *Tugurios: La cultura de los marginados*. Lima: Instituto Nacional de Cultura.

Mishkin, Bernard

1946 "The Contemporary Quechua," in *The Handbook of South American Indians*, vol. 2, *The Andean Civilizations*, edited by Julian Steward. Washington, D.C.: Government Printing Office.

Montoya, Rodrigo

1986 "Identidad étnica y luchas agrarias en los Andes peruanos," in *Identidades andinas y lógicas del campesinado*. Lima: Mosca Azul Editores.

1987 *La cultura quechua hoy*. Lima: Hueso Húmero Ediciones.

Montoya, Rodrigo, and Edwin and Luis Montoya

1987 *La sangre de los cerros: Antología de la poesía quechua que se canta en el Perú*. Lima: Centro Pernano de Estudios Sociales, Mosca Azul Editores, and Universidad Nacional Mayor de San Marcos.

Moscoso, Susana, and Patricia Mostajo

n.d. "Perú: Guía demográfica y socio-económica." (chart). Lima: Consejo Nacional de Población.

Murra, John

1975 "El control vertical de un máximo de pisos ecológicos en la economía de las sociedades andinas," in *Formaciones económicas y políticas del mundo andino*. Lima: Instituto de Estudios Peruanos.

Necker, Luís
1986   "A propósito de algunas tesis recientes sobre la indianidad," in *Identidades andinas y lógicas del campesinado*. Lima: Mosca Azul Editores.

Neira Samanez, Hugo
1974   *Huillca: Habla un campesino peruano*. Lima: Ediciones Promoción Editorial Inca S.A.

Nettl, Bruno
1974   "Thoughts on Improvisation: A Comparative Approach." *Musical Quarterly* 60(1):1–19.
1978   *Eight Urban Musical Cultures*. Urbana: University of Illinois Press.
1983   *The Study of Ethnomusicology: Twenty-nine Issues and Concepts*. Urbana: University of Illinois Press.
1985   *The Western Impact on World Music: Change, Adaptation, and Survival*. New York: Schirmer Books.

North, Liisa L.
1983   "Ideological Orientations of Peru's Military Rulers," in *The Peruvian Experiment Reconsidered*, edited by Cynthia McClintock and Abraham F. Lowenthal. Princeton, N.J.: Princeton University Press.

Nuñez, Lucy
1985   "La vigencia de la danza de las tijeras en Lima metropolitana." Master's thesis, Pontificia Universidad Católica del Peru, Lima.

Nuñez, Lucy, and José Antonio Lloréns
1981   "Lima: De la jarana criolla a la fiesta andina." *Quehacer* 9:107–27.

Palmer, David Scott
1980   *Peru: The Authoritarian Tradition*. New York: Praeger.

Palomino, Salvador
1984   *El sistema de oposiciones en la comunidad de Sarhua*. Lima: Editorial Pueblo Indio.

Paniagua, Felix
1982   "El kh'ajhelo." *Tarea* 6:65–69.

Patterson, Orlando
1975   "Context and Choice in Ethnic Allegiance: A Theoretical Framework and Caribbean Case Study," in *Ethnicity: Theory and Experience*, edited by Nathan Glazer and Daniel P. Moynihan. Cambridge, Mass.: Harvard University Press.

Peirce, Charles Sanders
1955   *Philosophical Writings of Peirce*. Edited by Justus Buchler. New York: Dover Books.

Pinilla, Enrique
1980   "Informe sobre la música en el Perú," in *Historia del Perú*, vol. 9. Lima: Editorial Mejía Baca.
1985   "La música en el siglo XX," in *La música en el Perú*. Lima: Patronato Popular y Porvenir Pro Música Clasica.

Quezada M., José
1985   "La música en el virreinato," in *La música en el Perú*. Lima: Patronato Popular y Porvenir Pro Musica Clásica.
Quijano, Anibal
1980   *Dominación y cultura: El cholo y el conflicto cultural en el Perú*. Lima: Mosca Azul Editores.
Razuri, Jaime
1983   "La chicha: Identitidad chola en la gran ciudad." *Debate* 24:72–76.
Rénique, José Luis
1987   "De la fe en el progreso al mito andino: Los intelectuales cusqueños." *Margenes* 1:9–33.
1991   *Los sueños de la sierra: Cusco en el siglo XX*. Lima: Centro Pernano de Estudios Sociales.
República, La
1985   "Comunicado, la voz del ambulante: No a la ordenanza no. 002." *La República*, 25 May, National section, p. 7.
1985   "No hay error: La municipalidad defiende a los vendedores ambulantes." *La República*, 26 May, Local section, p. 11.
Rice, Timothy
1987   "Toward the Remodeling of Ethnomusicology." *Ethnomusicology* 31(3):469–88.
Roberts, Bryan R.
1974   "The Interrelationships of City and Provinces in Peru and Guatemala," in *Latin American Urban Research: Anthropological Perspectives on Latin American Urbanization*, edited by Wayne A. Cornelius and Felicity M. Trueblood. Beverly Hills, Calif.: Sage Publishers.
Roel, Josafat
1959   "El wayno del Cusco." *Folklore Americano* 6/7:129–245.
Romero, Raúl
1985   "La música tradicional y popular," in *La música en el Perú*. Lima: Patronato Popular y Porvenir Pro Musica Clásica.
1990   "Musical Change and Cultural Resistance in the Central Andes of Peru." *Latin American Music Review* 11(1):1–35.
Rosaldo, Renato
1989   *Culture and Truth: The Remaking of Social Analysis*. Boston: Beacon Press.
Rossel, Alberto
1977   *Arqueología sur del Perú*. Lima: Editorial Universo S.A.
Rowe, John H.
1946   "Inca Culture at the Time of the Spanish Conquest," in *Handbook of South American Indians*, vol. 2, *The Andean Civilizations*, edited by Julian H. Steward. Washington, D.C.: Government Printing Office.
Royce, Anya
1982   *Ethnic Identity*. Bloomington: Indiana University Press.

Rozas, Abel
1985   *Antología de la música cusqueña: Siglos XIX y XX.* Cusco, Peru: Comité de Servicios Integrados Turísticos Culturales Cusco.
Ryo Hirabayashi, Lane
1986   "The Migrant Village Association in Latin America: A Comparative Analysis." *Latin American Research Review* 21(3):7–29.
Sahlins, Marshall
1981   *Historical Metaphors and Mythical Realities.* Ann Arbor: University of Michigan Press.
Said, Edward
1989   "Representing the Colonized: Anthropology's Interlocutors." *Critical Inquiry* 15:205–25.
Salcedo, José María
1984   "El Perú informal." *Quehacer* 31:74–97.
Salomon, Frank
1987   "Ancestor Cults and Resistance to the State in Arequipa, ca. 1748–1754," in *Resistance, Rebellion, and Consciousness in the Andean Peasant World: 18th to 20th Centuries,* edited by Steve J. Stern. Madison: University of Wisconsin Press.
Santo Tomás, Domingo de
1951   *Lexicon o vocabulario de la lengua general del Perú.* Lima: Instituto de Historia.
Schaedel, Richard P.
1974   "The Anthropological Study of Latin American Cities in Intra- and Interdisciplinary Perspectives." *Urban Anthropology* 3(2):139–70.
1979   "From Homogenization to Heterogenization in Lima, Peru." *Urban Anthropology* 8(3/4):399–420.
Schaedel, Richard P., Gabriel Escobar, and Antonio Rodríguez
1959   *Human Resources in the Department of Puno.* Lima: Southern Peru Regional Development Project.
Schafer, R. Murray
1977   *The Tuning of the World.* New York: Alfred A. Knopf.
Schechter, John
1979   "The Inca *Cantar Histórico:* A Lexico-Historical Elaboration on Two Cultural Themes." *Ethnomusicology* 23(2):191–204.
1984   "Diatonic Harp in Ecuador: Historical Background and Modern Traditions, Part 1." *Journal of the American Musical Instrument Society* 10:97–118.
1991   *The Indispensable Harp: Historical Development, Modern Roles, Configurations, and Performance Practices in Ecuador and Latin America.* Kent, Ohio: Kent State Press.
Seeger, Anthony
1979   "What Can We Learn When They Sing? Vocal Genres of the Suya Indians of Central Brazil." *Ethnomusicology* 23(3):373–94.
1980   "Sing for Your Sister: The Structure and Performance of Suya Akia,"

in *Ethnography of Musical Performance,* edited by Marcia Herndon and Norma McLeod. Darby, Pa.: Norwood Editions.

1987   *Why Suyá Sing: A Musical Anthropology of an Amazonian People.* Cambridge, U.K.: Cambridge University Press.

Seeger, Charles

1977   "Music and Class Structure in the United States," in *Studies in Musicology, 1935–1975.* Berkeley: University of California Press.

1977   "Music and Society: Some New-World Evidence of Their Relation-
(1951)   ship," in *Studies in Musicology, 1935–1975.* Berkeley: University of California Press.

Silverblatt, Irene

1988   "Political Memories and Colonizing Symbols: Santiago and the Mountain Gods of Colonial Peru," in *Rethinking History and Myth: Indigenous South American Perspectives on the Past,* edited by Jonathan D. Hill. Urbana: University of Illinois Press.

Smith, Robert J.

1975   *The Art of Festival As Exemplified by the Fiesta to the Patroness of Otuzco: La Virgen de la Puerta.* Lawrence: University of Kansas Press.

Solc, Vaclav

1969   *Los aymaras de las islas del Titicaca.* Mexico: Instituto Indigenista Interamericano.

Stern, Steve J., ed.

1987   *Resistance, Rebellion, and Consciousness in the Andean Peasant World: 18th to 20th Centuries.* Madison: University of Wisconsin Press.

Stevenson, Robert

1968   *Music in Aztec and Inca Territory.* Berkeley: University of California Press.

Sugarman, Jane

1989   "The Nightingale and the Partridge: Singing and Gender among Prespa Albanians." *Ethnomusicology* 33(2):191–215.

Tamayo, José

1980   *Historia del indigenismo cusqueño, siglos XVI–XX.* Lima: Instituto Nacional de Cultura.

1982   *Historia social e indigenismo en el altiplano.* Lima: Ediciones Treintaitres.

Tello, Julio

1959   *Paracas, primera parte.* Lima: Institute of Andean Research of New York.

Thompson, John B.

1984   *Studies in the Theory of Ideology.* Berkeley: University of California Press.

Tschopik, Harry, Jr.

1946   "The Aymara," in *Handbook of South American Indians,* vol. 2, *The Andean Civilizations,* edited by Julian H. Steward. Washington, D.C.: Government Printing Office.

1968   *Magia en Chucuito*. Mexico: Instituto Indigenista Interamericano.

Turino, Thomas

1982   "Communication in Performance: The Fiesta of the Virgen del Carmen, Paucartambo, Peru." Master's thesis, University of Texas at Austin.

1983   "The Charango and the Sirena: Music, Magic, and the Power of Love." *Latin American Music Review* 4(1):81–119.

1984   "The Urban-Mestizo Charango Tradition in Southern Peru: A Statement of Shifting Identity." *Ethnomusicology* 28(2):253–69.

1987   "Power Relations, Identity, and Musical Choice: Music in a Peruvian Altiplano Village and among Its Migrants in the Metropolis." Ph.D. diss., University of Texas at Austin.

1988   "The Music of Andean Migrants in Lima, Peru: Demographics, Social Power and Style." *Latin American Music Review* 9(2):127–50.

1989   "The Coherence of Social Style and Musical Creation among the Aymara in Southern Peru." *Ethnomusicology* 33(1):1– 30.

1990a   "Structure, Context, and Strategy in Musical Ethnography." *Ethnomusicology* 34(3):399–412.

1990b   " 'Somos el Perú': Cumbia Andina and the Children of Andean Migrants in Lima, Peru." *Studies in Latin American Popular Culture* 9:15–37.

1991a   "The State and Andean Musical Production in Peru," in *Nation-State and Indian in Latin America*, edited by Joel Sherzer and Greg Urban. Austin: University of Texas Press.

1991b   "The History of a Peruvian Panpipe Style and the Politics of Interpretation," in *Ethnomusicology and Modern Music History*, edited by Stephen Blum, Philip Bohlman, and Daniel Neuman. Urbana: University of Illinois Press.

Turner, Victor

1969   *The Ritual Process*. Chicago: Aldine Publishing.

Turner, Victor W., and Edward M. Bruner, eds.

1986   *The Anthropology of Experience*. Urbana: University of Illinois Press.

Universidad del Pacífico

1983   "Decomposición del cambio en el empleo en la industria manufacturera, 1975–1979." Universidad del Pacífico, Lima. Typescript.

Urton, Gary

1984   "Chuta: El espacio de la práctica social en Pacariqtambo, Perú." *Revista Andina* 2(1):7–43.

Uzzell, Douglas

1974a   "Cholos and Bureaus in Lima." *International Journal of Comparative Sociology* 15(3/4):143–50.

1974b   "A Strategic Analysis of Social Structure in Lima, Peru, Using the Concept of 'Plays.' " *Urban Anthropology* 3(1):34–45.

1979   "Conceptual Fallacies in the Rural-Urban Dichotomy." *Urban Anthropology* 8(3/4):333–50.

1980   "Mixed Strategies and the Informal Sector: Three Faces of Reserve Labor." *Human Organization* 39(1):40–49.

Valcarcel, Luis E.
1946   "The Andean Calendar," in *Handbook of South American Indians*, vol. 2, *The Andean Civilizations*, edited by Julian H. Steward. Washington, D.C.: Government Printing Office.

Valdivia, Oscar
1970   *Migración interna a la metrópoli: Contraste cultural, conflicto, y desadaptación*. Lima: Imprenta de la Universidad Nacional Mayor de San Marcos.

Valencia, Américo
1980   "Los sikuris de la isla de Taquile." *Separata del Boletín de Lima* 8/9:1–23.
1981   "Los chiriguanos de Huancané." *Separata del Boletín de Lima* 12/13/14:1–28.
1982   "El siku bipolar en el antiguo Perú." *Boletín de Lima* 4(23):29–48.
1983   *El siku bipolar altiplánico. vol. 1: Los sikuris y sikumorenos*. Lima: Artex E.I.R.L.

Van den Berghe, Pierre L., and George P. Primov
1977   *Inequality in the Peruvian Andes: Class and Ethnicity in Cuzco*. Columbia: University of Missouri Press.

Vargas Urgarte, Rubén
1953   *Historia de la iglesia en el Perú (1511–1568)*. Vol. 1. Lima: Imprenta Santa María.
1951   *Concilios limenses (1551–1772)*. Vol. 1. Lima: n.p.

Vásquez, Rosa Elena
1982   *La práctica musical de la población negra en Perú*. Havana: Casa de las Américas.

Vásquez Rodríguez, Chalena, and Abilio Vergara Figueroa
1988   *Chayraq! Carnaval ayacuchano*. Lima: Centro de Desarrollo Agropecuario.

Velasco Alvarado, Juan
1971   *La voz de la revolución: Discursos del Presidente de la República, General de División, Juan Velasco Alvarado, 1968–1970*. Vol. 1. Lima: Ediciones Participación.
1972   *La voz de la revolución: Discursos del Presidente de la República, General de División, Juan Velasco Alvarado, 1970–1972*. Vol. 2. Lima: Ediciones Participación.

Verger, Pierre
1945   *Fiestas y danzas en el Cuzco y en los Andes*. Buenos Aires: Editorial Sudamericana.

Vilca, Dante
1982   "La Asociación Juvenil Puno." *Tarea* 6:61–64.

Vivanco, J. Alejandro
1973   "El migrante de provincias como intérprete del folklore andino en

Lima." B.A. thesis, Universidad Nacional Mayor de San Marcos, Lima.

1976   "La difusión del folklore y la formación de actitudes." Ph.D. diss., Universidad Nacional Mayor de San Marcos, Lima.

Wallace, Anthony F. C.

1956   "Revitalization Movements." *American Anthropologist* 58(2):264–81.

Wallace, James M.

1984   "Urban Anthropology in Lima: An Overview." *Latin American Research Review* 19(3):57–85.

Waterman, Christopher

1990a   *Juju: A Social History and Ethnography of an African Popular Music.* Chicago: University of Chicago Press.

1990b   " 'Our Tradition Is a Very Modern Tradition': Popular Music and the Construction of Pan-Yoruba Identity." *Ethnomusicology* 34(3):367–79.

Waterman, Richard

1952   "African Influence on American Negro Music," in *Acculturation in the Americas,* edited by Sol Tax. Chicago: University of Chicago Press.

Wendorff, Carlos

1985   "Sector informal urbano y crisis económica: Diagnóstico y alternativas de política," in *Lima: Población, trabajo, y política,* edited by Narda Henríquez et al. Lima: Pontificia Universidad Católica del Perú.

ANNOTATED

DISCOGRAPHY

This brief discography primarily lists commercial records readily available in the United States which have selections that pertain to genres, styles, instruments, and ensemble types that I have discussed in the book.

Huayno Music of Peru, vol. 1 (1949–1989), Arhoolie (CD 320), edited with notes by John Cohen (1989). This recording includes reissues of Peruvian recordings of the type that I have called the "commercial wayno style" (or "urban-country" style) from the 1950s and 1960s in Lima. Selections 1 (Jilguero del Huascarán) and 3 (Pastorita Huaracina) are by particularly important "country music" stars from Ancash; selection 2 is by a Junín orquesta with harp, violin, saxes, and clarinets.

Kingdom of the Sun: Peru's Inca Heritage, Nonesuch (H-72029), recorded by David Lewiston (n.d.). This recording includes an excellent example of a sikumoreno ensemble (side 1, band 4) of the type heard in the city of Puno and in the Province of Chucuito, Puno. It also includes a wayno that I refer to in chapter 9, "Adios pueblo de Ayacucho" (side 1, band 1), played in Ayacuchano style, and waynos from other regions. Side 2, band 2 is a good example of a kena solo.

Music of Peru, Folkways (FE 4415), notes by Harry Tschopik, Jr. (1950 [1959]). The recordings on side 1, bands 1 and 3, and side 2, band 1, demonstrate the ensemble sound approximating early estudiantinas (especially side 1, band 3); the bass support provided by the guitars is particularly typical. Wayno (huayno) and marinera genres are included.

Música Andina del Perú, Patronato Popular y Porvenir Pro Música Clásica (write: Proyecto de Preservación de la Música Tradicional Andina, Pontificia Universidad Católica del Perú, Instituto Riva Agüero, Jr., Camaná 459-Lima 1, for this and other recordings from Junín, Cajamarca, and Arequipa), edited with notes by Raúl Romero (1987). This excellent survey of highland Peruvian music includes examples of charango music from Cusco (side 1, band 1); the unison pitu style from Cusco (side 3, band 8—this style is quite different from the sound of pitu ensembles in Conima); the music for the Puneño traje de luz dance, "La Diablada," performed by a brass band (side 3, band 9); chiriguano panpipe music from Huancané (side 3, band 10); and choquela (chokela) music from Puno (side 3, band 11), a tradition previously performed in Conima.

315

Mountain Music of Peru, Folkways (FE 4539), collected with notes by John Cohen (1966). This recording includes examples of music by highland migrants in Lima (side 1, bands 6 and 7); Junín orquestas (side 3, band 10); and a panpipe ensemble from Chucuito, Puno, that is related to the sound of a sikumoreno ensemble (side 4, bands 5 and 10).

Mountain Music of Peru, Vol. 2, Smithsonian/Folkways (SF 40406), recordings and notes by John Cohen and Thomas Turino. This expanded compact disc reissue of Cohen's *Mountain Music of Peru* (1966) includes sikuri performances by Qhantati Ururi (a choclo and a lento) and Centro Social Conima (the lento "Manuelita"; see transcription A.2). It also contains a tarka performance by Tarkas de Putina, a pitu performance of achachk'umu by Ayllu Checasaya, and a five-hole pinkillu Carnival piece. The chiriguano and ayarachi panpipe styles may also be heard on this recording.

Peru: Ayarachi and Chiriguano, UNESCO/IMC (MTC1; write to 1 rue Miollis, 75015 Paris, France), recordings and notes by Xavier Bellenger (1983). This recording includes excellent examples of ayarachi panpipe music from Lampa, Puno, and chiriguano panpipe music from Huancané, Puno.

Peru: Music from the Land of Macchu Picchu, Lyrichord (LLST 7294), recordings by Verna Gillis with David Moisés Pérez Martínez (n.d.). This record includes waynos and marineras played on a variety of instruments (harp, kena, guitar, violin), and a Junín orquesta selection (side 1, band 2).

Your Struggle Is Your Glory: Songs of Struggle, Huayno and Other Peruvian Music, Arhoolie (3025), recorded and edited with notes by John Cohen (1988). Included are performances by Máximo Damián (mentioned in chapter 9, the "Anniversary of Lima"), one of which is a scissors dance piece (side 1, band 6).

INDEX

317